W9-BRV-269

Teach Yourself VISUALLY™

iPad®
6th Edition

Teach Yourself VISUALLY™

iPad®
6th Edition

by Guy Hart-Davis

Visual®
A Wiley Brand

Teach Yourself VISUALLY™ iPad® 6th Edition

Published by
John Wiley & Sons, Inc.
10475 Crosspoint Boulevard
Indianapolis, IN 46256

www.wiley.com

Published simultaneously in Canada

Copyright © 2018 by John Wiley & Sons, Inc., Indianapolis, Indiana

No part of this publication may be reproduced, stored in a retrieval system or transmitted in any form or by any means, electronic, mechanical, photocopying, recording, scanning or otherwise, except as permitted under Sections 107 or 108 of the 1976 United States Copyright Act, without either the prior written permission of the Publisher, or authorization through payment of the appropriate per-copy fee to the Copyright Clearance Center, 222 Rosewood Drive, Danvers, MA 01923, (978) 750-8400, fax (978) 646-8600. Requests to the Publisher for permission should be addressed to the Permissions Department, John Wiley & Sons, Inc., 111 River Street, Hoboken, NJ 07030, 201-748-6011, fax 201-748-6008, or online at www.wiley.com/go/permissions.

Wiley publishes in a variety of print and electronic formats and by print-on-demand. Some material included with standard print versions of this book may not be included in e-books or in print-on-demand. If this book refers to media such as a CD or DVD that is not included in the version you purchased, you may download this material at http://booksupport.wiley.com. For more information about Wiley products, visit www.wiley.com.

Library of Congress Control Number: 2017955901

ISBN: 978-1-119-46389-4

Manufactured in the United States of America

10 9 8 7 6 5 4 3 2 1

Trademark Acknowledgments

Wiley, the Wiley logo, Visual, the Visual logo, Teach Yourself VISUALLY, Read Less - Learn More and related trade dress are trademarks or registered trademarks of John Wiley & Sons, Inc. and/or its affiliates. iPad, iPad mini, iPad Air, and iPad Pro are trademarks or registered trademarks of Apple, Inc. All other trademarks are the property of their respective owners. John Wiley & Sons, Inc. is not associated with any product or vendor mentioned in this book. *Teach Yourself VISUALLY™ iPad® 6th Edition* is an independent publication and has not been authorized, sponsored, or otherwise approved by Apple, Inc.

LIMIT OF LIABILITY/DISCLAIMER OF WARRANTY: THE PUBLISHER AND THE AUTHOR MAKE NO REPRESENTATIONS OR WARRANTIES WITH RESPECT TO THE ACCURACY OR COMPLETENESS OF THE CONTENTS OF THIS WORK AND SPECIFICALLY DISCLAIM ALL WARRANTIES, INCLUDING WITHOUT LIMITATION WARRANTIES OF FITNESS FOR A PARTICULAR PURPOSE. NO WARRANTY MAY BE CREATED OR EXTENDED BY SALES OR PROMOTIONAL MATERIALS. THE ADVICE AND STRATEGIES CONTAINED HEREIN MAY NOT BE SUITABLE FOR EVERY SITUATION. THIS WORK IS SOLD WITH THE UNDERSTANDING THAT THE PUBLISHER IS NOT ENGAGED IN RENDERING LEGAL, ACCOUNTING, OR OTHER PROFESSIONAL SERVICES. IF PROFESSIONAL ASSISTANCE IS REQUIRED, THE SERVICES OF A COMPETENT PROFESSIONAL PERSON SHOULD BE SOUGHT. NEITHER THE PUBLISHER NOR THE AUTHOR SHALL BE LIABLE FOR DAMAGES ARISING HEREFROM. THE FACT THAT AN ORGANIZATION OR WEBSITE IS REFERRED TO IN THIS WORK AS A CITATION AND/OR A POTENTIAL SOURCE OF FURTHER INFORMATION DOES NOT MEAN THAT THE AUTHOR OR THE PUBLISHER ENDORSES THE INFORMATION THE ORGANIZATION OR WEBSITE MAY PROVIDE OR RECOMMENDATIONS IT MAY MAKE. FURTHER, READERS SHOULD BE AWARE THAT INTERNET WEBSITES LISTED IN THIS WORK MAY HAVE CHANGED OR DISAPPEARED BETWEEN WHEN THIS WORK WAS WRITTEN AND WHEN IT IS READ.

FOR PURPOSES OF ILLUSTRATING THE CONCEPTS AND TECHNIQUES DESCRIBED IN THIS BOOK, THE AUTHOR HAS CREATED VARIOUS NAMES, COMPANY NAMES, MAILING, E-MAIL AND INTERNET ADDRESSES, PHONE AND FAX NUMBERS AND SIMILAR INFORMATION, ALL OF WHICH ARE FICTITIOUS. ANY RESEMBLANCE OF THESE FICTITIOUS NAMES, ADDRESSES, PHONE AND FAX NUMBERS AND SIMILAR INFORMATION TO ANY ACTUAL PERSON, COMPANY AND/OR ORGANIZATION IS UNINTENTIONAL AND PURELY COINCIDENTAL.

Contact Us

For general information on our other products and services please contact our Customer Care Department within the U.S. at 877-762-2974, outside the U.S. at 317-572-3993 or fax 317-572-4002.

For technical support please visit https://hub.wiley.com/community/support.

Credits

Executive Editors
Riley Harding
Jody Lefevere

Project Editor
Lynn Northrup

Technical Editor
Galen Gruman

Copy Editor
Lynn Northrup

Production Editor
Barath Kumar Rajasekaran

Manager, Content Development & Assembly
Mary Beth Wakefield

Vice President, Professional Technology Strategy
Barry Pruett

About the Author

Guy Hart-Davis is the author of *Teach Yourself VISUALLY iPhone 8, iPhone 8 Plus, and iPhone X; Teach Yourself VISUALLY MacBook, 4th Edition; Teach Yourself VISUALLY Android Phones and Tablets, 2nd Edition; Teach Yourself VISUALLY Apple Watch; Teach Yourself VISUALLY Samsung Galaxy S6; Teach Yourself VISUALLY iMac, 3rd Edition; iMac Portable Genius, 4th Edition;* and *iWork Portable Genius, 2nd Edition*.

Author's Acknowledgments

My thanks go to the many people who turned my manuscript into the highly graphical book you are holding. In particular, I thank Riley Harding and Jody Lefevere for asking me to write the book; Lynn Northrup for keeping me on track and skillfully editing the text; Galen Gruman for reviewing the book for technical accuracy and contributing helpful suggestions; and SPi Global for laying out the book.

How to Use This Book

Who This Book Is For

This book is for the reader who has never used this particular technology or software application. It is also for readers who want to expand their knowledge.

The Conventions in This Book

1 Steps

This book uses a step-by-step format to guide you easily through each task. **Numbered steps** are actions you must do; **bulleted steps** clarify a point, step, or optional feature; and **indented steps** give you the result.

2 Notes

Notes give additional information — special conditions that may occur during an operation, a situation that you want to avoid, or a cross reference to a related area of the book.

3 Icons and Buttons

Icons and buttons show you exactly what you need to tap to perform a step.

4 Tips

Tips offer additional information, including warnings and shortcuts.

5 Bold

Bold type shows command names, options, and text or numbers you must type.

6 Italics

Italic type introduces and defines a new term.

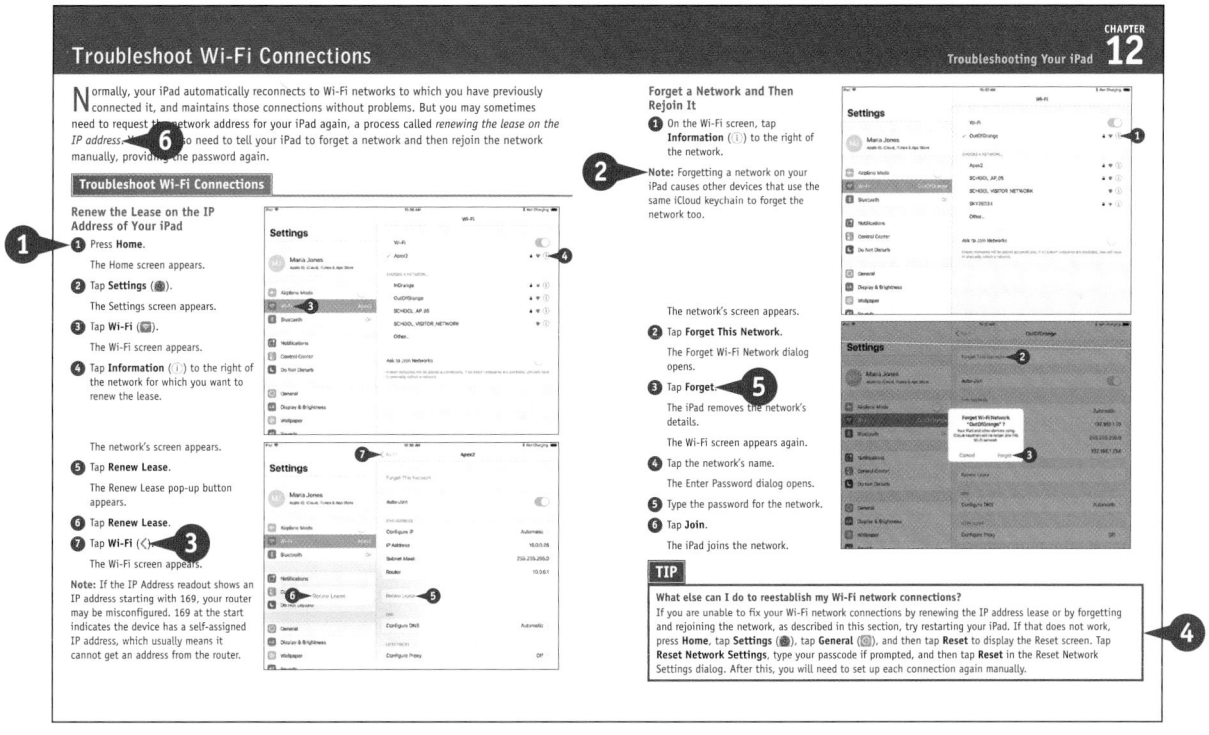

Troubleshoot Wi-Fi Connections

Troubleshooting Your iPad CHAPTER 12

Normally, your iPad automatically reconnects to Wi-Fi networks to which you have previously connected it, and maintains those connections without problems. But you may sometimes need to request the network address for your iPad again, a process called *renewing the lease on the IP address*. You also need to tell your iPad to forget a network and then rejoin the network manually, providing the password again.

Troubleshoot Wi-Fi Connections

Renew the Lease on the IP Address of Your iPad

1. Press **Home**.
   The Home screen appears.
2. Tap **Settings**.
   The Settings screen appears.
3. Tap **Wi-Fi**.
   The Wi-Fi screen appears.
4. Tap **Information** to the right of the network for which you want to renew the lease.
   The network's screen appears.
5. Tap **Renew Lease**.
   The Renew Lease pop-up button appears.
6. Tap **Renew Lease**.
7. Tap **Wi-Fi**.
   The Wi-Fi screen appears.

Note: If the IP Address readout shows an IP address starting with 169, your router may be misconfigured. 169 at the start indicates the device has a self-assigned IP address, which usually means it cannot get an address from the router.

Forget a Network and Then Rejoin It

1. On the Wi-Fi screen, tap **Information** to the right of the network.
   Note: Forgetting a network on your iPad causes other devices that use the same iCloud keychain to forget the network too.
   The network's screen appears.
2. Tap **Forget This Network**.
   The Forget Wi-Fi Network dialog opens.
3. Tap **Forget**.
   The iPad removes the network's details.
   The Wi-Fi screen appears again.
4. Tap the network's name.
   The Enter Password dialog opens.
5. Type the password for the network.
6. Tap **Join**.
   The iPad joins the network.

TIP

What else can I do to reestablish my Wi-Fi network connections?
If you are unable to fix your Wi-Fi network connections by renewing the IP address lease or by forgetting and rejoining the network, as described in this section, try restarting your iPad. If that does not work, press **Home**, tap **Settings**, tap **General**, and then tap **Reset** to display the Reset screen. Tap **Reset Network Settings**, type your passcode if prompted, and then tap **Reset** in the Reset Network Settings dialog. After this, you will need to set up each connection again manually.

Table of Contents

Chapter 1 Getting Started with Your iPad

Identify and Compare the iPad Models 4
Meet Your iPad's Controls 8
Download, Install, and Set Up iTunes 10
Begin Setup and Activate Your iPad 12
Set Up Your iPad as New Using iCloud 16
Set Up Your iPad from an iCloud Backup 20
Set Up Your iPad Using iTunes 22
Choose Which Items to Sync from Your Computer 24
Sync Your iPad with Your Computer via Wi-Fi 28
Explore the Interface and Launch Apps 30
Using Cover Sheet and Today View 32
Using Control Center 34
Using the Dock 36

Chapter 2 Personalizing Your iPad

Find the Settings You Need 40
Set Up and Configure iCloud 42
Choose Which Apps Can Give Notifications 46
Choose Sounds Settings 48
Configure Display, Brightness, and Night Shift 50
Set Home Screen and Lock Screen Wallpaper 52
Choose Privacy and Location Settings 54
Configure Search and Find What You Need 56
Choose Locking and Control Center Settings 58
Set Up and Use Do Not Disturb Mode 60
Secure Your iPad with Touch ID or a Passcode 62

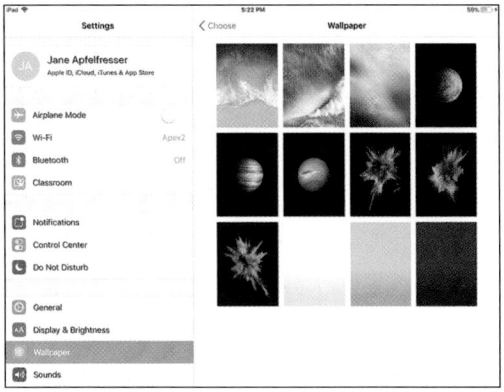

Configure Restrictions and Parental Controls 64
Set Up Family Sharing and Add Members 66
Choose Date, Time, and Region Settings 68

Chapter 3 Working with Voice and Accessibility

Give Commands with Siri 72
Dictate Text Using Siri 74
Gather and Share Information with Siri 76
Configure Siri to Work Your Way 78
Using VoiceOver to Identify Items On-Screen 80
Configure Other Accessibility Features 82
Using a Hardware Keyboard 88
Using Your iPad with Your Mac 90

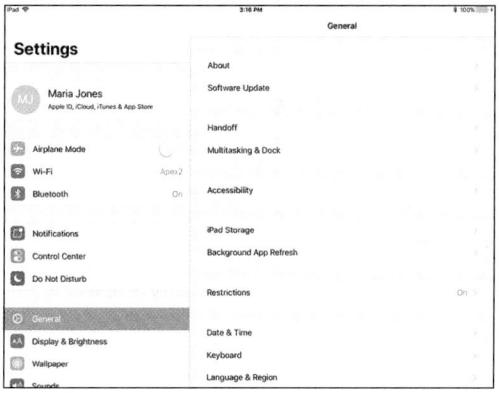

Chapter 4 Setting Up Communications

Set Up Your Mail Accounts 94
Set Up an Exchange Server Account 96
Set Your Default Account and Create Signatures 98
Choose How Your iPad Gets Your E-Mail 100
Control How Your iPad Displays Your E-Mail 102
Organize Your E-Mail Messages by Threads 104
Add People to the VIP Inbox 106
Choose How Your iPad Displays Your Contacts 108
Choose Alert Options for Calendar Events 110
Choose Your Default Calendar and Time Zone 112
Choose Settings for Notes 114

Table of Contents

Chapter 5 Networking and Communicating

Using Airplane Mode 118
Connect Bluetooth Devices to Your iPad 120
Control Cellular Data and Background Refresh 122
Connect Your iPad to a Different Carrier 124
Specify Your iPad's Cellular Access Point 125
Share Items via AirDrop 126
Share Your Cellular iPad's Internet Access 128
Connect to Wi-Fi Networks and Hotspots 130
Connect to a Network via VPN 134
Send Text and Multimedia Messages 136
Using Emoji and Other iMessage Features 138
Manage Your Instant Messages 140
Mute a Conversation or Share Your Location 142
Choose Settings for Messages 144
Block and Unblock Senders 146
Chat Face-to-Face Using FaceTime 148

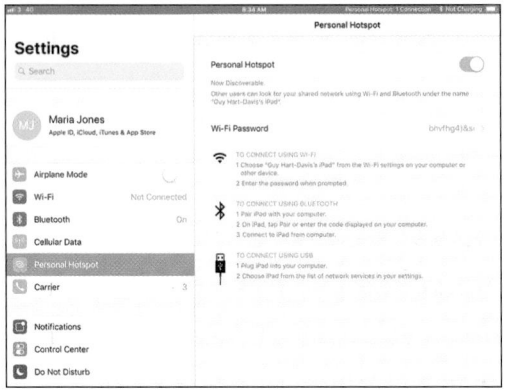

Chapter 6 Working with Apps and Files

Customize the Home Screen and the Dock 152
Organize Apps with Folders 154
Switch Quickly from One App to Another 156
Multitask with Split-Screen Views 158
Find the Apps You Need 164
Update and Remove Apps 166
Manage Automatic Downloads and Your Apple ID 168
Manage Files with the Files App 170
Enter Text Quickly in Apps 174

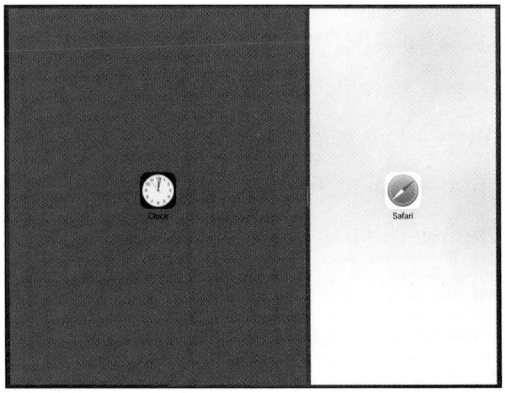

Cut, Copy, and Paste Text.....176
Bold, Italicize, Underline, and Replace Text.....178
Take Screenshots and Use Instant Markup.....180

Chapter 7 Browsing the Web and Sending E-Mail

Browse the Web with Safari.....184
Access Websites Quickly with Bookmarks.....186
Create Bookmarks to Access Pages Quickly.....188
Keep a Reading List of Web Pages.....190
Fill In Forms Quickly with AutoFill.....192
Tighten Up Safari's Security.....194
Read Your E-Mail Messages.....196
Reply To or Forward an E-Mail Message.....198
Organize Your Messages in Mailbox Folders.....200
Write and Send E-Mail Messages.....202
View Files Attached to Incoming Messages.....204

Chapter 8 Keeping Your Life Organized

Browse or Search for Contacts.....208
Create a New Contact.....210
Share Contacts via E-Mail and Messages.....212
Browse Existing Events in Your Calendars.....214
Create New Events in Your Calendars.....216
Work with Calendar Invitations.....218
Track Your Commitments with Reminders.....220
Take Notes.....224
Find Your Location with the Maps App.....230

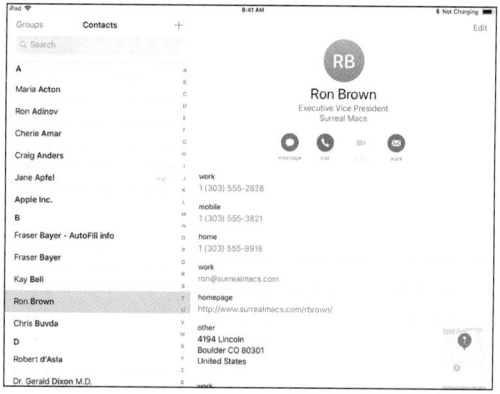

Table of Contents

Find Directions with the Maps App 232
Using the Maps App's Favorites and Contacts 234
Using the Clock App 236
Using Apple Pay 238

Chapter 9 Playing Music and Videos

Navigate the Music App and Set Preferences 242
Play Music Using the Music App 246
Play Videos Using the TV App 248
Play Music and Videos Using AirPlay 250
Create a Music Playlist 254
Configure iPad Audio Settings 256
Listen to Apple Music Radio 258

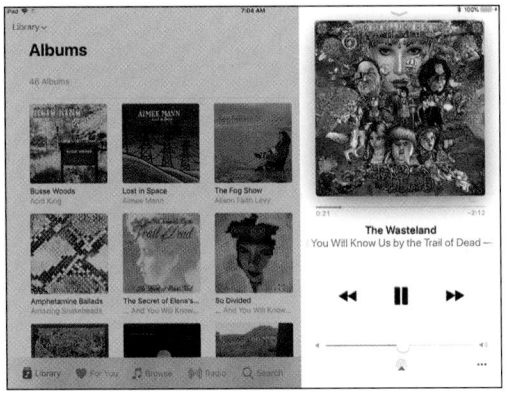

Chapter 10 Working with Photos and Books

Browse Photos Using Years, Collections, and Moments 264
Browse Shared Photos 266
Browse Photos Using Albums 268
Create Albums 270
Share Photos Across Your Devices and Computers 272
Share Photo Albums with Other People via iCloud 274
Share and Use Your Photos 276
Play Slide Shows of Photos 278
Read Digital Books with iBooks 280

Chapter 11 Taking Photos and Videos

Take Photos with the Camera App 284
Take HDR Photos and Square Photos 286
Using the Self-Timer and the Grid 288
Take Time-Lapse Movies 290
Take Fun Photos with Photo Booth 292
Crop, Rotate, and Straighten Photos 294
Enhance Photos 296
Reduce Red-Eye in Photos 297
Adjust the Colors in Photos 298
Apply Filters to Photos 300
Capture Video 302

Chapter 12 Troubleshooting Your iPad

Close an App That Has Stopped Responding 306
Update the Software on Your iPad 308
Extend Your iPad's Runtime on the Battery 310
Back Up and Restore Your iPad Using iTunes 312
Back Up and Restore Your iPad Using iCloud 314
Restore the Operating System Using iTunes 316
Restore Your iPad to Factory Settings 318
Troubleshoot Wi-Fi Connections 320
Locate Your iPad with Find My iPad 322

Index 326

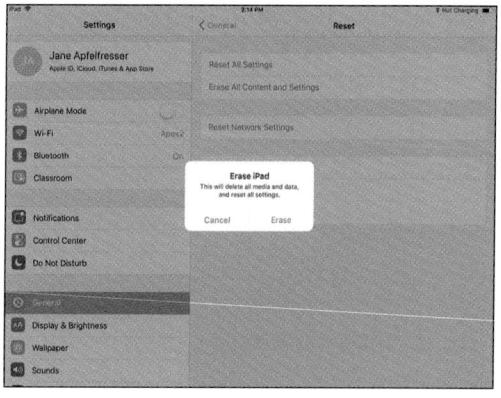

CHAPTER 1

Getting Started with Your iPad

The iPad is a series of powerful and extremely popular touch-screen tablet computers created by Apple. You can use an iPad either as a full-powered computing device on its own or as a companion device to your Mac or PC. In this chapter, you set up your iPad, sync data to it, and learn to use the user interface.

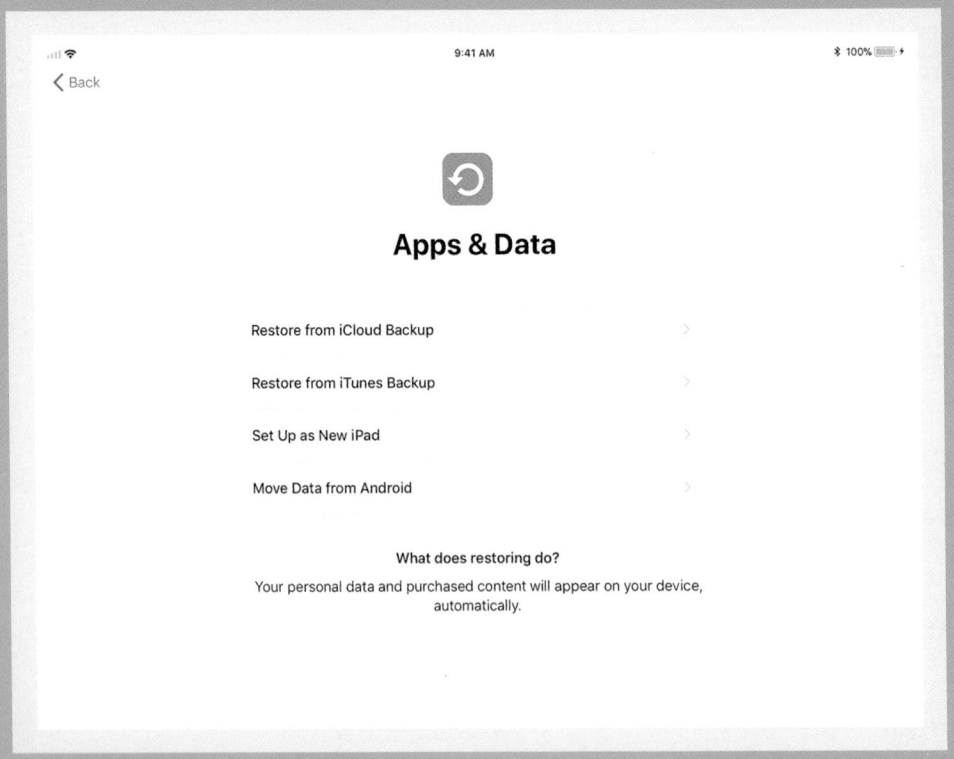

Identify and Compare the iPad Models 4
Meet Your iPad's Controls 8
Download, Install, and Set Up iTunes 10
Begin Setup and Activate Your iPad 12
Set Up Your iPad as New Using iCloud 16
Set Up Your iPad from an iCloud Backup. 20
Set Up Your iPad Using iTunes 22
Choose Which Items to Sync from Your Computer 24
Sync Your iPad with Your Computer via Wi-Fi 28
Explore the Interface and Launch Apps 30
Using Cover Sheet and Today View 32
Using Control Center 34
Using the Dock. 36

Identify and Compare the iPad Models

The Apple iPad is the most popular tablet computer on the market. Powerful, elegantly designed, and easy to use, the iPad can take over many of the tasks you normally perform on your desktop or laptop computer, such as surfing the web, exchanging e-mail messages, performing desktop publishing, and playing video games.

Understand the Choice of iPad Models

The iPad comes in three sizes: small, medium, and large. The small size consists of the iPad mini models. The medium size includes the model called simply "iPad" and the smaller iPad Pro model. The large size is the full-size iPad Pro.

Compare Screen Size and Device Size

Recent iPad mini models have a 7.9-inch screen with 2048 × 1536 pixels at a resolution of 326 pixels per inch, or ppi. The iPad has a 9.7-inch screen with 2048 × 1536 pixels at a resolution of 264 ppi. The smaller iPad Pro has a 10.5-inch screen with 2224 × 1668 pixels at a resolution of 264 ppi. The full-size iPad Pro has a 12.9-inch screen with 2732 × 2048 pixels at a resolution of 264 ppi. All of these screen measurements are diagonal.

Although the difference in diagonal measurements sounds small — less than 2 inches between the iPad mini and the iPad, and just over 3 inches between the iPad and the full-size iPad Pro — the difference in screen size is dramatic. The iPad screen is one-and-a-half times as large as the iPad mini screen. The full-size iPad Pro screen is one-and-three-quarter times as large as the iPad screen, and more than two-and-a-half times as large as the iPad mini screen.

The iPad mini measures 8 inches tall × 5.3 inches wide and weighs around two-thirds of a pound. The iPad measures 9.4 inches tall × 6.6 inches wide and weighs around 1 pound. The 10.5-inch iPad Pro measures 9.8 inches tall × 6.8 inches wide and weighs just over 1 pound. The full-size iPad Pro measures 12 inches tall × 8.68 inches wide and weighs around 1.5 pounds.

iPad mini

10.5-inch iPad Pro

iPad

12.9-inch iPad Pro

Compare iPad Storage Capacity

Apple offers the various iPad models with storage capacities ranging from 32GB to 256GB. The storage capacities available vary by model. For example, as of this writing, the iPad comes in 32GB and 128GB capacities; the iPad Pro models have capacities of 64GB, 256GB, and 512GB; whereas the iPad mini offers only a single choice, 128GB.

Having more storage enables you to install more apps and carry more music, movies, and other files with you. More storage is especially valuable if you plan to shoot videos on your iPad.

Higher capacities command substantially higher prices, so you must decide how much you are prepared to spend. Generally speaking, higher-capacity devices get more use in the long run and are worth the extra cost.

Compare iPad Processors and Coprocessors

Each iPad has a main processor from Apple's A series of processors plus a coprocessor from Apple's M series of coprocessors. A *coprocessor* is a supplementary processor that speeds up specific tasks, such as rendering graphics and interpreting input from the iPad's sensors.

- The iPad mini 4 has an A8 processor with a non-embedded M8 coprocessor.
- The iPad model has an A9 processor and an embedded M9 coprocessor. The processor is 1.6× faster than the A8, and graphics performance is 1.8× faster.
- The iPad Pro models have an A10X Fusion processor and an embedded M10 coprocessor. The processor is 2.5× faster than the A8, and graphics performance is 4.3× faster.

Choose Between a Wi-Fi–Only iPad and a Cellular-and–Wi-Fi iPad

The iPad mini, iPad, and iPad Pro all come in Wi-Fi–only and cellular-and–Wi-Fi models.

With a Wi-Fi–only iPad, you can connect to the Internet only through wireless networks, such as those at your home or workplace, or wireless hotspots that are open to the public or to customers of the establishments that host them.

With a cellular-and–Wi-Fi iPad, you can connect both through the cellular network and through wireless networks, giving you Internet access no matter where you go. This option costs more both in the purchase price of the iPad and in the cellular service fees with either a monthly or a pay-as-you-go plan.

continued ▶

The front of each iPad contains a touch screen that you use for most of your interaction with the device and its interface. The front of the iPad also contains a camera, located above the screen and sometimes called the "selfie camera," for taking self-portraits and for video chat. The rear of the iPad contains a higher-resolution camera capable of taking good-quality photos and videos.

Apart from being larger and designed for professional use, the iPad Pro models have features and accessories that the iPad mini and iPad do not have, such as the Apple Pencil stylus and the Smart Keyboard.

Touch Screen

Each iPad model has a touch screen that takes up most of the space on the front of the tablet. You use the touch screen to access everything on the iPad with your fingers and to view content. The iPad software uses gestures to scroll, rotate, and zoom in on objects on-screen.

All current iPad models have what Apple calls a Retina display, which has very high resolution.

Cameras

Each iPad has one camera on the front — the screen side — and another on the back.

The front camera is for FaceTime video calling and self-portraits. This camera's specifications vary depending on the iPad model, but in all models the camera's video capabilities are high enough to provide a good-quality video picture for FaceTime calls. In general, the front camera captures photos and videos at lower resolutions and has fewer capabilities than the rear camera.

The back camera is for taking photos and videos of other subjects, much as you would use a stand-alone digital camera. As with the front camera, the back camera's specifications vary depending on the iPad model. The back camera on some iPad models can capture slow-motion video at 120 frames per second and can take bursts of photos.

Apple Pencil for iPad Pro

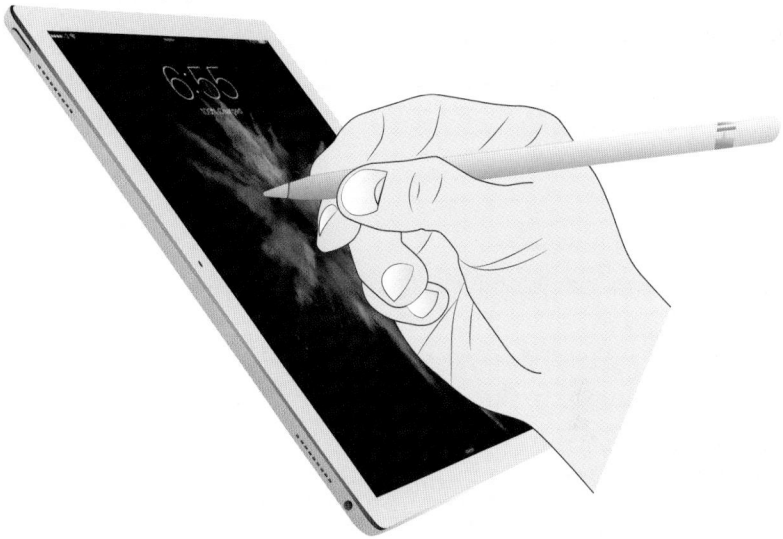

You can use your fingers on the touch screen to control the iPad Pro models just as you can with the other iPad models, but the iPad Pro models are also designed to use a custom stylus called the Apple Pencil. The Apple Pencil enables you to draw and make selections much more precisely than you can with a finger, giving you finer control over the documents you create and edit on the iPad Pro. The Apple Pencil and the iPad Pro screens are pressure sensitive, so you can draw lines of different thicknesses by varying the amount of pressure you apply.

The Apple Pencil contains a rechargeable battery that you can charge by plugging the Apple Pencil into an iPad Pro.

Smart Keyboard for iPad Pro

Like the iPad mini and iPad, the iPad Pro models have an on-screen keyboard that you can use to enter text as needed. You can also connect a Bluetooth keyboard to the iPad Pro models to enter text, as you can for any iPad.

But if you need to enter large amounts of text, you may prefer a Smart Keyboard, the custom keyboard models that double as covers for the iPad Pro models. The Smart Keyboard connects to the iPad Pro via the Smart Connector interface on the side of the device, which allows the Smart Keyboard not only to provide input to the iPad Pro, but also to draw power from it.

Meet Your iPad's Controls

Your iPad has four hardware controls for essential actions: the Sleep/Wake button to control power, the Volume Up button and the Volume Down button for controlling audio volume, and the Home button below the screen.

If your iPad has cellular connectivity, it needs a SIM card. Some iPad models come with an Apple SIM that works with most carriers. Some carriers do not support the Apple SIM or impose restrictions on its use, so you must verify that your carrier does support it before you activate the iPad using the Apple SIM.

Meet Your iPad's Controls

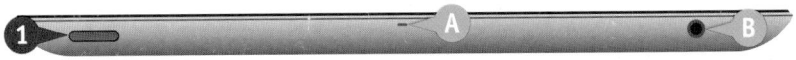

1. Press and hold the **Sleep/Wake** button on top of the iPad for a couple of seconds.

   The top of the iPad also contains:

   - A The microphone.
   - B The headphone socket.

   As the iPad starts, the Apple logo appears on the screen.

   - C Above the iPad screen is the front-facing camera.
   - D Below the iPad screen is the Home button, which you press to display the Home screen.

   At the bottom of the iPad are:

   - E The Lightning Connector.
   - F The speakers.

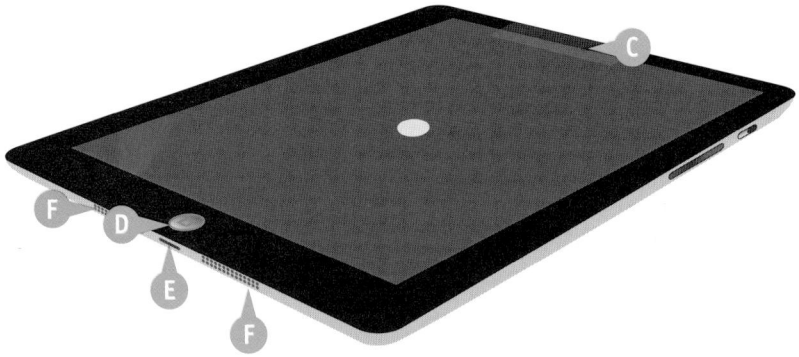

2. Turn the iPad so that you can see its right side.

3. On an iPad model that has the side switch, move the side switch down, so that an orange dot appears, when you want to mute the iPad notifications, alerts, and sound effects.

Note: On iPad models that have the side switch, you can configure the side switch to lock the screen rotation. To do so, tap **Settings** (), tap **General** (), and then tap **Lock Rotation** in the Use Side Switch To area.

4. Press the **Volume Up** (+) button to increase the sound volume.

Note: When the Camera app is active, you can press the **Volume Up** (+) button to take a picture with the camera.

5. Press the **Volume Down** (–) button to decrease the volume.

6. When the lock screen appears, press **Home** to unlock the iPad.

   The iPad unlocks, and the Home screen appears.

TIPS

How do I insert a SIM card in my iPad?
If you have a cellular iPad that does not yet contain a SIM card, get a suitable nano-SIM. Then insert the SIM removal tool or the straightened end of a paper clip in the SIM hole at the top of the left side of the iPad. Push the tool gently straight in until the tray pops out, and then pull the tray with your fingernails. Insert the SIM in the tray, and then push the tray in fully.

What do I do if my carrier does not support the Apple SIM?
If your carrier does not support the Apple SIM, get an approved SIM from the carrier and use it to activate your iPad. Do not activate your iPad using the Apple SIM, or you may not be able to use the iPad with that carrier in the future.

Download, Install, and Set Up iTunes

To sync your iPad with your computer, you use Apple's iTunes application. iTunes comes preinstalled on every Mac but not on PCs; to get iTunes for Windows, you download it from the Apple website and then install it on your PC.

If you do not have a computer, or you do not want to sync your iPad with your computer, you can set up and sync your iPad using Apple's iCloud service, as described later in this chapter.

Download, Install, and Set Up iTunes

1. On your PC, open the web browser. This example uses Microsoft Edge, the browser that comes with Windows 10.
2. Click the Address box, type **www.apple.com/itunes/download**, and then press Enter.

   The Download iTunes web page appears.
3. Click the check boxes (☑ changes to ☐) if you do not want to receive e-mail from Apple.
4. Click **Download now.**
5. When the download finishes, click **Run** in the pop-up panel that appears.

   The iTunes installation begins, and the Welcome to iTunes dialog opens.
6. Click **Next**, and then follow the steps of the installer.

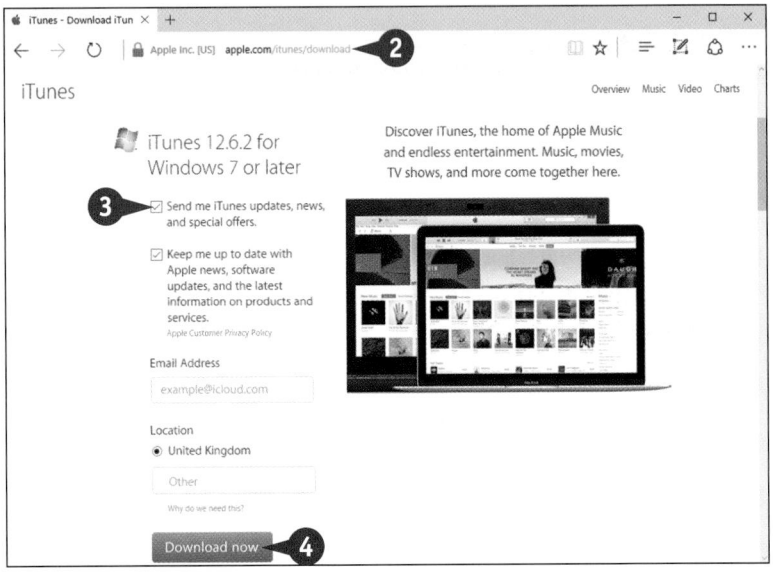

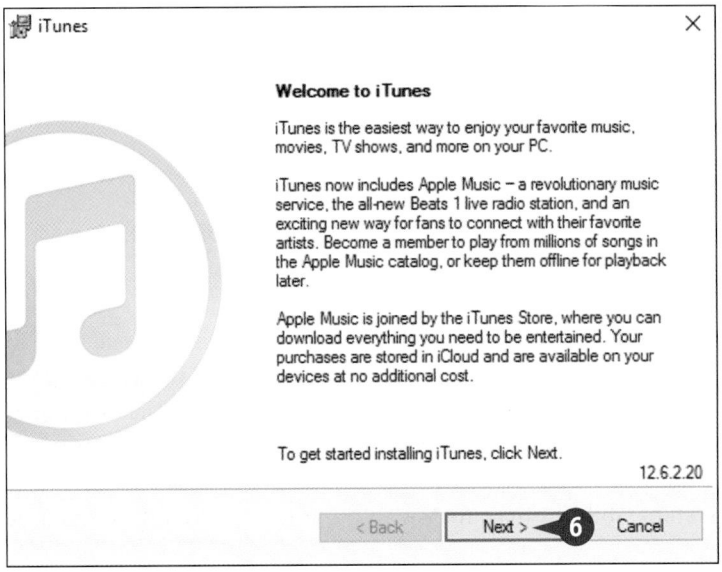

Note: You must accept the license agreement to install iTunes.

7. Click **Add iTunes shortcut to my desktop** (☑ changes to ☐) unless you want this shortcut.
8. Click **Use iTunes as the default player for audio files** (☑ changes to ☐) if you do not want to use iTunes as the default audio player.
9. Click **Automatically update iTunes and other Apple software** (☑ changes to ☐) if you do not want automatic updates.
10. Click **Install.**

    When the installation finishes, the installer displays the Congratulations dialog.

11. Click **Open iTunes after the installer exits** (☑ changes to ☐) if you do not want iTunes to launch automatically when you close the installer.
12. Click **Finish.**

    The installer closes.

    Unless you chose not to open iTunes automatically, iTunes opens.

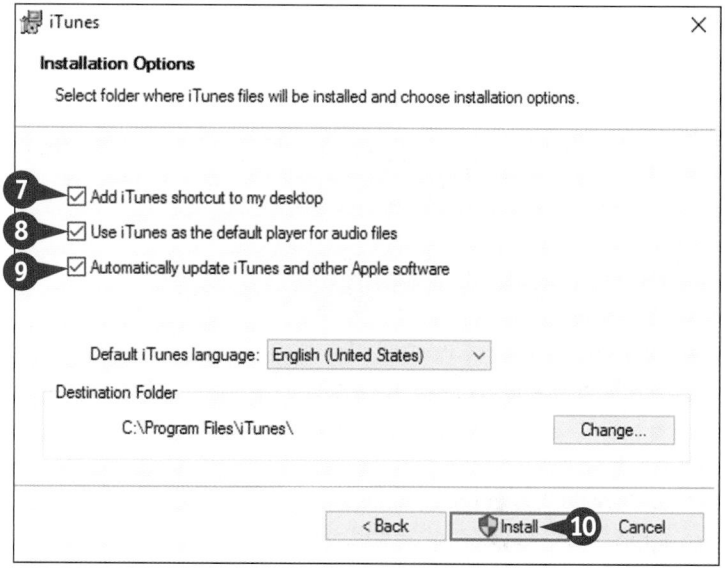

TIPS

Should I allow Apple to install updates automatically on my PC?
If this is your own PC, installing updates automatically is usually helpful. The updates may include fixes to bugs or vulnerabilities, new features, or both.

How do I set up iTunes on a Mac?
If you have not run iTunes already, click the **iTunes** icon (♫) that appears on the Dock by default. If the Dock contains no iTunes icon, click **Launchpad** (🚀) on the Dock, and then click **iTunes** (♫) on the Launchpad screen. The iTunes Setup Assistant launches. Follow the steps to set up iTunes.

Begin Setup and Activate Your iPad

Before you can use your iPad, you must set it up and activate it. First, you choose your language and specify your country or region. You then choose between manual setup and using the Quick Start feature to sign in to the iPad using your existing iPhone or iPad running iOS 11. In manual setup, you connect the iPad to the Internet through either a Wi-Fi network or the cellular network, and activate the iPad, registering it with the Apple servers.

Begin Setup and Activate Your iPad

1. Turn on the iPad by pressing and holding the **Sleep/Wake** button for a couple of seconds until the Apple logo appears.

   The Hello screen appears.

2. Press **Home**, the button below the screen.

   The Language screen appears.

3. Tap the language you want to use for the interface.

   The Select Your Country or Region screen appears.

4. Tap the country or region.

   The Quick Start screen appears.

5. If you have an iPhone or an iPad running iOS 11, you can bring it close to the iPad to sign in automatically using your Apple ID. Skip the rest of these steps. Otherwise, tap **Set Up Manually** and follow the rest of these steps.

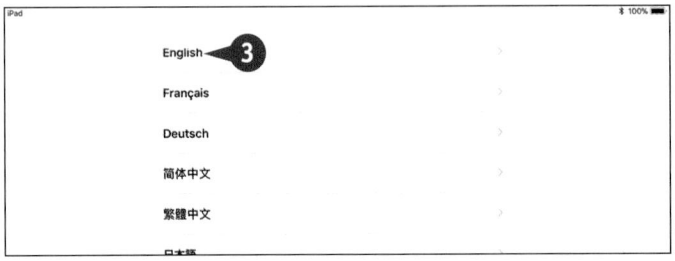

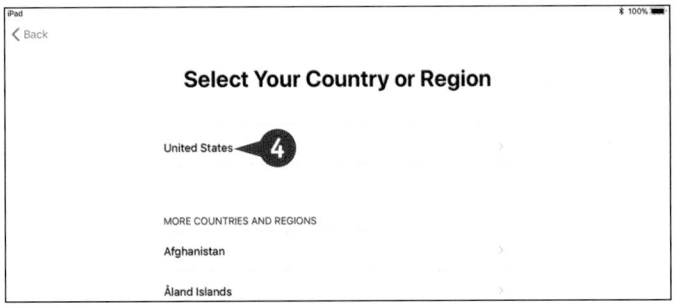

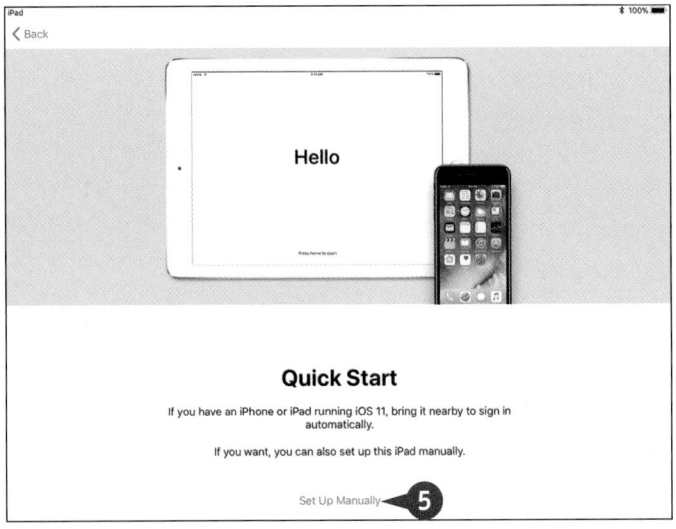

The Choose a Wi-Fi Network screen appears.

6 Tap the wireless network you want to use.

A Tap **Choose Another Network** to connect to a network that does not broadcast its name.

Note: On a cellular iPad, you can tap **Use Cellular Connection** to connect to the Internet via the cellular network and set up your iPad.

B If the Connect to iTunes button appears, you can tap it to stop the setup process here. You can then continue as explained in the section "Set Up Your iPad Using iTunes," later in this chapter.

The Enter Password dialog opens.

7 Type the password.

8 Tap **Join**.

Your iPad joins the wireless network and connects to the Internet.

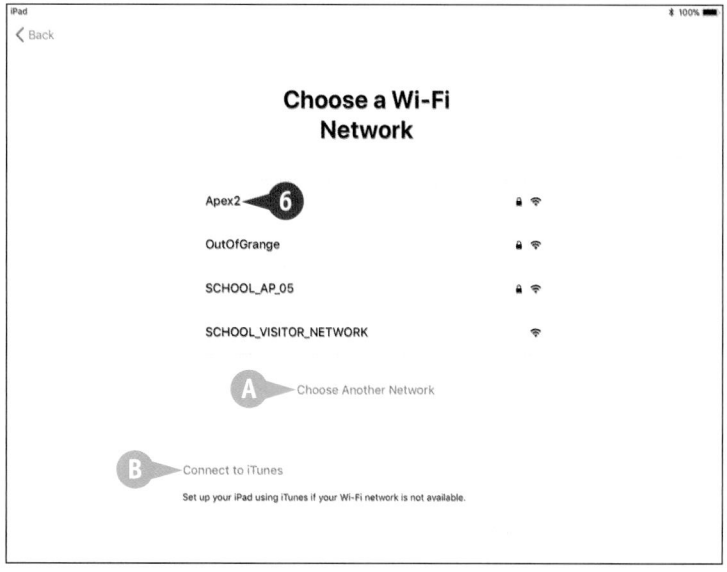

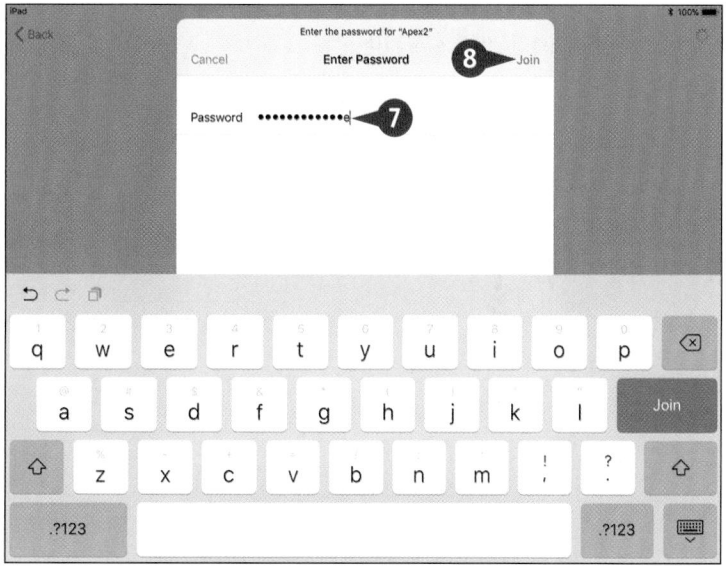

TIP

Why does my network's name not appear on the Choose a Wi-Fi Network screen?
If the network is within range of your iPad, the most likely reason is that the network does not broadcast its network name. Tap **Choose Another Network**. You can then type the network's name, choose the security type, enter the security information — such as a password — and connect to the network.

continued ▶

During setup, you secure your iPad with a passcode. On most iPad models, you can also set up the Touch ID feature, which enables you to unlock the iPad quickly using your fingerprint or thumbprint.

After this first stage of setup, you choose among setting up the iPad as a new iPad, restoring it from an iCloud backup, restoring it from an iTunes backup, or moving data from an Android device.

Begin Setup and Activate Your iPad (continued)

The Touch ID screen appears.

Note: If your iPad does not support Touch ID, the Touch ID screen does not appear. Instead, the Passcode screen appears, prompting you to set a passcode to secure the iPad.

C You can tap **Set Up Touch ID Later** if you prefer not to set up Touch ID now.

9 Tap **Continue**, and then follow the prompts to scan your fingerprint or thumbprint.

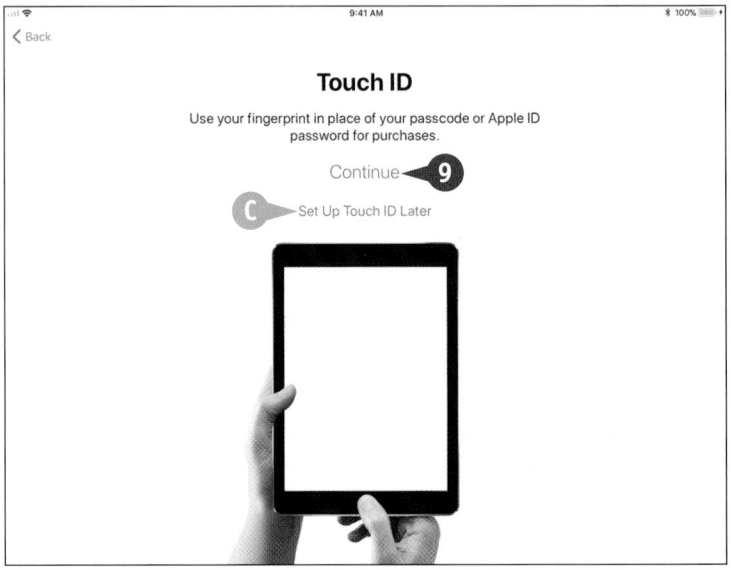

The Complete screen appears.

10 Tap **Continue**.

The Create a Passcode screen appears.

D You can tap **Passcode Options** to create a custom alphanumeric code or a four-digit code instead of a six-digit code.

11 Type a six-digit passcode, and then repeat it on the Re-Enter Your Passcode screen.

The Apps & Data screen appears.

12 Tap the appropriate button:

E Tap **Restore from iCloud Backup** to set up your iPad using a backup stored in iCloud. See the later section, "Set Up Your iPad from an iCloud Backup," for details.

F Tap **Restore from iTunes Backup** to set up your iPad using a backup stored on your computer. See the later section, "Set Up Your iPad Using iTunes," for details.

G Tap **Set Up as New iPad** to set up your iPad from scratch using iCloud. See the next section, "Set Up Your iPad as New Using iCloud," for details.

H Tap **Move Data from Android** to transfer data from an Android device.

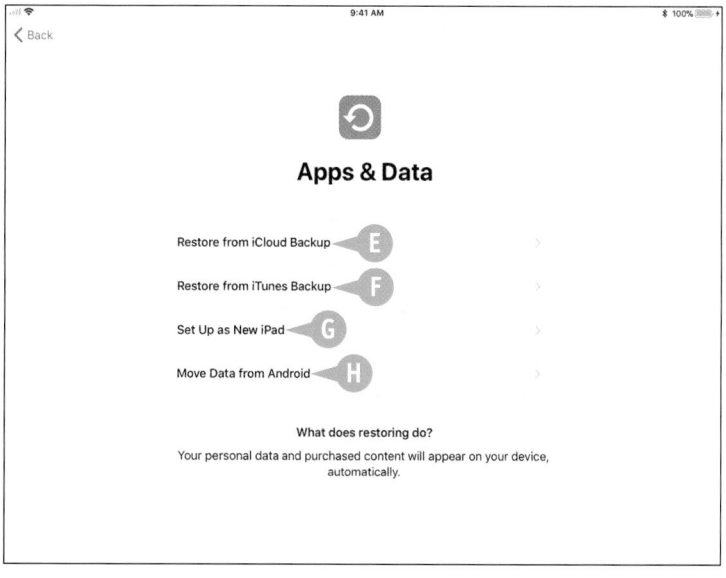

TIP

Should I use Touch ID to secure my iPad?

This is entirely your decision, but most people find Touch ID a fast and convenient way to unlock the iPad. Touch ID is generally considered to offer good security, because it is difficult for an attacker to copy your fingerprint in a way that will deceive the sensor. However, law enforcement may be able to compel you legally — or someone else may be able to compel you by force — to touch the sensor and unlock the iPad.

Set Up Your iPad as New Using iCloud

If you want to set up and use your iPad without syncing it to your computer, you can set it up using Apple's iCloud online service. With this approach, you sync your data to your account on iCloud, from which you can access it using other iOS devices, a Mac or a Windows PC, or a web browser on any computer.

To set up a new iPad to use iCloud, follow the instructions in the previous section to begin setup, and then continue with the instructions in this section. If you have backed up your iPad to iCloud and want to restore it from that backup, turn to the next section instead.

Set Up Your iPad as New Using iCloud

1. Begin setup as explained in the previous section, "Begin Setup and Activate Your iPad."
2. On the Apps & Data screen, tap **Set Up as New iPad.**

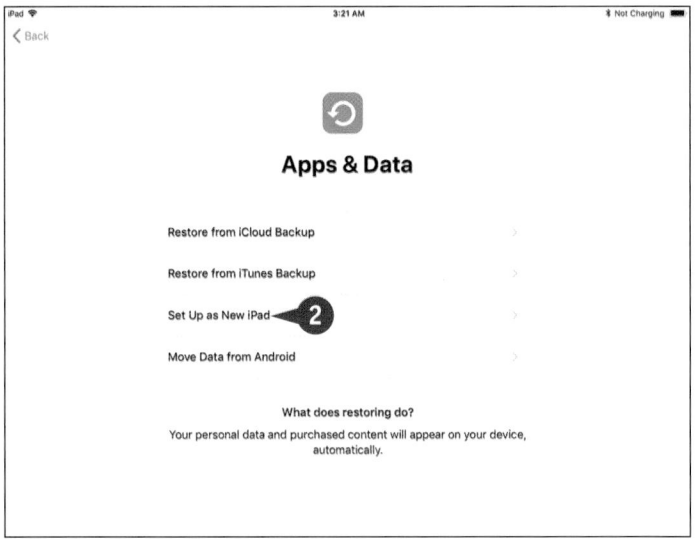

The Apple ID screen appears.

A If you do not yet have an Apple ID, tap **Don't have an Apple ID or forgot it?** and follow the screens that appear.

3. Type your Apple ID.
4. Type your password.

Note: If the Apple ID Security screen appears, prompting you to create new security questions, tap **Add Security Questions**, tap **Next**, and then create the questions.

5. Tap **Next.**

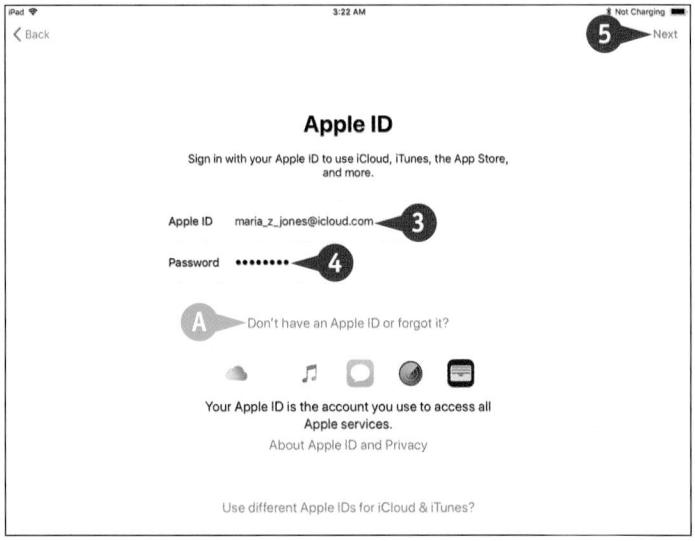

If you have enabled two-factor verification on your account, as Apple and security experts recommend, the Apple ID Verification Code dialog opens.

6 Type the six-digit verification code sent to the iPhone, other iOS device, or Mac specified as the verification device in your account.

B You can tap **Didn't Get a Code?** if you did not receive a code or if you dismissed it by accident.

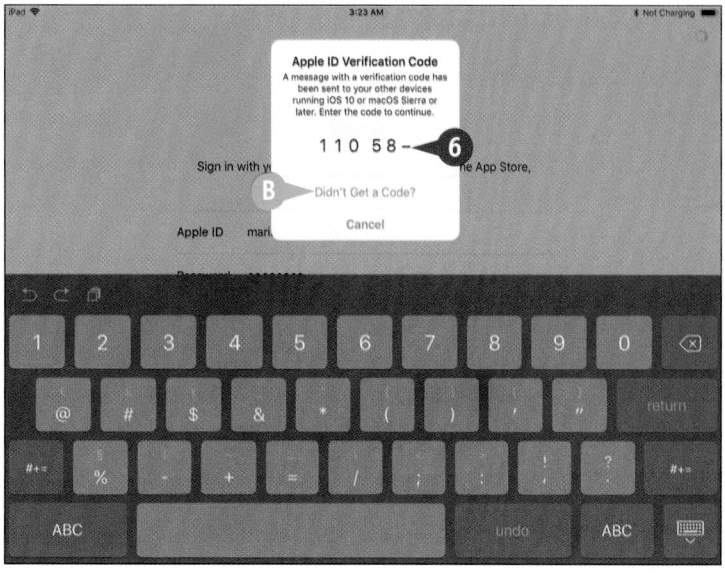

The Terms and Conditions screen appears.

7 Tap **Agree** in the lower-right corner of the screen if you want to proceed.

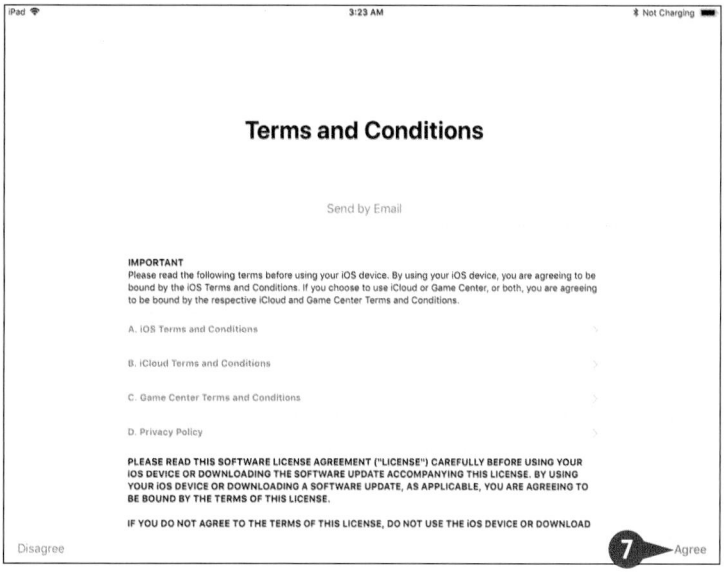

TIP

What is Siri and should I enable it?

Siri is Apple's voice-driven assistant, which enables you to interact with your iPad by voice. Many people find Siri useful, but if you do not, you can turn Siri off at any time. See Chapter 3 for instructions on using and customizing Siri.

continued ▶

When you set up your iPad using iCloud, use an e-mail address that you intend to keep for the long term. This is especially important if you use the same e-mail address for the Apple ID that you use for the App Store; each app you buy is tied to that e-mail address, so if you change the address, you will need to authenticate again for each app update.

Set Up Your iPad as New Using iCloud (continued)

The Express Settings screen appears.

8 Tap **Continue** if you want to proceed with the default values or your current values for the items listed on the screen, such as Siri and Location Services.

C You can tap **Customize Settings** if you want to customize all the settings.

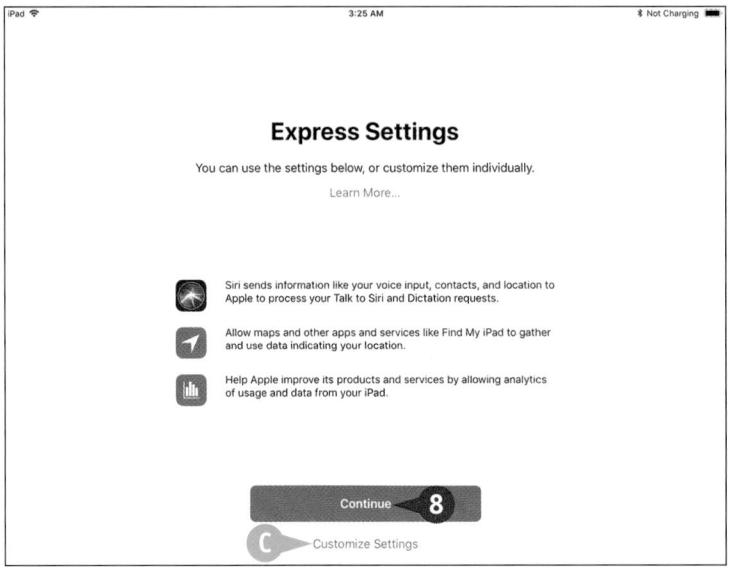

The Apple Pay screen appears.

9 Tap **Continue**, and then follow the prompts on the Add Card screen to add your card. You can either point the iPad's rear camera lens at your card and have iOS recognize the details, or tap **Enter Card Details Manually** and type in the details on the Card Details screen.

D You can tap **Set Up Later in Settings** if you do not want to set up Apple Pay now.

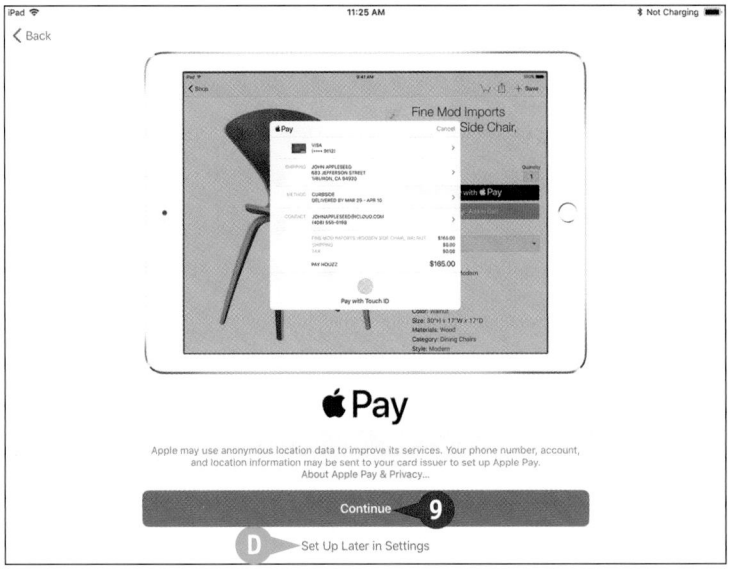

Several information screens appears, such as the Access the Dock from Anywhere screen.

10 On each information screen, read the details and tap **Continue** to proceed.

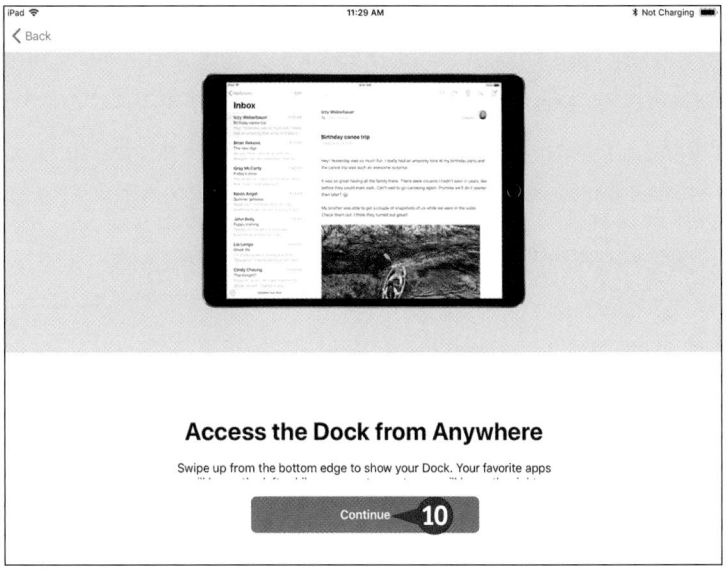

The App Analytics screen appears.

11 Tap **Share with App Developers** if you want to share usage statistics and crash data with the developers of the apps you use. Otherwise, tap **Don't Share**.

The Welcome to iPad screen appears.

12 Tap **Get Started**.

The Home screen appears, and you can begin using your iPad.

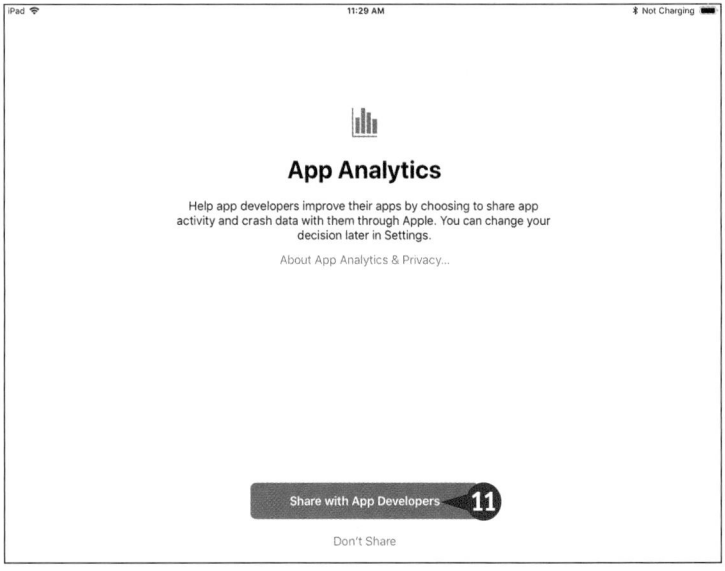

TIP

What is iCloud Keychain?

iCloud Keychain gives you an easy way to store your passwords and credit card information securely on your iPad, other iOS devices, and Mac. Instead of having to remember the password for each website, or needing to look at a credit card so that you can enter its details, you can have iCloud Keychain automatically provide the details.

Set Up Your iPad from an iCloud Backup

Instead of setting up your iPad as new using iCloud, you can set it up by restoring it from an iCloud backup of either another iPad or iOS device or the same iPad. For example, if you are upgrading to a new iPad, you can restore the backup of your previous iPad.

When you restore your iPad from an iCloud backup, you choose which backup to use. iOS automatically restores your settings, downloads your apps from the App Store, and then installs them on the iPad.

Set Up Your iPad from an iCloud Backup

1. Begin setup as explained in the section "Begin Setup and Activate Your iPad," earlier in this chapter.
2. On the Apps & Data screen, tap **Restore from iCloud Backup**.

Note: On a cellular iPad, use a Wi-Fi network rather than the cellular network to restore your iPad from backup so as not to run through your data plan.

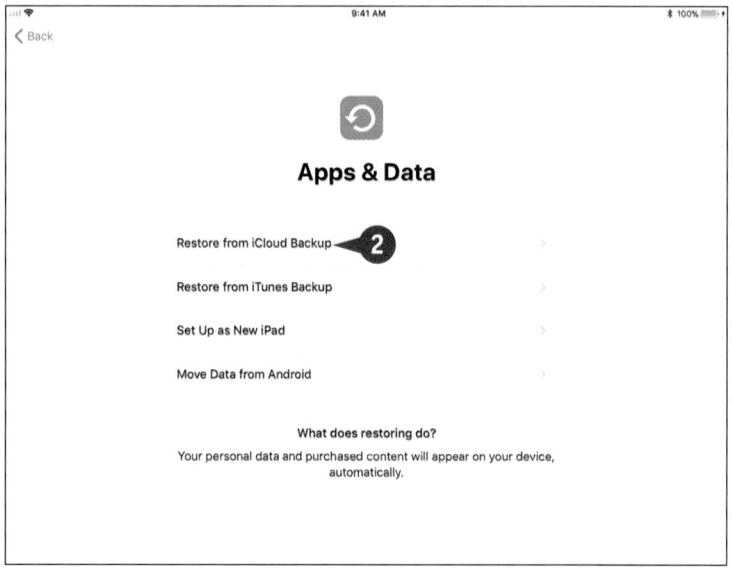

The iCloud Sign In screen appears.

3. Type your Apple ID.
4. Type your password.
5. Tap **Next**.

The Terms and Conditions screen appears.

6. Tap **Agree** in the lower-right corner of the screen.

iOS verifies your Apple ID.

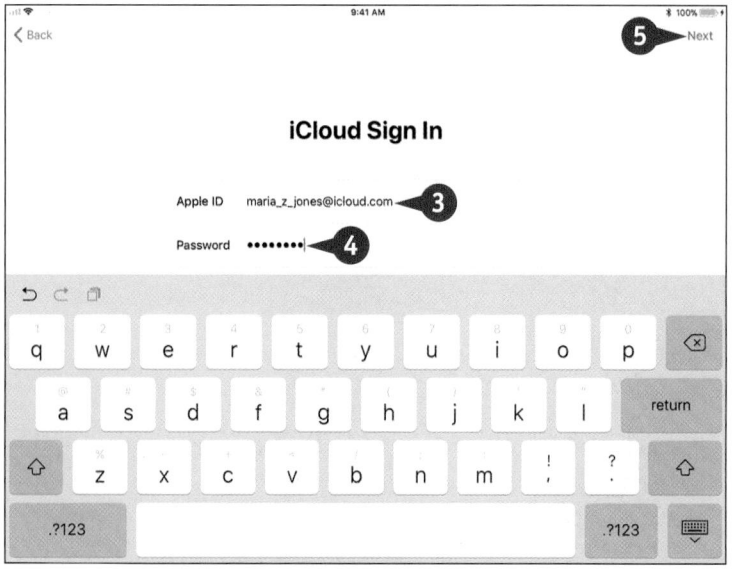

The Choose Backup screen appears.

7 Tap the backup you want to use.

A If the backup you want to use does not appear, tap **Show All Backups** to display other backups, and then tap the appropriate backup.

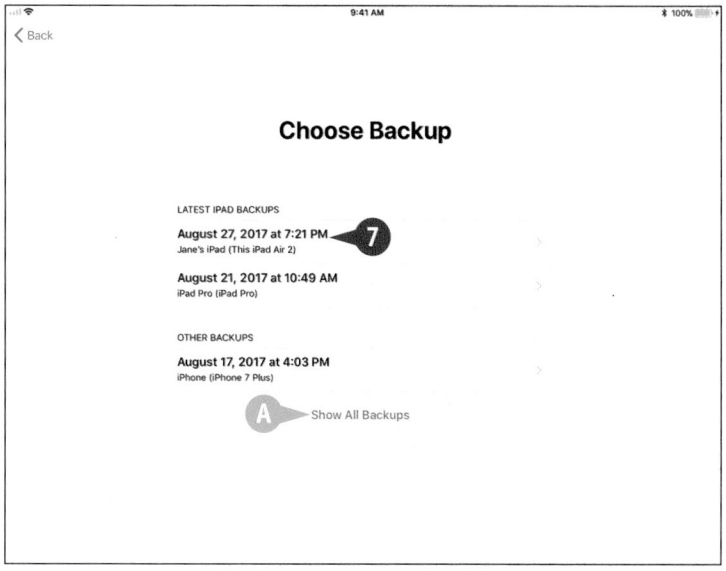

The Settings from Your Backup screen appears.

8 Tap **Continue** to restore the backup and include the settings shown in the list.

B You can tap **Customize Settings** if you want to customize the settings shown in the list.

The Restore from iCloud screen appears while iOS restores the backup to your iPad.

After iOS completes the restoration, your iPad restarts.

The lock screen appears.

9 Press **Home** to unlock your iPad, and follow any security prompts that appear. You can then start using the iPad.

TIP

Which iPad backup should I use?

Normally, it is best to use the most recent backup available for this iPad or for the iPad whose backups you are using. But sometimes you may find there is a problem with the latest backup. If this happens, try the previous backup.

Set Up Your iPad Using iTunes

Instead of setting up your iPad using iCloud, as described in the previous two sections, you can set it up using iTunes. You can either restore an iTunes backup to the device or set up the iPad from scratch using iTunes.

When setting up your iPad for the first time, you can restore it from an iTunes backup of another iPad — for example, your previous iPad — or another iOS device. If you have already set up this iPad, you can restore it from its own backup.

Set Up Your iPad Using iTunes

1. Begin setup as explained in the section "Begin Setup and Activate Your iPad," earlier in this chapter.
2. On the Apps & Data screen, tap **Restore from iTunes Backup**.

   The Connect to iTunes screen appears.
3. Connect your iPad to your computer via the USB cable.

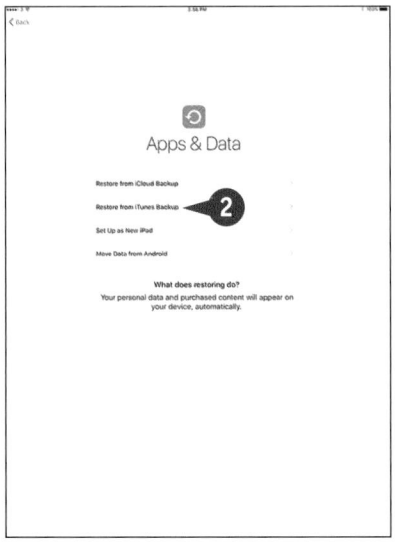

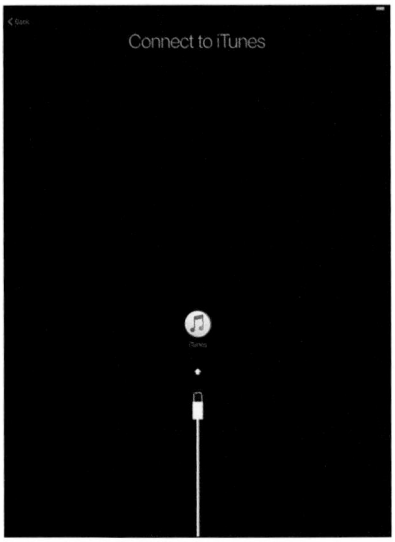

   On your computer, iTunes opens or becomes active.

   The Welcome to Your New iPad screen appears.
4. Make sure the **Restore from this backup** radio button is selected (◉).
5. Click the pop-up menu (⬍), and select the appropriate iPad.
6. Click **Continue**.

iTunes restores your iPad from the backup.

When the restore is complete, your iPad restarts.

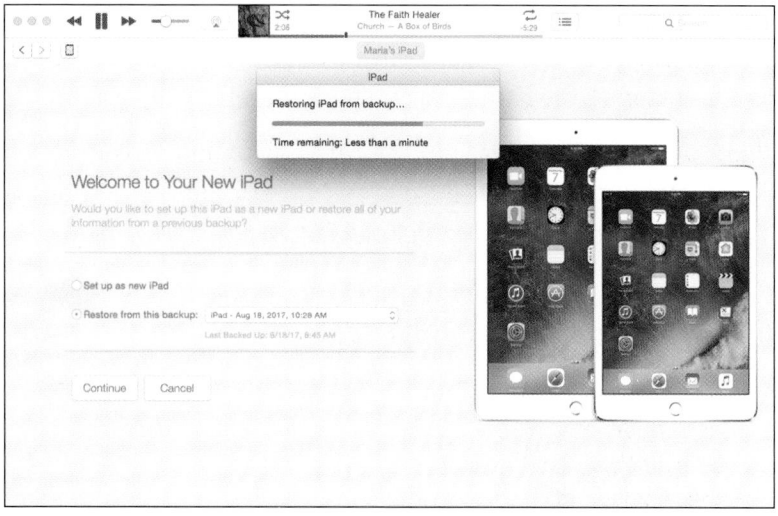

The control screens for your iPad appear in the iTunes window.

You can now choose sync settings for the iPad as explained in the next section, "Choose Which Items to Sync from Your Computer."

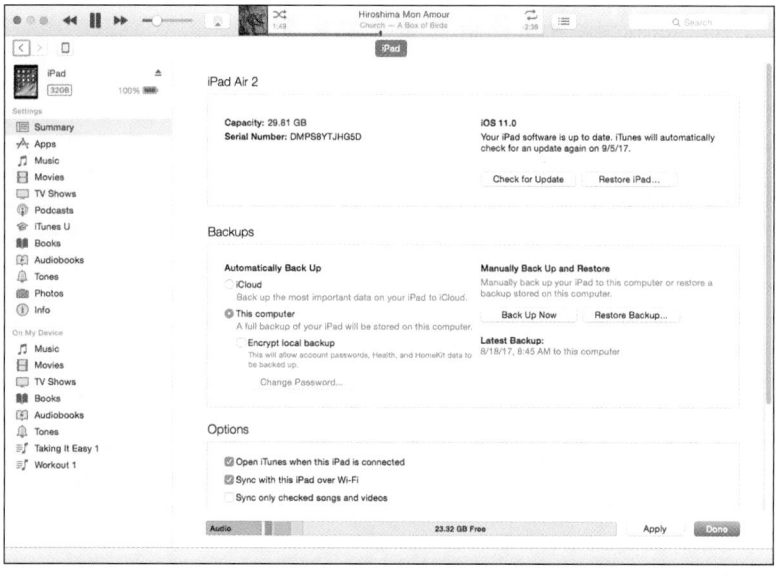

TIP

How do I set up my iPad from scratch using iTunes?

On the Apps & Data screen, tap **Restore from iTunes Backup**, and then connect your iPad to your computer via the USB cable. When the Welcome to Your New iPad screen appears in iTunes on your computer, click **Set up as new iPad** (○ changes to ◉). Click **Continue**. On the Sync with iTunes screen that appears, click **Get Started**. The iPad control screens appear, and you can set up sync as described in the next section, "Choose Which Items to Sync from Your Computer."

Choose Which Items to Sync from Your Computer

After setting up your iPad, you can use the iPad control screens in iTunes to choose which items to sync from your computer. When setting your sync preferences, start on the Summary tab. Here, you can change the iPad's name, choose whether to back up the iPad to iCloud or to your computer, decide whether to encrypt the backup, and set general options for controlling syncing.

Choose Which Items to Sync from Your Computer

Connect Your iPad and Choose Options on the Summary Tab

1. Connect your iPad to your computer via the USB cable.

   The iTunes window appears.

2. If the iPad control screens do not automatically appear, click the **iPad** button ( ) on the navigation bar at the top of the screen.

Note: Your iPad appears in iTunes with either a default name or the name you have given it.

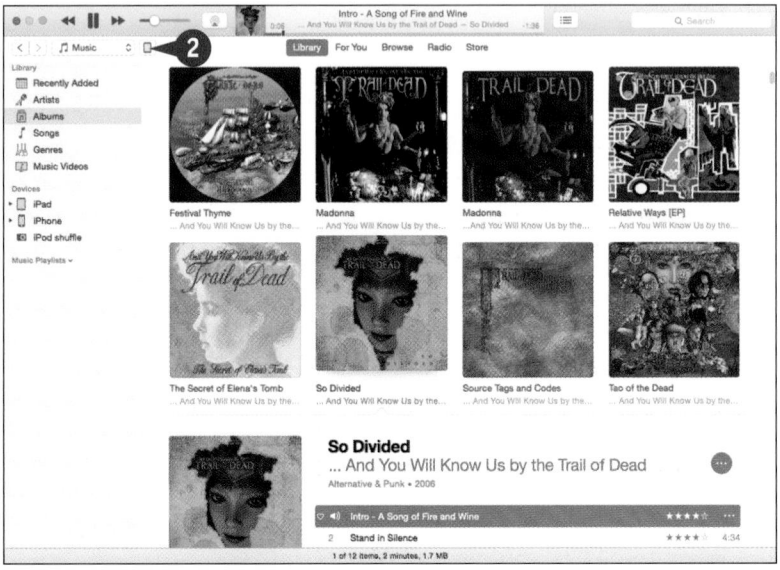

   The iPad control screens appear.

3. Click **Summary**.

   The Summary screen appears.

4. To change the name of your iPad, click the existing name, type the new name, and press Enter or Return.

5. In the Automatically Back Up area, click **iCloud** (changes to) or **This computer** (changes to) to specify where to back up your iPad.

6. If you choose to back up to this computer, click **Encrypt local backup** (changes to).

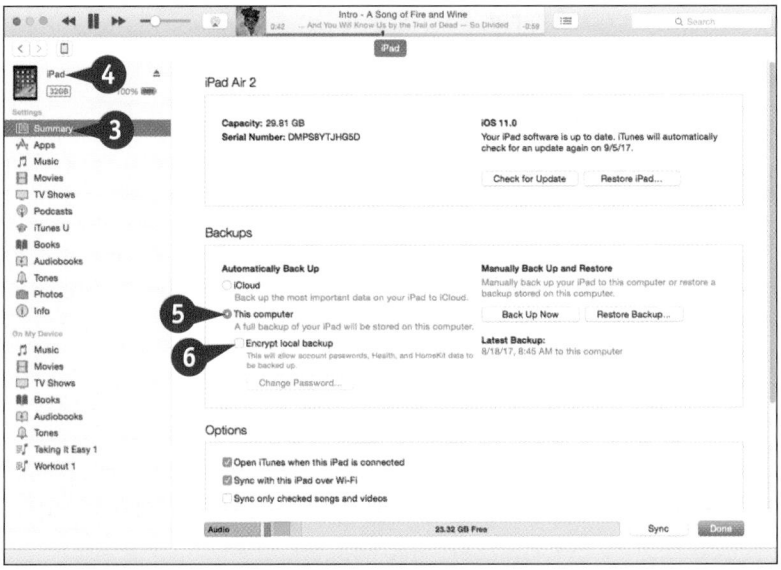

7. In the Set Password dialog, type a password twice.
8. On a Mac, click **Remember this password in my keychain** (☐ changes to ☑) if you want to save the password in your keychain.
9. Click **Set Password**.

The Set Password dialog closes.

10. Click **Open iTunes when this iPad is connected** (☐ changes to ☑) if you want iTunes to open automatically when you connect the iPad.
11. Click **Sync only checked songs and videos** (☐ changes to ☑) if you want syncing to omit any song or video whose check box you have deselected (☐).
12. Select **Convert higher bit rate songs to AAC** (☐ changes to ☑) if you want to compress high-quality song files to fit more on your iPad. In the pop-up menu, choose the bit rate.

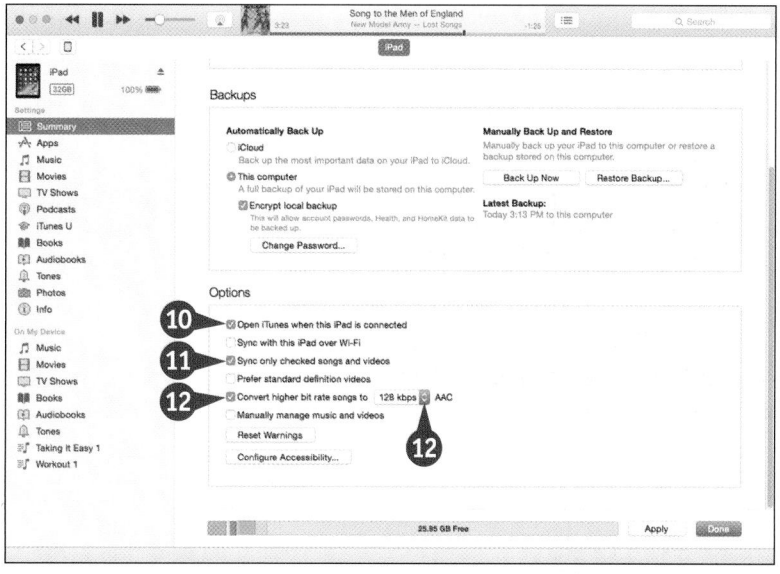

TIP

Should I back up my iPad to my computer or to iCloud?

If you plan to use your iPad mostly with your computer, back up the iPad to the computer. iTunes stores a full backup, so you can restore all the data to your iPad, or to a replacement iPad, if necessary. You can also encrypt the backup; this enables you to back up and restore your passwords as well, which can save you time and effort. To keep your data safe, you must back up your computer as well. For example, you can use the Time Machine feature on the Mac to back up your iPad's backup along with your other files.

Backing up your iPad to iCloud enables you to access the backups from anywhere via the Internet, but make sure your iCloud account has enough storage to contain the backups. An iCloud backup stores less information than an iTunes backup.

continued ▶

iTunes makes it easy to choose which items to sync to your iPad. By selecting the iPad in the navigation bar in iTunes and then clicking the appropriate item in the Settings area of the Source list, you can quickly choose which apps, music, movies, and other items to sync from your computer.

After choosing the items to sync, you click the Apply button to apply your changes or the Sync button to run the sync.

Choose Which Items to Sync from Your Computer (continued)

Choose Which Apps to Sync

1. Click **Apps**.

   A You can click the pop-up menu (⬍) and choose how to sort the apps: Click **Sort by Name**, **Sort by Kind**, **Sort by Category**, **Sort by Date Added**, or **Sort by Size**, as needed.

2. Click **Install** for each app you want to sync to the iPad (Install changes to Will Install).

3. Further down the screen, click **Automatically install new apps** (☐ changes to ☑) if you want to sync new apps automatically. Click the pop-up menu (⬍) and click **iPad** or **iPad and iPhone**, as needed.

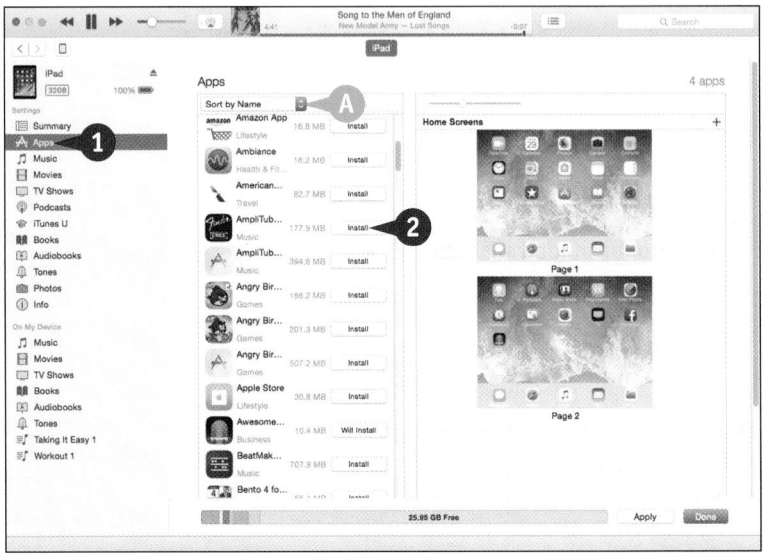

Choose Which Music to Sync

1. Click **Music**.
2. Click **Sync Music** (☐ changes to ☑).
3. To load a selection of music, click **Selected playlists, artists, albums, and genres** (○ changes to ◉) instead of **Entire music library**.

   B Click **Automatically fill free space with songs** (☐ changes to ☑) if you want to put as much music as possible on your iPad.

4. Click the check box (☐ changes to ☑) for each playlist, artist, genre, or album to include.

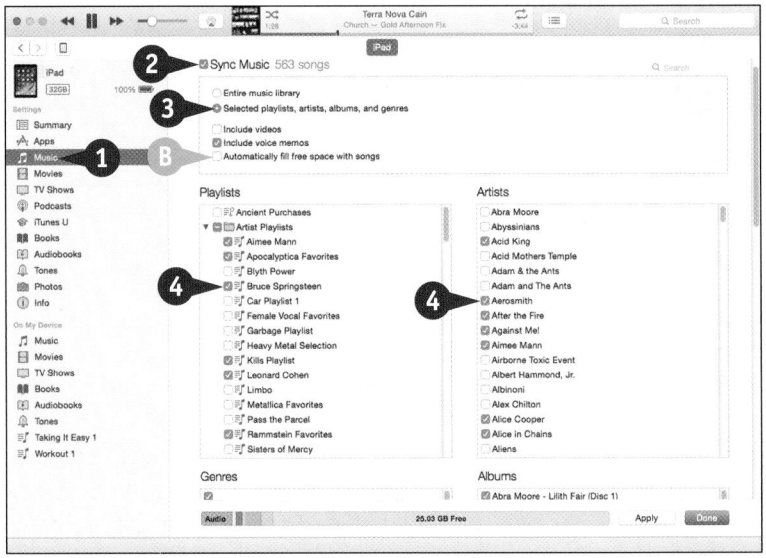

Sync Books

1. Click **Books**.

   The Books controls appear.

2. Click **Sync Books** (☐ changes to ☑).

3. Click **All books** (○ changes to ◉) or **Selected books** (○ changes to ◉).

4. If you click **Selected books**, use the controls in the Books box to choose which books to sync.

Note: You can sync photos from your computer only if you are not using the iCloud Photos feature. If you have enabled iCloud Photos, your iPhone syncs your photos through iCloud instead.

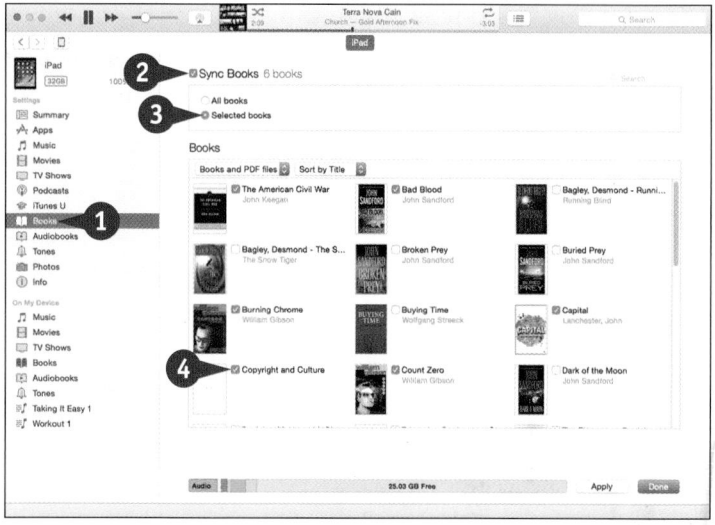

Apply Your Changes and Sync

1. Click **Apply** or **Sync**.

Note: The Apply button appears when you have made changes to the times you will sync. Click **Apply** to apply the changes and sync them.

   iTunes syncs the items to your iPad.

   C The readout shows you the sync progress.

   D If you need to stop the sync, click **Stop** (✕).

2. When the sync finishes, disconnect your iPad.

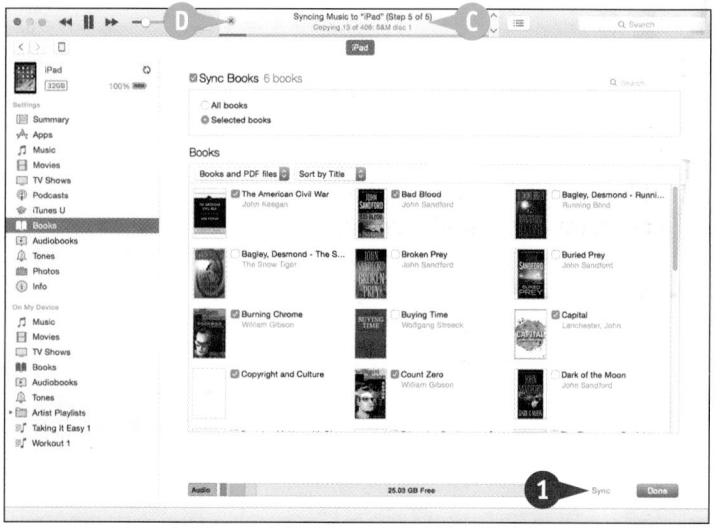

TIP

How can I fit more content on my iPad?

You cannot increase your iPad's storage capacity, but you can use the iPad Storage feature to remove items you do not need.

Press **Home**, tap **Settings** (⚙) to display the Settings screen, and then tap **General** (⚙). On the General screen, tap **iPad Storage** to display the iPad Storage screen. You can then follow suggestions in the Recommendations box, such as tapping **Enable** for Optimize Photos or for Offload Unused Apps, or tap buttons in the lower section to see which apps and files are consuming the most space.

Sync Your iPad with Your Computer via Wi-Fi

Instead of syncing your iPad via the USB-to-Lightning cable, you can sync it wirelessly, or "over the air." To do so, you must connect both your computer and your iPad to the same network and enable wireless sync in iTunes. You can then have the iPad sync automatically when it is connected to a power source and to the same wireless network as the computer, and when iTunes is also running on your Mac or PC. You can also start a sync manually from the iPad even if it is not connected to a power source.

Sync Your iPad with Your Computer via Wi-Fi

Set Your iPad to Sync with iTunes via Wi-Fi

1. Connect your iPad to your computer with the USB cable.

   The iTunes window appears.

2. Click **iPad** ( ) on the navigation bar.

   The iPad control screens appear.

3. Click **Summary**.

4. Click **Sync with this iPad over Wi-Fi** (changes to).

5. Click **Apply**.

6. Disconnect your iPad from your computer.

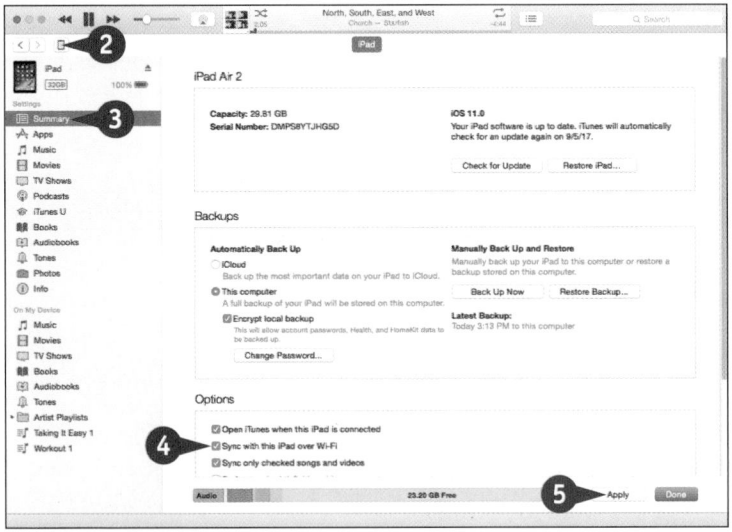

Perform a Manual Sync via Wi-Fi

1. Press **Home**.

   The Home screen appears.

2. Tap **Settings** ( ).

The Settings screen appears.

3. Tap **General** (⚙).

The General screen appears.

4. Tap **iTunes Wi-Fi Sync**.

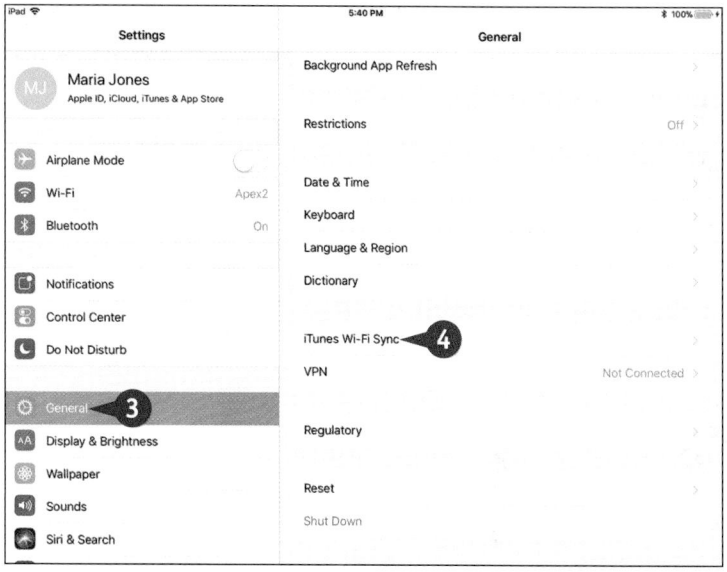

The iTunes Wi-Fi Sync screen appears.

5. Tap **Sync Now**.

The sync runs.

The Sync symbol (🔄) appears in the iPad status bar.

The readout shows which part of the sync is currently running.

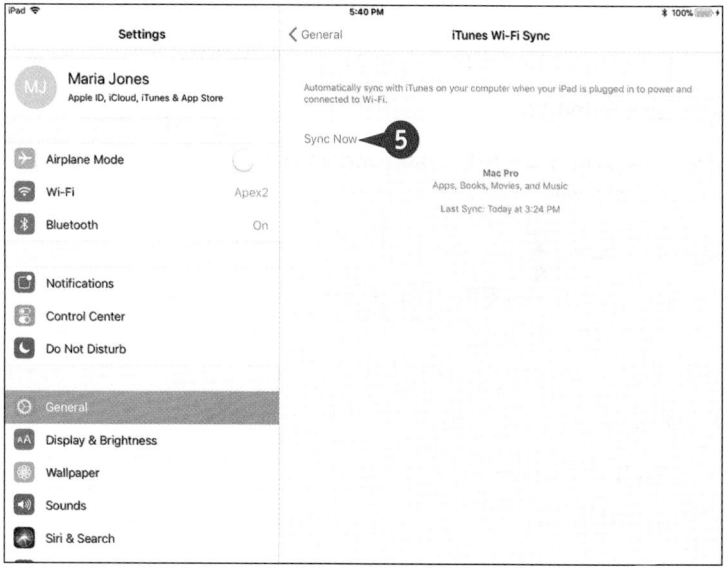

TIP

Should I sync my iPad via Wi-Fi or via USB?

Try both means of syncing and see which suits you best. You can use USB sync even after enabling Wi-Fi syncing, so you do not have to choose one means or the other.

Even though modern Wi-Fi networks and iPads can transfer data at high speeds, you may find that USB sync is still faster and more reliable.

Explore the Interface and Launch Apps

After you sync the iPad with your computer or set it up with iCloud, you are ready to start using the iPad. When you press the Sleep/Wake button or open the Smart Cover — or the Smart Keyboard on an iPad Pro — the iPad displays the lock screen. You then unlock the iPad to reach the Home screen, which contains icons for running the apps installed on the iPad.

You can quickly launch an app by tapping its icon on the Home screen. From the app, you can return to the Home screen by pressing the Home button. You can then launch another app as needed.

Explore the Interface and Launch Apps

1. Press **Home** with a finger or thumb you have registered for Touch ID fingerprint recognition.

   The iPad wakes and reads your fingerprint.

   The iPad unlocks, and the Home screen appears.

   A The iPad has two or more Home screens, depending on how many apps are installed and how you arrange them. The gray dots at the bottom of the Home screen show how many Home screens you have. The white dot shows the current Home screen.

2. Tap **Notes** ( ).

   The Notes app opens.

Note: If you chose to sync notes with your iPad, the synced notes appear in the Notes app. Otherwise, the list is empty until you create a note.

3. Tap **New** ( ) to create a new note.

   The on-screen keyboard appears automatically.

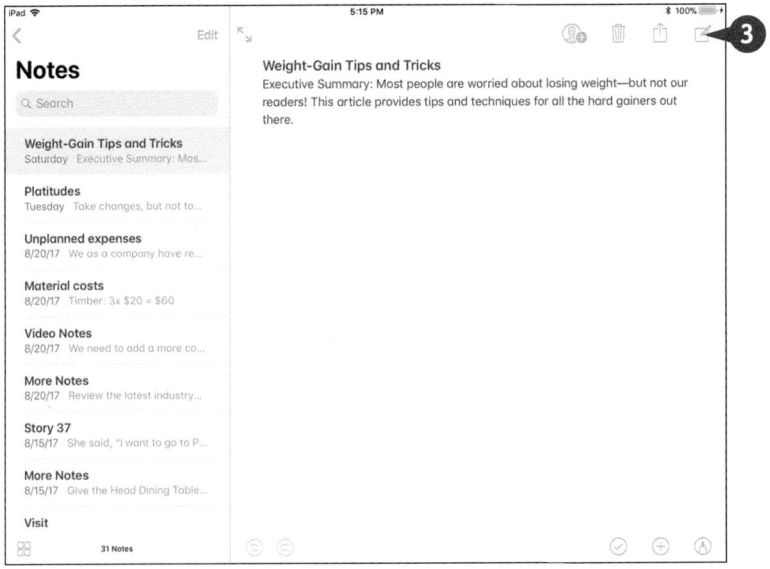

4. Type a short note.

   B The note appears in the Notes list.

   C If the suggestion bar shows the word or phrase you want, tap it to enter it.

Note: If the suggestion is in the center, you can enter it by tapping Spacebar or another punctuation character.

   D If you need to hide the keyboard, tap **Hide Keyboard** ( ).

   E To delete the note, tap **Delete** ( ) and then tap **Delete Note** on the pop-up panel.

5. Press **Home**.

   The Home screen appears.

6. Swipe left to display the second Home screen.

   You can now launch another app by tapping its icon.

7. Press the **Sleep/Wake** button.

Note: If your iPad has a Smart Cover, you can also put it to sleep by closing the Smart Cover.

   Your iPad goes to sleep.

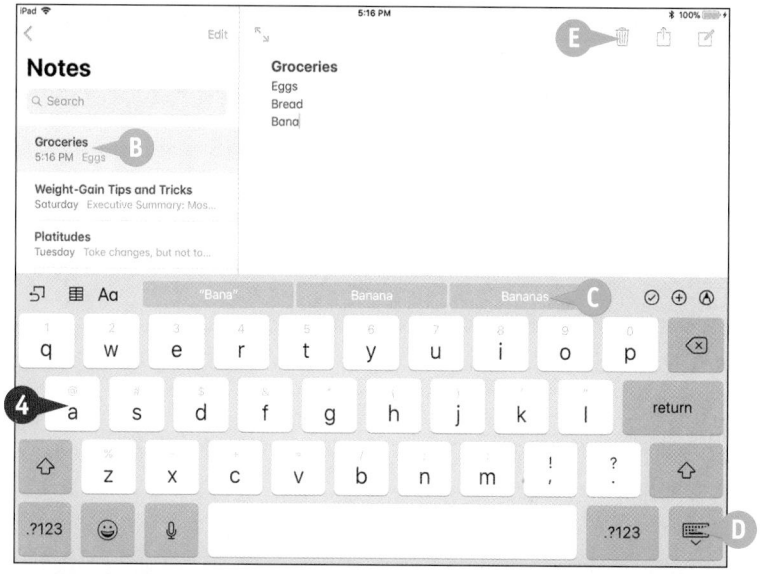

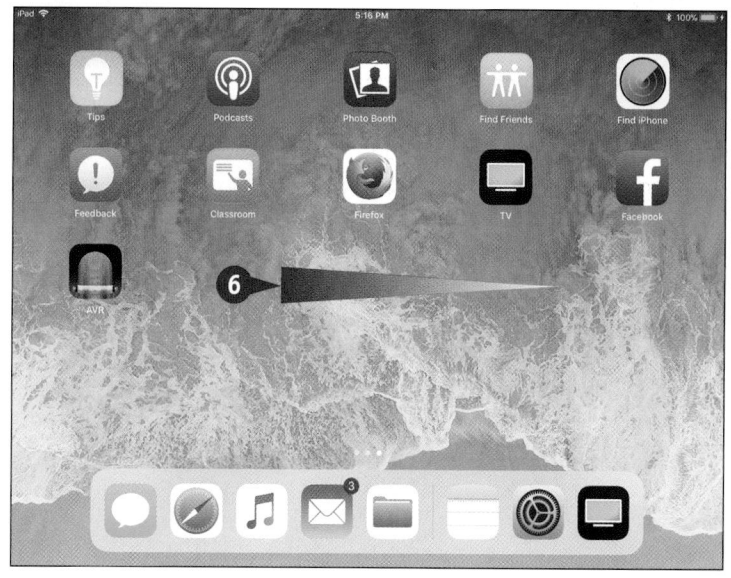

TIP

Where do I get more apps to perform other tasks?

You can find an amazingly wide selection of apps — both free and those you pay for — on the Apple App Store. See Chapter 6 for instructions on finding and downloading the apps you need.

Using Cover Sheet and Today View

Your iPad handles many different types of alerts, such as missed FaceTime calls, text messages, and invitations to events such as meetings. Your iPad integrates these alerts into Cover Sheet so that you can review them easily.

The iPad's Today View enables you to view snippets of important and helpful information, such as weather, calendar appointments, and stock updates. You can access Today View either via Cover Sheet or directly from the Home screen.

Using Cover Sheet and Today View

1. Swipe down from the top of the screen.

Cover Sheet appears.

A You can tap **Clear** (⊗) to clear all notifications in a category, such as Earlier Today.

B You can tap a notification to go to the app that raised it. For example, if you tap the notification for a message, the Messages app appears.

2. Swipe a notification left.

The View button and the Clear button appear.

3. Tap **Clear**.

The notification disappears from Cover Sheet.

4. Swipe right.

Note: You can also open Today View by swiping right on the first Home screen.

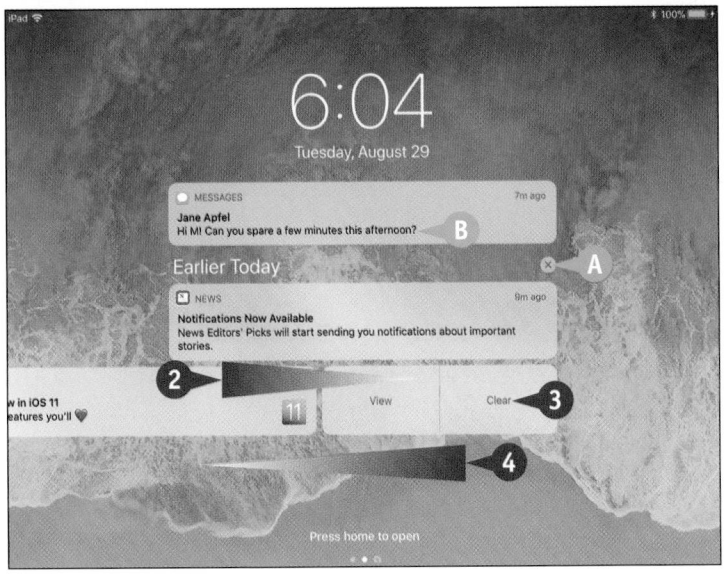

Today View appears, showing current information such as weather, calendar appointments, news, and reminders.

Other items appear.

C You can tap a widget to go straight to the related app.

D You can tap **Search** (🔍) and type a search term to search for items.

Note: You can tap an item such as a reminder to mark it as done.

5 To edit Today View, tap **Edit**.

The Add Widgets screen appears, showing current widgets in the top section and available widgets in the More Widgets section.

6 Drag a handle (☰) to move an item from one section to another or to a different position within its current section.

7 Tap **Remove** (⊖) to remove a widget from the current widgets, moving it to the More Widgets section.

8 Tap **Add** (⊕) to move a widget from the More Widgets section to the current widgets.

9 Tap **Done**.

Today View appears again.

10 Swipe up from the bottom of the screen.

Today View closes, and the screen appears that you were using before.

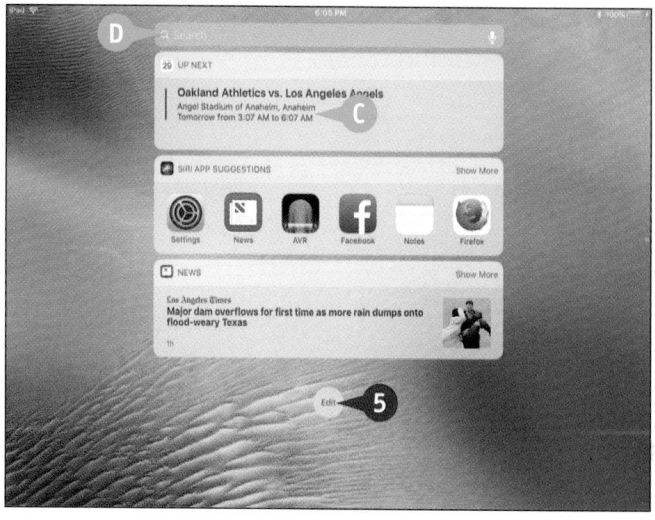

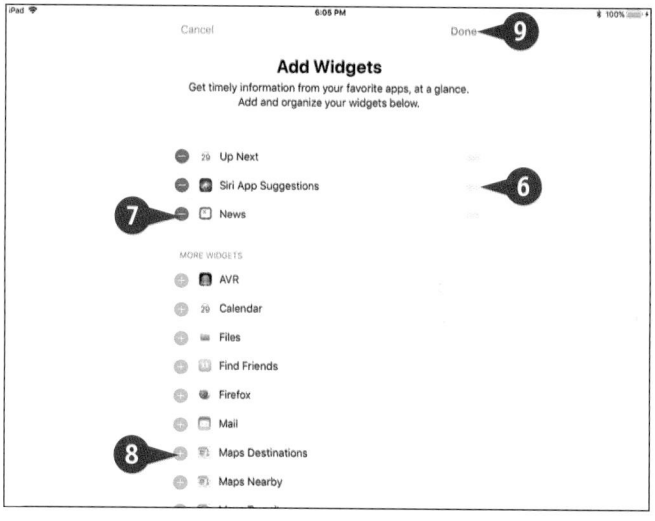

TIP

What happens if I receive a notification when my iPad is locked?

What happens when you receive a notification while the screen is locked depends on the type of notification. For most types of notifications, your iPad displays an alert on the lock screen to alert you to the notification. Unlocking your iPad while the alert is displayed takes you directly to the notification in whatever app it belongs to — for example, to an instant message in the Messages app. If there are multiple alerts, drag across the one you want to open.

Using Control Center

Control Center enables you to turn on or off Airplane Mode, Wi-Fi, Bluetooth, Do Not Disturb Mode, Mute, Orientation Lock, and Night Shift; adjust the screen brightness; control music playback and volume, and direct the audio output to AirPlay devices; change the setting for the AirDrop sharing feature; and quickly access the Clock and Camera apps.

When the iPad is locked, Control Center appears on its own. When the iPad is unlocked, the Dock appears, as do thumbnails for your open apps.

Using Control Center

Open Control Center

1. Swipe up from the bottom of the screen.

   The Dock appears when the iPad is unlocked.

   Control Center opens.

Note: You can open Control Center from most apps and screens.

- A You can drag the **Brightness** slider (☀) up or down to adjust the brightness.
- B You can drag the **Volume** slider (🔊) up or down to adjust the volume.
- C You can tap **Timer** (⏲) to display the Timer screen in the Clock app.
- D You can tap **Camera** (📷) to display the Camera app.

Control Essential Settings

1. Tap **Airplane Mode** (✈) to turn Airplane Mode on or off.
2. Tap **Wi-Fi** (📶) to turn Wi-Fi on or off.
3. Tap **Bluetooth** (✱) to turn Bluetooth on or off.
4. Tap **Orientation Lock** (🔒) to turn Orientation Lock on or off.
5. Tap **Mute** (🔔) to turn muting on or off.
6. Tap **Do Not Disturb** (☾) to turn Do Not Disturb Mode on or off.

Use AirPlay Devices and Control Music Playback

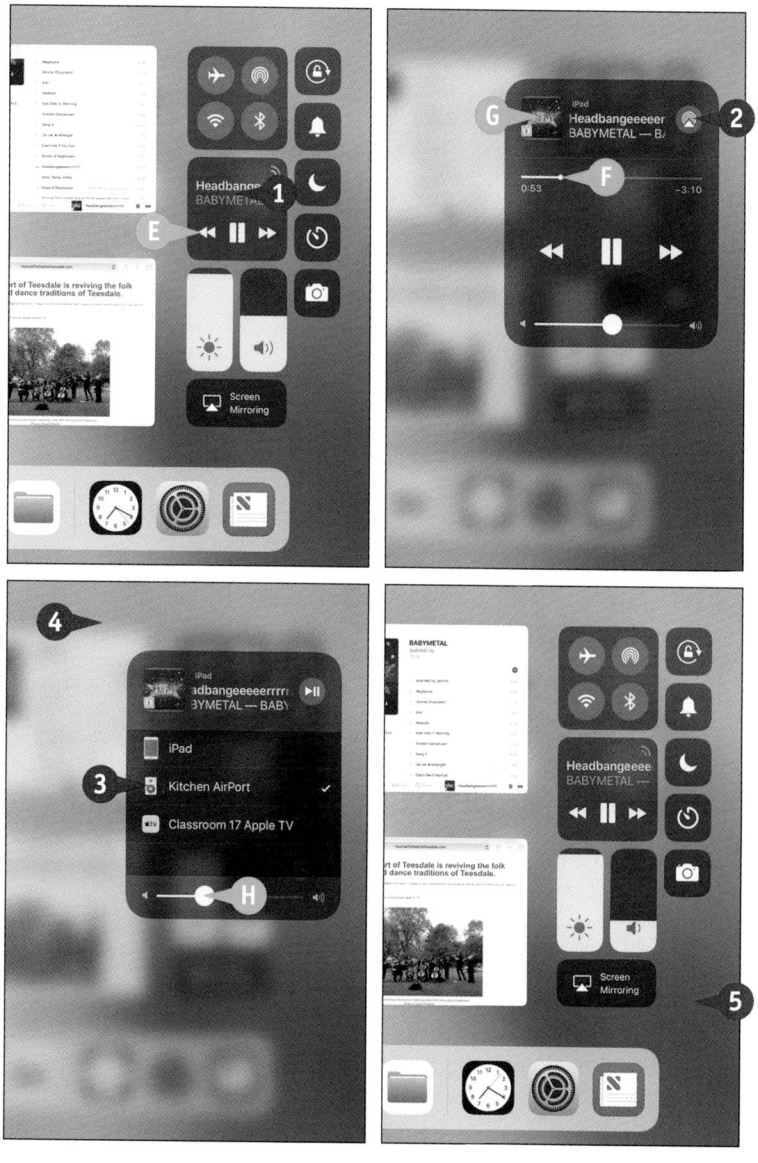

(E) You can use the playback controls to control playback.

1. Press and hold the Music box.

   The Music box expands, showing additional controls.

(F) You can drag the Playhead to move through the song.

(G) You can tap the song art or the song details to go to the Music app.

2. Tap **AirPlay** ( ).

   The AirPlay dialog opens.

3. Tap the AirPlay device you want to use.

   The music starts playing on the AirPlay device.

(H) You can drag the **Volume** slider to adjust the playback volume on the current device.

4. Tap outside the AirPlay dialog.

   The AirPlay dialog closes.

5. Tap open space on the screen or press **Home**.

   Control Center closes.

Note: Instead of closing Control Center, you can tap an app's thumbnail to go straight to that app.

TIP

How do I enable or disable Night Shift from Control Center?

Swipe up from the bottom of the screen to open Control Center, and then tap and hold the **Brightness** slider ( ). The Brightness slider expands, and the Night Shift icon appears. Tap **Night Shift** (or) to turn Night Shift on (changes to) or off (changes to). Tap outside the Brightness slider or the Night Shift icon to return to Control Center.

Using the Dock

The Dock enables you to launch apps and switch quickly among them. The Dock appears on the Home screen, but you can also open it from other screens with a short swipe up from the bottom of the screen. A longer swipe up opens Control Center as well.

The Dock is divided into two sections by a vertical line. The left section contains apps fixed to the Dock, which you can customize as needed. The right section contains recent apps and suggested apps, which change as you work.

Using the Dock

Open the Dock and Launch an App

1. With an app displayed on the screen, swipe up from the bottom of the screen.

Note: If you have a keyboard connected to your iPad, you can press ⌘+Option+D to display or hide the Dock.

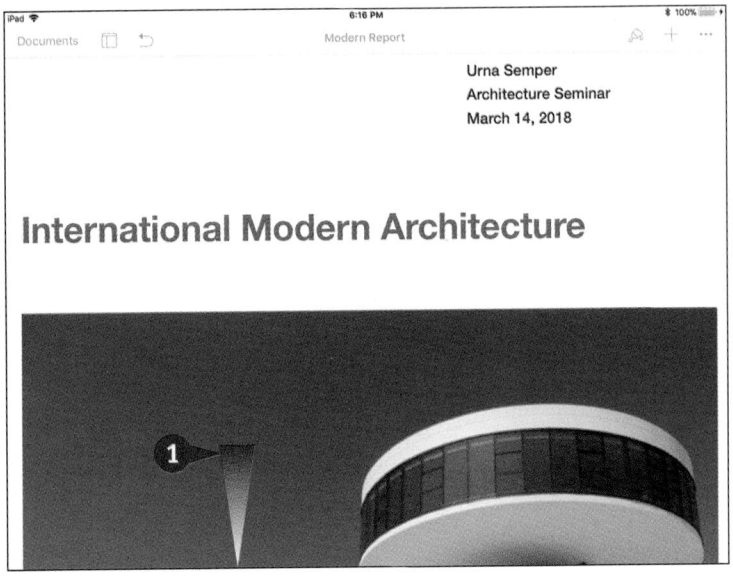

The Dock appears.

- A Icons on the left side of the Dock are fixed to the Dock. You can add, remove, and rearrange the fixed icons as needed.
- B This faint line divides the left side from the right side.
- C Icons on the right side of the Dock are for recent apps and suggested apps.

2. Tap the icon for the app you want to launch.

The app opens.

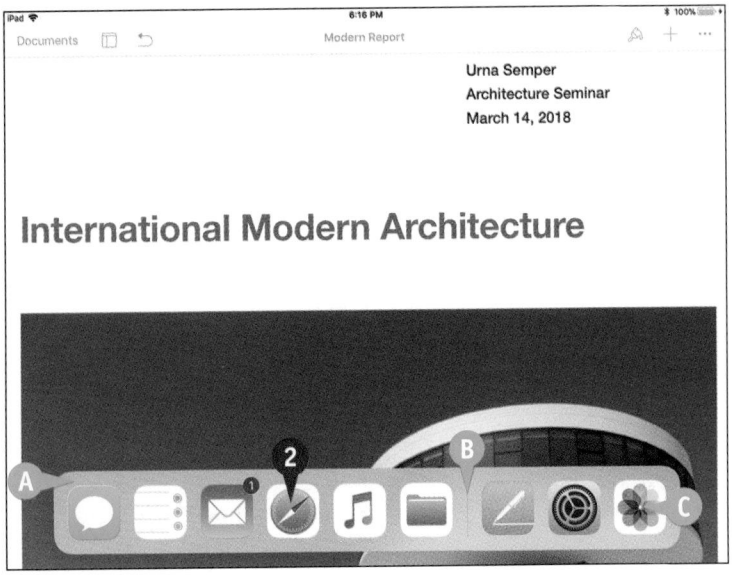

Open a Recent File

1. Tap and hold the icon for the appropriate app on the Dock. This example uses **Pages** ( ).

Note: This technique works for only some apps.

A list of recent files appears.

Note: If you tap and hold for too long with the Home screen displayed, the icons start jiggling so that you can customize the layout. Press **Home** to stop the icons from jiggling.

2. Tap the icon for the file you want to open.

The file opens.

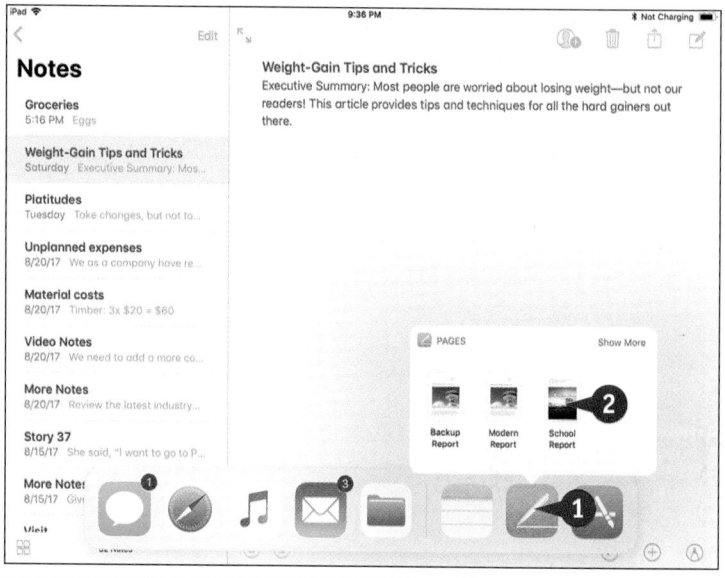

Open an App in Slide-Over View

1. With an app displayed, open the Dock and drag the app's icon up off it.
2. When the icon becomes a button, release it.

The app appears in Slide-Over view on the right side of the screen.

Note: See the section "Multitask with Split-Screen Views and Spaces" in Chapter 6 for more coverage of multitasking.

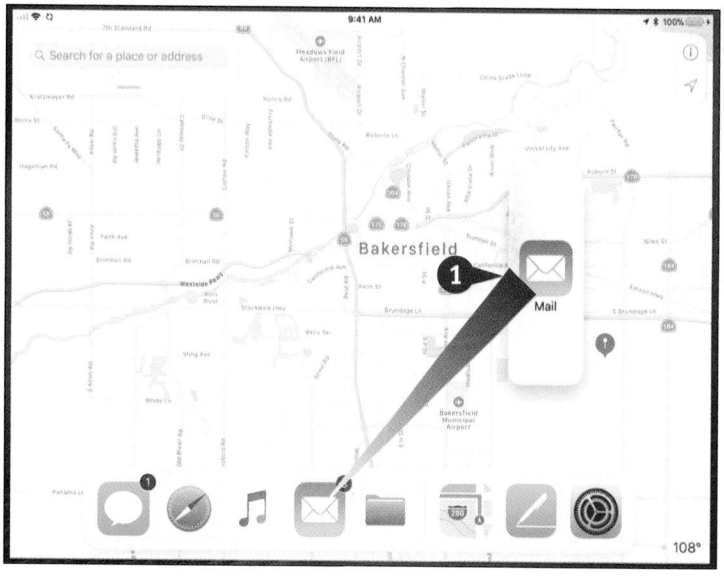

TIP

How do I customize the Dock to contain the icons I need?

You can rearrange the icons on the left side of the Dock by tapping and holding an icon and then dragging it to its new destination. To add an icon, drag it from the Home screen to the Dock. To remove an icon, drag it from the Dock to the Home screen.

To remove recent apps and suggested apps, press **Home**, tap **Settings** ( ), tap **General** ( ), tap **Multitasking & Dock**, and then set the **Show Suggested and Recent Apps** switch to Off ( ).

CHAPTER 2

Personalizing Your iPad

In this chapter, you learn how to control notifications, audio preferences, screen brightness, and other key iPad behaviors.

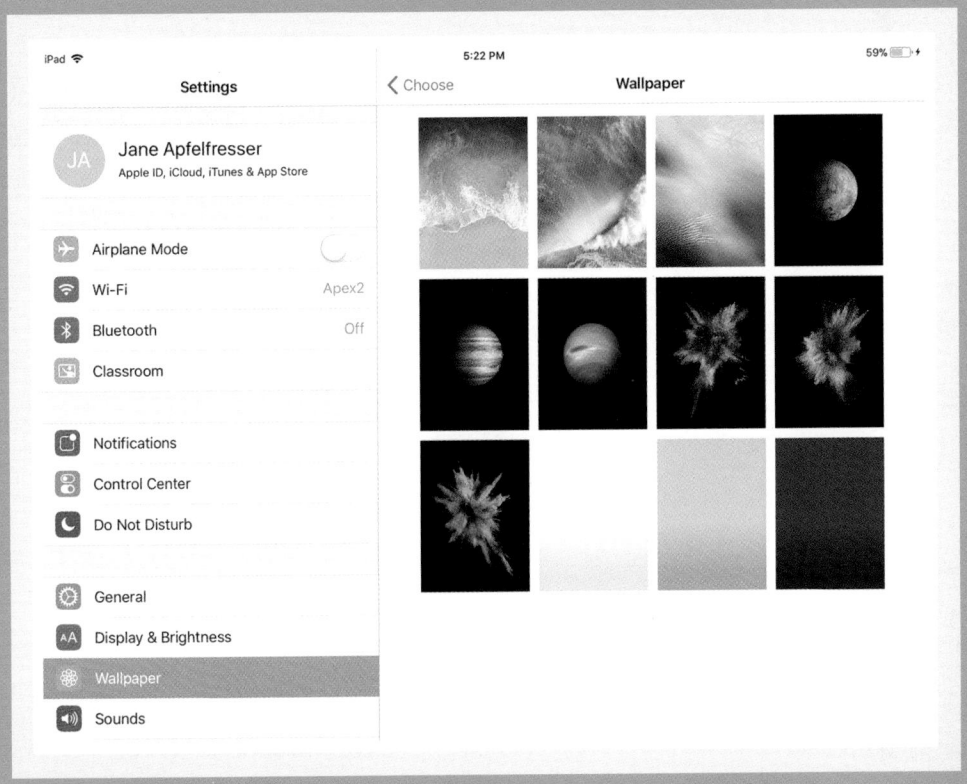

Find the Settings You Need 40
Set Up and Configure iCloud 42
Choose Which Apps Can Give Notifications 46
Choose Sounds Settings 48
Configure Display, Brightness, and Night Shift. 50
Set Home Screen and Lock Screen Wallpaper. 52
Choose Privacy and Location Settings 54
Configure Search and Find What You Need. 56
Choose Locking and Control Center Settings 58
Set Up and Use Do Not Disturb Mode 60
Secure Your iPad with Touch ID or a Passcode 62
Configure Restrictions and Parental Controls 64
Set Up Family Sharing and Add Members 66
Choose Date, Time, and Region Settings. 68

Find the Settings You Need

To configure your iPad, you work with its settings using the Settings app. This app contains settings for the iPad system software, the apps the iPad includes, and third-party apps you have added.

To reach the settings, you first display the Settings screen, and then display the category of settings you want to configure. In this section, you learn how to open the Settings screen to display the main categories of settings it contains.

Find the Settings You Need

Display the Settings Screen

1. Press **Home**.

   The Home screen appears.

2. Tap **Settings** ( ).

   A You can also tap **Settings** ( ) on the Dock.

   The Settings screen appears.

   B You can tap **Search** ( ) and type a keyword to search for the setting you need. You may need to swipe your finger down the left column, scrolling the column up, to display the Settings box.

3. Tap in the left column and drag up to scroll down the screen to locate the settings category you need.

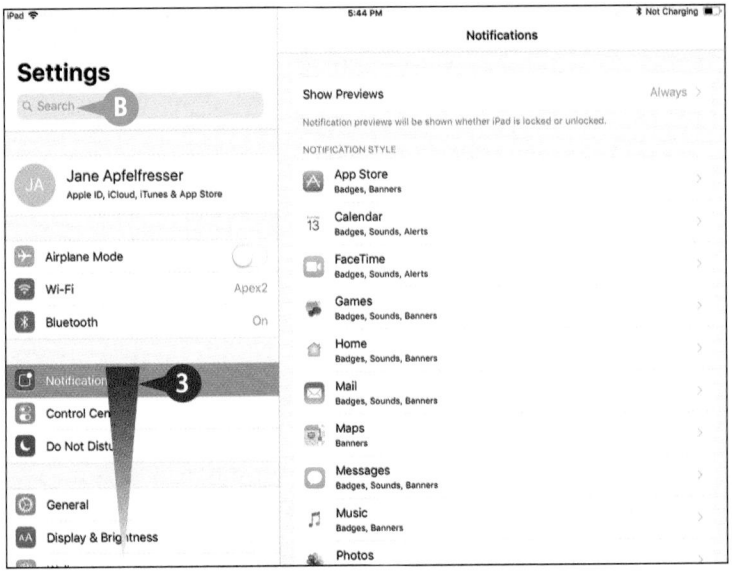

Display a Settings Screen

1. In the left column on the Settings screen, tap the button for the settings you want to display. For example, tap **Display & Brightness** (AA) to show the Display & Brightness screen.

C Tap a button that has > at its right end to display another screen of settings.

D Set a switch to On (◯) or Off ( ) to enable or disable a setting.

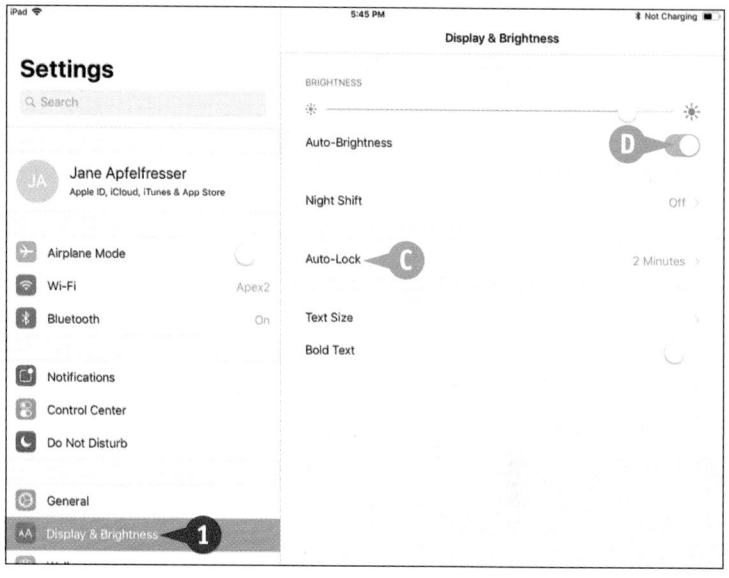

Display the Settings for an App

1. On the Settings screen, tap and drag up the left column to scroll down the screen.
2. Tap the button for the app whose settings you want to display. For example, tap **iBooks** (📖) to display the settings for the iBooks app.
3. When you finish using the Settings app, press **Home**.

   The Home screen appears again.

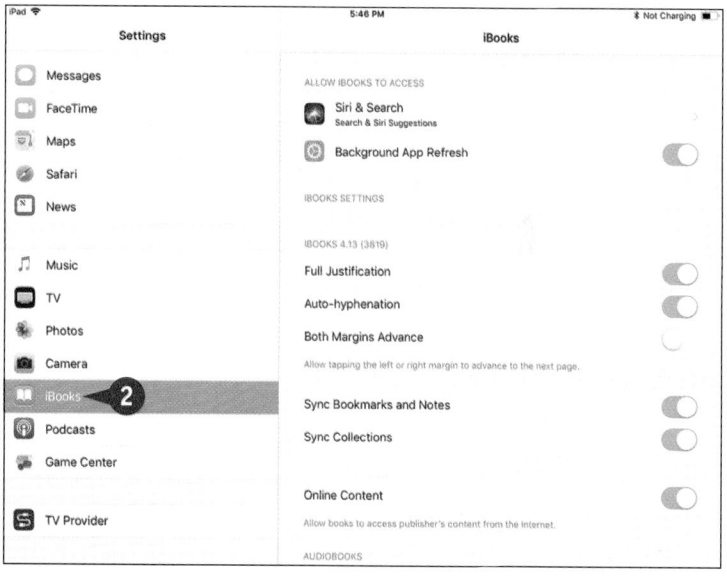

TIP

Where do I find other settings for an app?

As well as the settings that you access by tapping the button bearing the app's name on the Settings screen, some apps include settings that you configure directly within the app. For such apps, look for a Settings icon or menu item.

To configure notifications for an app, tap **Notifications** (🔔) on the Settings screen, and then tap the app's button. To configure Location Services settings for an app, tap **Privacy** (✋) on the Settings screen, tap **Location Services** (➚), and then tap the app's button.

Set Up and Configure iCloud

Apple's iCloud service enables you to sync items such as your e-mail, contacts, calendars and reminders, Safari bookmarks, photos, and documents and data online. You can also use the Find My iPad feature to locate your iPad when it goes missing.

To use iCloud, you set your iPad to use your Apple ID, and then choose which features to use. If you set up your iPad using iCloud, your account is already active, but you may want to choose different settings for iCloud.

Set Up and Configure iCloud

1. Press **Home**.

   The Home screen appears.

2. Tap **Settings** (◉).

   The Settings screen appears.

3. Tap **Sign in to your iPad**.

   The Sign In dialog opens.

4. Type your Apple ID.

   A If you do not yet have an Apple ID, tap **Don't have an Apple ID or forgot it?**, and then follow the prompts.

5. Type your password.

6. Tap **Sign In**.

   Your iPad starts signing in to iCloud.

   If your Apple ID uses two-step verification, as Apple and security experts recommend, the Apple ID Verification Code dialog opens.

7. Type the six-digit code sent to the iOS device or Mac you use for verification.

   The iPad completes the sign-in process.

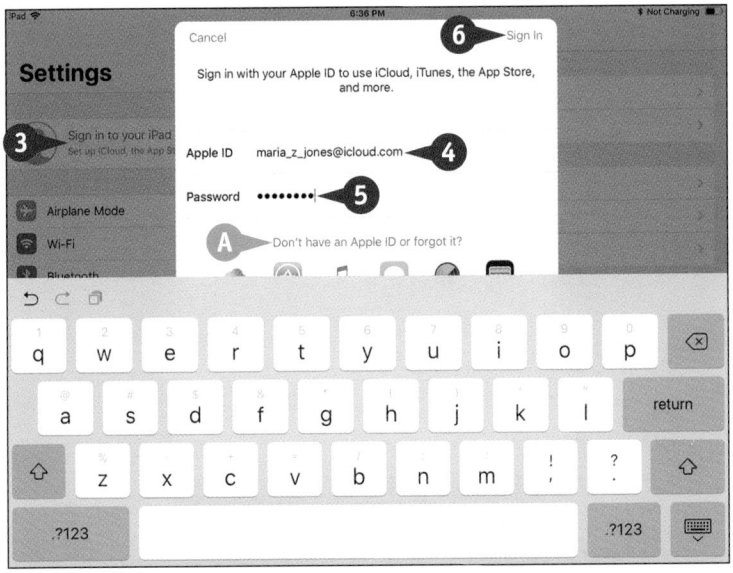

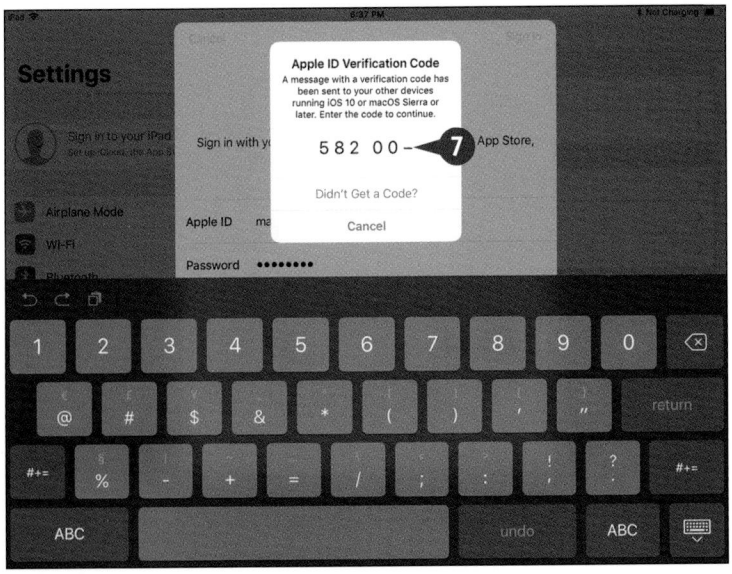

Note: When you sign into iCloud, iOS automatically enables Find My iPad, enabling you to locate your iPad by signing in to your account on the iCloud website, www.icloud.com. See the section "Locate Your iPad with Find My iPad" in Chapter 12 for details.

The Apple ID screen appears.

B You can tap **Name, Phone Numbers, Email** to change your contact information.

C You can tap **Password & Security** to change your security details.

D You can tap **Payment & Shipping** to change your payment and shipping options.

E You can tap **Family Sharing** ( ) to configure sharing. See the section "Set Up Family Sharing and Add Members," later in this chapter, for details.

8 Tap **iCloud** ( ).

The iCloud screen appears.

F The Storage readout shows how much iCloud storage you have and how much is in use.

9 In the Apps Using iCloud list, set each app's switch to On ( ) or Off ( ), as needed, to control which apps can use iCloud.

10 Tap **Photos** ( ).

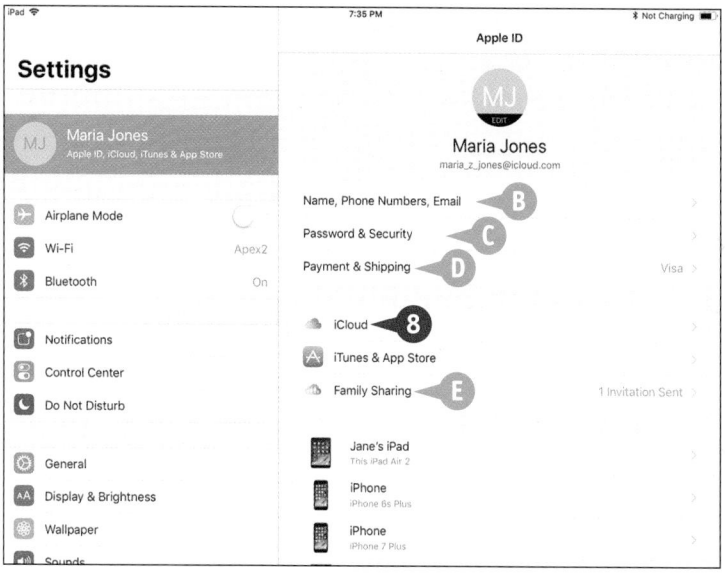

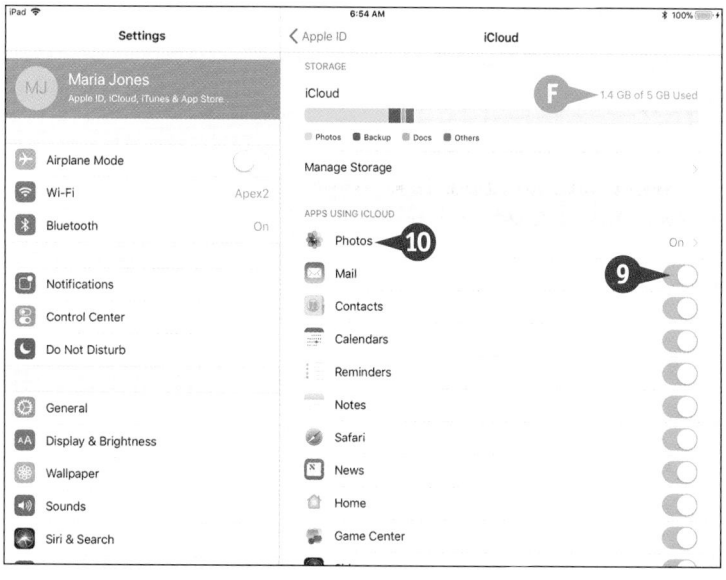

TIP

What does the Look Me Up By Email feature do?

This feature enables you to control which apps can look you up by the e-mail address you use for your Apple ID. Tap **Look Me Up By Email** on the iCloud Drive screen to display the Look Me Up By Email screen, which displays a list of the apps that have requested permission to look you up. You can then set the switch for an app to Off (changes to) if you want to prevent the app from looking you up.

continued ▶

On the Photos screen in iCloud Settings, you can choose to store your entire photo library in iCloud so that you can access your photos and videos from all your devices. You can also decide whether to upload photos automatically, whether to upload bursts of photos, and whether to share photos with other people via iCloud Photo Sharing.

Your other options include iCloud Keychain, which gives you a secure way to store passwords and credit card information across your Apple devices.

Set Up and Configure iCloud (continued)

The Photos screen appears.

11. Set the **iCloud Photo Library** switch to On (◐) to upload all your photos to iCloud.
12. Tap **Optimize iPad Storage** to store lower-resolution versions of photos on your iPad to save space. Tap **Download and Keep Originals** if you prefer to keep original, full-quality photos on your iPad.
13. Set the **Upload to My Photo Stream** switch to On (◐) to use Photo Stream.
14. Set the **Upload Burst Photos** switch to On (◐) to upload bursts you have shot.
15. Set the **iCloud Photo Sharing** switch to On (◐) to enable album sharing with other people.
16. Tap **iCloud** (<).

    The iCloud screen appears again.
17. Toward the bottom of the screen, set the **iCloud Drive** switch to On (◐) to enable iCloud Drive.
18. In the lower part of the screen, set each app's switch to On (◐) or Off (○) to control which apps can use iCloud.

G You can tap **Keychain** (🔑) to display the Keychain screen, on which you can enable or disable iCloud Keychain.

19. Tap **Find My iPad** (◉).

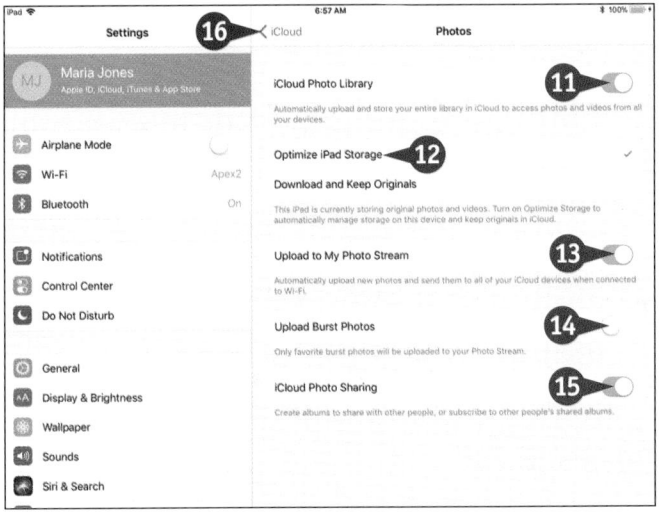

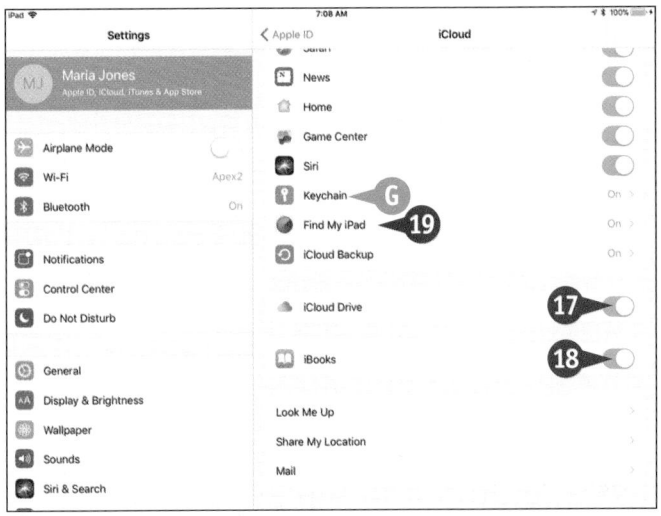

The Find My iPad screen appears.

H You can set the **Find My iPad** switch to Off (◯ changes to ◯) to turn off Find My iPad, such as when preparing to erase the iPad so that you can sell it.

20 Set the **Send Last Location** switch to On (◯) if you want the iPad to send Apple its location when the battery runs critically low.

21 Tap **iCloud** (<).

The iCloud screen appears again.

22 Tap **iCloud Backup** (⟲).

The Backup screen appears.

23 Set the **iCloud Backup** switch to On (◯).

I You can tap **Back Up Now** to start a backup immediately.

24 Tap **iCloud** (<).

The iCloud screen appears again.

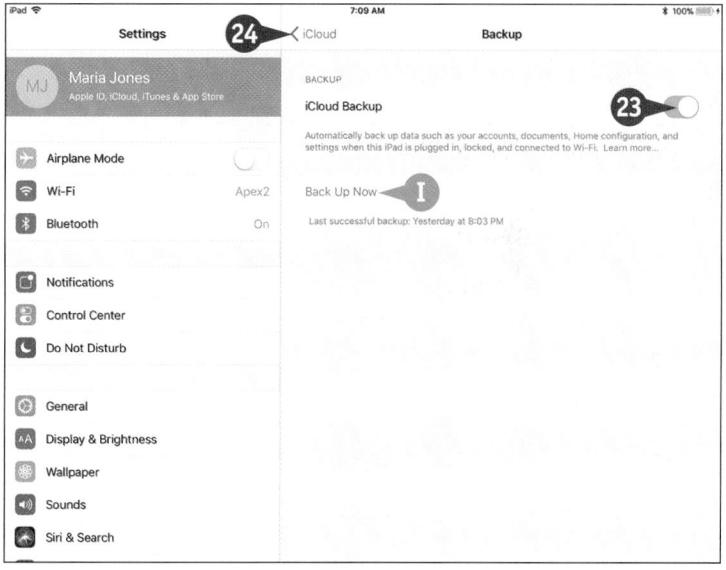

TIP

How much space does iCloud provide?
iCloud provides 5GB of space for a free account. Content and apps you acquire from Apple do not count against this space. You can buy more space by tapping **Manage Storage** on the iCloud screen, tapping **Upgrade** on the iCloud Storage screen, and then following the prompts.

Choose Which Apps Can Give Notifications

Many apps can notify you when events occur, such as a message arriving for you in the Messages app. You can choose which apps give notifications for events and which events those notifications concern. You can also control notification previews and choose which notifications appear on Cover Sheet, the iOS screen for current notifications, and in History, which contains older notifications.

iOS apps use three types of notifications: badges on app icons, temporary banners, and persistent banners. See the tip for details.

Choose Which Apps Can Give Notifications

1. Press **Home**.

   The Home screen appears.

2. Tap **Settings** ( ).

   The Settings screen appears.

3. Tap **Notifications** ( ).

   The Notifications screen appears.

   A To choose your default setting for notification previews, tap **Show Previews**, and then tap **Always**, **When Unlocked**, or **Never**, as needed.

4. In the Notification Style list, tap the app for which you want to configure notifications. This example uses Messages ( ).

   The screen for the app appears.

5. Set the **Allow Notifications** switch to On ( ) to receive notifications from the app.

6. Set the **Badge App Icon** switch to On ( ) or Off ( ), as needed.

7. Set the **Show on Cover Sheet** switch to On ( ) or Off ( ), as needed.

8. Set the **Show in History** switch to On ( ) or Off ( ), as needed.

9. To have notifications appear as banners, set the **Show as Banners** switch to On ( ), then tap **Temporary** or **Persistent**, as appropriate.

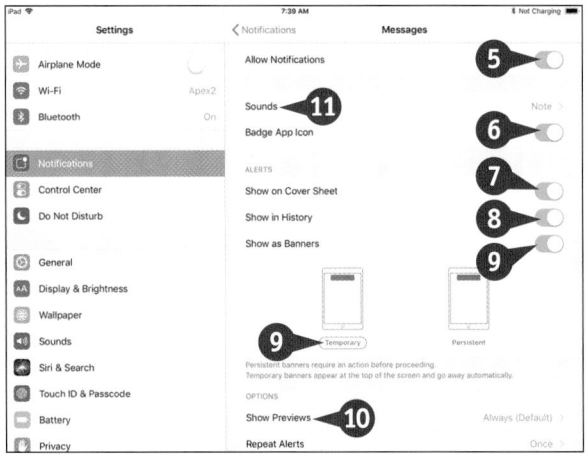

10. To exempt this app from your default preview setting, tap **Show Previews**, and then tap **Always**, **When Unlocked**, or **Never**.

11. Tap **Sounds**.

The Sounds screen appears.

12 Tap the sound you want to hear for the notification.

B You can tap **None** for no sound.

C You can tap **Tone Store** to browse and buy tones.

Note: Scroll down the Sounds screen to display the list of ringtones. Tap **Classic**, at the bottom of the Alert Tones list or at the bottom of the Ringtones list, to see the selection of alert tones or ringtones from early versions of iOS.

13 Tap the **Back** button (<) — in this case, the **Messages** button.

The screen for the app appears again.

14 Tap **Repeat Alerts**.

The Repeat Alerts screen appears.

15 Tap the repetition frequency you want, such as **Twice**.

16 Tap the **Back** button (<) — in this case, the **Messages** button.

The screen for the app appears again.

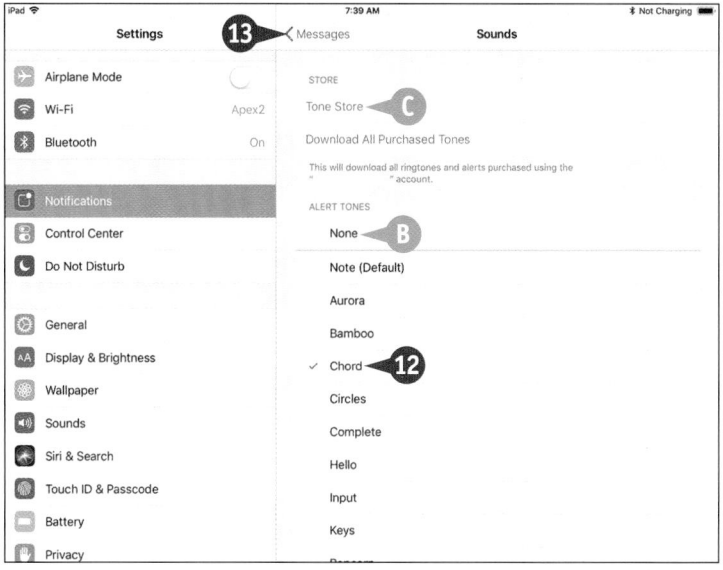

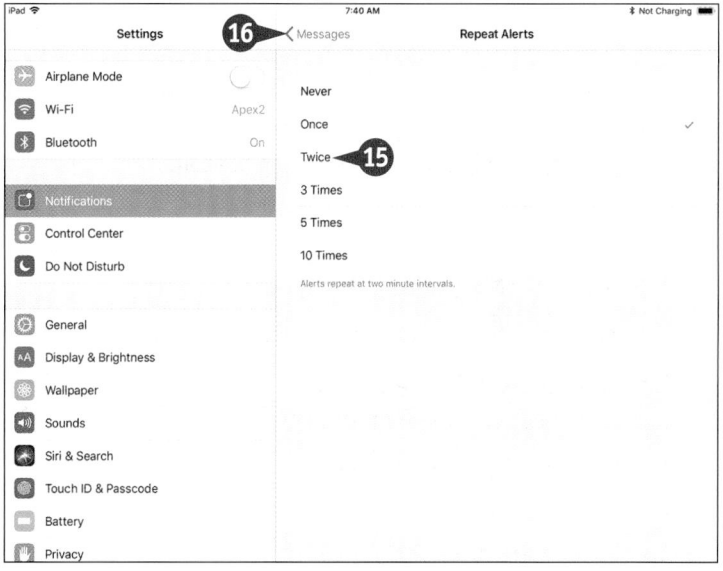

TIP

What are the three types of notifications?

A *badge* is a red circle or rounded rectangle that appears on the app's icon on the Home screen and shows a white number indicating how many notifications there are. A *temporary banner* is a pop-up notification that appears briefly at the top of the screen and then disappears automatically. A *persistent banner* — previously called an *alert* — is like a temporary banner, but you must dismiss it before you can take other actions on your iPad. Whichever notification type you choose, you can set the **Sounds** switch to On (◯) to have your iPad play a sound to get your attention.

Choose Sounds Settings

To control how your iPad gives you audio feedback, choose settings on the Sounds screen. Here, you can set the volume for the ringer and for alerts, choose your default ringtone for FaceTime and text tone for Messages, and choose whether to receive alerts for calendar items and reminders.

Playing lock sounds helps confirm that you have locked or unlocked your iPad as you intended. Playing keyboard clicks confirms each key press on the on-screen keyboard.

Choose Sounds Settings

1. Press **Home**.

   The Home screen appears.

2. Tap **Settings** ( ).

   The Settings screen appears.

3. Tap **Sounds** ( ).

   The Sounds screen appears.

4. Drag the **Ringer and Alerts** slider to set the volume.

5. Set the **Change with Buttons** switch to On ( ) if you want to be able to change the Ringer and Alerts volume by pressing the volume buttons on the side of the iPad.

6. Tap **Ringtone**.

The Ringtone screen appears.

7. Tap the ringtone you want to hear for FaceTime calls.

   Your iPad plays the ringtone so you can decide whether to use it.

   A You can tap **Tone Store** to buy extra ringtones or alert tones.

Note: Scroll down the Ringtone screen to display the list of alert tones. Tap **Classic**, at the bottom of the Ringtones list or the Alert Tones list, to see the selection of ringtones or alert tones from early versions of iOS.

8. Tap **Sounds** (<).

   The Sounds screen appears again.

9. Repeat steps **6** to **8** to set other tones, such as text tones.

10. Set the **Keyboard Clicks** switch to On (◐) or Off ( ), as needed.

11. Set the **Lock Sound** switch to On (◐) or Off ( ), as needed.

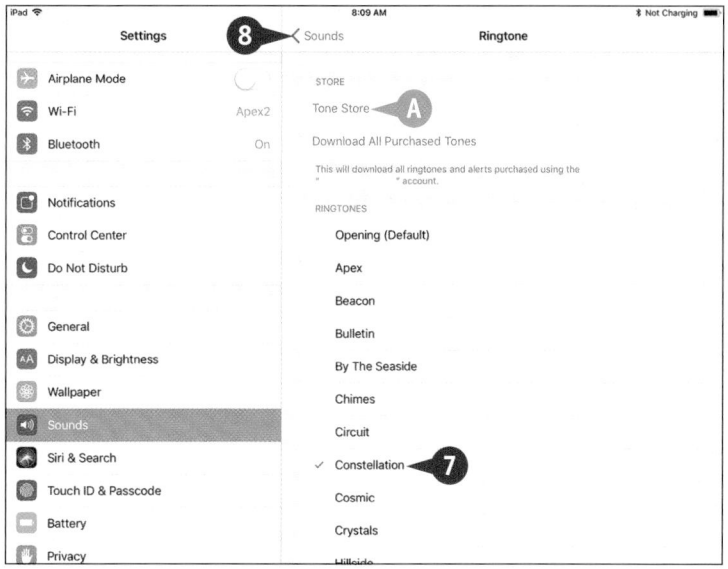

TIP

How do I use different ringtones for different callers?

The ringtone you set in the Ringtone area of the Sounds screen is your default tone for FaceTime calls; the text tone is the default for messaging calls. To set different tones to identify a contact, press **Home** and tap **Contacts** ( ). In the Contacts app, tap the contact, tap **Edit**, and then tap **Ringtone**. In the Ringtone dialog, tap the ringtone, and then tap **Done**. You can also change the text tone for the contact. Tap **Done** when you finish editing the contact.

Configure Display, Brightness, and Night Shift

To make the screen easy to see, you can change its brightness. You can let the iPad's Auto-Brightness feature automatically set the screen's brightness based on ambient light. You can enable the Night Shift feature to reduce the screen's output of blue light, which can disrupt your sleep.

To make text on the screen easier to read, you can increase or decrease the text size as needed. You can also turn on the Bold Text setting and adjust the Display Zoom setting.

Configure Display, Brightness, and Night Shift

1. Press **Home**.

   The Home screen appears.

2. Tap **Settings** ( ).

   The Settings screen appears.

3. Tap **Display & Brightness** ( ).

   The Display & Brightness screen appears.

4. Drag the **Brightness** slider left or right to set brightness.

5. Set the **Auto-Brightness** switch to On ( ) or Off ( ), as needed.

6. Tap **Night Shift**.

   The Night Shift screen appears.

7. Set the **Scheduled** switch to On ( ) to run Night Shift each night.

8. Tap **From, To** to display the Schedule screen. In the Automate Schedule box, either tap **Sunset to Sunrise** or tap **Custom Schedule**. If you tap Custom Schedule, tap **Turn On At** and set the start time, then tap **Turn Off At** and set the end time. Tap **Night Shift** ( ) to return to the Night Shift screen.

9. Drag the **Color Temperature** slider along the Less Warm–More Warm axis to set the color temperature.

10. Tap **Display & Brightness** ( ).

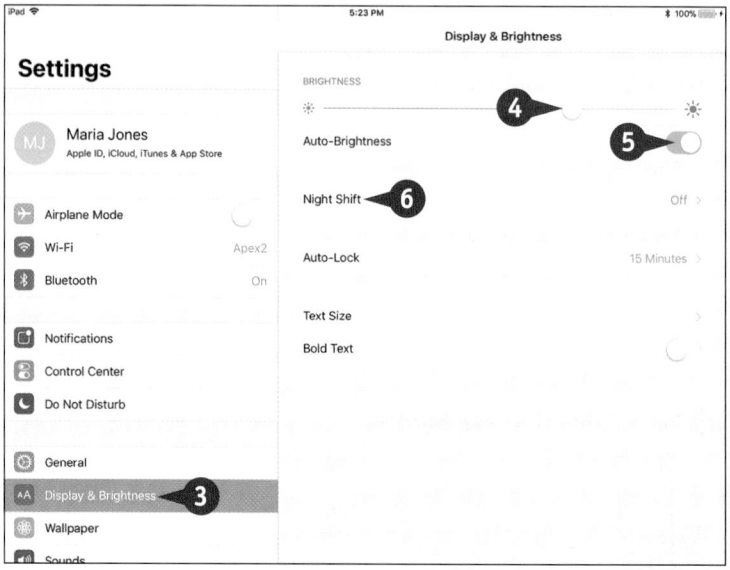

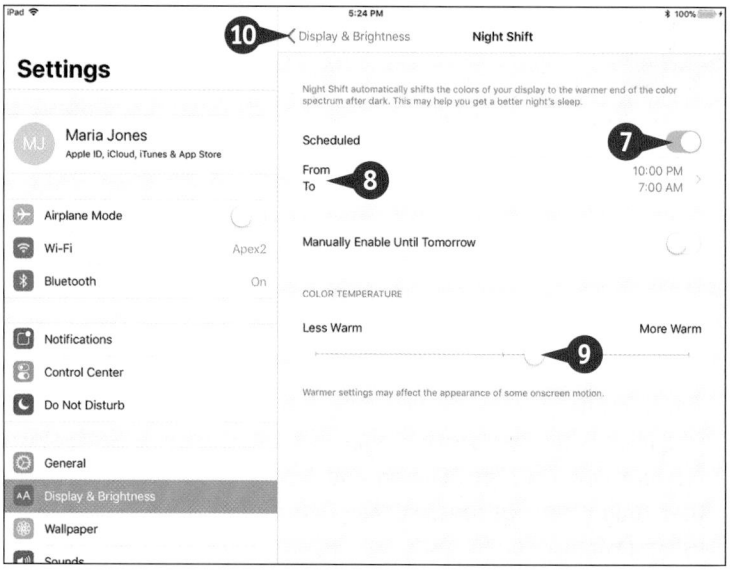

The Display & Brightness screen appears again.

11 Tap **Text Size** to display the Text Size screen, drag the slider left or right to adjust the text size, and then tap **Display & Brightness** (<) to return to the Display & Brightness screen.

Note: Adjusting the text size works only for apps that support the Dynamic Type feature, not for all apps.

A If you want to use bold text, set the **Bold Text** switch to On (◯) and tap **Continue** in the Applying This Setting Will Restart Your iPad dialog.

12 Tap **View**.

The Display Zoom dialog opens.

13 Tap **Standard** or **Zoomed**, as needed.

Note: You can swipe left once or twice to view other example previews.

14 If you change the display zoom, tap **Set**, and then tap **Use Standard** in the Use Standard? dialog or tap **Use Zoomed** in the Use Zoomed? dialog to effect the change.

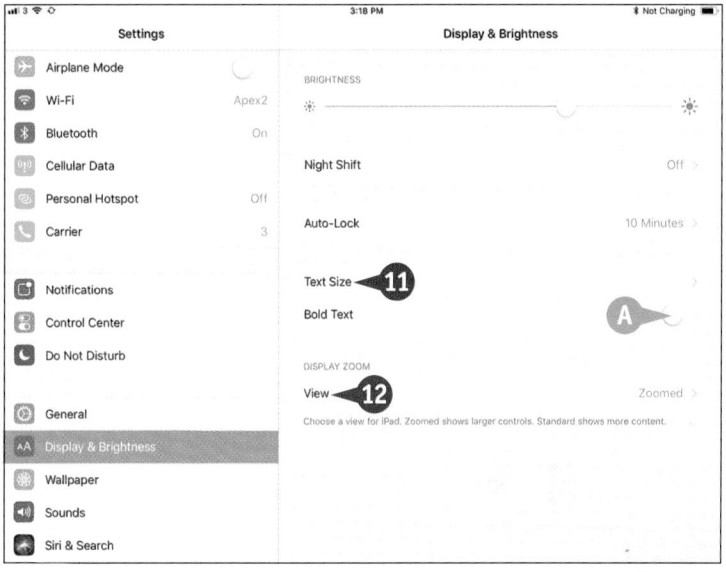

TIPS

How else can I change the screen brightness?

Swipe up from the bottom of the screen to open Control Center, and then drag the **Brightness** slider (☀) up or down.

How do I turn on Night Shift manually?

Swipe up from the bottom of the screen to open Control Center. Press and hold the **Brightness** slider (☀) to expand the slider, and then tap **Night Shift** (◉). You can also set the **Manually Enable Until Tomorrow** switch on the Night Shift screen in the Settings app to On (◯), but Control Center is usually quicker and easier.

Set Home Screen and Lock Screen Wallpaper

You can choose which picture to use as the wallpaper that appears in the background. You can use either a static wallpaper or a dynamic, changing wallpaper. You can set different wallpaper for the lock screen — the screen you see when the iPad is locked — and for the Home screen.

When setting the wallpaper, you can choose whether to turn perspective zoom on or off. Perspective zoom gives the three-dimensional effect when you tilt the iPad when looking at the wallpaper.

Set Home Screen and Lock Screen Wallpaper

1. Press **Home**.

   The Home screen appears.

2. Tap **Settings** ( ).

   The Settings screen appears.

3. Tap **Wallpaper** ( ).

   The Wallpaper screen appears.

4. Tap **Choose a New Wallpaper**.

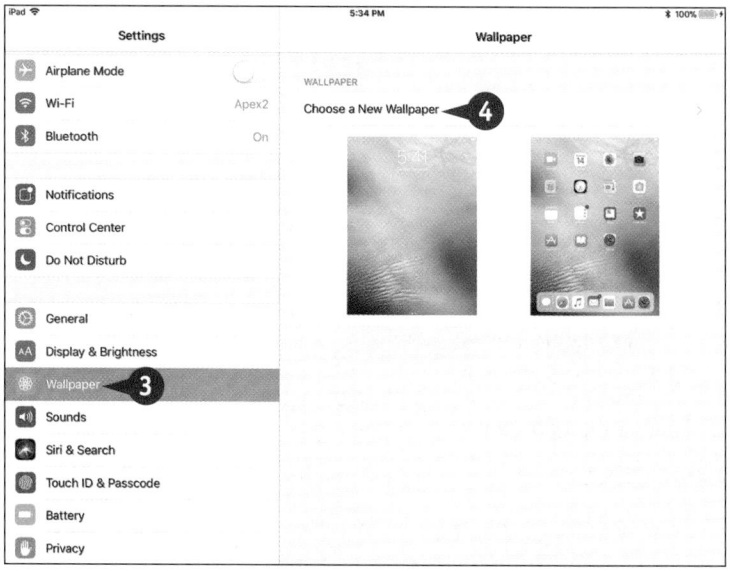

   The Choose screen appears.

5. At the top of the screen, tap **Dynamic** or **Stills**. This example uses Stills.

   A To choose a picture from a different picture category, tap that category. For example, tap **All Photos** to display pictures you have taken with the iPad camera or saved from e-mail messages, multimedia messages, or web pages.

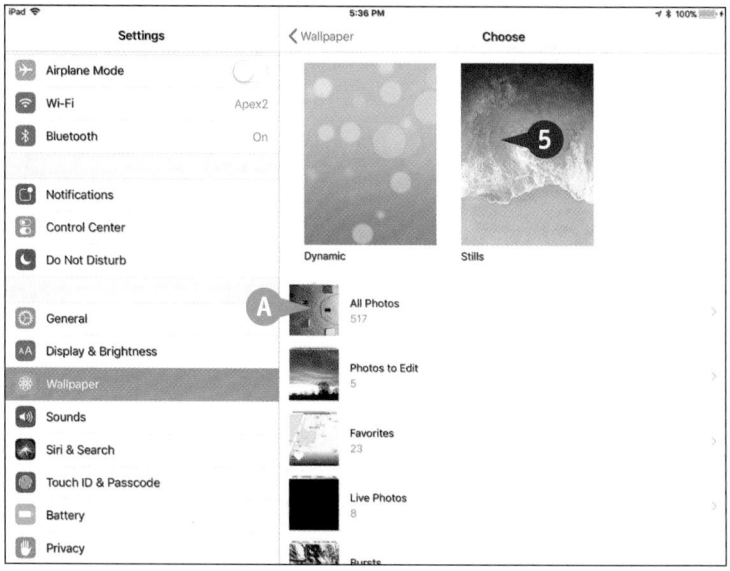

The Wallpaper screen appears.

6 Tap the wallpaper you want.

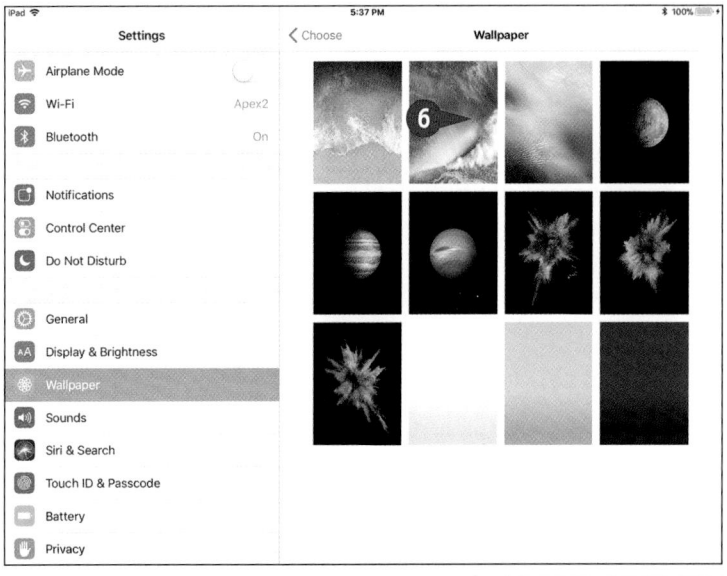

The Wallpaper Preview screen appears.

7 Tap **Perspective Zoom: On** or **Perspective Zoom: Off** to toggle the perspective zoom on or off.

8 Tap **Set Lock Screen**, **Set Home Screen**, or **Set Both**.

The Wallpaper screen appears.

9 Tap **Choose** (<).

The Choose screen appears.

10 Tap **Wallpaper** (<).

The Wallpaper screen appears.

Note: To see the wallpaper, press **Home** to display the Home screen or press the **Sleep/Wake** button twice to display the lock screen.

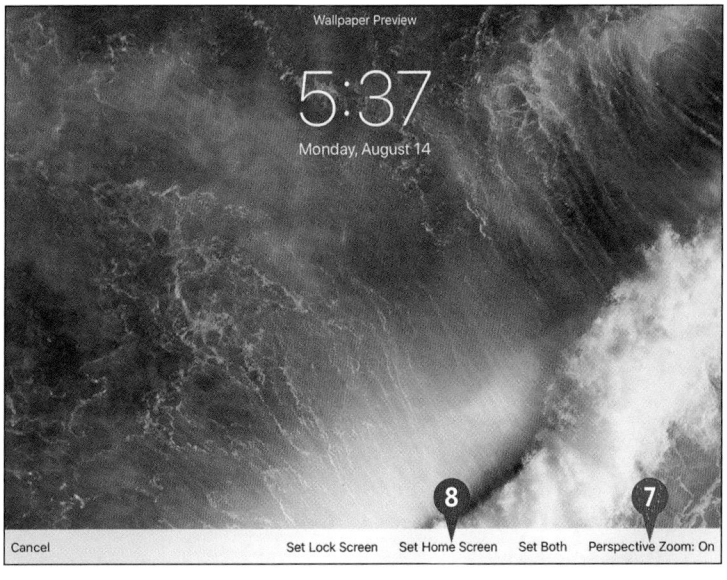

TIP

How do I use only part of a picture as the wallpaper?

The iPad wallpapers are the right size for the screen, so you do not need to resize them. But when you choose a photo for the wallpaper, the iPad displays the Move and Scale screen. Pinch in or out to zoom the photo out or in, and drag to move the picture around. When you have chosen the part you want, tap **Set Lock Screen**, **Set Home Screen**, or **Set Both**. Moving and scaling a photo does not edit the original image.

Choose Privacy and Location Settings

Your iPad contains a huge amount of information about you, the people you communicate with, what you do, and where you go. To keep this information safe, you need to choose suitable privacy and location settings.

Privacy settings enable you to control which apps may access your contacts, calendars, reminders, and photos. You can also choose which apps can use location services, which track your iPad's location using known wireless networks and the Global Positioning System, or GPS, on cellular iPads.

Choose Privacy and Location Settings

1. Press **Home**.

   The Home screen appears.

2. Tap **Settings** ( ).

   The Settings screen appears.

3. Tap **Privacy** ( ).

   The Privacy screen appears.

4. Tap **Location Services** ( ).

Note: To minimize advertisers tracking you, tap **Advertising** at the bottom of the Privacy screen and set the **Limit Ad Tracking** switch to On ( ). Then tap **Reset Advertising Identifier** and tap **Reset Identifier** in the confirmation dialog.

   The Location Services screen appears.

   A If you need to turn location services off completely, set the **Location Services** switch to Off ( ).

5. To control location sharing, tap **Share My Location**. On the Share My Location screen, set the **Share My Location** switch to On ( ) or Off ( ), as needed. If you set it to On, tap **From** and choose the sharing device on the Share Location From screen.

6. Tap an app or feature. This example uses Camera.

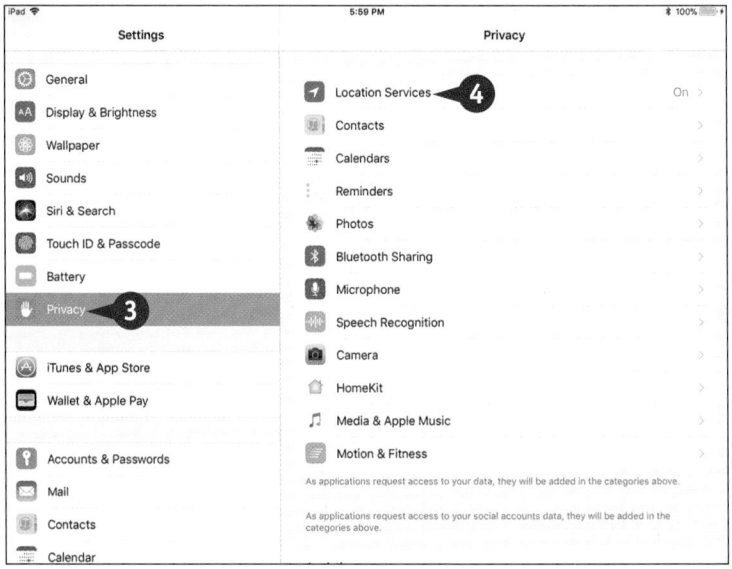

The screen for the app or feature appears.

7. In the Allow Location Access list, tap the appropriate button, such as **Never** or **While Using the App**.

8. Tap **Location Services** (<).

   The Location Services screen appears.

9. Tap **System Services**.

Note: For privacy, you may want to set the **Location-Based Alerts** switch, the **Location-Based Apple Ads** switch, and the **Location-Based Suggestions** switch on the System Services screen to Off ( ).

   The System Services screen appears.

10. Set the switch for each system service to On ( ) or Off ( ).

11. Set the **Status Bar Icon** switch to On ( ) to display an arrow in the status bar when the iPad is being tracked.

12. Tap **Location Services** (<).

    The Location Services screen appears.

13. Tap **Privacy**.

    The Privacy screen appears.

14. Tap each app or service and choose the apps that can access that app's information.

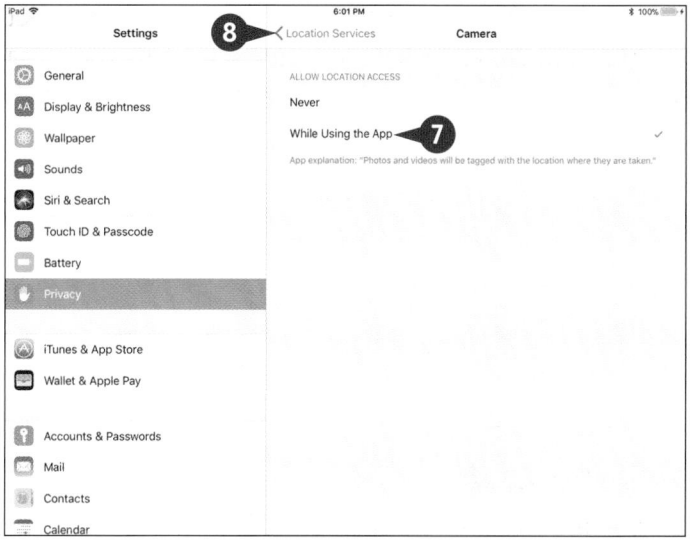

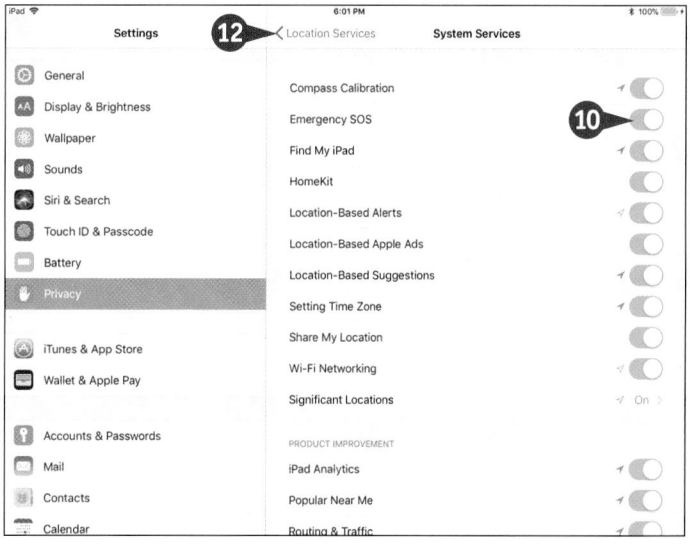

TIP

Why do some apps need to use location services?

Some apps and system services need to use location services to determine where you are. The Maps app uses location services to display your location, and the Compass app needs your position to display accurate compass information. If you allow the Camera app to use location services, it stores location data in your photos. You can sort the photos by location in apps such as Photos or Photoshop Elements on your computer. Other apps use location services to provide context-specific information, such as information about nearby restaurants. For security, review which apps are using location services and turn off any that do not have a compelling reason for doing so.

Configure Search and Find What You Need

Your iPad can put a huge amount of data in your hand, and you may often have to search to find what you need. To make your search results more accurate and helpful, you can configure the Search feature on your iPad.

You can enable or disable suggestions from Siri, the search assistant. You can also turn off searching for items you do not want to see in your search results.

Configure Search and Find What You Need

Configure Search

1. Press **Home**.

   The Home screen appears.

2. Tap **Settings** ( ).

   The Settings screen appears.

3. Tap **Siri & Search** ( ).

   The Siri & Search screen appears.

4. Set the **Suggestions in Search** switch to On ( ) to see Search suggestions when you search.

5. Set the **Suggestions in Look Up** switch to On ( ) to see Search suggestions when you use Look Up.

6. Tap the button for the app you want to configure. This example uses **Calendar** ( ).

   The screen for that app appears.

7. Set the **Search & Siri Suggestions** switch to On ( ) if you want Calendar content to appear in Search and Look Up and for Siri to access your Calendar data.

8. Set the **Find Events in Other Apps** switch to On ( ) if you want iOS to try to identify events.

Note: The Find in Other Apps switch appears for only some apps. Its name varies depending on the app. For example, the Find Contacts in Other Apps switch appears for the Contacts app.

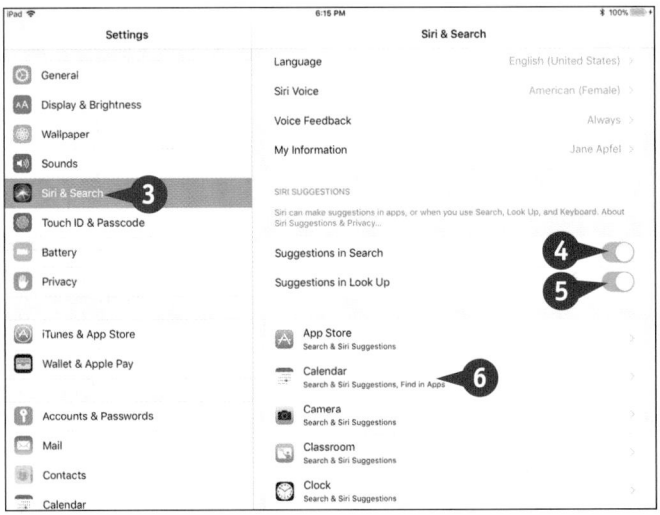

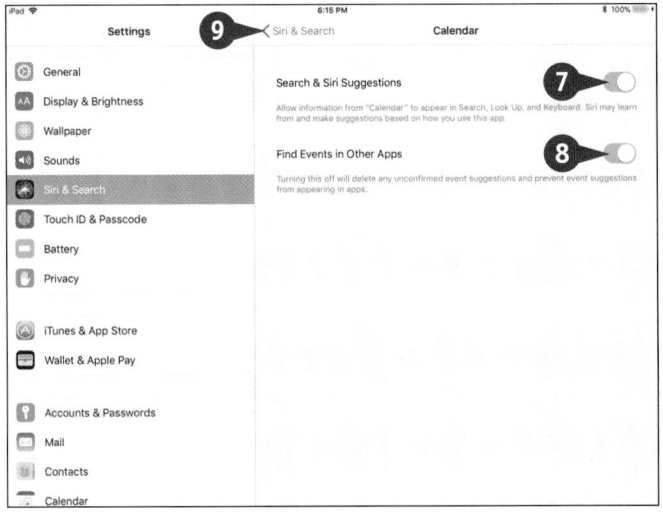

9. Tap **Siri & Search** ( ).

   The Siri & Search screen appears again, and you can configure other apps.

Search for Items

1. Press **Home**.

   The Home screen appears.

2. Draw your finger down the screen a short way.

   The Search screen appears.

3. Tap in the Search field.

   The keyboard appears.

4. Type your search term.

   A list of results appears.

   A You can tap a suggested search to perform that search.

5. Tap the result you want to view.

TIP

Which items should I set the Search feature to search?

This depends on what you need to be able to search for. For example, if you do not need to search for music, videos, or podcasts, you can exclude the Music app, the Videos app, and the Podcasts app from Siri & Search Suggestions.

Choose Locking and Control Center Settings

To avoid unintentional taps on the screen, your iPad automatically locks itself after a period of inactivity. After locking itself, your iPad turns off its screen and goes to sleep to save battery power.

You can choose how long your iPad waits before locking itself. You may prefer to leave your iPad on longer so that you can continue working, and then lock your iPad manually. You can also choose which controls appear in Control Center and customize their order.

Choose Locking and Control Center Settings

1. Press **Home**.

   The Home screen appears.

2. Tap **Settings** ( ).

   The Settings screen appears.

3. Tap **Display & Brightness** ( ).

   The Display & Brightness screen appears.

4. Tap **Auto-Lock**.

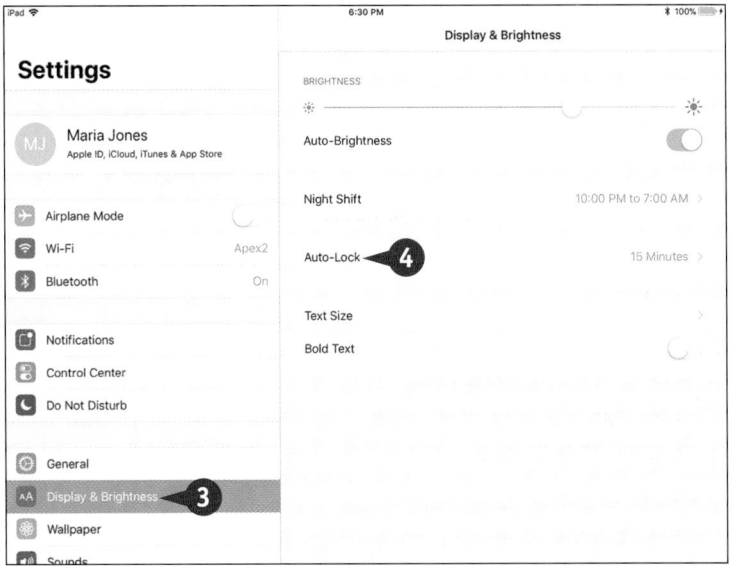

   The Auto-Lock screen appears.

5. Tap the interval — for example, **5 Minutes**.

Note: Choose the **Never** setting for Auto-Lock if you need to make sure the iPad never goes to sleep. For example, if you are playing music with the lyrics displayed, turning off auto-locking may be helpful.

6. Tap **Control Center** ( ).

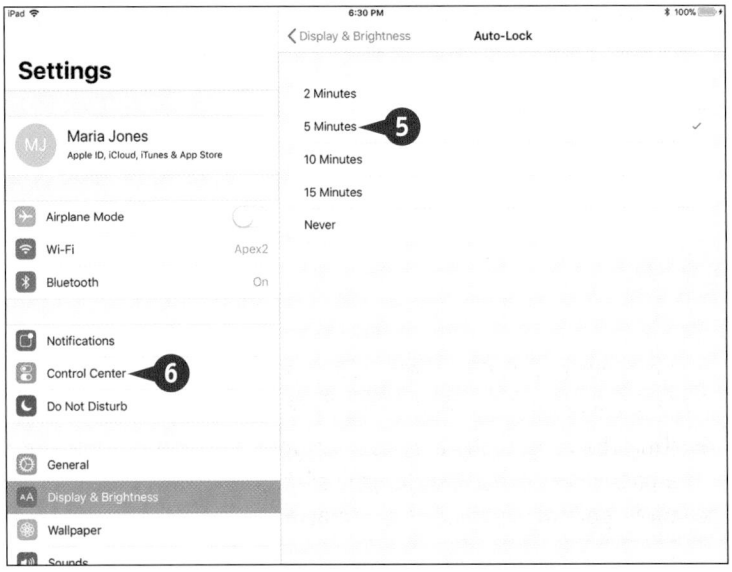

The Control Center screen appears.

7 Tap **Customize Controls**.

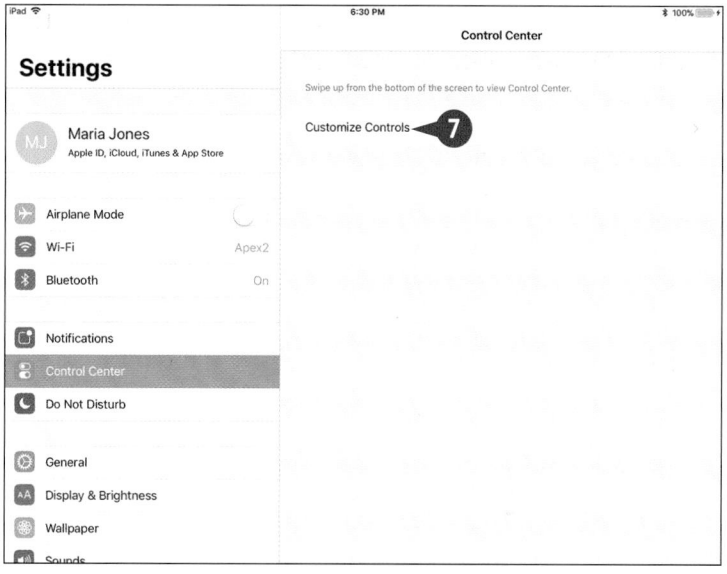

The Customize screen appears.

A The Include section shows current controls you can remove.

B The More Controls section shows controls you can add.

8 To remove a control from Control Center, tap **Remove** (⊖), and then tap the textual **Remove** button that appears.

9 To change the order, drag a control by its handle (≡).

10 To add a control to Control Center, tap **Add** (⊕).

11 Tap **Control Center** (<).

The Control Center screen appears again.

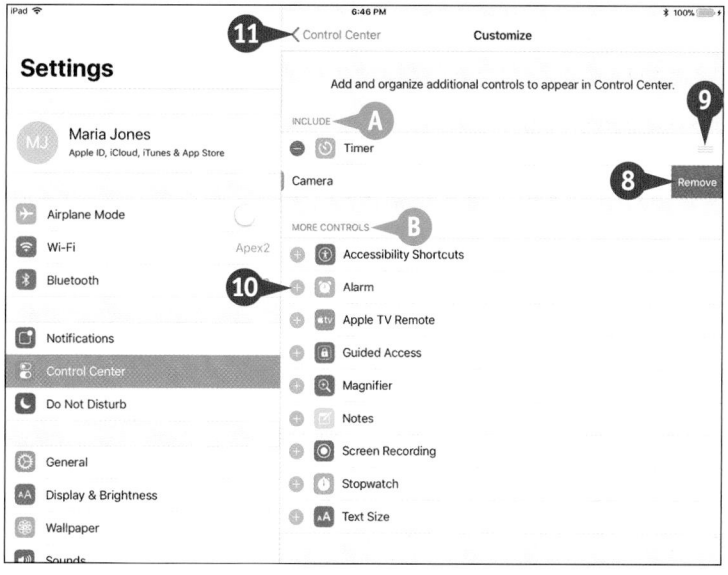

TIP

How do I put the iPad to sleep manually?

You can put the iPad to sleep at any point by pressing the Sleep/Wake button for a moment. If your iPad has a Smart Cover or Smart Case, close the cover or case.

Putting the iPad to sleep as soon as you stop using it helps to prolong battery life. If you apply Touch ID or a passcode, as discussed in the section "Secure Your iPad with Touch ID or a Passcode," later in this chapter, putting the iPad to sleep also protects your data sooner.

Set Up and Use Do Not Disturb Mode

When you do not want your iPad to disturb you, turn on Do Not Disturb Mode. You can configure Do Not Disturb Mode to turn on and off automatically at set times each day; you can also turn Do Not Disturb Mode on and off manually. You can allow particular groups of contacts to bypass Do Not Disturb Mode. You can also allow repeated calls to ring when Do Not Disturb is on.

Set Up and Use Do Not Disturb Mode

Configure Do Not Disturb Mode

1. Press **Home**.

   The Home screen appears.

2. Tap **Settings** ( ).

   The Settings screen appears.

3. Tap **Do Not Disturb** ( ).

   The Do Not Disturb screen appears.

4. To schedule regular quiet hours, set the **Scheduled** switch to On ( ).

5. Tap **From, To**.

   The Quiet Hours dialog opens.

6. Tap **From**.

7. Set the From time.

8. Tap **To**.

9. Set the To time.

10. Tap **Allow Calls From**.

    The Allow Calls From screen appears.

11. Tap the group you will allow to call you via FaceTime during quiet hours.

12. Tap **Do Not Disturb** ( ).

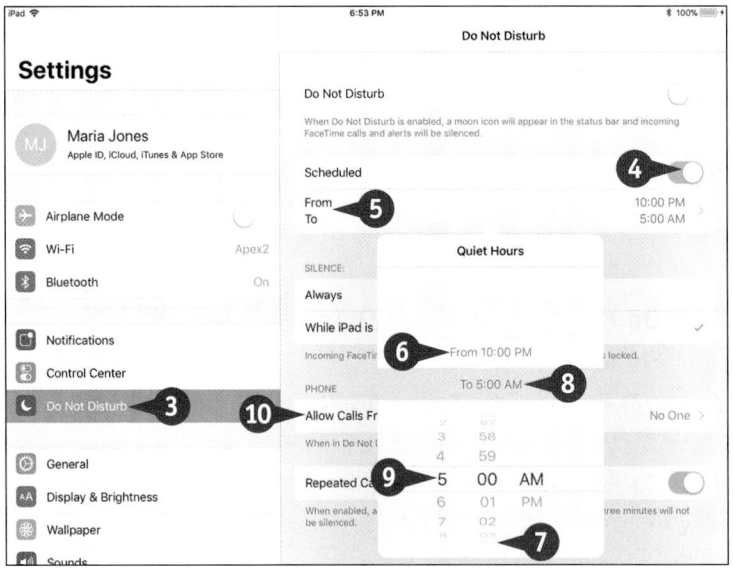

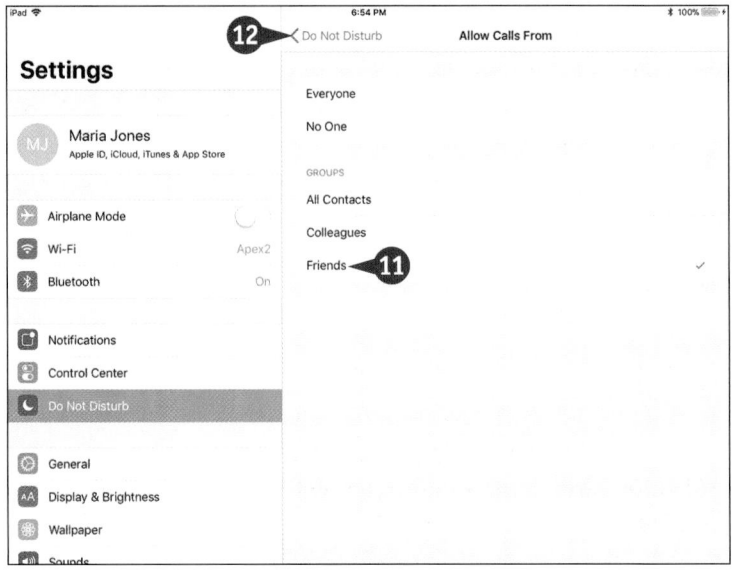

The Do Not Disturb screen appears again.

Ⓐ You can set the **Manual** switch to On ( ) to turn on Do Not Disturb Mode from this screen. It is usually easier to use Control Center to toggle Do Not Disturb Mode on and off.

13 In the Silence area, tap **Always** or **While iPad is locked**, as needed.

14 Set the **Repeated Calls** switch to On ( ) or Off ( ), as needed.

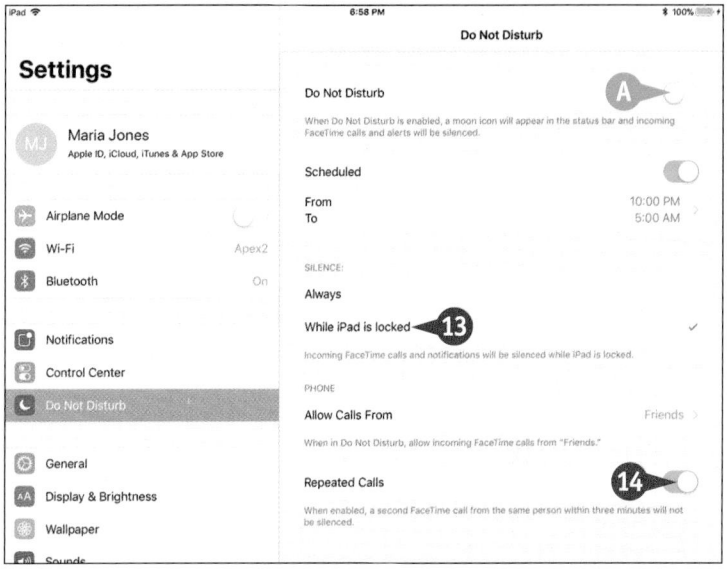

Turn Do Not Disturb Mode On or Off Manually

1 Swipe up from the bottom of the screen.

Note: You can open Control Center from the Home screen or from most other screens.

Control Center opens.

2 Tap **Do Not Disturb** to turn Do Not Disturb on (changes to) or off (changes to).

3 Tap the screen outside Control Center.

Control Center closes.

TIP

How can I tell whether Do Not Disturb is on?
When Do Not Disturb is on, a crescent moon symbol appears in the status bar to the left of the battery readout.

Secure Your iPad with Touch ID or a Passcode

During setup, you secure your iPad using Touch ID or a passcode. Touch ID uses your fingerprint to unlock the iPad, with a passcode as a backup unlock method. All recent iPad models have Touch ID; older models without Touch ID use a passcode instead. Even with Touch ID enabled, you must enter your passcode after restarting your iPad or after not using it for 48 hours or longer.

For added security, you can set the iPad to automatically erase its data after ten failed passcode attempts.

Secure Your iPad with Touch ID or a Passcode

1. Press **Home**.

   The Home screen appears.

2. Tap **Settings** (⚙).

   The Settings screen appears.

3. Tap **Touch ID & Passcode.**

Note: If your iPad does not support Touch ID, tap **Passcode Lock** to display the Passcode Lock screen.

   The Enter Passcode dialog opens.

4. Type your passcode.

   The Passcode Lock screen appears.

5. Set the **iPad Unlock** switch to On (◯) to use Touch ID for unlocking.

6. Set the **Apple Pay** switch to On (◯) to use Touch ID for Apple Pay.

7. Set the **iTunes & App Store** switch to On (◯) to use Touch ID for store purchases.

A You can tap a button in the Fingerprints box to change the button name or delete the fingerprint.

B You can tap **Add a Fingerprint** to add another fingerprint to Touch ID.

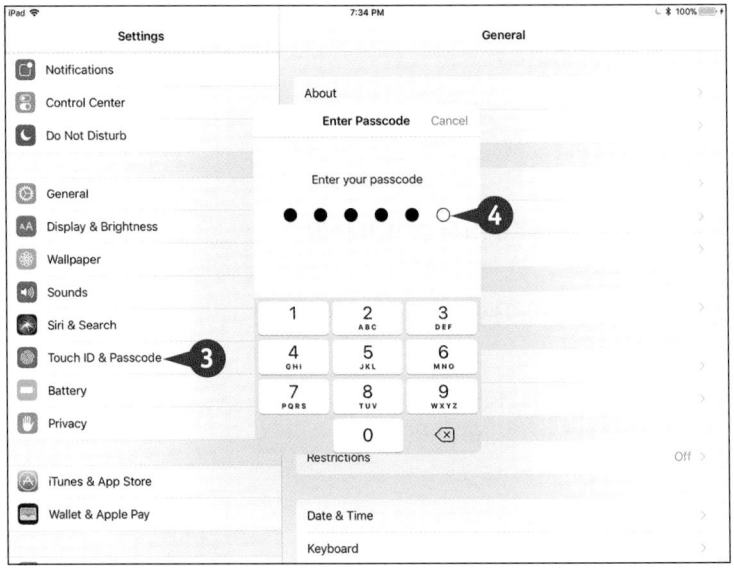

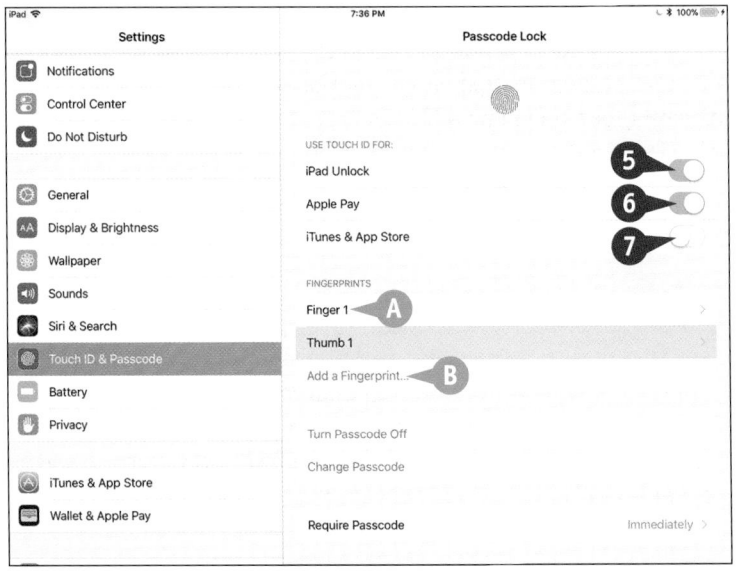

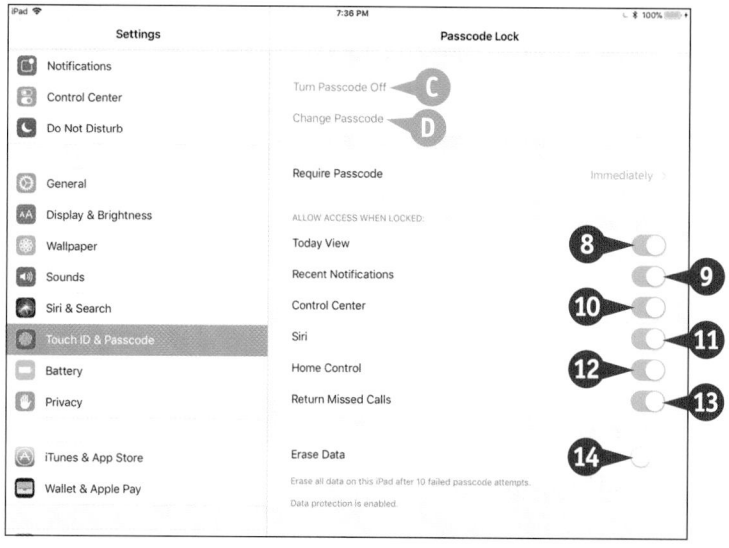

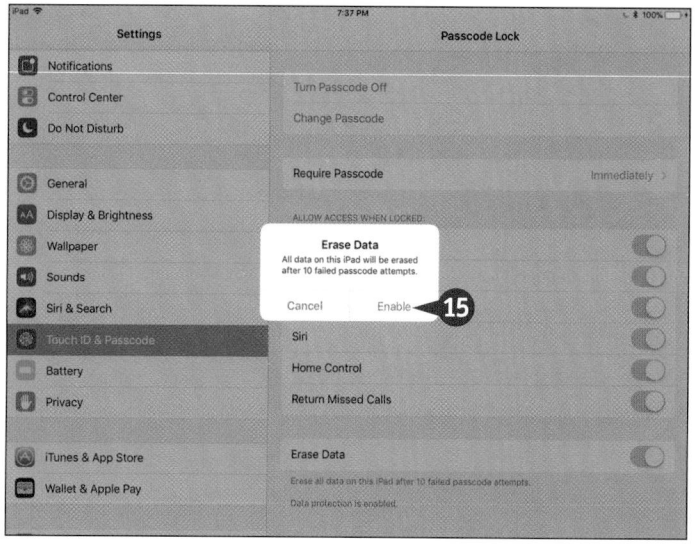

C You can tap **Turn Passcode Off** to turn the passcode off; however, this is seldom wise.

D You can tap **Change Passcode** to change your passcode. See the tip for information on changing the passcode type.

8 Set the **Today View** switch to On (◐) or Off ( ), as needed.

9 Set the **Recent Notifications** switch to On (◐) or Off ( ), as needed.

10 Set the **Control Center** switch to On (◐) or Off ( ), as needed.

11 Set the **Siri** switch to On (◐) or Off ( ), as needed.

12 Set the **Home Control** switch to On (◐) or Off ( ), as needed.

13 Set the **Return Missed Calls** switch to On (◐) or Off ( ), as needed.

14 If you want the iPad to erase all its data after ten failed passcode attempts, set the **Erase Data** switch to On (◐).

The Erase Data dialog opens.

15 Tap **Enable**.

Note: The Erase Data feature provides effective protection against conventional attackers, but some law-enforcement agencies can defeat it.

TIP

How do I change the type of passcode my iPad uses?

On the Touch ID & Passcode screen, tap **Change Passcode** to open the Change Passcode dialog. Type your existing passcode to authenticate yourself, and then tap **Passcode Options** to display the Passcode Options pop-up panel. You can then tap **Custom Alphanumeric Code** to create an ultra-secure passcode using letters and numbers; tap **Custom Numeric Code** to create a numeric passcode whose length you choose; or tap **4-Digit Numeric Code** to create a four-digit numeric code, which is easier to type but does not provide serious security.

Configure Restrictions and Parental Controls

Like any other computer that can access the Internet, the iPad can reach vast amounts of content not suitable for children or business contexts.

You can restrict the iPad from accessing particular kinds of content. You can use the restrictions to implement parental controls — for example, you can prevent the iPad user from buying content in apps or watching adult-rated movies.

Configure Restrictions and Parental Controls

1. Press **Home**.

   The Home screen appears.

2. Tap **Settings** (⚙).

   The Settings screen appears.

3. Tap **General** (⚙).

   The General screen appears.

4. Tap **Restrictions**.

   The Restrictions screen appears.

5. Tap **Enable Restrictions**.

   The Set Passcode dialog appears.

Note: The passcode you set to protect restrictions is separate from the passcode you use to lock the iPad. Do not use the same code.

6. Type the passcode.

Note: The iPad shows dots instead of your passcode digits in case someone is watching.

   The iPad displays the Set Passcode dialog again, this time with the message "Re-enter your Restrictions Passcode."

7. Type the passcode again.

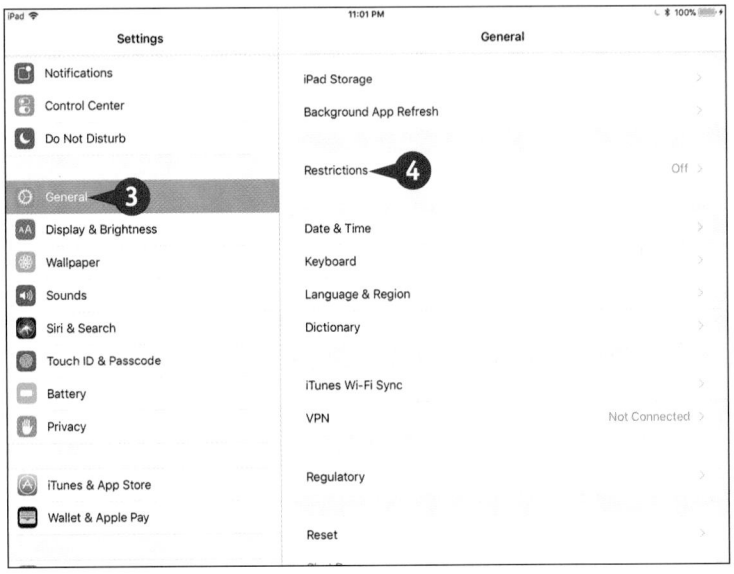

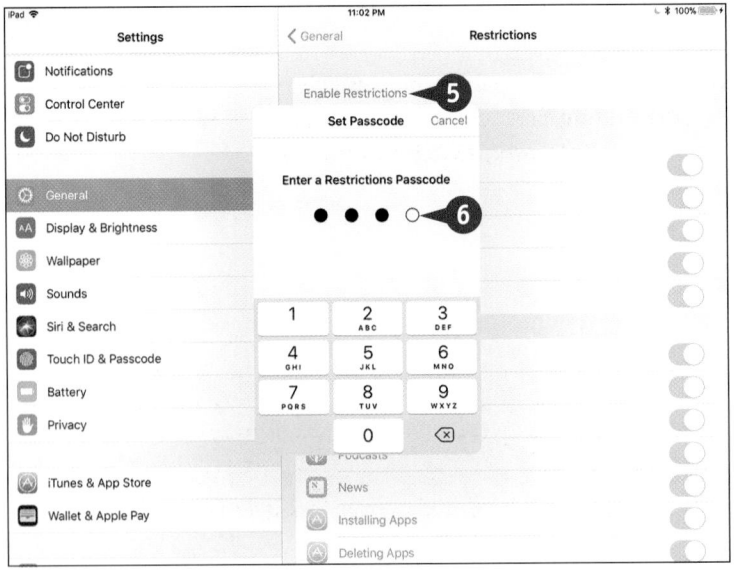

The Restrictions screen appears with the controls in the Allow area now available.

8. In the Allow area, set each switch to On (◐) or Off ( ), as needed.
9. If you need to change the country used for rating content, tap **Ratings For**. On the Ratings For screen, tap the country, and then tap **Restrictions**.
10. Choose settings for items in the Allowed Content box. For example, tap **Movies**.

    The Movies screen appears.
11. On the Movies screen, tap the highest rating you will permit.
12. Tap **Restrictions** (<).

    The Restrictions screen appears again.
13. Set the **In-App Purchases** switch to On (◐) or Off ( ), as needed.
14. Choose other settings in the Privacy box.
15. Choose settings in the Allow Changes box.
16. Set the **Multiplayer Games** switch, the **Adding Friends** switch, and the **Screen Recording** switch to On (◐) or Off ( ), as needed.

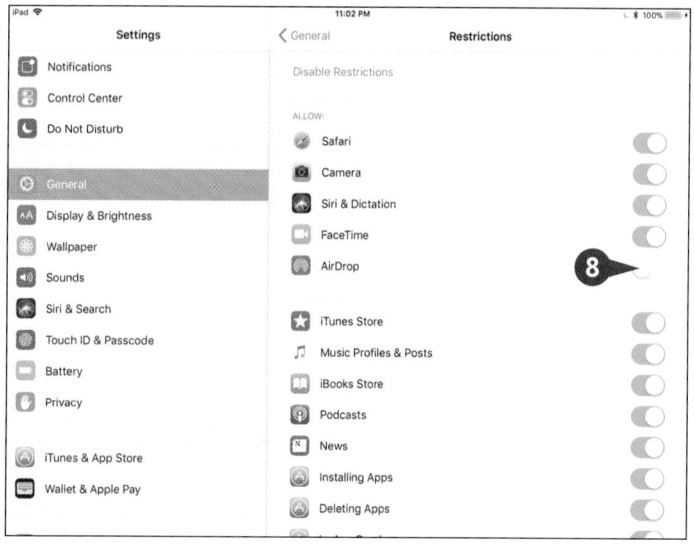

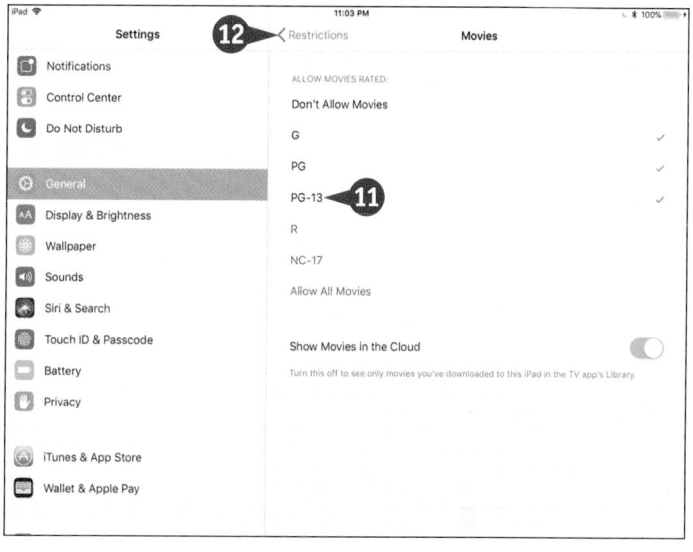

TIPS

What are in-app purchases?

In-app purchases are items that you can buy within apps without needing to use the App Store app. These are a popular and easy way for developers to sell extra features for apps, especially low-cost apps or free apps. They are also an easy way for the iPad user to spend money.

What do the Privacy settings in Restrictions do?

The Privacy settings in Restrictions enable you to control which apps can access the location information, contacts, calendars, reminders, photos, and other features on your iPad.

Set Up Family Sharing and Add Members

Apple's Family Sharing feature enables you to share purchases from Apple's online services with other family members. You can also share photos and calendars, and you can use the Find My iPhone feature to find your iOS devices and Macs when they go missing.

This section assumes that you are the Family organizer, the person who sets up Family sharing, invites others to participate, and pays for the content they buy on the iTunes Store, the iBooks Store, and the App Store.

Set Up Family Sharing

To set up Family Sharing, press **Home** and then tap **Settings** ( ) to open the Settings app. Tap **Apple ID** — the button bearing your Apple ID name — at the top of the Settings screen to display the Apple ID screen, and then tap **Set Up Family Sharing** ( ) to display the Family Sharing dialog.

Tap **Get Started** to display the Get Started dialog, and then tap the first feature you want to share. Your choices are **Apple Music** ( ), **iCloud Storage** ( ), **iTunes & App Store Purchases** ( ), or **Location Sharing** ( ).

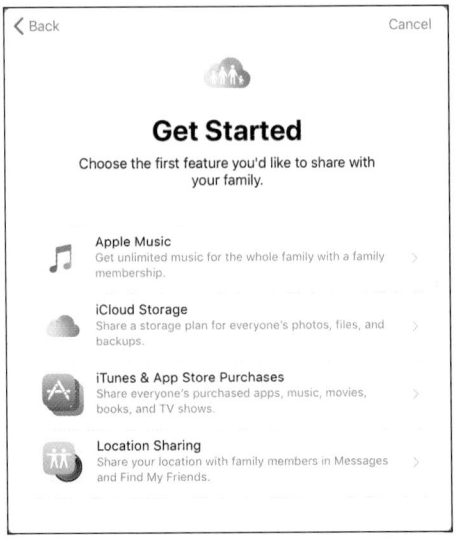

After making your choice, follow the prompts to choose the service type and set up your means of payment. For example, if you tap **Apple Music** ( ), the Apple Music dialog opens, and you can choose among Individual, Family, and College Student plans; assuming you are not yet paying for the service, you may be able to start with a free trial.

Once you have enabled Family Sharing on your account, the Family Sharing screen appears. You can then add a family member to Family Sharing, as explained in the next section.

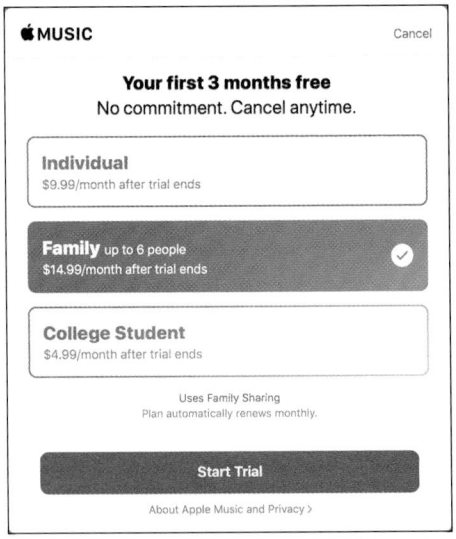

Add a Family Member to Family Sharing

To add a family member, first display the Family Sharing screen in the Settings app by pressing **Home**, tapping **Settings** (), tapping **Apple ID** — the button bearing your Apple ID name — and then tapping **Family Sharing** ( ).

On the Family Sharing screen, tap **Add Family Member** to display the Add Family Member dialog, and then tap **Invite via iMessage**, **Invite in Person**, or **Create a Child Account**, as appropriate. Follow the prompts to create the invitation. If the Verify Security Code screen appears, enter your card's security code and then tap **Next**.

Accept an Invitation to Family Sharing

When someone sends you an invitation to Family Sharing, tap **Get Started** in the e-mail message. If you are using an iOS device, the Family Sharing Invitation screen appears, and you can simply tap **Accept** to accept the invitation.

If you do not want to accept the invitation, tap **Decline** instead.

Choose Date, Time, and Region Settings

To keep yourself on time and your data accurate, you need to make sure your iPad is using the correct date and time. You can choose between having your iPad set the date and time automatically or setting them yourself. To choose date and time settings, you use the Date & Time screen in the Settings app. To make dates, times, and other data appear in the formats you prefer, you may need to change the Language & Region settings on your iPad.

Choose Date, Time, and Region Settings

Choose Date and Time Settings

1. Press **Home**.

   The Home screen appears.

2. Tap **Settings** ( ).

   The Settings screen appears.

3. Tap **General** ( ).

   The General screen appears.

4. Tap **Date & Time.**

   The Date & Time screen appears.

5. Set the **24-Hour Time** switch to On ( ) if you want to use 24-hour times.

6. To set the date and time manually, set the **Set Automatically** switch to Off (changes to).

7. Tap the button showing the date and time.

   The controls for setting the date and time appear.

8. Set the date and time.

9. Tap **General** ( ).

   The General screen appears.

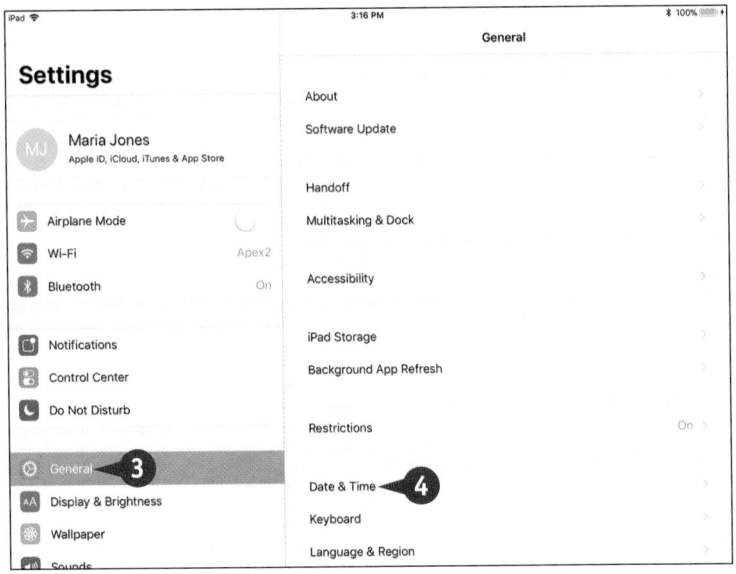

Choose Language & Region Settings

1. From the General screen, tap **Language & Region**.

   The Language & Region screen appears.

   A If you want to change the language used for the iPad user interface, tap **iPad Language**, tap the language in the iPad Language dialog that opens, and then tap **Done**.

2. Tap **Region**.

   The Region dialog opens.

3. Tap the region you want, which places a check mark next to it.

4. Tap **Done**.

   The Region dialog closes.

Note: From the Language & Region screen, you can also tap **Calendar** and then tap **Gregorian**, **Japanese**, or **Buddhist** to select the calendar system; or tap **Temperature Unit** and then tap **Celsius (°C)** or **Fahrenheit (°F)** to set the temperature unit.

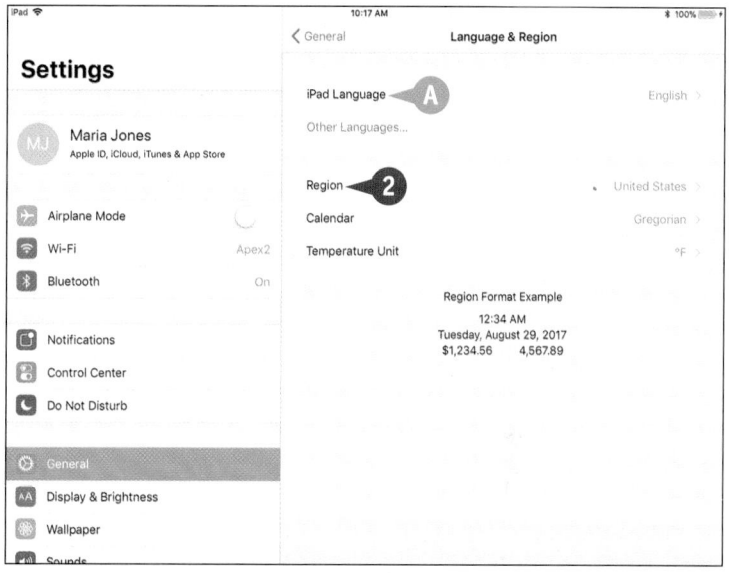

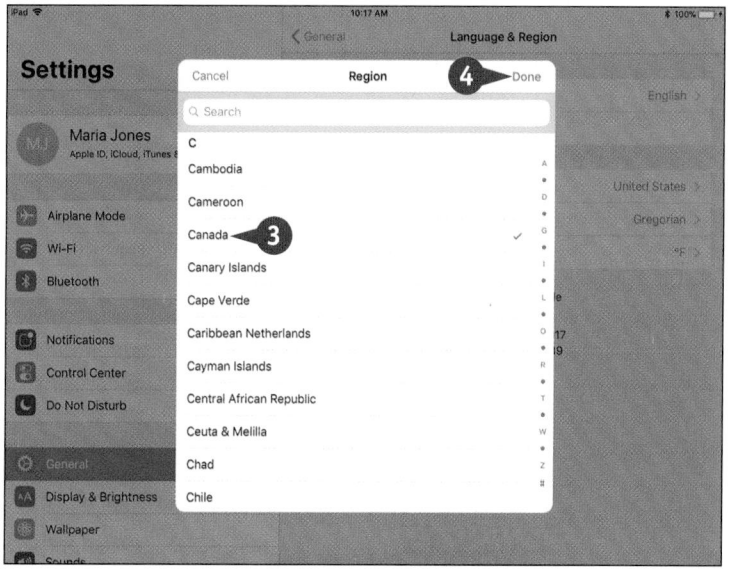

TIP

How does the iPad set the date and time automatically?
The iPad sets the date and time automatically by using time servers, which are computers on the Internet that provide date and time information to computers that request it. The iPad automatically determines its geographical location so that it can request the right time zone from the time server.

CHAPTER 3

Working with Voice and Accessibility

Your iPad includes the Siri personal assistant, helpful accessibility features, and integration with your Mac.

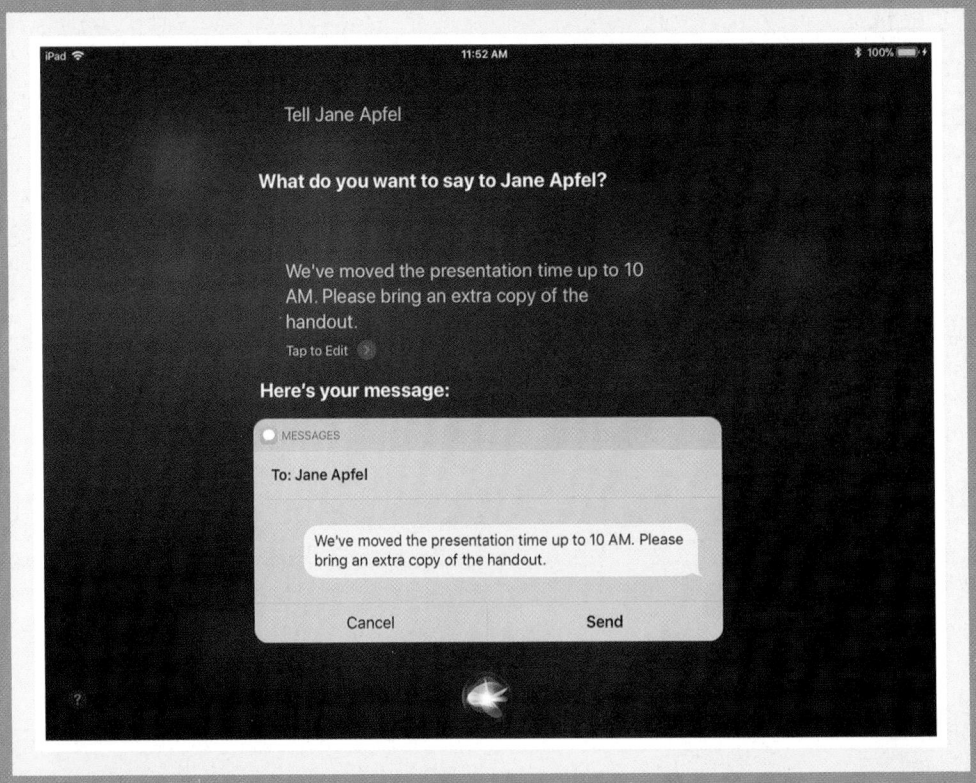

Give Commands with Siri 72
Dictate Text Using Siri 74
Gather and Share Information with Siri 76
Configure Siri to Work Your Way 78
Using VoiceOver to Identify Items On-Screen 80
Configure Other Accessibility Features 82
Using a Hardware Keyboard. 88
Using Your iPad with Your Mac 90

Give Commands with Siri

The powerful Siri feature on your iPad enables you to take essential actions by using your voice to tell your iPad what you want. Siri requires an Internet connection, because the speech recognition runs on servers in Apple's data center.

You can use Siri either with the iPad's built-in microphone or with a headset microphone. You can get good results from the built-in microphone if you are in a quiet environment and you speak loudly and clearly, or if you can speak as close to the built-in microphone as possible. Otherwise, use a headset microphone, which will usually provide better results.

Open Siri

From the Home screen or any app, press the **Home** button or the headset clicker button — if the headset has one — for several seconds.

The Siri screen appears, showing the "What can I help you with?" prompt. Siri also plays a tone to indicate that it is ready to take your commands.

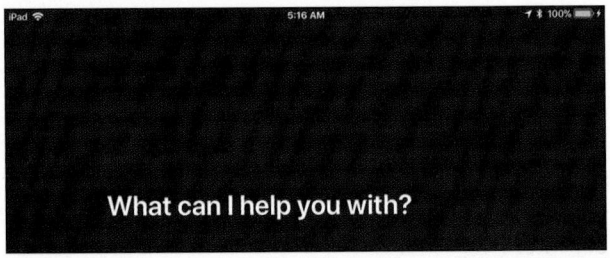

When your iPad is connected to a power source, you can also activate Siri by saying "Hey Siri" if the Allow "Hey Siri" feature is turned on in Settings.

Send an E-Mail Message

Say "E-mail" and the contact's name, followed by the message. Siri creates an e-mail message to the contact and enters the text. Review the message, and then tap **Send** to send it.

You can also say "E-mail" and the contact's name and have Siri prompt you for the various parts of the message. This approach gives you more time to collect your thoughts.

If your Contacts list has multiple e-mail addresses for the contact, Siri prompts you to choose the address to use.

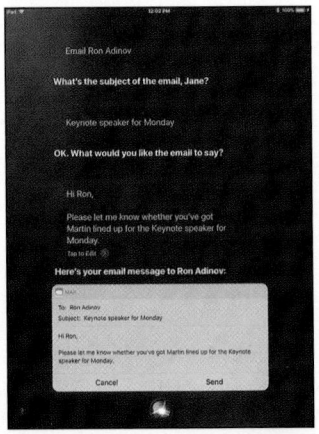

Set an Alarm

Say "Set an alarm for 5AM" and check the alarm that Siri displays.

You can turn the alarm off by tapping its switch (changes to).

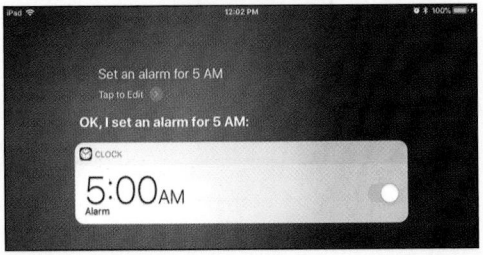

Send a Text Message

Say "Tell" or "Text" and the contact's name. When Siri responds, say the message you want to send. For example, say "Tell Kelly Wilson" and then "I am stuck in traffic, but I'll be there in an hour." Siri creates a text message to the contact, enters the text, and sends the message when you say "Send" or tap **Send**.

You can also say "Tell" and the contact's name followed immediately by the message. For example, "Tell Bill Sykes the package will arrive at 10AM."

Set a Reminder for Yourself

Say "Remind me" and the details of what you want Siri to remind you of. For example, say "Remind me to take the wireless transmitter to work tomorrow morning." Siri listens to what you say and creates a reminder. Check what Siri has written; if the reminder is correct, you need do nothing more, but if it is incorrect, tap **Remove** to remove it.

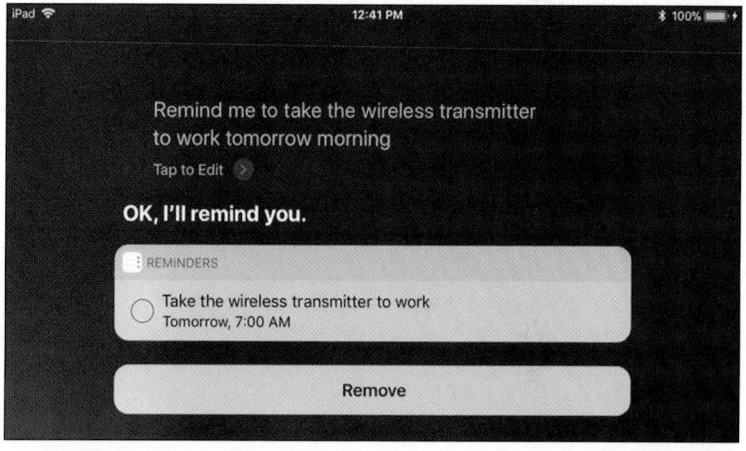

Set Up a Meeting

Say "Meet with" and the contact's name, followed by brief details of the appointment. For example, say "Meet with Don Williamson for lunch at noon on Thursday." Siri listens and warns you of any scheduling conflict. Siri then displays the appointment for you to check.

If you tap **Confirm**, Siri sends a meeting invitation to the contact if it finds an e-mail address. Siri adds the meeting to your calendar.

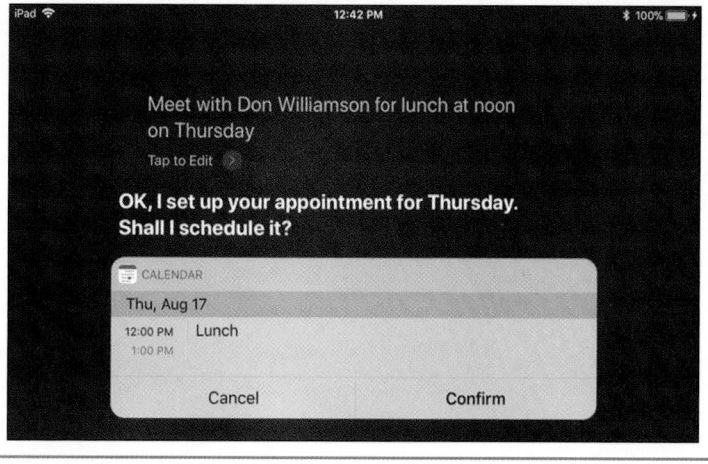

Dictate Text Using Siri

One of Siri's strongest features is its capability to transcribe your speech quickly and accurately into correctly spelled and punctuated text. Using your iPad, you can dictate into any app whose keyboard displays the microphone icon (🎙), so you can dictate e-mail messages, notes, documents, and more. To dictate, simply tap the microphone icon (🎙), speak after Siri beeps, and then tap **Done**.

To get the most out of dictation, it is helpful to know the standard terms for dictating punctuation, capitalization, symbols, layout, and formatting.

Insert Punctuation

To insert punctuation, use standard terms: "comma," "period" (or "full stop"), "semicolon," "colon," "exclamation point" (or "exclamation mark"), "question mark," "hyphen," "dash" (for a short dash, –), or "em dash" (for a long dash, —).

You can also say "asterisk" (*), "ampersand" (&), "open parenthesis" and "close parenthesis," "open bracket" and "close bracket," and "underscore" (_).

For example, say "buy eggs comma bread comma and cheese semicolon and maybe some milk period nothing else exclamation point" to enter the text shown here.

Insert Standard Symbols

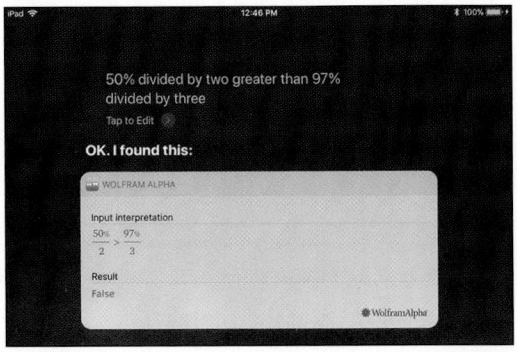

To insert symbols, use these terms: "at sign" (@), "percent sign" (%), "greater-than sign" (>) and "less-than sign" (<), "forward slash" (/) and "backslash" (\), "registered sign" (®), and "copyright sign" (©).

For example, say "fifty percent forward slash two greater than ninety-seven percent forward slash three" to enter the computation shown here.

Insert Currency Symbols

To insert currency symbols, say the currency name and "sign." For example, say "dollar sign" to insert $, "cent sign" to insert ¢, "euro sign" to insert €, "pound sterling sign" to insert £, and "yen sign" to insert ¥.

For example, say "the cost is dollar sign six or euro sign five per person" to enter the text shown here.

Control Layout

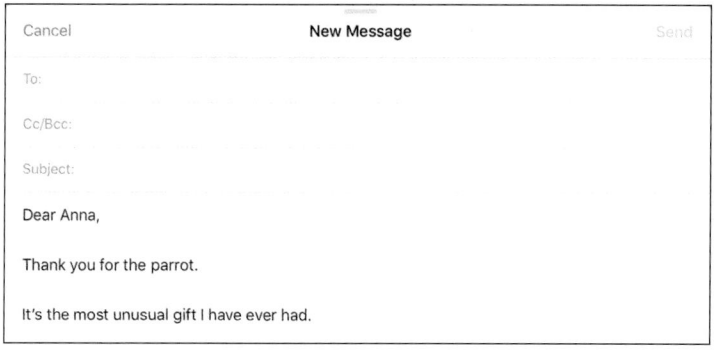

You can control layout by creating new lines and new paragraphs as needed. A new paragraph enters two line breaks, creating a blank line between paragraphs.

To create a new line, say "new line." To create a new paragraph, say "new paragraph."

For example, say "dear Anna comma new paragraph thank you for the parrot period new paragraph it's the most unusual gift I have ever had period" to enter the text shown here.

Control Capitalization

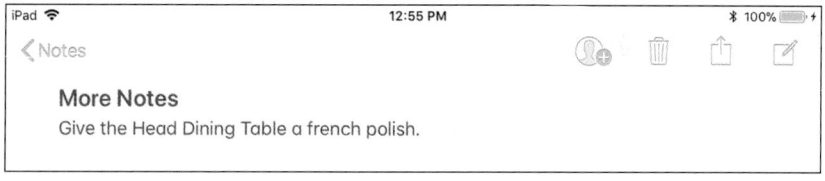

You can apply capitalization to the first letter of a word or to a whole word. You can also switch capitalization off temporarily to force lowercase:

Say "cap" to capitalize the first letter of the next word.

Say "caps on" to capitalize all the words until you say "caps off."

Say "no caps" to prevent automatic capitalization of the next word — for example, "no caps Monday" produces "monday" instead of "Monday."

Say "no caps on" to force lowercase of all words until you say "no caps off."

For example, say "give the cap head cap dining cap table a no caps french polish period" to enter the text shown here.

Insert Quotes and Emoticons

To insert double quotes, say "open quotes" and "close quotes." To insert single quotes, say "open single quotes" and "close single quotes."

To enter standard emoticons, say "smiley face," "frown face," and "wink face."

For example, say "she said comma open quotes I want to go to Paris next summer exclamation point close quotes" to enter the text shown here.

Gather and Share Information with Siri

You can use Siri to research a wide variety of information online — everything from sports and movies to restaurants worth visiting or worth avoiding. You can also use Siri to perform hands-free calculations.

When you need to share information quickly and easily, you can turn to Siri. By giving the right commands, you can quickly change your Facebook status or post on your wall. Similarly, you can send tweets using your Twitter account.

Find Information About Sports

Launch Siri and ask a question about sports. For example:

"Siri, when's the next Patriots game?"

"Did the Lakers win their last game?"

"When's the end of the NBA season?"

"Can you show me the roster for the Maple Leafs?"

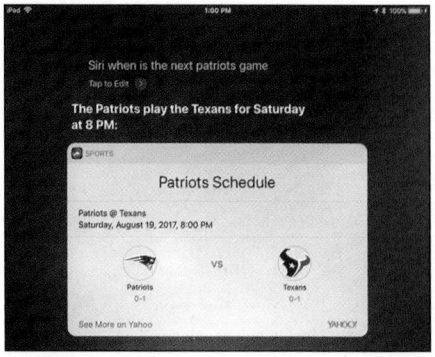

Find Information About Movies

Launch Siri and ask a question about movies. For example:

"How good is the movie *Hell or High Water*?"

"Siri, where is the movie *Let's Be Evil* playing in Indianapolis?"

"What's the name of Jason Statham's latest movie?"

"Who's the star of *Nine Lives*?"

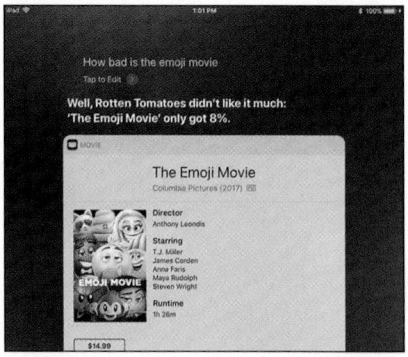

Find a Restaurant

Launch Siri, and then tell Siri what type of restaurant you want. For example:

"Where's the best Mexican food in Spokane?"

"Where can I get sushi in Albuquerque?"

"Is there a brewpub in Minneapolis?"

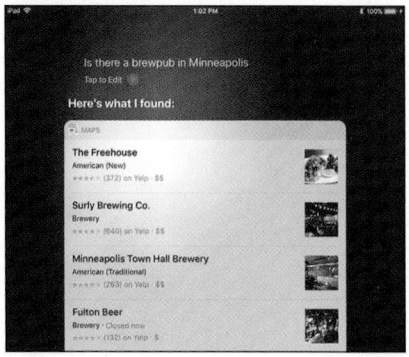

Address a Query to the Wolfram Alpha Computational Knowledge Engine

Launch Siri, and then say "Wolfram" and your question. For example:

"Wolfram, what is the cube of 27?"

"Wolfram, minus 20 Centigrade in Kelvin."

"Wolfram, tangent of 60 degrees."

"Wolfram, give me the chemical formula of formaldehyde."

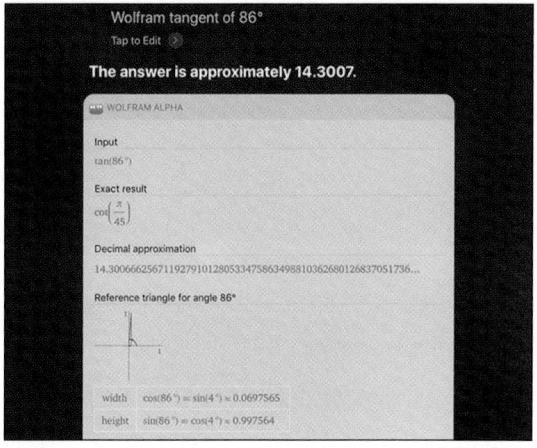

Find Out What Music You Are Listening To

Launch Siri and ask a question such as "What song is this?" or "Do you know what this music is called?" Siri monitors the microphone's input, consults the Shazam music-recognition service, and returns a result if there is a match.

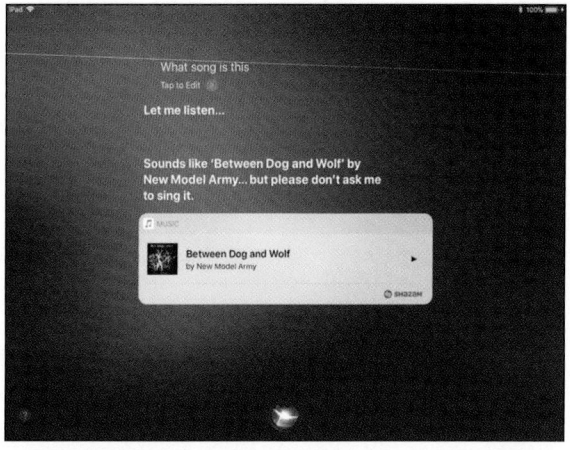

Translate to Another Language

Launch Siri, and then say "Translate to" and the name of the language, such as "Translate to Spanish." When Siri prompts you for the text, speak it. Siri announces the translated text and displays it on-screen, together with a Play button (▶) that you can tap to play the audio again.

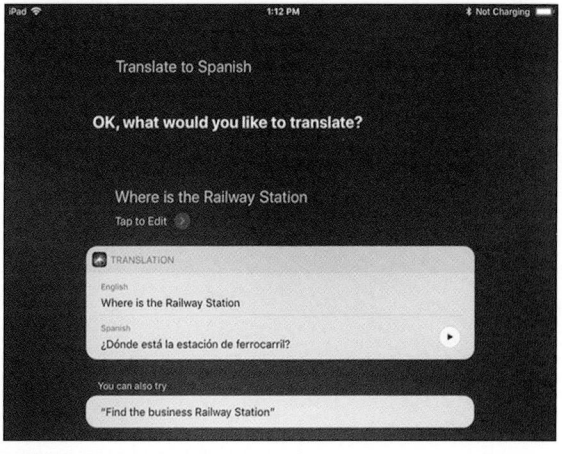

Configure Siri to Work Your Way

To get the most out of Siri, spend a few minutes configuring it. You can set the language Siri uses, choose between using a female voice and a male voice, and control when Siri should give you voice feedback. You can also enable or disable the "Hey Siri" feature, use Siri via the on-screen keyboard, or temporarily turn Siri off.

Most important, you can tell Siri which contact record contains your information, so that Siri knows your name, address, phone numbers, e-mail address, and other essential information.

Configure Siri to Work Your Way

1. Press **Home**.

   The Home screen appears.

2. Tap **Settings** ( ).

   The Settings screen appears.

3. Tap **Siri & Search** ( ).

   The Siri & Search screen appears.

4. Set the **Listen for "Hey Siri"** switch to On ( ) to activate Siri by saying "Hey, Siri!"

5. Set the **Press Home for Siri** switch to On ( ) to be able to press Home to summon Siri.

6. Set the **Allow Siri When Locked** switch to On ( ) to use Siri from the lock screen.

7. Tap **Language**.

   The Language screen appears.

8. Tap the language you want to use.

9. Tap **Siri & Search** ( ).

   The Siri & Search screen appears again.

10. Tap **Siri Voice**.

Note: To use Siri via the keyboard, press **Home**, tap **Settings** ( ), tap **General** ( ), tap **Accessibility**, tap **Siri**, and then set the **Type to Siri** switch to On ( ).

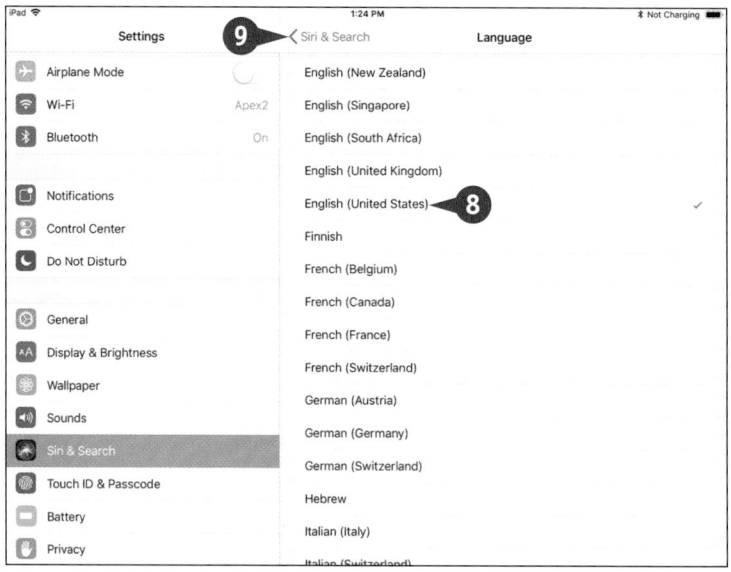

The Siri Voice screen appears.

11. In the Accent box, tap the accent you want, such as **American**.

12. In the Gender box, tap **Male** or **Female**.

13. Tap **Siri & Search** (<).

    The Siri & Search screen appears again.

14. Tap **Voice Feedback**.

    The Voice Feedback screen appears.

15. Tap **Always On**, **Control with Mute Setting**, or **Hands-Free Only** to specify when you want to receive voice feedback from Siri.

16. Tap **Siri & Search** (<).

    The Siri & Search screen appears again.

17. Tap **My Info**.

    The Contacts dialog appears.

Note: To change which contacts appear in the Contacts dialog, tap **Groups**, select the groups to display, and then tap **Done**.

18. Tap the contact record that contains your information.

    The name appears on the My Info button.

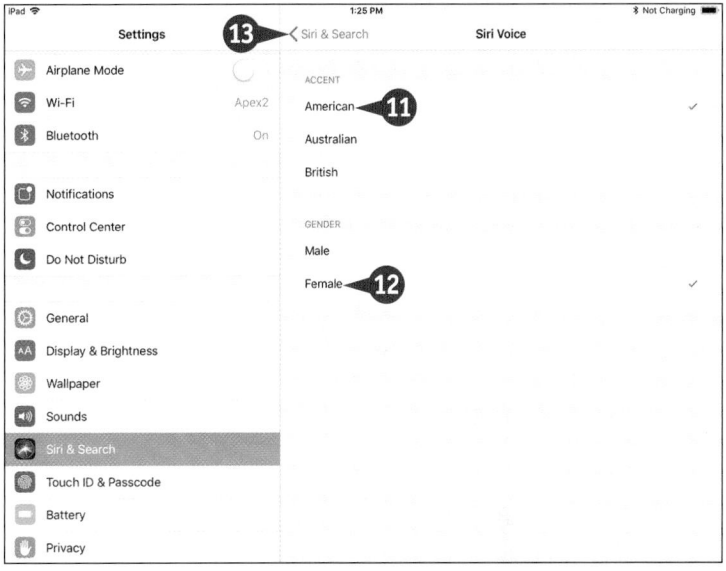

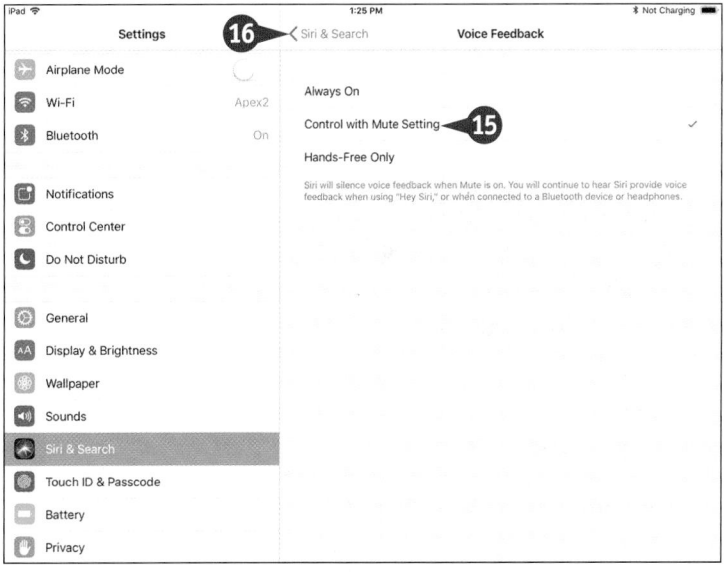

TIP

Does Apple store the details of what I ask Siri?

Yes, but not in a way that will come back to haunt you. When you use Siri, your iPad passes your input to servers in the Apple data center in North Carolina, USA, for processing. The servers analyze your request and tell Siri how to respond to it. The Apple data center stores the details of your request and may analyze them to determine what people use Siri for and work out ways of making Siri more effective. Apple does not associate your Siri data with other data Apple holds about you — for example, the identity and credit card data you used to pay for iTunes Match.

Using VoiceOver to Identify Items On-Screen

If you have trouble identifying the iPad controls on-screen, you can use the VoiceOver feature to read them to you. VoiceOver changes the standard iPad finger gestures so that you tap to select the item whose name you want it to speak, double-tap to activate an item, and flick three fingers to scroll. VoiceOver can make your iPad easier to use. Your iPad also includes other accessibility features, which you can learn about in the next section.

Using VoiceOver to Identify Items On-Screen

1. Press **Home**.

   The Home screen appears.

2. Tap **Settings** ( ).

   The Settings screen appears.

3. Tap **General** ( ).

   The General screen appears.

4. Tap **Accessibility**.

   The Accessibility screen appears.

5. Tap **VoiceOver**.

Note: You cannot use VoiceOver and Zoom at the same time. If Zoom is on when you try to switch VoiceOver on, your iPad prompts you to choose which to use.

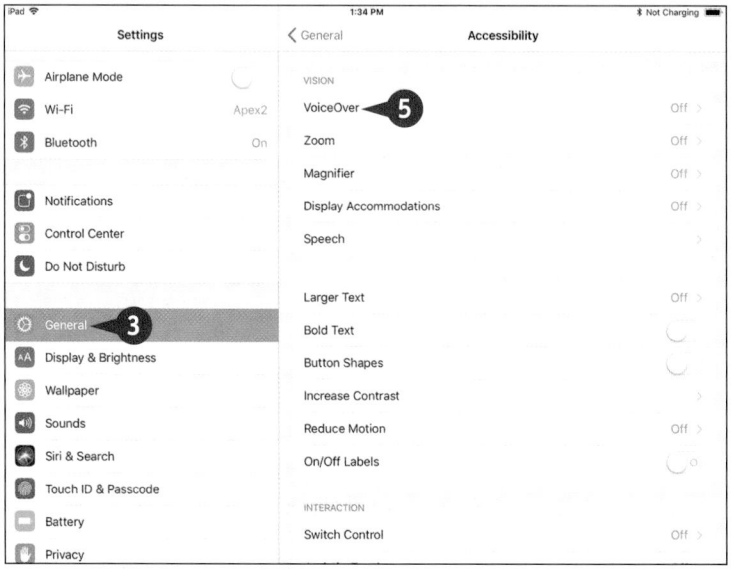

   The VoiceOver screen appears.

6. Set the **VoiceOver** switch to On ( ).

7. Tap **VoiceOver Practice**.

   A. A selection border appears around the button, and VoiceOver speaks its name.

8. Double-tap **VoiceOver Practice**.

9. Practice tapping, double-tapping, triple-tapping, and swiping.

10. Tap **Done** to select the button, and then double-tap **Done**.

11. On the VoiceOver screen, tap **Speaking Rate** to select it, and then swipe up or down to adjust the rate. Swiping up or down is the VoiceOver gesture for adjusting the slider.

12 Swipe up with three fingers.

The screen scrolls down.

13 Tap and then double-tap **Speech** and choose voice, pronunciations, and pitch options on the Speech screen.

14 Tap and then double-tap **Verbosity** and choose which items to have VoiceOver announce.

15 Set the **Always Speak Notifications** switch to On (◐) or Off ( ), as needed.

16 Tap and then double-tap **Double-tap Timeout** and set the timeout for double-tapping.

17 Tap and then double-tap **Typing Feedback**.

The Typing Feedback screen appears.

18 In the Software Keyboards area, tap and then double-tap the feedback type you want: **Nothing**, **Characters**, **Words**, or **Characters and Words**.

19 In the Hardware Keyboards area, tap and then double-tap the feedback type you want: **Nothing**, **Characters**, **Words**, or **Characters and Words**.

20 Tap and then double-tap **VoiceOver** (<).

The VoiceOver screen appears again.

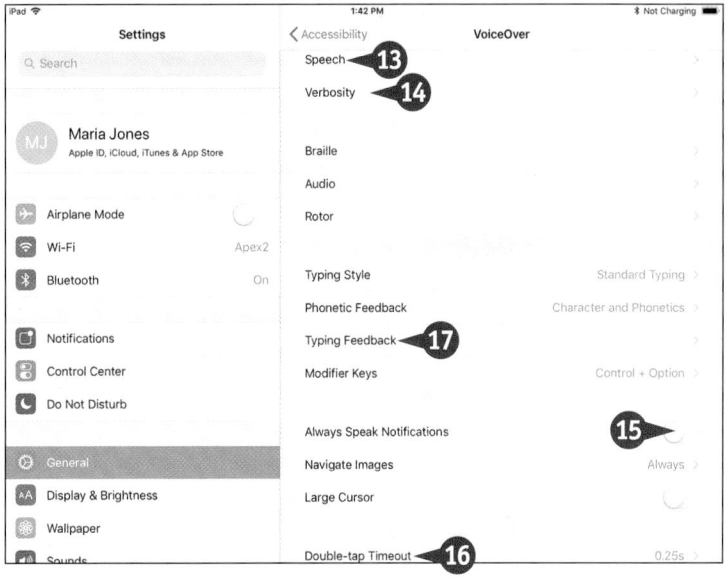

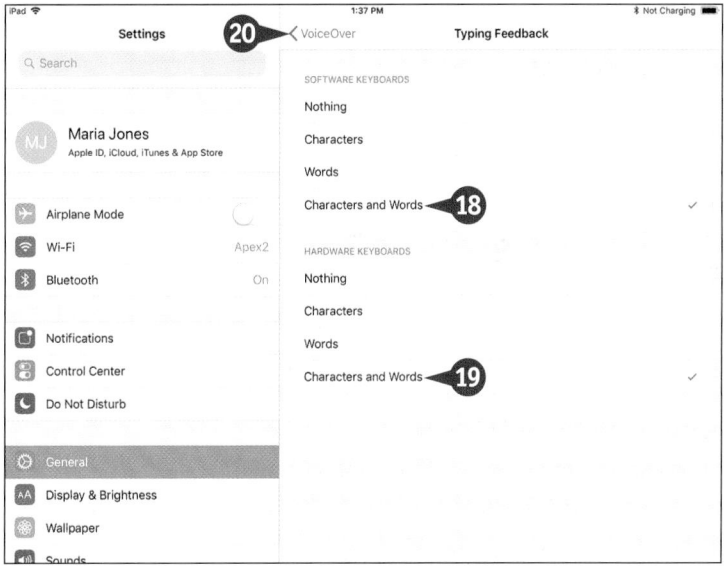

TIP

Is there an easy way to turn VoiceOver on and off?

Yes. You can set your iPad to toggle VoiceOver on or off when you use the accessibility shortcut, which is pressing the Home button three times in rapid sequence. At the bottom of the Accessibility screen, tap **Accessibility Shortcut** to display the Accessibility Shortcut screen, and then tap **VoiceOver** to place a check mark next to it.

Configure Other Accessibility Features

To help you see the screen better, iOS provides a full-featured zoom capability. After turning on zooming, you can display the Zoom Controller to give yourself easy control of zoom, choose the zoom region, and set the maximum zoom level.

The Follow Focus feature makes the zoomed area follow the focus on-screen. The Smart Typing feature makes iOS switch to Window Zoom when the keyboard appears, so that text is zoomed but the keyboard is regular size.

Configure Other Accessibility Features

Display the Accessibility Screen and Configure Zoom Settings

1. Press **Home**.

   The Home screen appears.

2. Tap **Settings** ( ).

   The Settings screen appears.

3. Tap **General** ( ).

   The General screen appears.

4. Tap **Accessibility**.

   The Accessibility screen appears.

5. Tap **Zoom**.

   The Zoom screen appears.

6. Set the **Zoom** switch to On ( ).

   A The Zoom window appears if the Zoom Region is set to Window Zoom.

7. Set the **Follow Focus** switch to On ( ) or Off ( ).

8. Set the **Smart Typing** switch to On ( ) or Off ( ).

9. Set the **Show Controller** switch to On ( ).

   B The Zoom Controller appears.

10. Drag the **Maximum Zoom Level** slider to set the maximum zoom level.

11. Tap **Idle Visibility**.

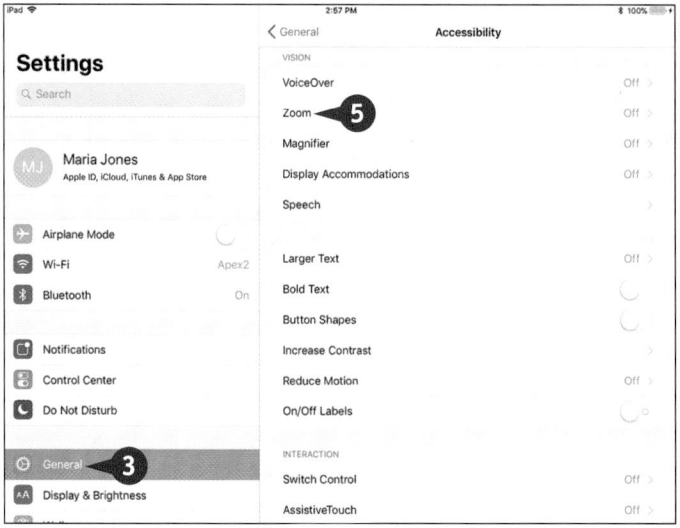

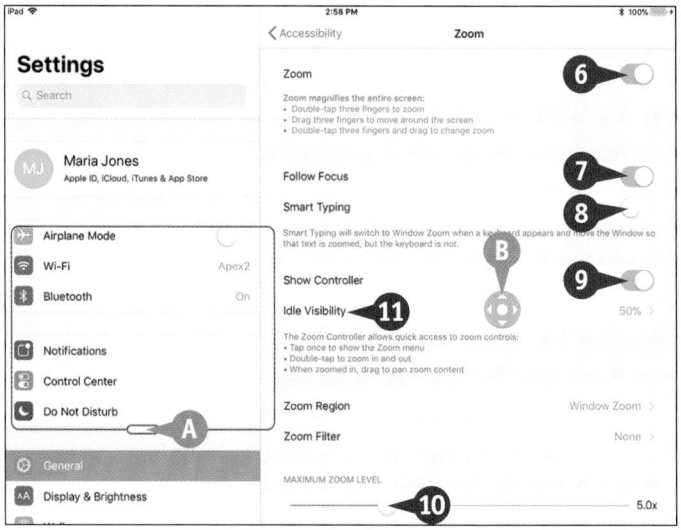

The Idle Visibility screen appears.

12 Drag the slider to set the visibility percentage for the Zoom Controller when it is idle.

Note: Move the slider on the Idle Visibility screen to the left to make the controller fade more after you have not used it for a while.

13 Tap **Zoom** (<).

The Zoom screen appears again.

14 Tap **Zoom Region**.

The Zoom Region screen appears.

15 Tap **Full Screen Zoom** or **Window Zoom**, as needed.

Note: Window Zoom displays a movable window frame that you can position over the area you want to zoom, leaving the rest of the screen unchanged.

16 Tap **Zoom** (<).

The Zoom screen appears again.

17 Tap **Zoom Filter**.

The Zoom Filter screen appears.

18 Tap the zoom filter you need: **None**, **Inverted**, **Grayscale**, **Grayscale Inverted**, or **Low Light**.

19 Tap **Zoom** (<).

The Zoom screen appears again.

20 Tap **Accessibility** (<).

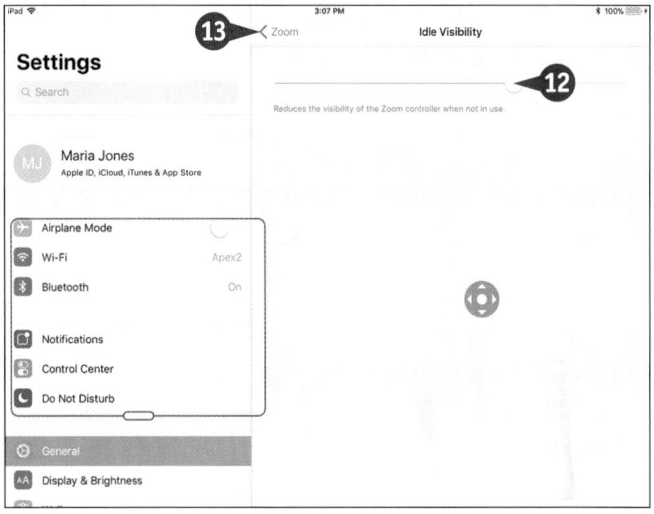

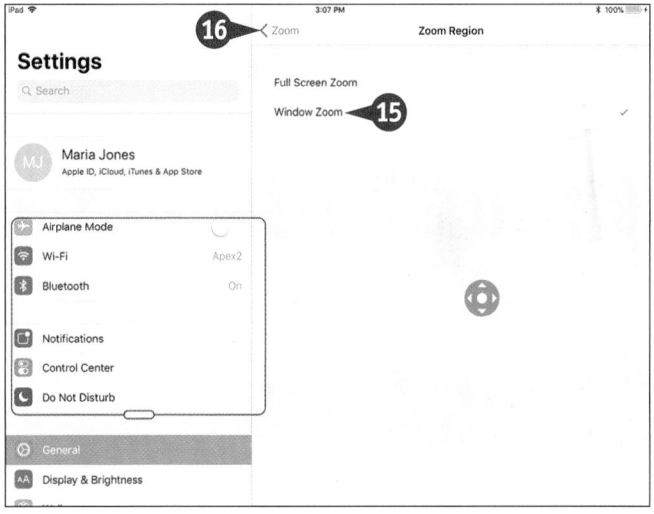

TIP

Is there an easy way to turn the Zoom feature on and off?

Yes. You can set your iPad to toggle Zoom on or off when you invoke the accessibility shortcut by pressing the **Home** button three times in rapid sequence. From the Accessibility screen, tap **Accessibility Shortcut** to display the Accessibility Shortcut screen. Tap **Zoom** to place a check mark next to it. You can also use the Home button triple-press to toggle the VoiceOver feature, the Invert Colors feature, the Grayscale feature, the Switch Control feature, or the AssistiveTouch feature.

continued ▶

Your iPad includes several "display accommodations" such as inverting the screen colors entirely, reducing the white point to lessen the intensity of bright colors, and applying color filters for grayscale or for the protanopia, deuteranopia, or tritanopia color blindnesses.

You can also set a larger text size, apply shading around text-only buttons, reduce the transparency of items, and darken colors.

Configure Other Accessibility Features (continued)

Configure Display Accommodations

1. On the Accessibility screen, tap **Display Accommodations**.

   The Display Accommodations screen appears.

2. Tap **Invert Colors** and set the **Smart Invert** switch or the **Classic Invert** switch to On (◐) to invert colors, as in this example.

Note: Inverting colors disables the Night Shift feature.

3. Set the **Reduce White Point** switch to On (◐) if you want to reduce the intensity of bright colors.

4. Drag the slider to adjust the white point.

5. Tap **Color Filters**.

   The Color Filters screen appears.

   C The color chart displays colors using the filtering you apply. Swipe left to see other color samples.

6. Set the **Color Filters** switch to On (◐).

   The list of color filters appears.

7. Tap the filter you want to apply: **Grayscale, Red/Green Filter, Green/Red Filter, Blue/Yellow Filter**, or **Color Tint**.

8. If the Intensity slider appears, drag it to adjust the intensity.

9. For Color Tint, drag the **Hue** slider to adjust the hue.

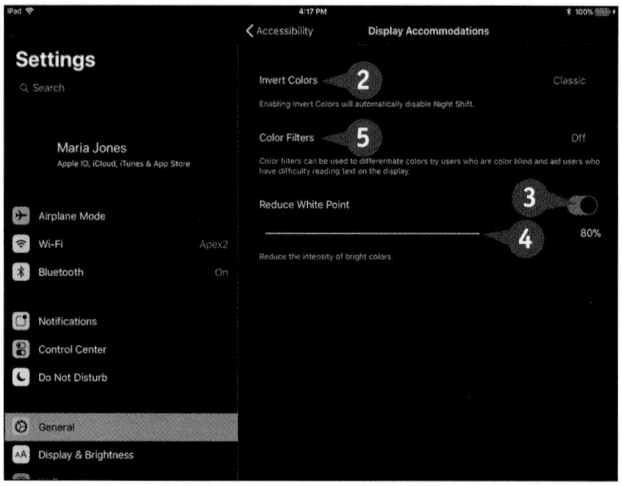

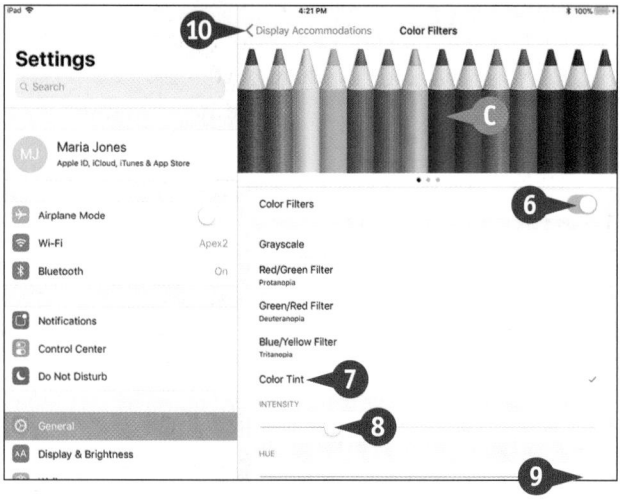

10. Tap **Display Accommodations** (<).

11. Tap **Accessibility** (<).

    The Accessibility screen appears again.

Configure Visual Interface Accessibility Settings

D On the Accessibility screen, you can set the **Bold Text** switch to On (◐) to make text appear bold. You must restart your iPad to effect this change.

E You can set the **Button Shapes** switch to On (◐) to make shapes appear around text buttons, as on the General button here.

F You can set the **On/Off Labels** switch to On (◐) to display I and O labels on the switches, as shown here.

1. Tap **Larger Text**.

   The Larger Text screen appears.

2. Set the **Larger Accessibility Sizes** switch to On (○ changes to ◐).

3. Drag the slider to set the text size.

4. Tap **Accessibility** (<).

   The Accessibility screen appears again.

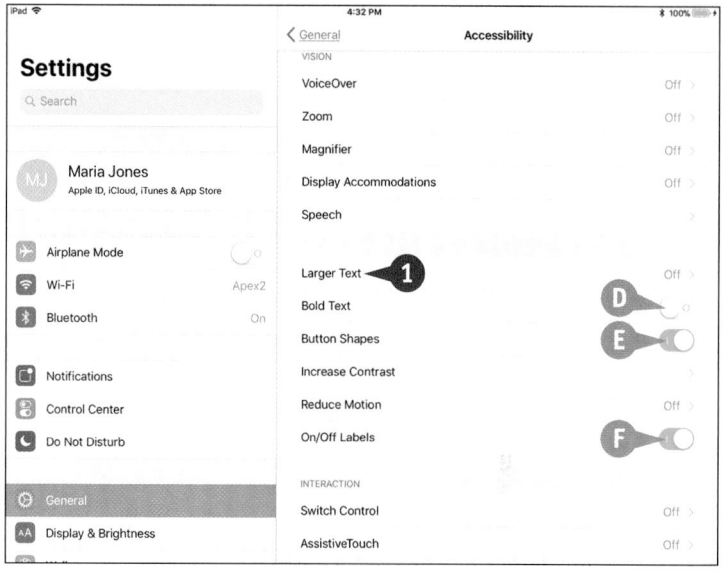

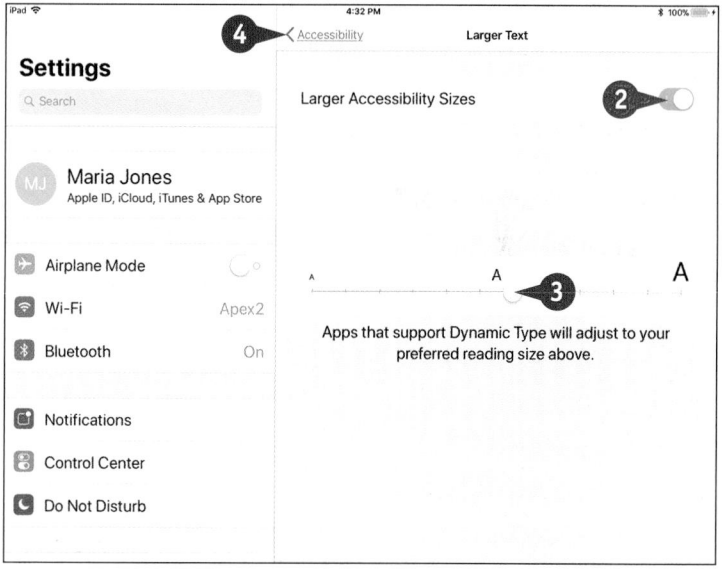

TIPS

What is the difference between Classic Invert and Smart Invert for inverting colors?

Classic Invert inverts the colors of everything on the display. Smart Invert inverts colors of everything except images, other media, and some dark-colored apps.

What does the Reduce Motion feature do?

The Reduce Motion feature reduces the amount of movement that occurs when you tilt the iPad when displaying a screen such as the Home screen, where the icons appear to float above the background. To turn Reduce Motion on, tap **Reduce Motion** on the Accessibility screen to display the Reduce Motion screen, and then set the **Reduce Motion** switch to On (◐).

continued ▶

Your iPad includes a suite of interaction features designed to make it easier for you to interact with the touch screen and other hardware components, such as the accelerometers that detect and analyze the device's movements. Changes you can make include setting the tap-and-hold duration, adjusting the repeat interval, and configuring the double- and triple-click speed for the Home button. You can also choose your default audio device for call audio.

Configure Other Accessibility Features (continued)

Configure Interaction Accessibility Features

1. On the Accessibility screen, tap **Touch Accommodations**.

   The Touch Accommodations screen appears.

2. Set the **Touch Accommodations** switch to On (◯) to enable touch accommodations.

Note: If the Important dialog opens, warning you that Touch Accommodations changes iPad-control gestures, tap **OK**.

3. Set the **Hold Duration** switch to On (◯) if you need to adjust the hold duration.
4. Tap **+** or **–** to set the Hold Duration time.
5. Set the **Ignore Repeat** switch to On (◯) if your iPad detects false repeat touches.
6. Tap **+** or **–** to set the Ignore Repeat interval.
7. In the Tap Assistance box, tap **Off**, **Use Initial Touch Location**, or **Use Final Touch Location**, as needed.
8. In the Tap Assistance Gesture Delay box, tap **+** or **–** to set the delay on tap assistance. This is the length of time you get to perform a tap; beyond this point, the iPad assumes you are making a gesture other than tapping.
9. Tap **Accessibility** (<).

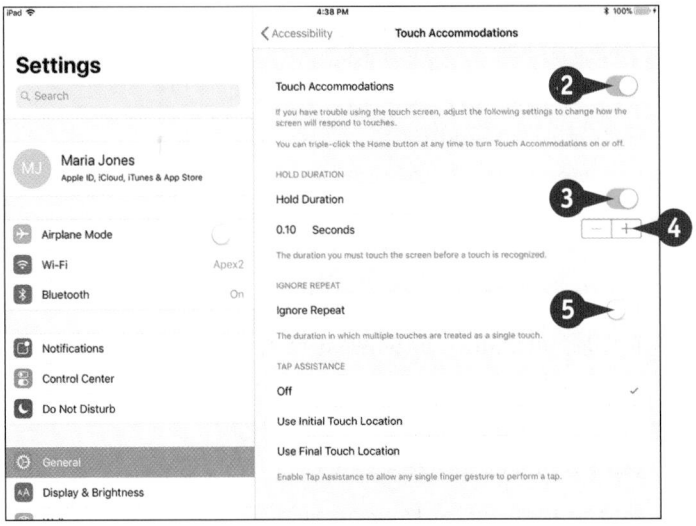

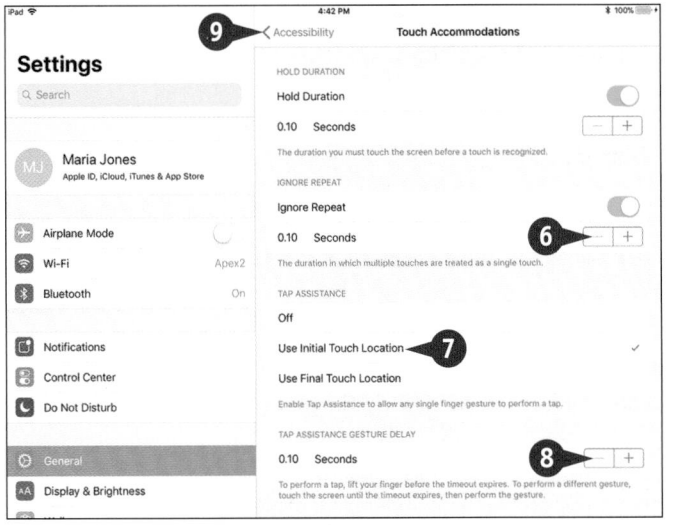

The Accessibility screen appears again.

10 Tap **Shake to Undo** to display the Shake to Undo screen, set the **Shake to Undo** switch to Off ( ) if the feature undoes actions by accident, and then tap **Accessibility** (<) to return to the Accessibility screen.

11 Tap **Call Audio Routing** to display the Call Audio Routing screen, tap the audio output device to use for FaceTime audio calls, such as **Bluetooth Headset**; and then tap **Accessibility** (<) to return to the Accessibility screen.

12 Tap **Home Button**.

The Home Button screen appears.

13 Tap **Default**, **Slow**, or **Slowest** to set the double-click speed.

14 In the Press and Hold to Speak section, tap **Siri** or **Off**, as needed.

15 Set the **Rest Finger to Open** switch to On ( ) if you want to be able to unlock the iPad using Touch ID by resting your finger on the Home button without having to press the Home button.

16 Tap **Accessibility** (<).

The Accessibility screen appears again.

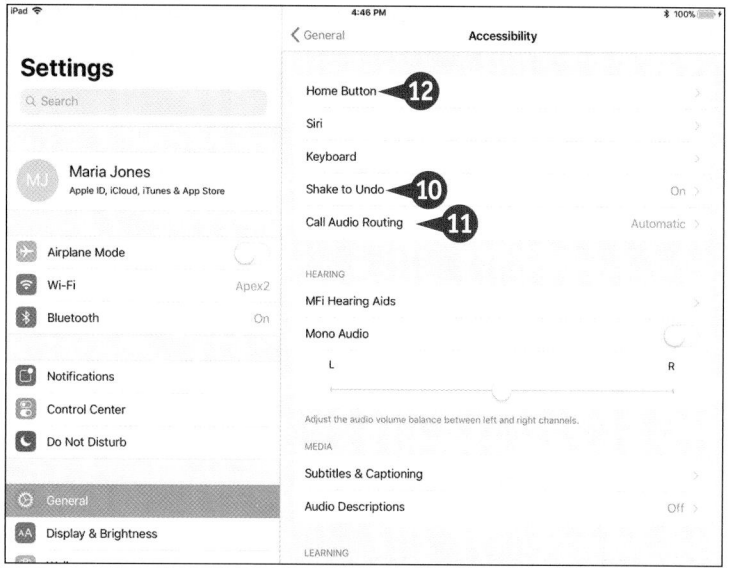

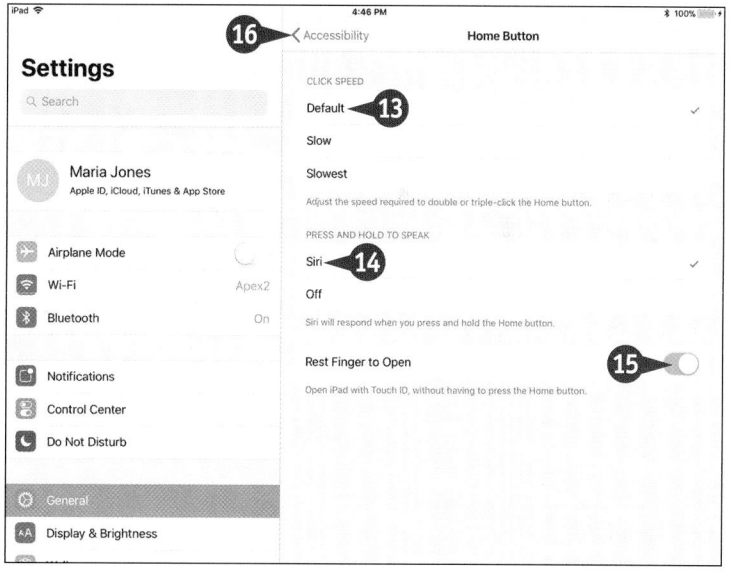

TIP

How do I set up a hearing aid with my iPad?

Tap **MFi Hearing Aids** on the Accessibility screen to display the MFi Hearing Aids screen. Here you can pair a hearing aid that conforms to the Made for iPad standard, MFi for short; connect other hearing aids via the Bluetooth settings screen, as for other Bluetooth devices.

Using a Hardware Keyboard

Your iPad includes several on-screen keyboards that appear automatically when you tap a text field on the screen. You can switch among the keyboards as necessary to type the characters you need, and you can undock the keyboard or split it so that you can type easily with two thumbs while holding the iPad.

If you need to type extensively, you may prefer to connect a hardware keyboard to your iPad. This section details your options for a hardware keyboard, explains how to connect it, and shows you how to use it.

Choose a Hardware Keyboard

You can connect a keyboard to any iPad by using Bluetooth, which is usually effective and convenient for most purposes. For the iPad Pro, you can get one of Apple's Smart Keyboard models, which connect via the custom Smart Connector on the iPad Pro models.

Many types of Bluetooth keyboards work well with iPads, but it is a good idea to verify the compatibility of any particular model before buying it. Keyboards designed specifically for the iPad, or for iOS devices in general, often include dedicated keys for functions such as displaying the Home screen, controlling the volume, and launching apps.

One option is to get a keyboard case designed specifically for the iPad model you have. This approach works well if you do not already have an iPad case, it is convenient for you to keep the iPad in the keyboard case, and you do not plan to switch iPad models in the near future. Some keyboard cases fully enclose the iPad, whereas others act as a protective cover for the screen but leave the iPad's back exposed.

For more flexibility, you can get a Bluetooth keyboard designed for use with iOS but not customized for any particular device. You can then use the keyboard with any iOS device.

For the greatest flexibility, you can use any Bluetooth keyboard that is compatible with iOS; this includes Apple's wireless keyboards for the Mac. For example, if you already have a Bluetooth keyboard, you may want to see if it works with your iPad. A Bluetooth keyboard can be active with only one device at a time.

Connect the Keyboard to the iPad

Once you have gotten your keyboard, connect it to your iPad. This section assumes you are using Bluetooth.

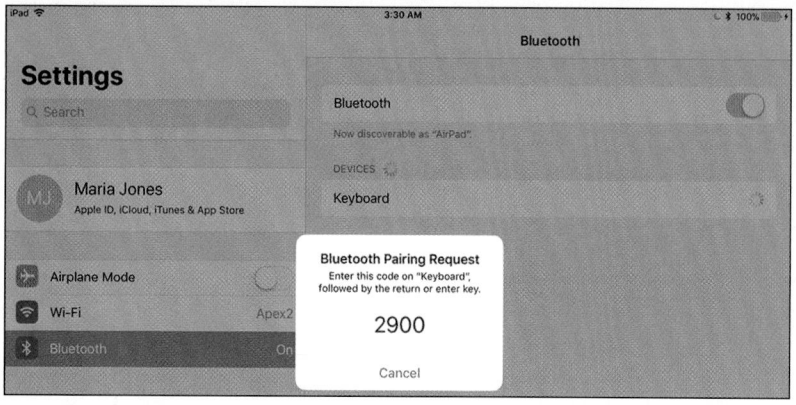

Unlock the iPad, press **Home** to display the Home screen, and then tap **Settings** (⚙) to display the Settings screen. Tap **Bluetooth** (✱) to display the Bluetooth screen, and set the **Bluetooth** switch to On (◯).

Turn the keyboard on, and then put the keyboard into pairing mode. How you do this depends on the keyboard, so you may need to read its documentation, but it often involves either pressing a dedicated pairing button or pressing and holding the power button until lights begin flashing in a particular pattern.

Tap the keyboard's button in the Devices list on the Bluetooth screen in Settings. The Bluetooth Pairing Request dialog opens, showing a pairing code. Type this code on the keyboard and press Enter or Return to authenticate the connection.

Configure the Keyboard

After connecting the keyboard, you can simply type on it after tapping a text field on the screen. But you can also change the keyboard layout if necessary.

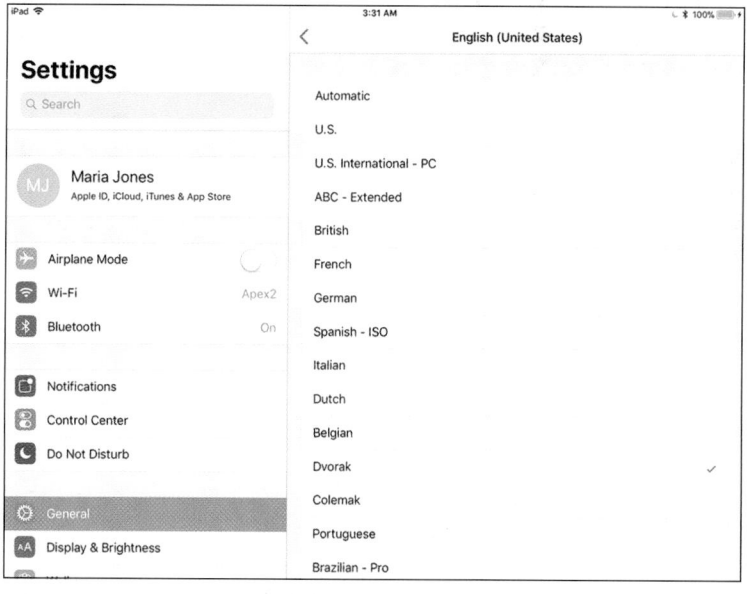

To change the keyboard layout, press **Home** to display the Home screen, and then tap **Settings** (⚙) to display the Settings screen. Tap **General** (⚙) to display the General screen, and then tap **Keyboard** to display the Keyboards screen. Tap **Hardware Keyboard** at the top of the screen to display the Hardware Keyboard screen, and then tap the language you are using, such as **English**. On the screen that appears, such as the English screen, tap the layout you want, such as **Dvorak** or **U.S. International – PC**.

Using Your iPad with Your Mac

If you have a Mac, you can enjoy the impressive integration that Apple has built into iOS and the Mac's operating system, which is now called macOS but was formerly called OS X. Apple calls this integration Continuity. Continuity involves several features including Handoff, which enables you to pick up your work or play seamlessly on one device exactly where you have left it on another device. For example, you can start writing an e-mail message on your Mac and then complete it on your iPad.

To use Continuity, your iPad must be running iOS 8, iOS 9, iOS 10, iOS 11, or a later version. Your Mac must be running Yosemite, El Capitan, Sierra, High Sierra, or a later version. Your Mac must have Bluetooth 4.0 hardware. In practice, this means a Mac mini or MacBook Air from 2011 or later, a MacBook Pro or iMac from 2012 or later, a MacBook from 2014 or later, or a Mac Pro from 2013 or later.

Enable Handoff on Your iPad

To enable your iPad to communicate with your Mac, you need to enable the Handoff feature. Press the **Home** button to display the Home screen, tap **Settings** ( ) to open the Settings app, and then tap **General** ( ) to display the General screen. Tap **Handoff** to display the Handoff screen, and then set the **Handoff** switch to On ( ).

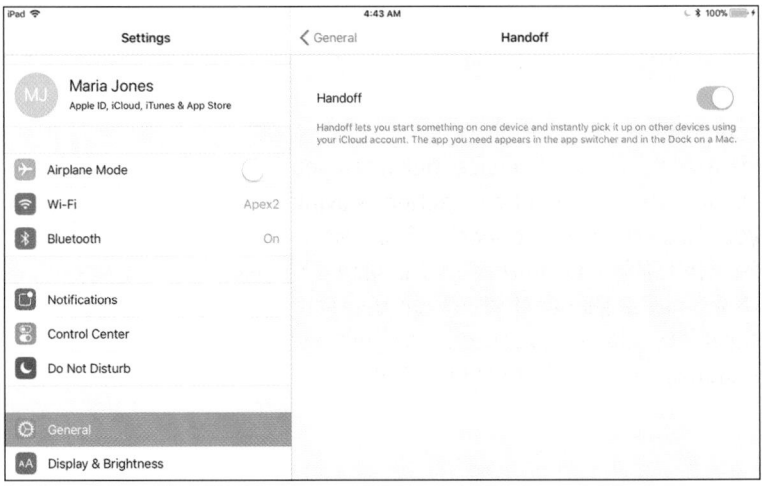

Enable Handoff on Your Mac

You also need to enable Handoff on your Mac. To do so, click **Apple** ( ) on the menu bar and then click **System Preferences** to open the System Preferences window. Click **General** to display the General pane. Click **Allow Handoff between this Mac and your iCloud devices** (changes to). You can then click **System Preferences** on the menu bar and click **Quit System Preferences** to quit System Preferences.

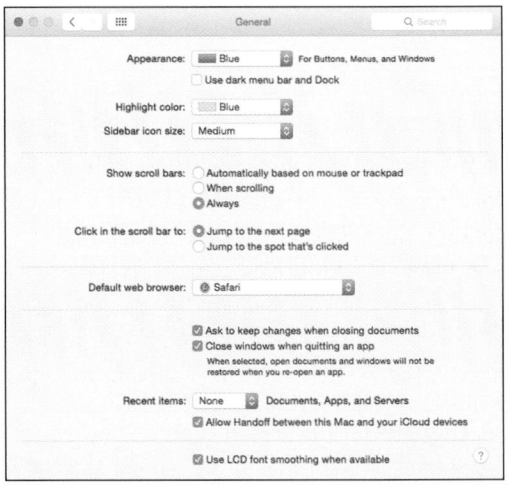

Work on the Same Task on Your Mac and Your iOS Devices

With Handoff enabled, you can easily start a task on one device, pick it up on another device, and finish it on a third. For example, you can start writing an e-mail message on your Mac at home, continue it on your iPhone as you commute, and then finish it on your iPad while waiting for a meeting to start. To perform a handoff, you click or tap the icon that appears on the Dock when a Handoff-compatible app is in use on another device.

Send and Receive Text Messages from Your Mac

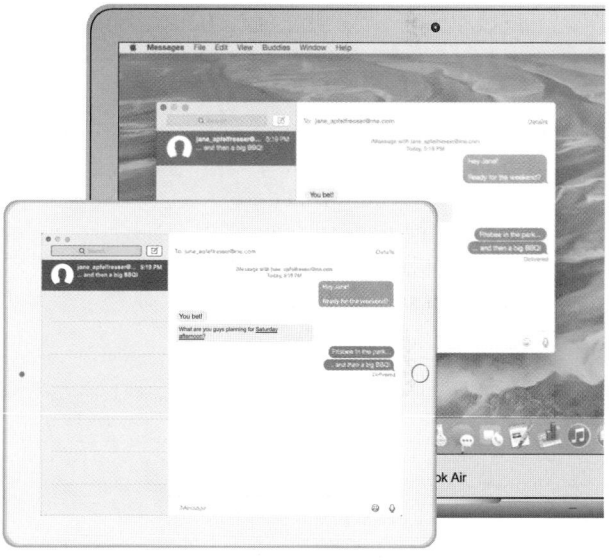

Your Mac can already send and receive messages via Apple's iMessage service, but when your cellular iPad's Internet connection is available, your Mac can send and receive Short Message Service (SMS) and Multimedia Messaging Service (MMS) messages directly through the iPad. This capability enables you to manage your messaging smoothly and tightly from your Mac.

Get Your Mac Online with Personal Hotspot

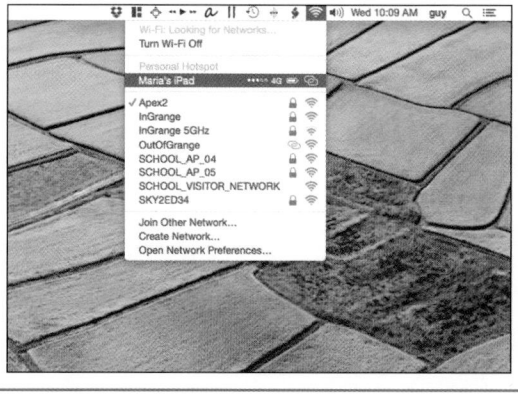

With Continuity, you can use your cellular iPad as a hotspot for your Mac without having to set up the Portable Hotspot feature. Click **Wi-Fi** (ᯤ) on the menu bar on your Mac and then click your iPad's entry on the pop-up menu to connect. The iPad's menu entry on the Wi-Fi pop-up menu shows the signal strength and battery life, enabling you to make sure you don't run your iPad down unusably low.

CHAPTER 4

Setting Up Communications

In this chapter, you learn how to add your e-mail accounts to the Mail app, choose how and when your iPad gets your mail, and control how the messages appear. You also learn how to make your contacts appear the way you prefer, choose alert options for calendar events, and set your default account for notes.

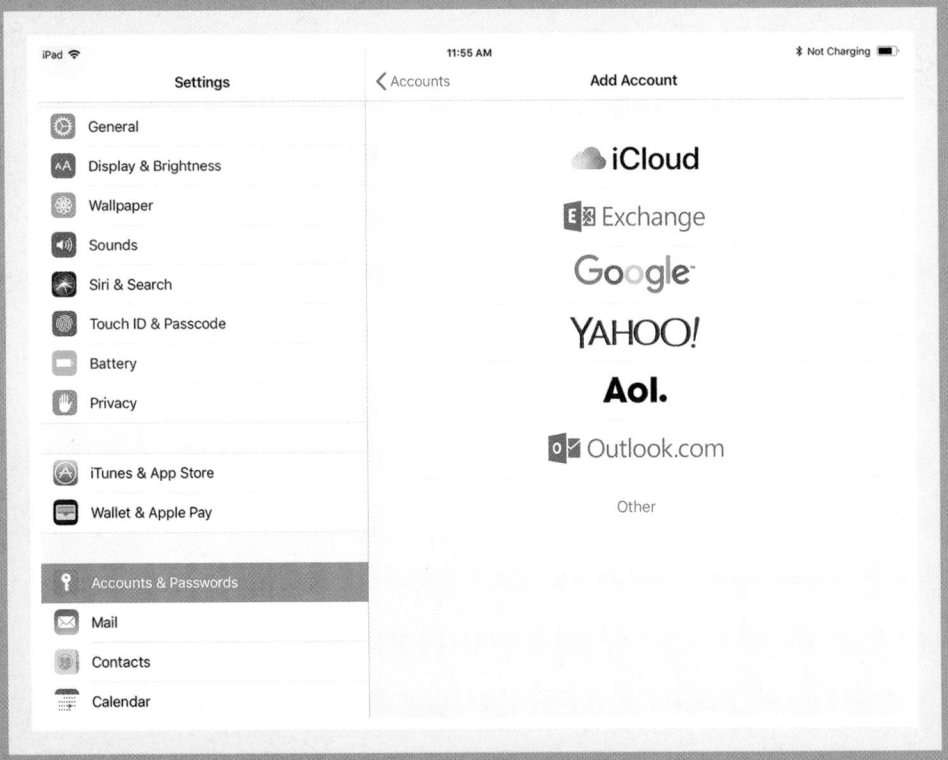

Set Up Your Mail Accounts 94
Set Up an Exchange Server Account 96
Set Your Default Account and Create Signatures 98
Choose How Your iPad Gets Your E-Mail 100
Control How Your iPad Displays Your E-Mail 102
Organize Your E-Mail Messages by Threads. 104
Add People to the VIP Inbox 106
Choose How Your iPad Displays Your Contacts 108
Choose Alert Options for Calendar Events 110
Choose Your Default Calendar and Time Zone 112
Choose Settings for Notes 114

Set Up Your Mail Accounts

You can set up your iCloud Mail account simply by setting up your iCloud account on your iPad. Beyond that, you can set up other e-mail accounts manually by working directly on the iPad, as explained in this section. To set up an e-mail account, you need to know the e-mail address and password, as well as the e-mail provider. You may also need to know the addresses of the mail servers the account uses. For Microsoft Exchange, you must know the domain name as well; see the next section, "Set Up an Exchange Server Account."

Set Up Your Mail Accounts

1. Press **Home**.

   The Home screen appears.

2. Tap **Settings** ( ).

   The Settings screen appears.

Note: If you have not yet set up an e-mail account on the iPad, you can also open the Add Account screen by tapping **Mail** ( ) on the Home screen.

3. Tap **Accounts & Passwords** ( ).

   The Accounts & Passwords screen appears.

4. Tap **Add Account**.

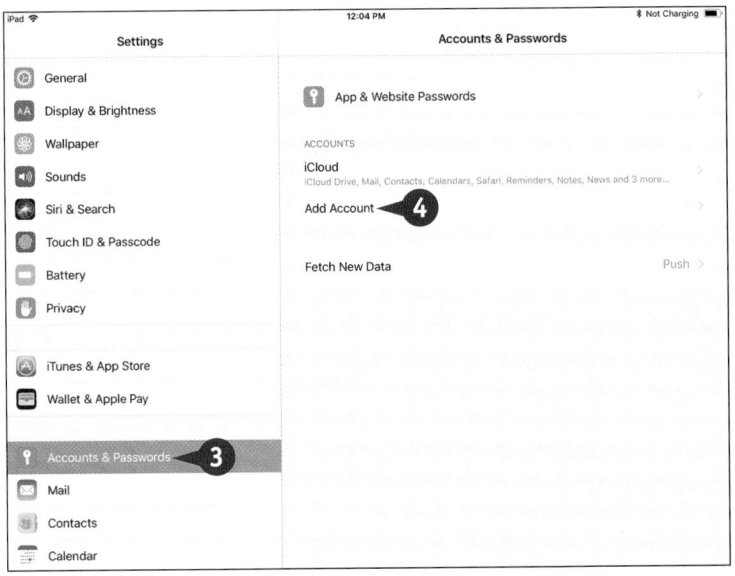

Note: This example uses a Google account. Different account types require you to enter different information. For example, for some account types, you must type a description for the e-mail account and your name the way you want it to appear in outgoing messages.

   The Add Account screen appears.

5. Tap the kind of account you want to set up.

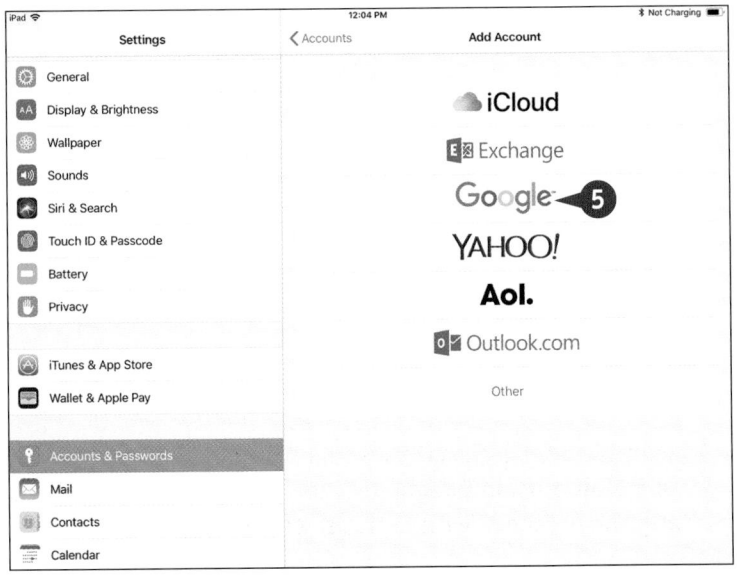

The screen for setting up that type of account appears.

6. Type the e-mail address.
7. Tap **Next**.
8. When prompted, type your password and tap **Next**.
9. If another security screen appears, such as the 2-Step Verification screen for a Google account, enter the required information and tap **Next**.

Note: For some e-mail account types, you tap a different button than Next, such as Sign In.

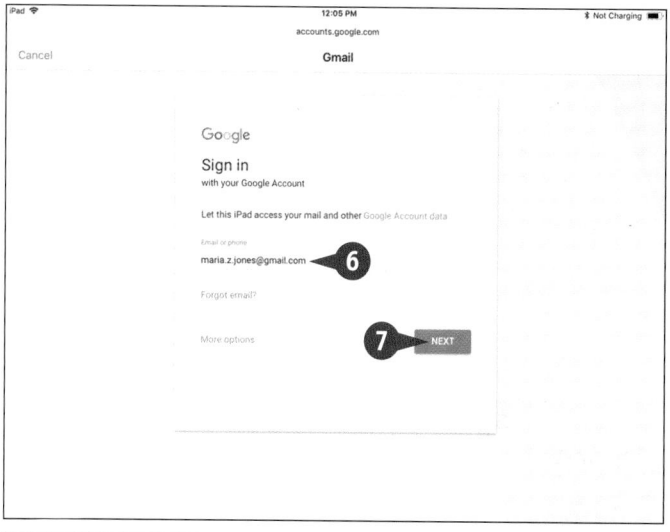

The configuration screen for the account appears. The options vary depending on the account type.

10. Make sure the **Mail** switch is set to On (◐).
11. Set the **Contacts** switch to On (◐) or Off (○).
12. Set the **Calendars** switch to On (◐) or Off (○).
13. Set the **Notes** switch to On (◐) or Off (○).

Note: If the Reminders switch appears, set it to On (◐) or Off (○), as needed.

14. Tap **Save**.

The account appears on the Accounts screen.

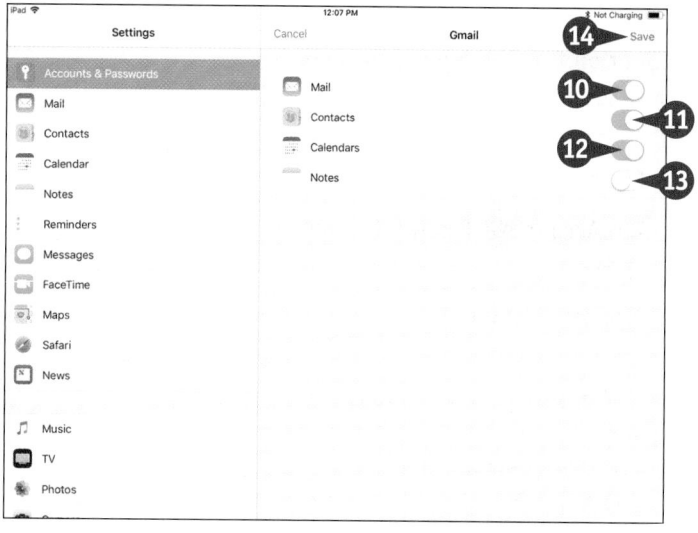

TIP

How do I change the name for an e-mail account?

To change the name displayed for the account, press **Home**, tap **Settings** (⚙), and then tap **Accounts & Passwords** (🔑). On the Accounts & Passwords screen, tap the account and then tap **Account** to open the Account dialog. Tap **Description** and type the name that you want to have appear for the account, such as **Work E-Mail** or **Main Google Account**. Tap **Done** to close the Account dialog, and then tap **Accounts** to display the Accounts & Passwords screen again.

Set Up an Exchange Server Account

You can set up your iPad to connect to Microsoft Exchange Server or Office 365 for e-mail, contacts, calendaring, reminders, and notes.

Before setting up your Exchange account, ask an administrator for the details you need. They include your e-mail address, your password, the server name, and the domain name, if required. You may be able to set up the account using only the e-mail address and password, but often you need the server name and domain as well.

Set Up an Exchange Server Account

1. Press **Home**.

   The Home screen appears.

2. Tap **Settings** ( ).

   The Settings screen appears.

3. Tap **Accounts & Passwords** ( ).

   The Accounts & Passwords screen appears.

4. Tap **Add Account**.

   The Add Account screen appears.

5. Tap **Exchange**.

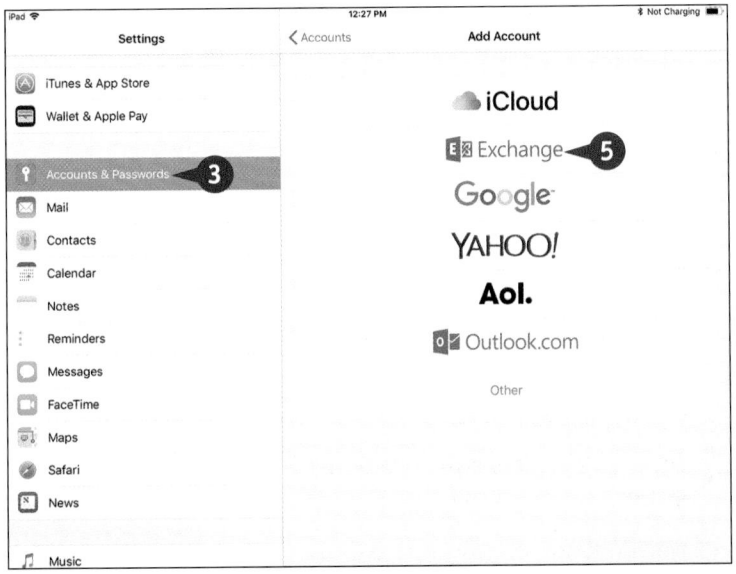

   The first Exchange dialog opens.

6. Tap **Email** and type your e-mail address.

7. Tap **Description** and type a descriptive name for the account.

Note: The description is to help you identify the account easily.

8. Tap **Next**.

   The Sign in to Your Exchange Account Using Microsoft? dialog opens.

9. Tap **Sign In**.

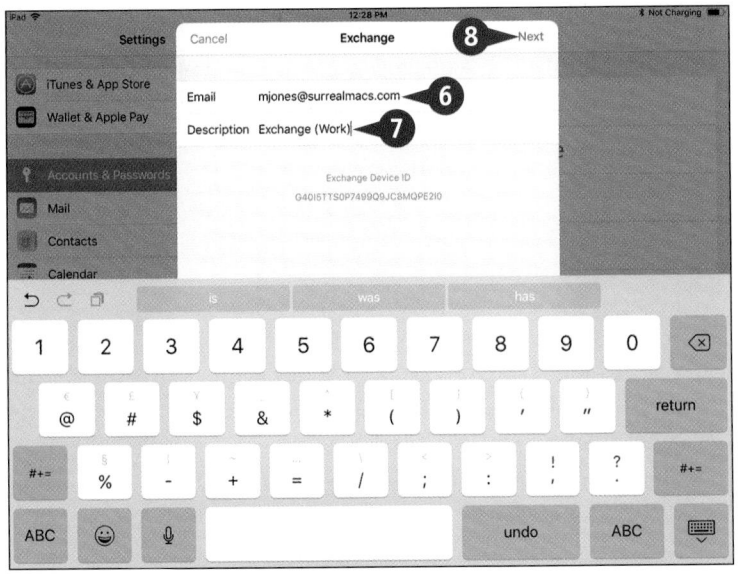

An untitled configuration dialog opens.

Note: If the second Exchange dialog opens at this point, go to step **14**.

10. Tap **Server** and type the server's address.
11. Tap **Domain** and type the domain, if it is needed.
12. Tap **Username** and type your username.
13. Tap **Next**.

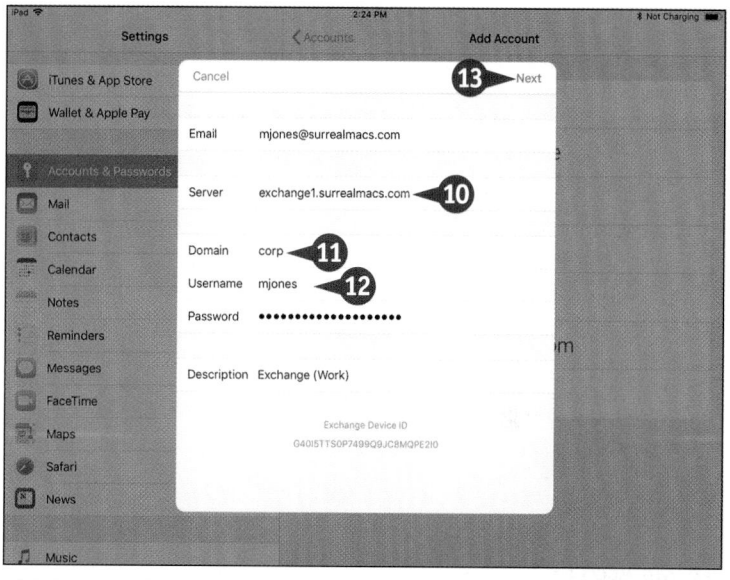

The second Exchange dialog opens.

14. Set the **Mail** switch to On (◐) or Off (◯), as needed.
15. Set the **Contacts** switch to On (◐) or Off (◯), as needed.
16. Set the **Calendars** switch to On (◐) or Off (◯), as needed.
17. Set the **Reminders** switch to On (◐) or Off (◯), as needed.
18. Set the **Notes** switch to On (◐) or Off (◯), as needed.
19. Tap **Save**.

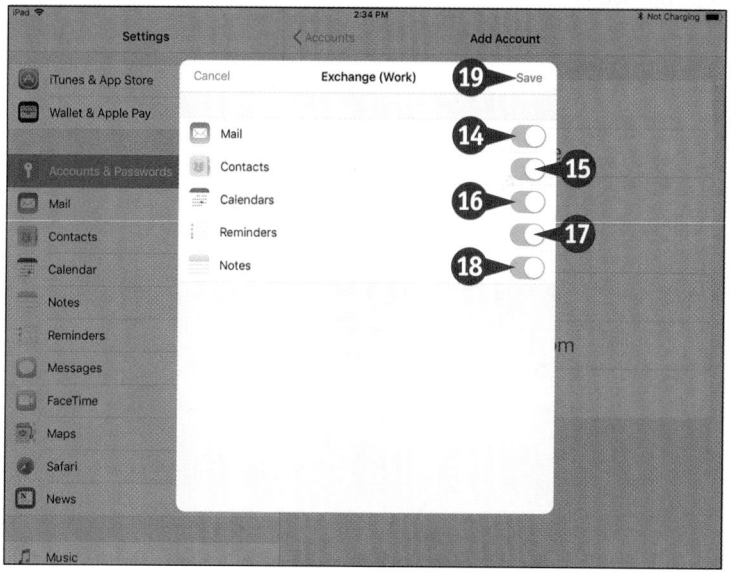

TIPS

How do I know whether to enter a domain name when setting up my Exchange account?
You need to ask an administrator, because some Exchange installations require you to enter a domain, whereas others do not.

How do I set up an Office 365 e-mail account?
Use the method explained in this section, but use outlook.office365.com as the server's address. Your username is typically your full e-mail address; if in doubt, ask an administrator.

Set Your Default Account and Create Signatures

If you set up multiple e-mail accounts on your iPad, you need to set your default account. This is the account from which the Mail app sends messages unless you choose to use another account for a particular message.

You can save time by using e-mail signatures. A signature is text that the Mail app automatically adds to each message you compose — for example, your name and contact information. The default iPad signature is "Sent from my iPad."

Set Your Default Account and Create Signatures

1. Press **Home**.

   The Home screen appears.

2. Tap **Settings** ( ).

   The Settings screen appears.

3. Tap **Mail** ( ).

   The Mail screen appears.

4. In the Composing section, tap **Default Account**.

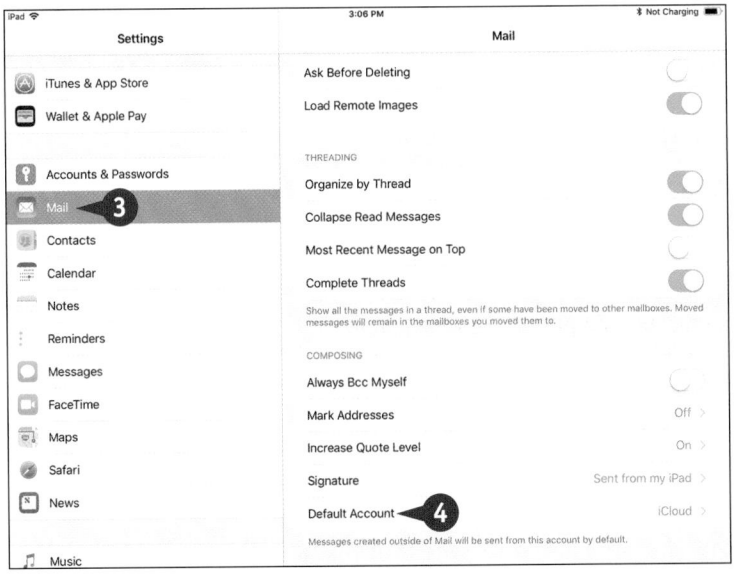

   The Default Account screen appears.

5. Tap the account you want to make the default.

6. Tap **Mail** ( ).

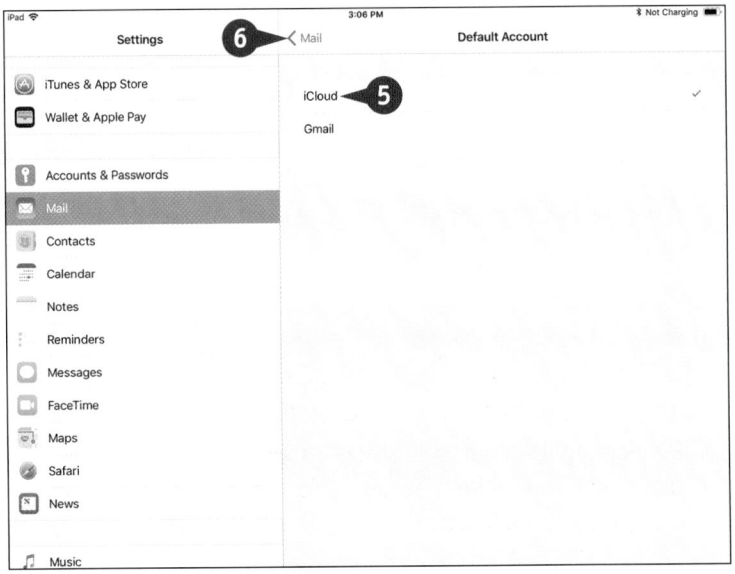

The Mail screen appears again.

7 Tap **Signature**.

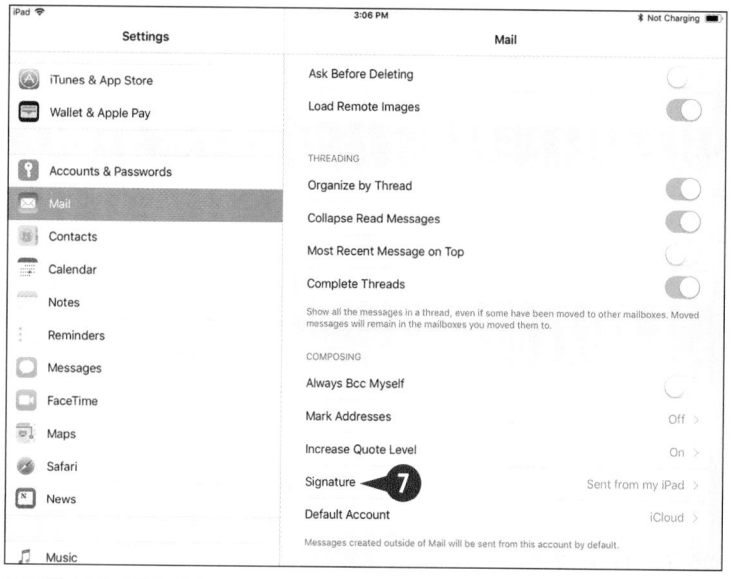

The Signature screen appears.

8 Tap **All Accounts** if you want to use the same signature for each e-mail account. Tap **Per Account** to use different signatures.

Note: If you do not want to use a signature, simply delete the default signature.

If you tap Per Account in step **8**, a separate area appears for each account.

9 Type the text of the signature or signatures.

Note: To make your signatures easy to read, keep them to four lines or fewer and use plain text without formatting.

10 Tap **Mail** (<).

The Mail screen appears.

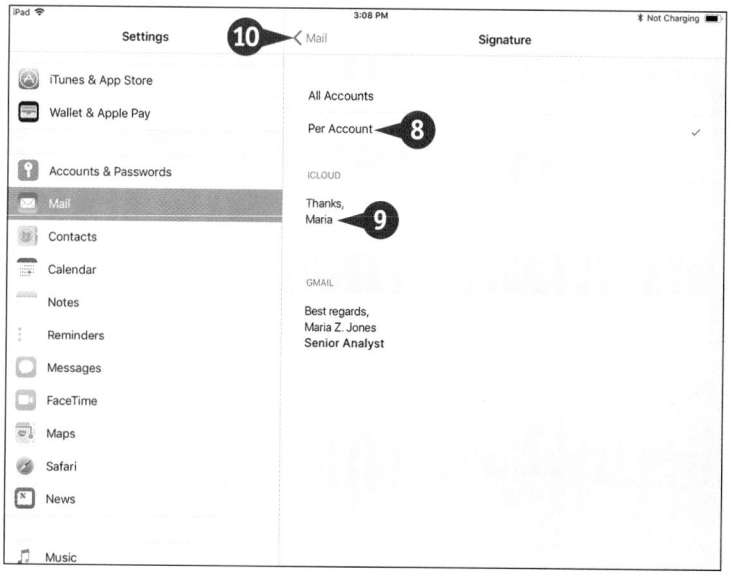

TIP

How do I send a message from an e-mail account other than the default account?

After starting to compose a message, tap **Cc/Bcc, From** to display the Cc, Bcc, and From lines. Tap **From** to display the pop-up menu of e-mail addresses, and then tap the address you want to use.

When you reply to a message, Mail sends the reply from the account to which the message was sent, even if this is not your default account. To send the reply from a different account, tap **Cc/Bcc, From**, tap **From**, and then tap the address.

Choose How Your iPad Gets Your E-Mail

Your iPad can get your e-mail messages by using two different technologies, Push and Fetch. With Push, the e-mail server "pushes" your new messages to your iPad as soon as the server receives them. With Fetch, your iPad checks in periodically with the server and downloads any new messages.

Push is normally more convenient than Fetch, but if your e-mail provider does not support Push, use Fetch and set a suitable interval for checking for messages. You can also check manually for e-mail at any point.

Choose How Your iPad Gets Your E-Mail

1. Press **Home**.

   The Home screen appears.

2. Tap **Settings** ( ).

Note: Push uses more battery power, especially if you receive many messages or large attachments.

   The Settings screen appears.

3. Tap **Accounts & Passwords** ( ).

   The Accounts & Passwords screen appears.

   A The Fetch New Data button shows Push if Push is enabled or Off if Push is disabled.

4. Tap **Fetch New Data**.

   The Fetch New Data screen appears.

5. To use Push for any of your e-mail accounts, set the **Push** switch to On ( ).

Note: The Fetch New Data screen shows only the options that are available for the accounts.

6. To control how frequently Fetch runs, tap **Automatically**, **Every 15 Minutes**, **Every 30 Minutes**, **Hourly**, or **Manually**.

7. If you need to use different settings for an account, tap that account.

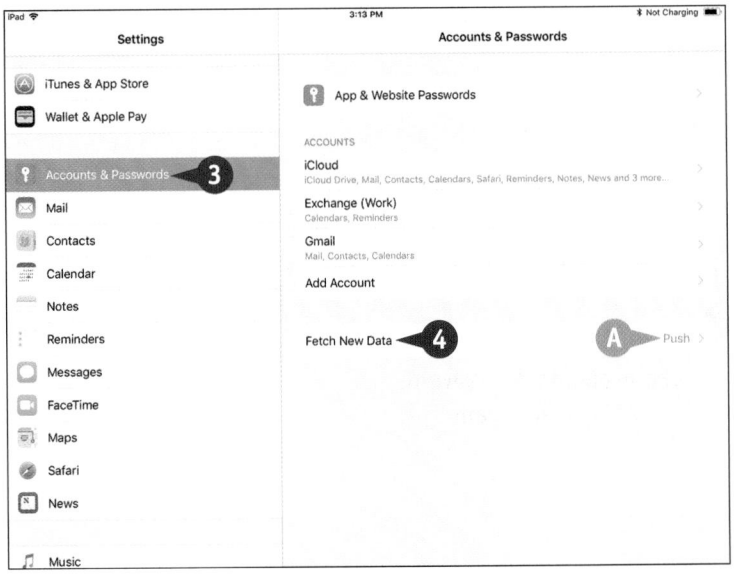

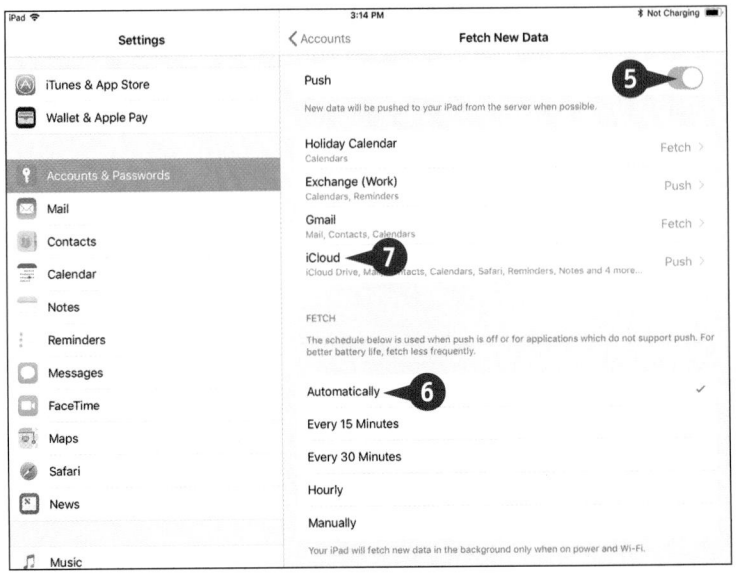

The account's screen appears.

8 Tap **Push**, **Fetch**, or **Manual**, as needed.

Note: Push is not available for some types of accounts.

B If the account displays the Pushed Mailboxes list, as iCloud and Exchange do, tap to select each mailbox you want to push.

9 Tap **Fetch New Data** (<).

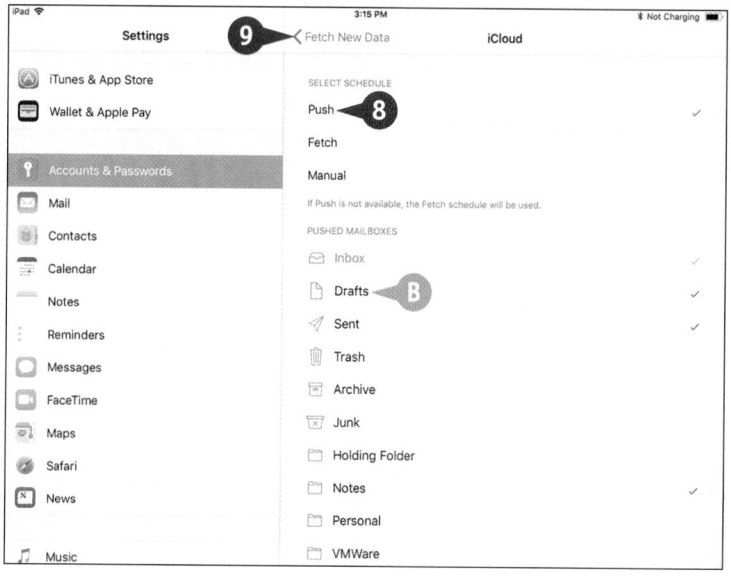

The Fetch New Data screen appears.

10 Tap **Accounts** (<).

The Accounts & Passwords screen appears again.

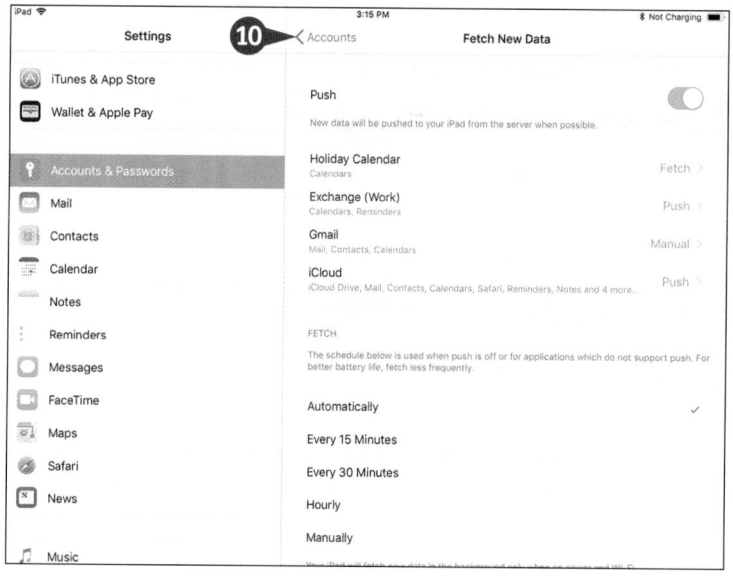

TIP

How do I check manually for new e-mail messages?
In a mailbox, tap the list of messages, drag down, and then release it. A progress icon indicates that Mail is checking for new messages.

Control How Your iPad Displays Your E-Mail

You can configure the Mail app to suit the way you work. You can choose how many lines to include in the message preview, decide whether to display the To/CC label, and control whether Mail prompts you before deleting a message.

To make messages easy to read, you can change the minimum font size. You can also choose whether to load remote images in messages and whether to increase the indentation on messages you reply to or forward to others.

Control How Your iPad Displays Your E-Mail

1. Press **Home**.

   The Home screen appears.

2. Tap **Settings** ( ).

   The Settings screen appears.

3. Tap **Mail** ( ).

   The Mail screen appears.

4. Set the **Show To/Cc Labels** switch to On ( ) or Off ( ).

5. Set the **Load Remote Images** switch to On ( ) or Off ( ).

6. Tap **Preview**.

   The Preview screen appears.

7. Tap the number of lines you want to see in previews.

8. Tap **Mail** ( ).

   The Mail screen appears again.

9. Tap **Flag Style**.

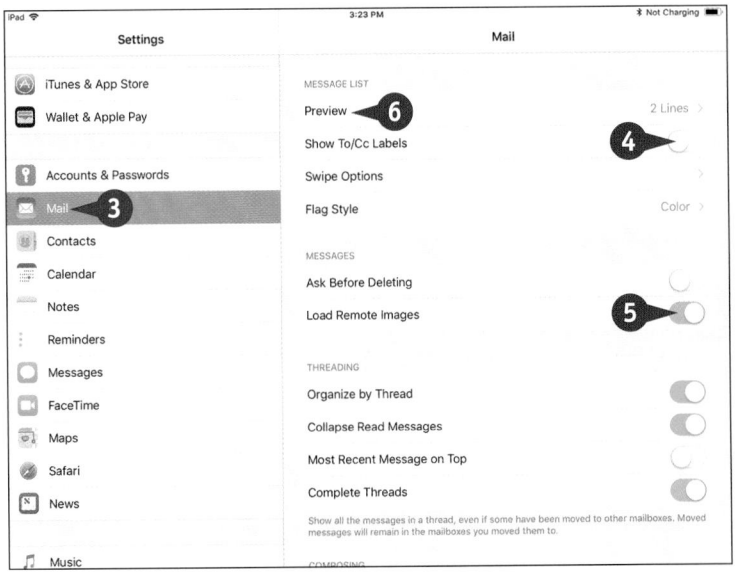

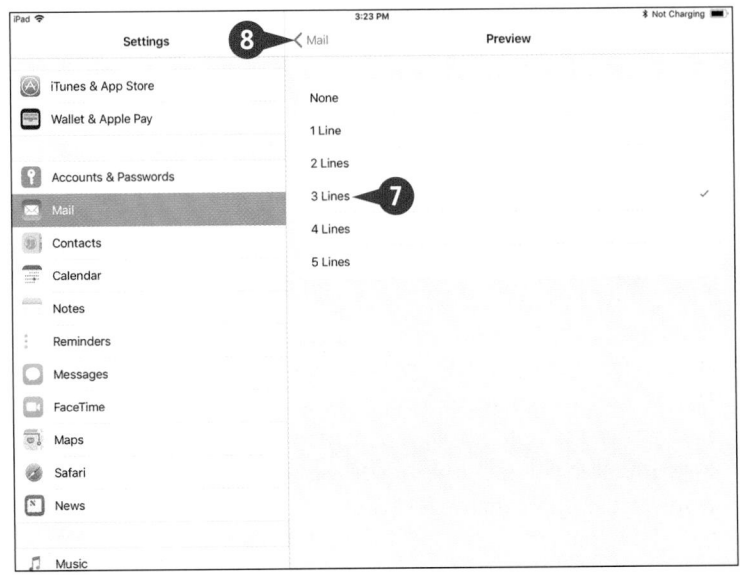

The Flag Style screen appears.

10 Tap **Color** or **Shape** to set the flag style.

11 Tap **Mail** (<).

The Mail screen appears again.

12 Tap **Increase Quote Level**.

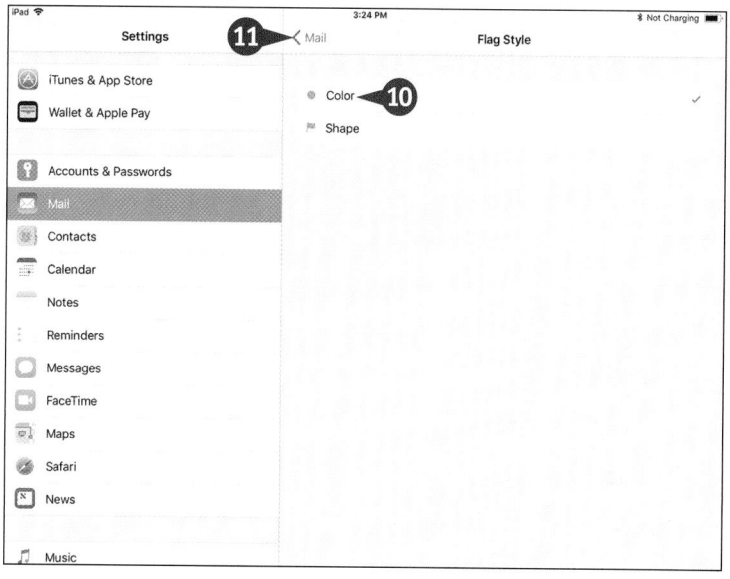

The Increase Quote Level screen appears.

13 Set the **Increase Quote Level** switch to On (◐) or Off ( ).

14 Tap **Mail** (<).

The Mail screen appears again.

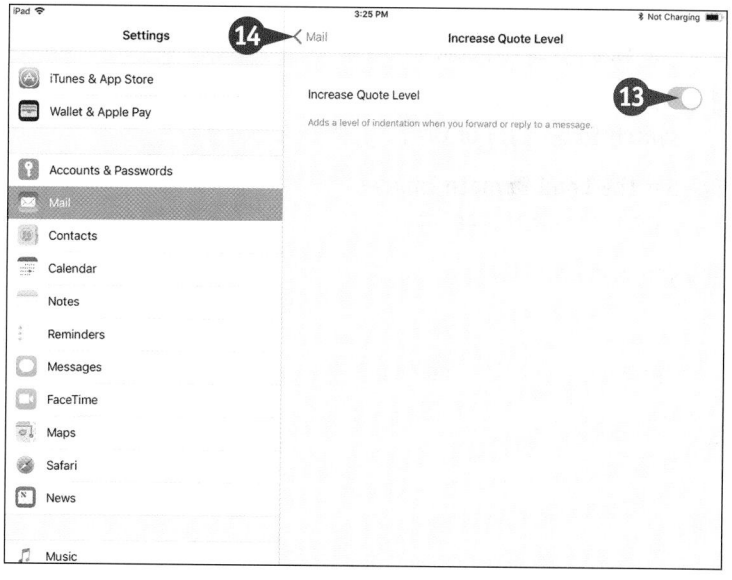

TIPS

Why turn off Load Remote Images?
Loading a remote image enables the sender to find out that you have opened the message. When Mail requests the remote image, the server that provides the image can log the date and time and your Internet connection's IP address, which reveals your approximate location.

What is Always Bcc Myself useful for?
Most e-mail services automatically put a copy of each message you send or forward into a folder with a name such as Sent. If your e-mail service does not use a Sent folder, set the **Always Bcc Myself** switch to On (◐) to send a bcc copy of each message to yourself. You can then file these messages for reference.

Organize Your E-Mail Messages by Threads

The Mail app gives you two ways to view e-mail messages. You can view the messages as a simple list, or you can view them with related messages organized into threads, which are sometimes called *conversations*.

Having Mail display your messages as threads can help you navigate your inbox quickly and find related messages easily. You may find threading useful if you tend to have long e-mail conversations, because threading reduces the number of messages you see at once.

Organize Your E-Mail Messages by Threads

Set Mail to Organize Your Messages by Thread

1. Press **Home**.

   The Home screen appears.

2. Tap **Settings** ( ).

   The Settings screen appears.

3. Tap **Mail** ( ).

   The Mail screen appears.

4. Set the **Organize by Thread** switch to On ( ).

5. Set the **Collapse Read Messages** switch to On ( ) if you want Mail to collapse read messages in the thread.

6. Set the **Most Recent Message on Top** switch to On ( ) if you want the newest message in each thread to appear at the top of the screen. This option is often helpful for keeping up with your messages.

7. Set the **Complete Threads** switch to On ( ) if you want each thread to show all its messages, even if you have moved some to other mailboxes. This option is usually helpful.

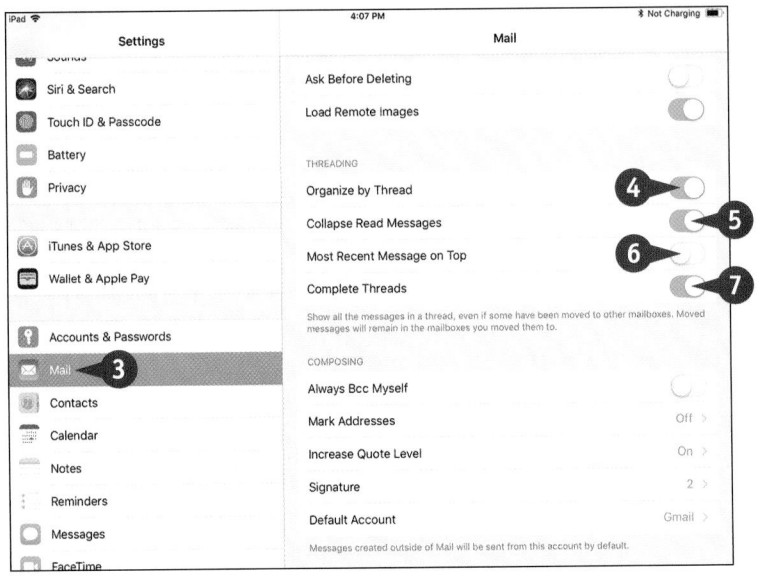

Read Messages Organized into Threads

1. Press **Home**.

   The Home screen appears.

2. Tap **Mail** (✉).

   The Mailboxes screen appears.

3. Tap the mailbox.

   The inbox for the account appears.

   A Two chevrons on the right (») indicate a threaded message.

4. Tap the threaded message.

   B The threaded messages appear in the right pane, with just the new part of each message displayed.

   C You can tap **See More** to display the entire message. Tap **Done** to return to the thread view.

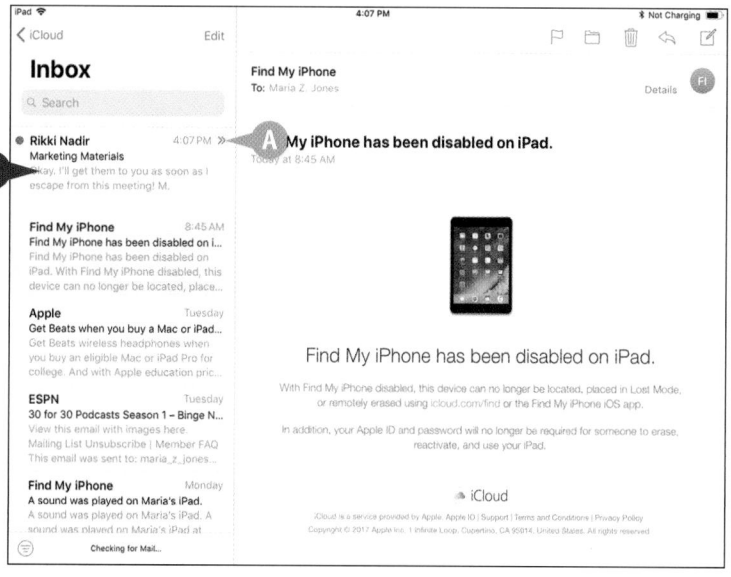

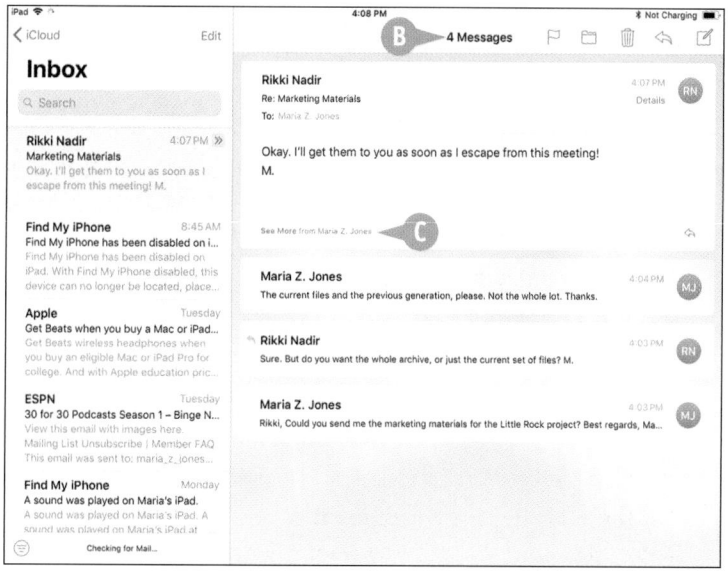

TIP

What does the Ask Before Deleting switch do?

This switch lets you control whether your iPad displays the Trash Message dialog to confirm deletion of a message by tapping **Delete** (🗑). Set **Ask Before Deleting** to On (◐) if you find you tap **Delete** (🗑) by accident sometimes — for example, when using your iPad on public transit.

Add People to the VIP Inbox

The Mail app includes an inbox named VIP for collecting your most important messages so that you do not miss any. Mail automatically monitors your incoming messages and adds those from your designated VIPs to the VIP inbox.

To start using your VIP inbox, you must add people to the VIP list. You can add people either from your Contacts list or from e-mail messages you receive. You can configure VIP notifications in Settings to enable you to distinguish incoming VIP messages from other messages.

Add People to the VIP Inbox

1. Press **Home**.

   The Home screen appears.

2. Tap **Mail** (✉).

   The Mailboxes screen appears.

3. Open the VIP list as follows:

   A. If Information (ⓘ) appears on the VIP button in the Mailboxes list, tap **Information** (ⓘ). Your VIP list already contains VIPs, so tapping the VIP button opens the mailbox rather than the VIP list.

   B. If Information (ⓘ) does not appear, tap **VIP**.

   The VIP List pane appears.

4. Tap **Add VIP**.

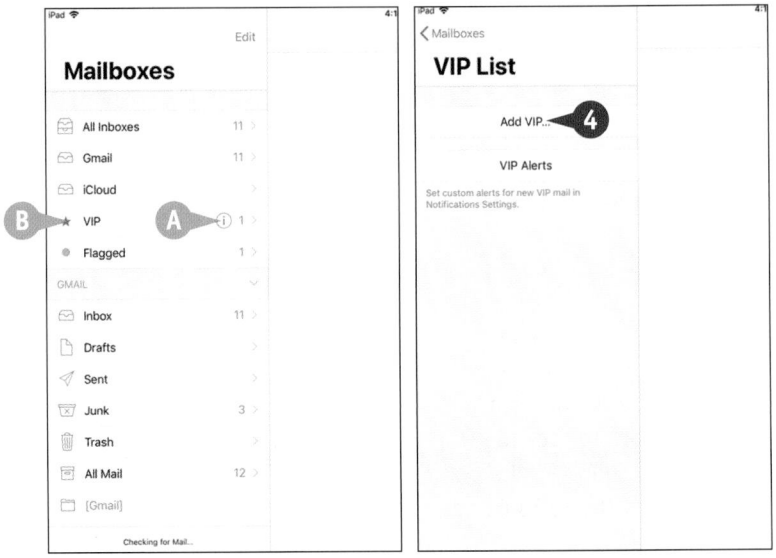

The Contacts list opens in the left pane. If All Contacts appears at the top, you are viewing all your contacts. If Contacts appears at the top, you are viewing only some groups.

C You can change the groups displayed by tapping **Groups**, making your choices on the Groups screen, and then tapping **Done**.

5 Tap the contact you want to make a VIP.

D The VIP List pane appears again, with the contact now added.

E You can tap **Add VIP** and repeat step **5** as needed to add all your VIPs to the VIP list.

6 Tap **VIP Alerts**.

The VIP pane in Settings appears.

7 Tap **Sounds**, tap the sound on the Sounds screen, and then tap **VIP** to return to the VIP screen.

8 Set the **Badge App Icon** switch to On (◐) to display a badge on the Mail icon.

9 Set the **Show on Cover Sheet** switch to On (◐) to display VIP messages on Cover Sheet.

10 Set the **Show in History** switch to On (◐) to include VIP messages in History.

11 To display banners for VIP messages, set the **Show as Banners** switch to On (◐) and then tap **Temporary** or **Permanent**, as needed.

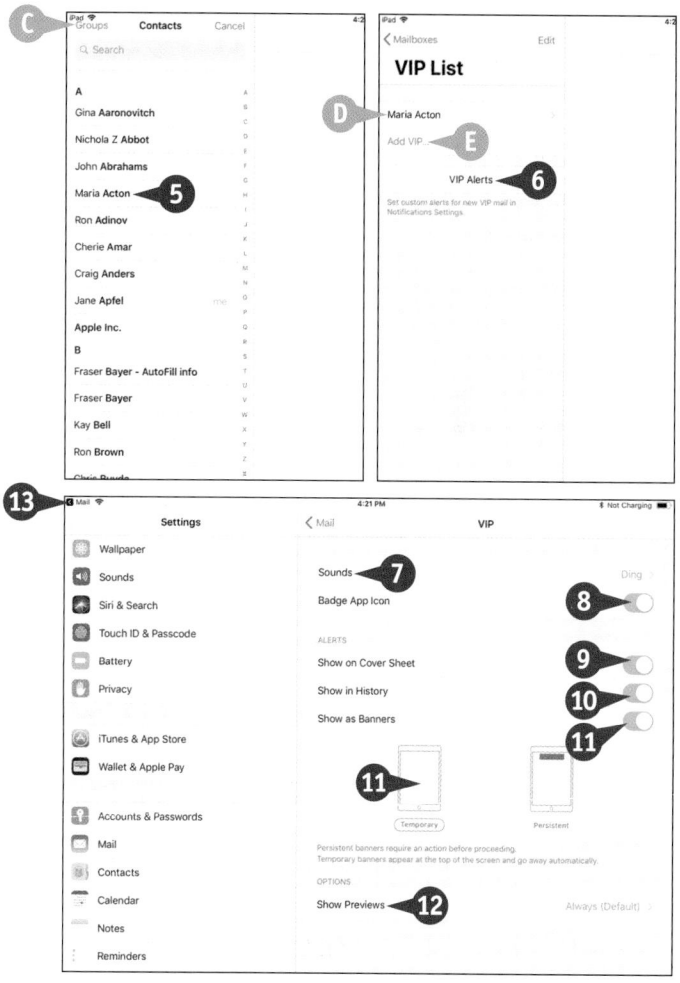

12 Tap **Show Previews** and choose which previews to display.

13 Tap **Mail**.

The VIP List screen in the Mail app appears.

TIPS

How do I remove a VIP?

Press Home, tap **Mail** (✉), and then tap **Information** (ⓘ) on the VIP button to display the VIP List pane. Tap **Edit** to open the list for editing, tap **Delete** (⊖) to the left of the VIP's name, and then tap the textual **Delete** button that appears to the right of the VIP's name.

Is there another way to add someone to my VIP list?

Yes. Open a message you have received, tap **Details**, and then tap the sender's name. In the Sender dialog, tap **Add to VIP** to add the sender to your VIP list.

Choose How Your iPad Displays Your Contacts

You can set your iPad to sort and display the contacts in your preferred order for easy browsing. You can sort contacts either by first name or by last name; you can display contacts either by first name or last name; and you can choose whether and how to shorten last names — for example, by using the first initial and last name.

You can also control whether iOS displays suggested contacts it has found in other apps. See the tip for details.

Choose How Your iPad Displays Your Contacts

1. Press **Home**.

   The Home screen appears.

2. Tap **Settings** (⚙).

   The Settings screen appears.

3. Tap **Contacts** (📇).

   The Contacts screen appears.

4. Tap **Sort Order**.

   The Sort Order screen appears.

5. Tap **First, Last** to sort by first name and then last name, or tap **Last, First** to sort by last name and then first name.

6. Tap **Contacts** (<).

7. On the Contacts screen, tap **Display Order**.

8. On the Display Order screen, tap **First, Last** to display the first name and then the last name, or tap **Last, First** to display the last name and then the first name.

9. Tap **Contacts** (<).

10. On the Contacts screen, tap **Short Name**.

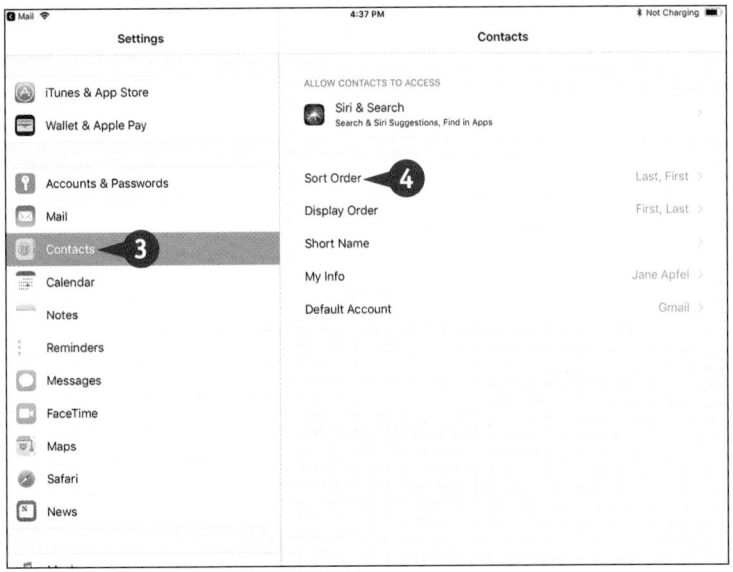

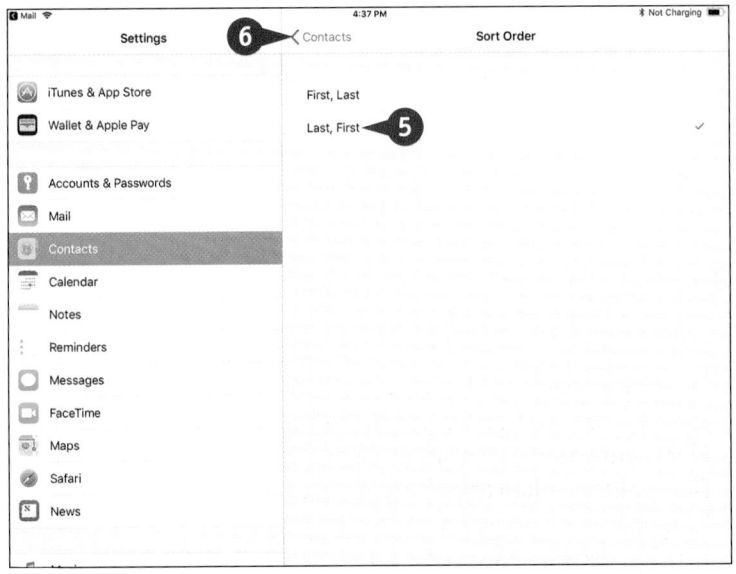

The Short Name screen appears.

11. Set the **Short Name** switch to On (◐) if you want to use name shortening.
12. Tap your preferred means of shortening names: **First Name & Last Initial**, **First Initial & Last Name**, **First Name Only**, or **Last Name Only**.
13. Set the **Prefer Nicknames** switch to On (◐) if you want Contacts to display nicknames instead of proper names.
14. Tap **Contacts** (<).

    The Contacts screen appears again.
15. Tap **Default Account**.

    The Default Account screen appears.
16. Tap the account to use for new contacts by default.
17. Tap **Contacts** (<).

    The Contacts screen appears again.

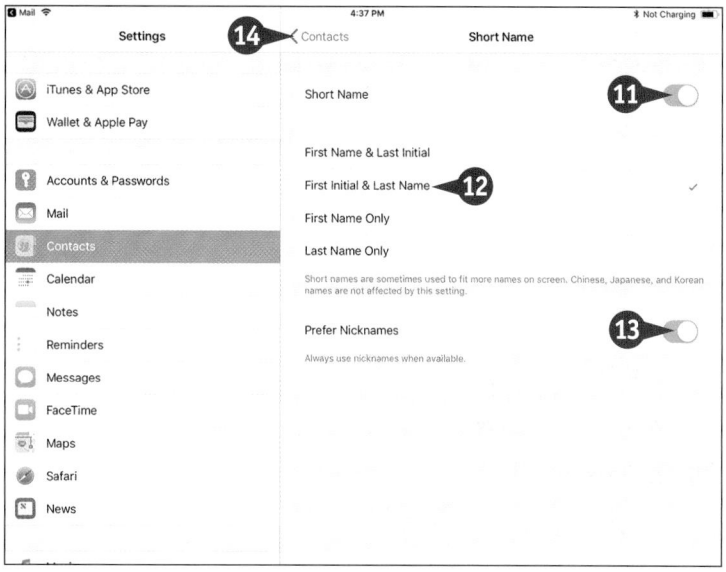

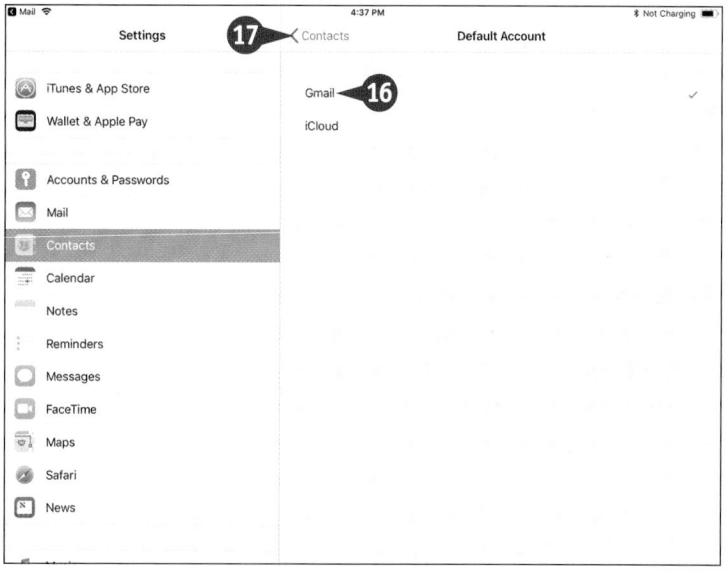

TIP

What does the Siri & Search button on the Contacts screen do?

Tap **Siri & Search** to display the Siri & Search screen. Here, you can set the **Search & Siri Suggestions** switch to On (◐) to allow your iPad to include contact information in suggestions. You can also set the **Find Contacts in Other Apps** switch to On (◐) if you want iOS to display suggestions for creating contacts from contact information that iOS has identified in other apps.

Choose Alert Options for Calendar Events

Your iPad enables you to sync your calendars via iCloud and other online services. To help keep on schedule, you can set default alert times for calendar events. You can set a different alert time for each type of event — for example, 15 minutes' notice for a regular event and a week's notice for a birthday. You can also turn on the Time to Leave feature to make the Calendar app allow travel time based on your location, the event's location, and current traffic.

Choose Alert Options for Calendar Events

1. Press **Home**.

   The Home screen appears.

2. Tap **Settings** ( ).

   The Settings screen appears.

3. Tap **Calendar** ( ).

   The Calendar screen appears.

4. Tap **Sync**.

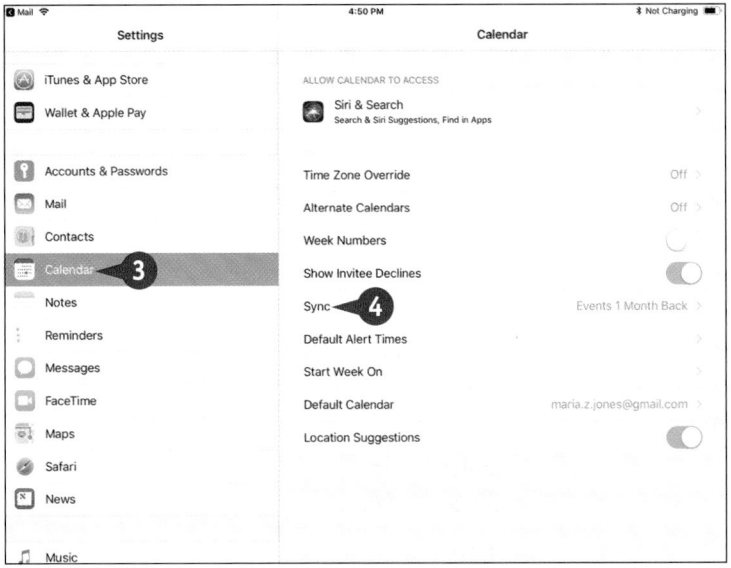

   The Sync screen appears.

5. Tap the period of events you want to sync. For example, tap **Events 1 Month Back**.

6. Tap **Calendar** (<).

   The Calendar screen appears again.

7. Tap **Default Alert Times**.

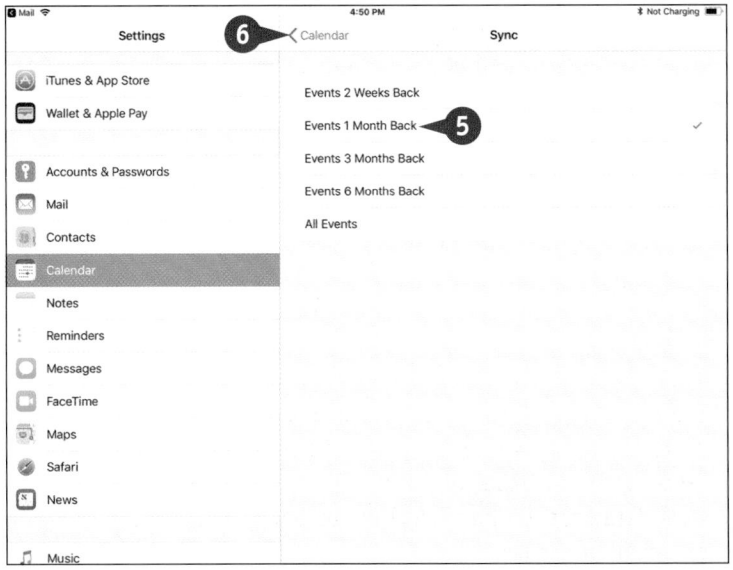

The Default Alert Times screen appears.

8 Set the **Time to Leave** switch to On (◐) to have your iPad use your location to determine a suitable departure time for events.

9 Tap the event type for which you want to set the default alert time. For example, tap **Events**.

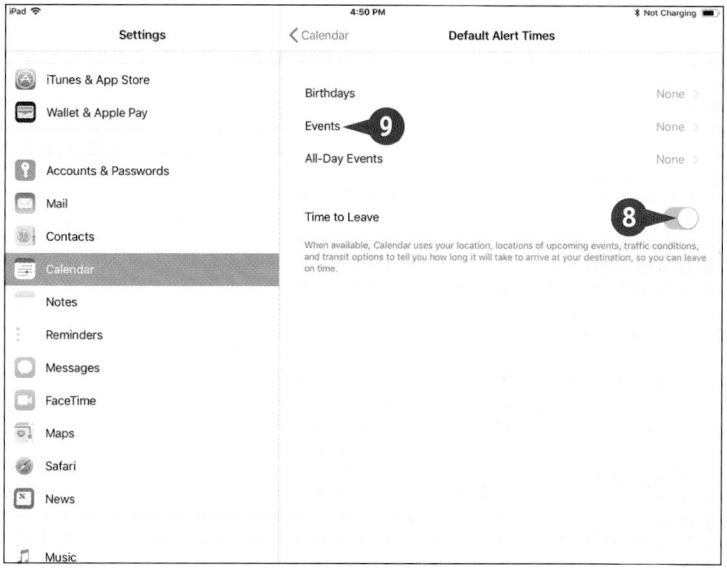

The corresponding screen appears — the Events screen, the Birthdays screen, or the All-Day Events screen.

10 Tap the amount of time for the warning. For example, for an event, tap **15 minutes before**.

11 Tap **Default Alert Times** (<).

The Default Alert Times screen appears again, and you can choose default alert times for other event types if you wish.

12 Tap **Calendar** (<).

The Calendar screen appears again.

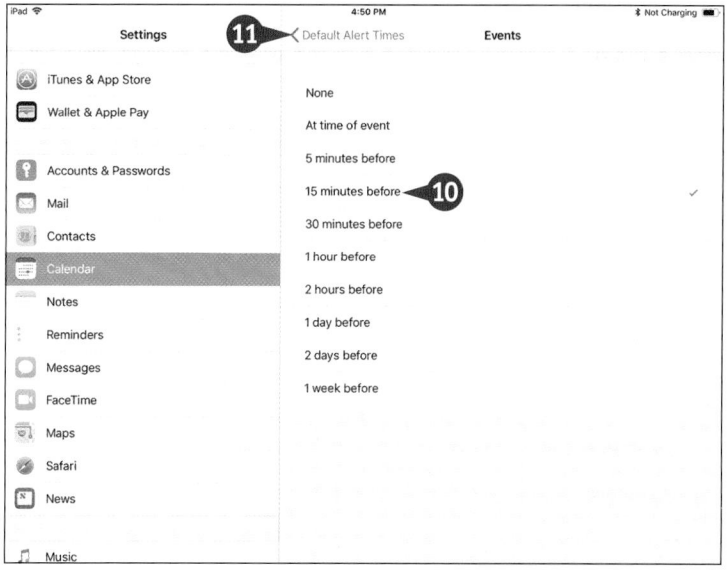

TIP

What does the Siri & Search button on the Calendar screen do?

Tap **Siri & Search** to display the Siri & Search screen. Here, you can set the **Search & Siri Suggestions** switch to On (◐) to allow your iPad to include calendar information in suggestions. You can also set the **Find Events in Other Apps** switch to On (◐) to have iOS display suggestions for creating Calendar events from data that iOS has identified as being possible events in incoming information, such as text messages or e-mail messages.

Choose Your Default Calendar and Time Zone

When you use multiple calendars on your iPad, you should set your default calendar. This is the calendar that receives events you create outside any specific calendar. For example, if you have a Work calendar and a Home calendar, you can set the Home calendar as the default calendar.

If you travel to different time zones, you may need to specify which time zone to show event dates and times in. Otherwise, Calendar uses the time zone for your current location.

Choose Your Default Calendar and Time Zone

1. Press **Home**.

   The Home screen appears.

2. Tap **Settings** ( ).

   The Settings screen appears.

3. Tap **Calendar** ( ).

   The Calendar screen appears.

4. Tap **Time Zone Override**.

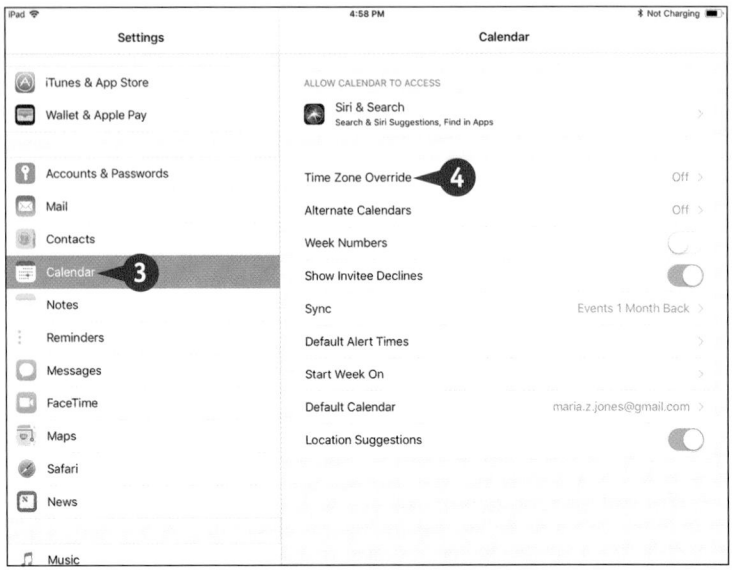

   The Time Zone Override screen appears.

5. Set the **Time Zone Override** switch to On ( ).

6. Tap **Time Zone**.

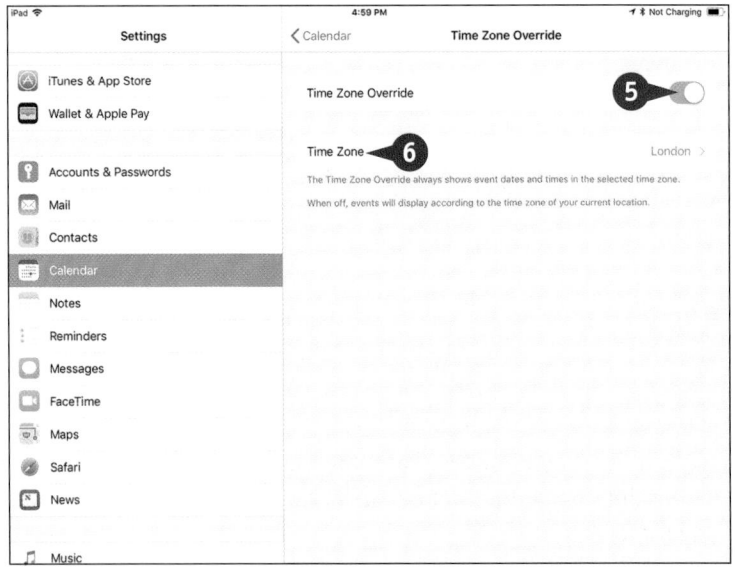

The Time Zone screen appears.

7. Type the first letters of a city in the time zone.
8. Tap the search result you want.

The Time Zone Override screen appears again.

9. Tap **Calendar** (<).

The Calendar screen appears again.

10. Tap **Default Calendar**.

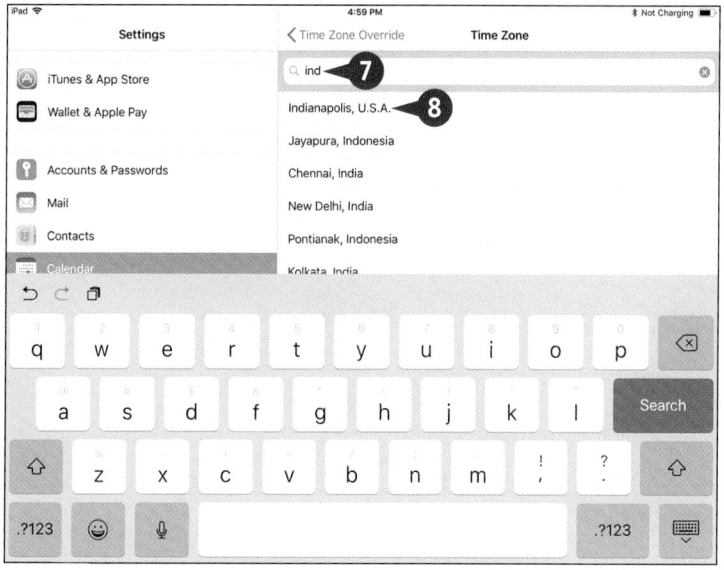

The Default Calendar screen appears.

11. Tap the calendar you want to make the default.
12. Tap **Calendar** (<).

The Calendar screen appears again.

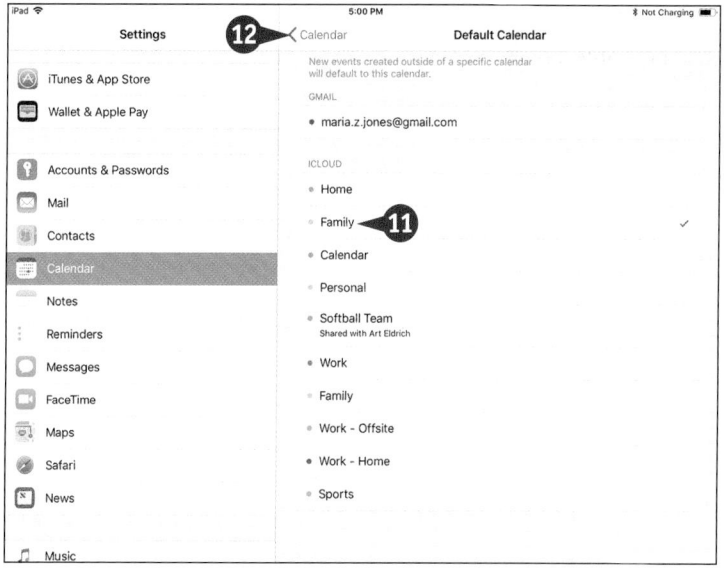

TIP

How do I choose which calendars to display in the Calendar app?

You choose the calendars in the Calendar app, not in the Settings app. Press **Home** to display the Home screen, tap **Calendar** (22), and then tap **Calendars**. In the Show Calendars dialog, tap to place a check mark on each calendar you want to display. Tap to remove a check mark from each calendar you want to hide, and then tap **Done**.

Choose Settings for Notes

As described earlier in this chapter, you can set up multiple e-mail accounts on your iPad. Each e-mail account can synchronize notes if the e-mail service supports them.

You can choose whether to store notes directly on your iPad as well as — or instead of — in online accounts. You can set the default account for notes you create using Siri. You can also choose other settings, such as the default style for the first line of new notes and the grid or lines in the background of notes.

Choose Settings for Notes

1. Press **Home**.

   The Home screen appears.

2. Tap **Settings** ( ).

   The Settings screen appears.

3. Tap **Notes** ( ).

   The Notes screen appears.

4. Set the **"On My iPad" Account** switch to On ( ) if you want to be able to store notes on your iPad instead of in online accounts. See the second tip.

5. Set the **Save to Photos** switch to On ( ) if you want photos and videos you take in Notes to appear in Photos.

6. Tap **Default Account**.

   The Default Account screen appears.

7. Tap the account in which you want to store new notes you create using Siri or the Notes widget in Today View.

8. Tap **Notes** ( ).

9. Tap **Sort Notes By** to display the Sort Notes By screen; tap **Date Edited**, **Date Created**, or **Title**; and then tap **Notes** ( ).

10. Tap **New Notes Start With**.

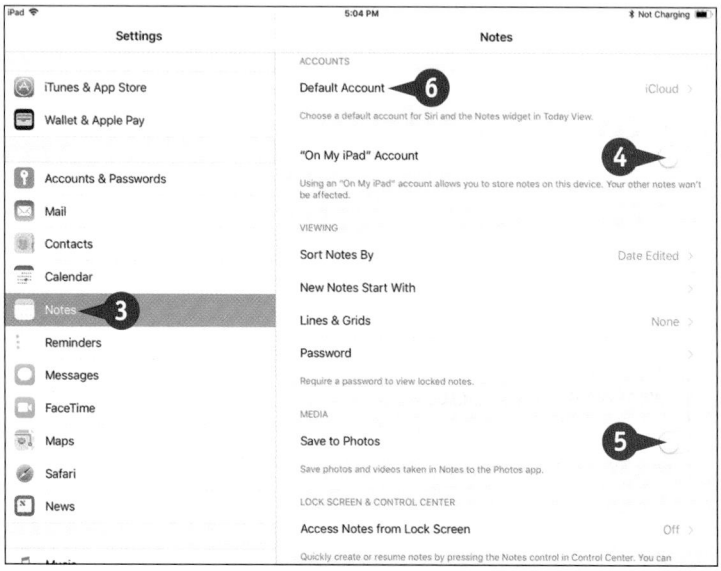

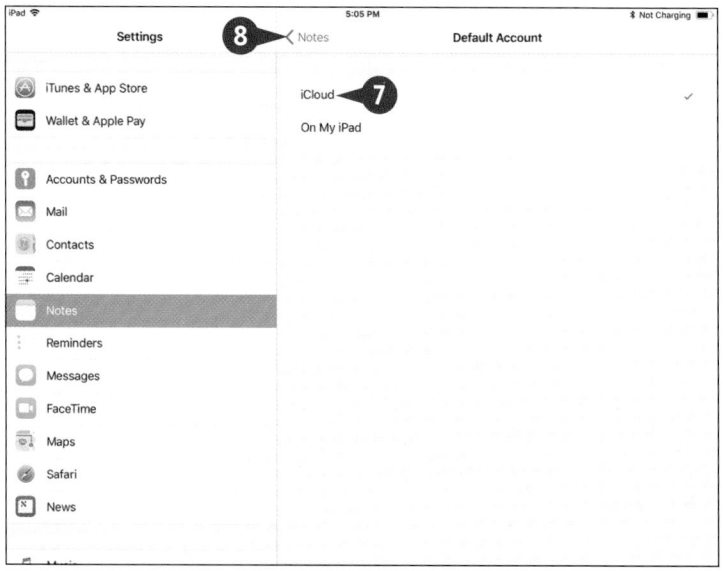

The New Notes Start With screen appears.

11 Tap **Title**, **Heading**, or **Body** to specify the style to use for the first paragraph of each note.

12 Tap **Notes** (<).

The Notes screen appears again.

13 Tap **Lines & Grids**, tap your preferred line or grid format, and then tap **Notes** (<).

14 Tap **Access Notes from Lock Screen.**

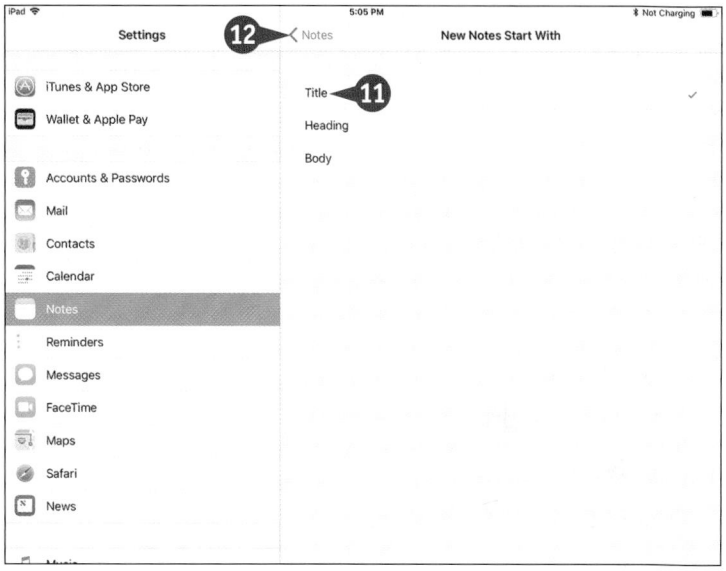

The Access Notes from Lock Screen screen appears.

15 Tap **Off**, **Always Create New Note**, **Resume Last Note Created on Lock Screen**, or **Resume Last Note Viewed in Notes App**, as appropriate.

16 Tap **Notes** (<).

The Notes screen appears again.

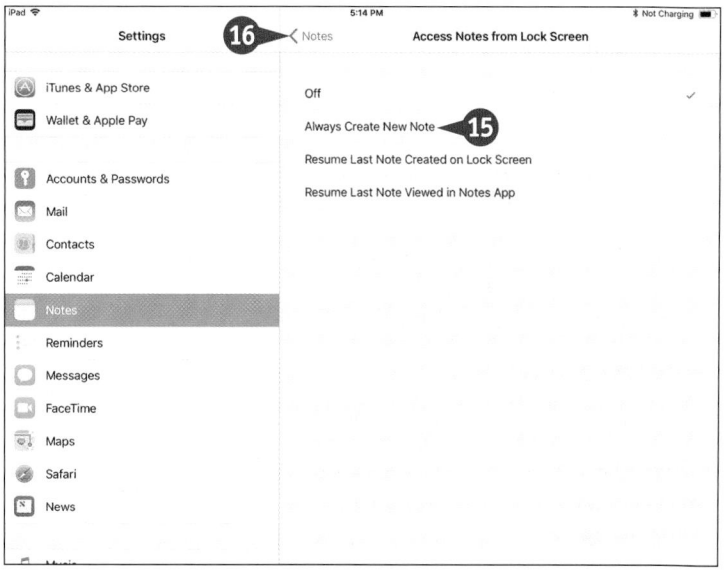

TIPS

How can I protect my notes against prying eyes?
Tap **Password** on the Notes screen in the Settings app and then use the Set Password dialog to set a password to protect your locked notes. You can set the **Use Touch ID** switch to On (◐) to enable yourself to unlock locked notes using your fingerprint.

Should I enable the "On My iPad" Account feature?
Usually, it is best to store your notes online, such as in your iCloud account, so that you can access them from all your iOS devices and your computers. But if you need to create private notes on the iPad without having them synced to online accounts, enable the "On My iPad" Account and store your notes in it.

CHAPTER 5

Networking and Communicating

Your iPad connects to the Internet through wireless networks and Wi-Fi hotspots; if it has cellular capability, it can connect through the cellular network as well. The iPad also has Bluetooth connectivity for connecting headsets and other devices. Once connected to the Internet, you can send instant messages via Apple's iMessage service or other services and make video calls with FaceTime.

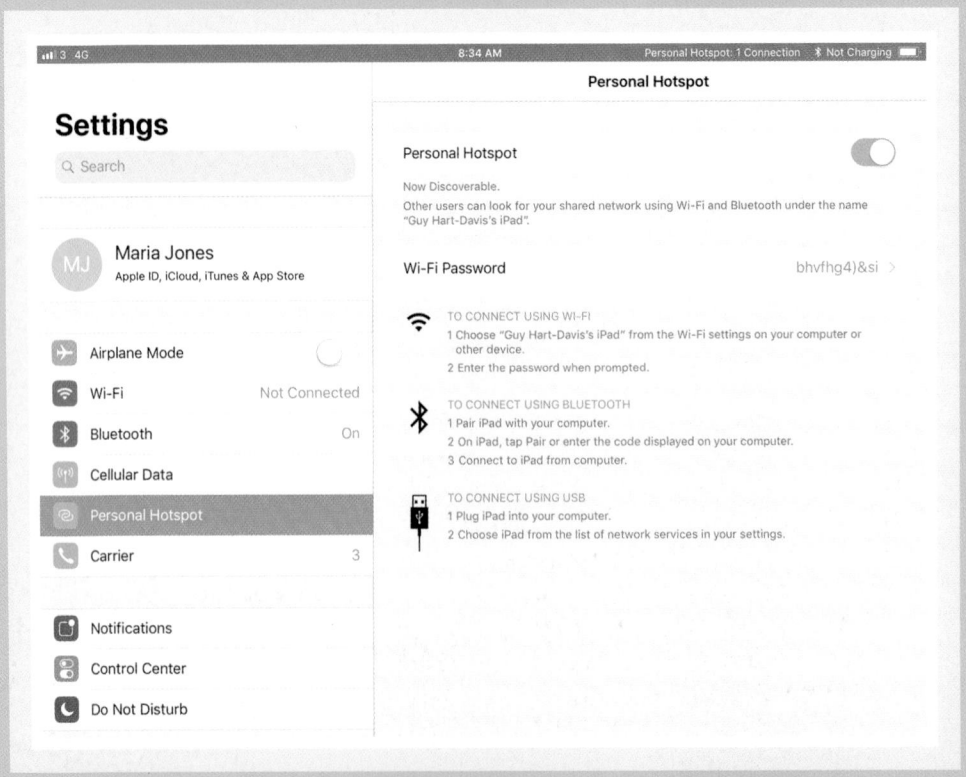

Using Airplane Mode 118
Connect Bluetooth Devices to Your iPad 120
Control Cellular Data and Background Refresh 122
Connect Your iPad to a Different Carrier 124
Specify Your iPad's Cellular Access Point 125
Share Items via AirDrop 126
Share Your Cellular iPad's Internet Access 128
Connect to Wi-Fi Networks and Hotspots 130
Connect to a Network via VPN 134
Send Text and Multimedia Messages 136
Using Emoji and Other iMessage Features 138
Manage Your Instant Messages 140
Mute a Conversation or Share Your Location 142
Choose Settings for Messages 144
Block and Unblock Senders 146
Chat Face-to-Face Using FaceTime 148

Using Airplane Mode

Normally, you will want to keep your iPad connected to the Internet so that you can send and receive messages and browse the web. But when you do not need or may not use the cellular network or Wi-Fi, you can turn on the Airplane Mode feature to cut off all connections.

Turning on Airplane Mode turns off Wi-Fi and Bluetooth connections as well. But you can also turn Wi-Fi and Bluetooth on and off separately when you need to.

Using Airplane Mode

1. Press **Home**.

   The Home screen appears.

2. Tap **Settings** ( ).

   The Settings screen appears.

3. To turn Airplane Mode on, set the **Airplane Mode** switch to On ( ).

Note: When a cellular iPad has a wireless network connection, it uses that connection instead of the cellular connection. This helps keep down your cellular network usage and often provides a faster connection.

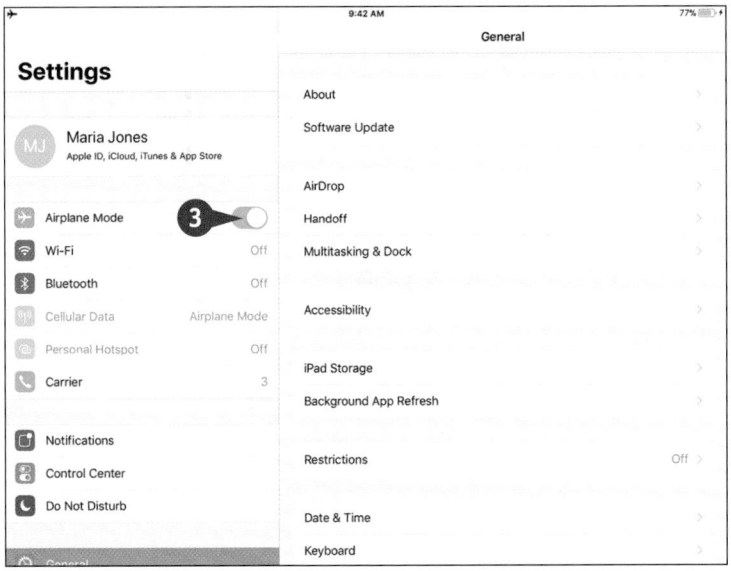

A The iPad turns off all cellular, Wi-Fi, and Bluetooth connections. An airplane icon ( ) appears in the status bar.

4. To turn on Wi-Fi, tap **Wi-Fi** ( ).

   The Wi-Fi screen appears.

5. Set the **Wi-Fi** switch to On ( ).

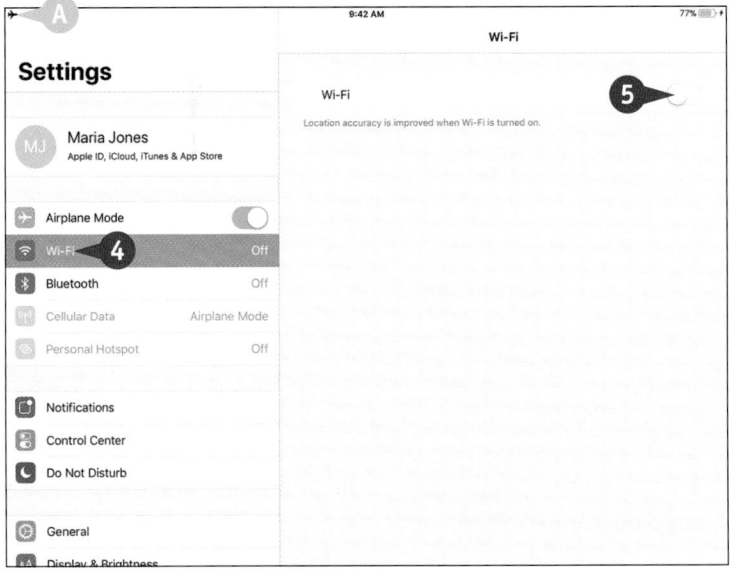

B The list of available networks appears in the Choose a Network section.

C If your iPad detects a known network, it connects automatically, and the network moves out of the Choose a Network list up to below the Wi-Fi switch. If not, you can connect to a network manually as described in the section "Connect to Wi-Fi Networks and Hotspots," later in this chapter.

6 Tap **Bluetooth** ( ).

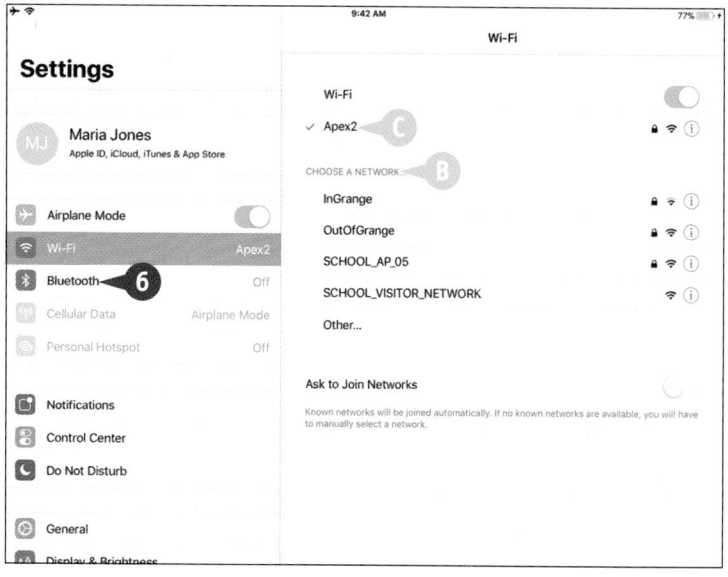

The Bluetooth screen appears.

7 Set the **Bluetooth** switch to On ( ) if you need to use Bluetooth devices while Airplane Mode is on.

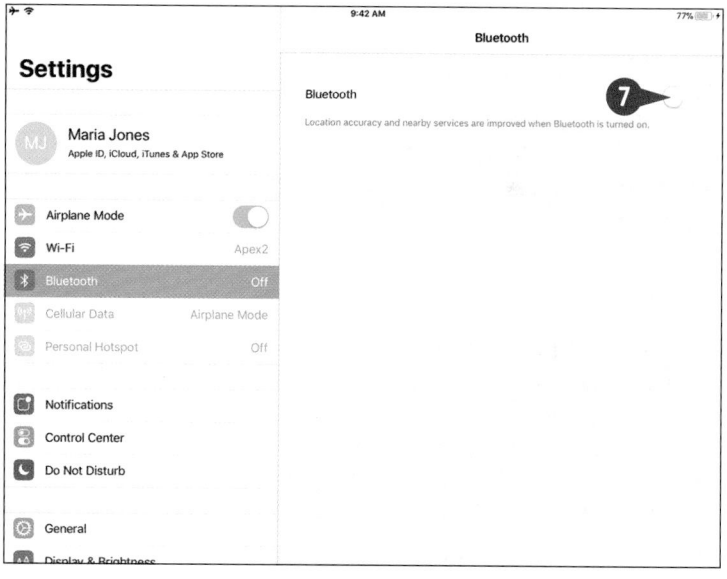

TIP

Is there another way to turn Airplane Mode on and off?

Yes, by using Control Center. Swipe up from the bottom of the screen to open Control Center, and then tap **Airplane Mode** (changes to or changes to). You can then enable or disable Wi-Fi by tapping **Wi-Fi** (changes to or changes to), but you cannot select a wireless network if your iPad does not find a known network. You can also enable or disable Bluetooth by tapping **Bluetooth** (changes to or changes to).

Connect Bluetooth Devices to Your iPad

To extend the functionality of your iPad, you can connect devices to it that communicate using the wireless Bluetooth technology. For example, you can connect a Bluetooth keyboard for faster typing or a Bluetooth headset for listening to music and making and receiving FaceTime calls. If you connect a Bluetooth headset or headphones, you need to tell the iPad which audio device to use.

Connect Bluetooth Devices to Your iPad

Set Up a Bluetooth Device

1. Press **Home**.

   The Home screen appears.

2. Tap **Settings** (⚙).

   The Settings screen appears.

3. Tap **Bluetooth** (✱).

   The Bluetooth screen appears.

4. Set the **Bluetooth** switch to On (◯).

5. Turn on the Bluetooth device and make it discoverable.

Note: Read the Bluetooth device's instructions to find out how to make the device discoverable via Bluetooth.

Ⓐ The My Devices list shows devices you have already paired with your iPad.

Ⓑ The Other Devices list shows unpaired devices.

6. Tap the device's button.

   Your iPad attempts to pair with the device.

Note: If the Bluetooth Pairing Request dialog opens, type the code to confirm the pairing request.

The iPad pairs with the device and then connects to it.

Ⓒ The device appears in the My Devices list.

Ⓓ The Connected readout indicates that the device is connected.

Choose the Device for Playing Audio

Note: This example shows the iPad playing music when locked. When the iPad is unlocked, swipe up from the bottom of the screen to open Control Center, tap and hold the **Music** box, and then tap **AirPlay** ( ) to open the AirPlay dialog.

1. Tap **AirPlay** ( ).

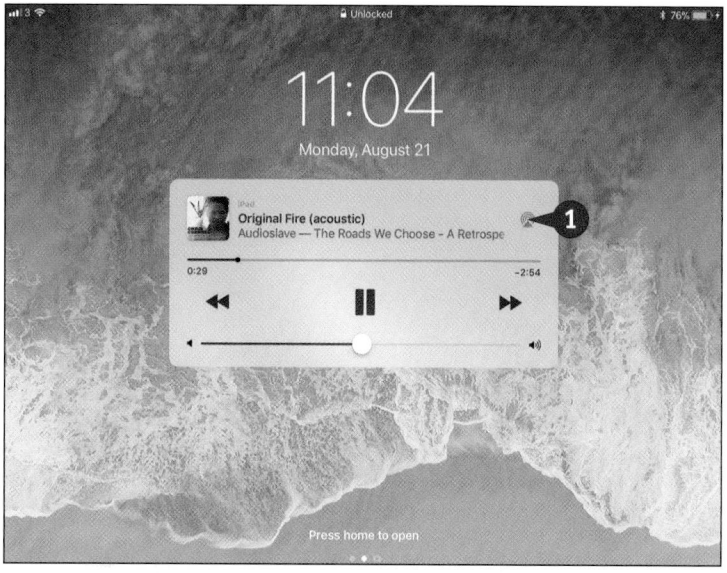

The AirPlay dialog opens.

2. Tap the AirPlay device you want to use.

The audio starts playing through the device you chose.

3. Drag the **Volume** slider to set the iPad's output volume.

4. Tap **Done**.

The AirPlay dialog closes.

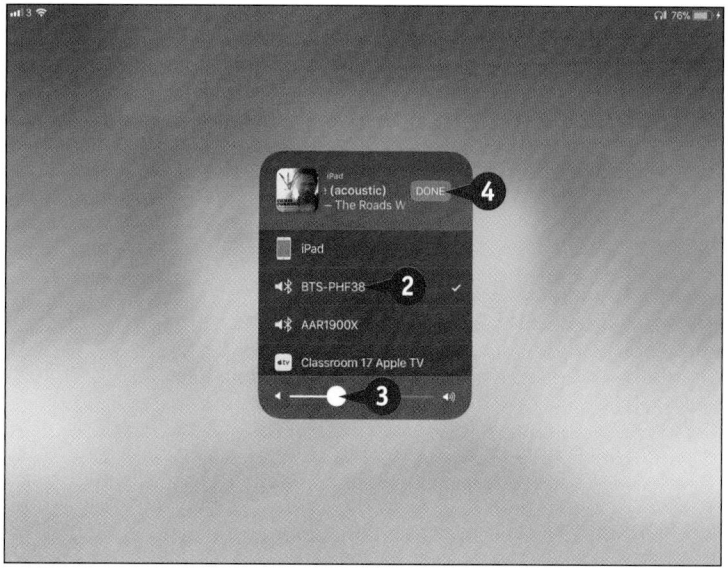

TIP

How do I stop using a Bluetooth device?

When you no longer need to use a particular Bluetooth device, tell your iPad to forget it. Press **Home**, tap **Settings** ( ), and then tap **Bluetooth** ( ). On the Bluetooth screen, tap **Information** (ⓘ) for the device. On the device's screen, tap **Forget This Device**, and then tap **Forget Device** in the confirmation dialog.

Control Cellular Data and Background Refresh

If you have a cellular iPad, you can monitor and control its use of cellular data using the Cellular screen in the Settings app to avoid incurring extra charges beyond your data plan. You can also turn on and off the Data Roaming feature, which enables some iPads to access the Internet using other carriers' networks, sometimes at an extra cost.

You can also use the Background App Refresh feature to control which apps refresh their content via Wi-Fi or cellular connections when running in the background rather than as the foreground app.

Control Cellular Data and Background Refresh

1. Press **Home**.

   The Home screen appears.

2. Tap **Settings** ( ).

   The Settings screen appears.

3. Tap **Cellular Data** ( ).

   The Cellular Data screen appears.

4. If you need to turn cellular data off altogether, set the **Cellular Data** switch to Off ( ). Normally, you will want to leave this switch set to On ( ).

   A The Current Period readout shows how much cellular data your iPad has used on your regular carrier since you last reset the statistics.

   B The Current Period Roaming readout shows data roaming usage since you last reset the statistics.

5. Tap **Cellular Data Options**.

   The Cellular Data Options screen appears.

6. If the **Enable 4G** switch is available, set it to On ( ) to enable 4G connectivity.

7. Set the **Data Roaming** switch to On ( ) if you need to use data roaming.

8. Tap **Cellular Data** ( ).

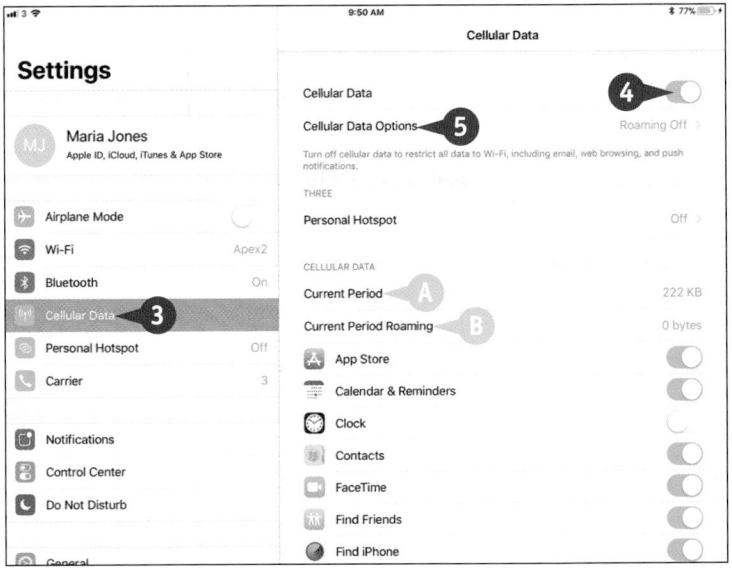

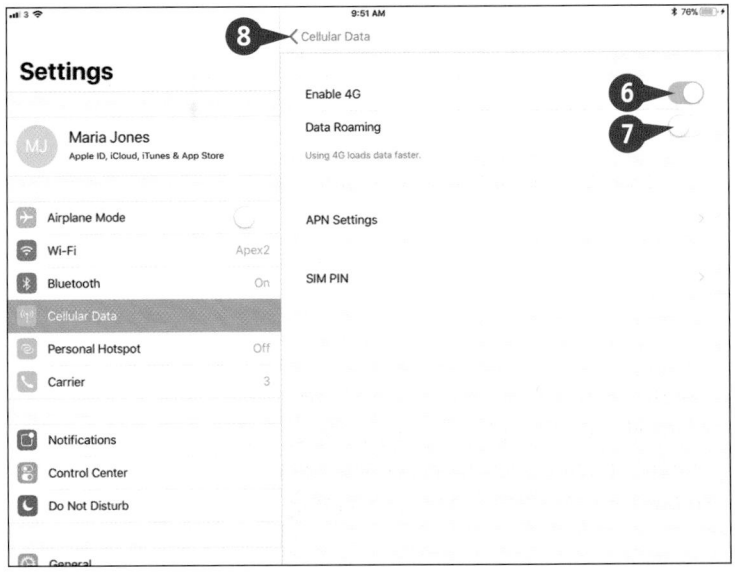

The Cellular Data screen appears again.

9. In the Use Cellular Data For area of the Cellular Data screen, set each app's switch to On (◐) or Off ( ), as needed.

10. At the bottom of the Cellular Data screen, set the **Wi-Fi Assist** switch to On (◐) to have your iPad automatically use cellular data when it detects that Wi-Fi connectivity is poor.

11. Set the **iCloud Drive** switch to On (◐) to use the cellular network to sync your iCloud Drive files.

C. You can tap **Reset Statistics** to reset your usage statistics.

12. Tap **General** (⚙).

    The General screen appears.

13. Tap **Background App Refresh**.

    The Background App Refresh screen appears.

14. Set the **Background App Refresh** switch to On (◐) or Off ( ), as needed.

15. Set each individual app switch to On (◐) or Off ( ), as needed.

16. Tap **General** (<).

    The General screen appears again.

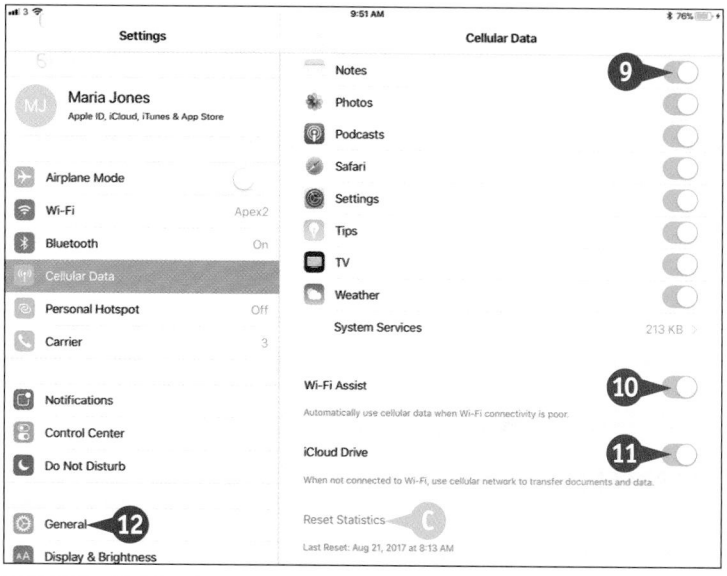

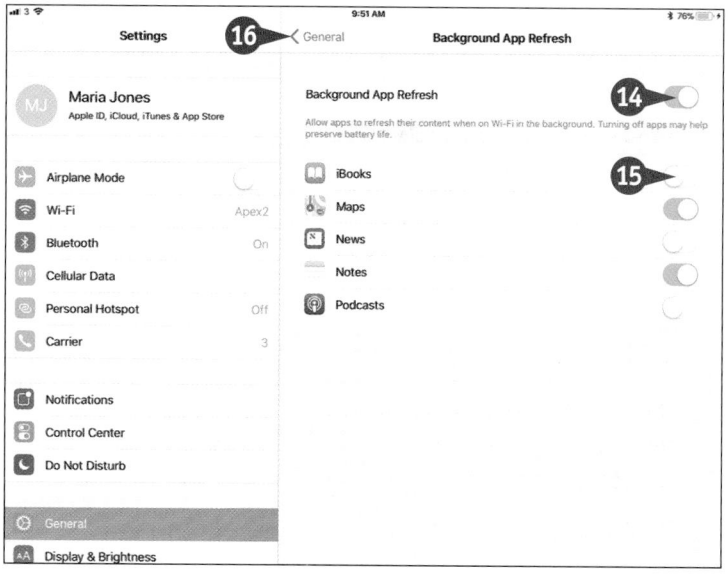

TIPS

Is the Current Period readout related to my plan's billing cycle?

No, it is not related. The Current Period readout shows the usage since you last tapped **Reset Statistics**. To make the Current Period readout relate to your data plan, you would need to tap **Reset Statistics** at the beginning of each billing cycle.

How can I monitor my data usage more closely?

See if your carrier provides an app for monitoring data usage. Such apps frequently offer extra features, such as warning you when your device is using data quickly.

Connect Your iPad to a Different Carrier

The SIM card in your cellular iPad makes it connect automatically to a particular carrier's network. Depending on whether your iPad is locked to your carrier — and if so, whether that carrier permits connections to different carriers — you may be able to connect manually to a different carrier's network when you are in a location, region, or country your carrier and its partners do not cover. You may need to set up an account with the other carrier, pay extra charges to your standard carrier, or change SIM cards.

Connect Your iPad to a Different Carrier

1. Press **Home.**

   The Home screen appears.

2. Tap **Settings** ( ).

   The Settings screen appears.

3. Tap **Carrier** ( ).

Note: If your cellular iPad does not show the controls discussed in this section, these features are not available to you.

   The Network Selection screen appears.

4. Set the **Automatic** switch to Off ( ).

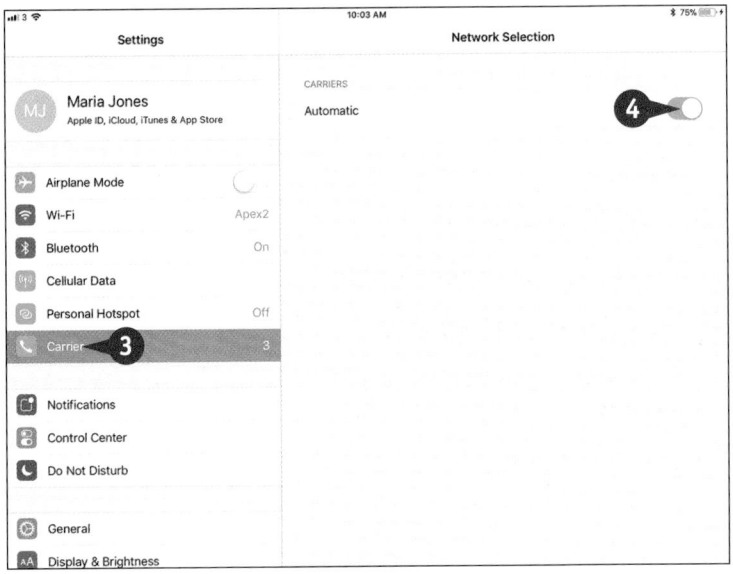

   The list of available carriers appears.

5. Tap the carrier you want to use.

Note: When you want to switch back to your regular carrier, set the **Automatic** switch on the Network Selection screen to On ( ).

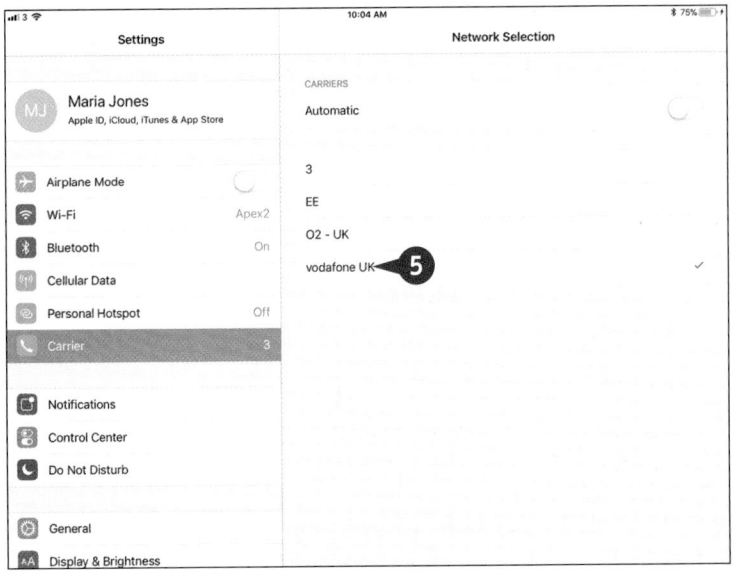

Specify Your iPad's Cellular Access Point

Normally, your cellular iPad connects automatically to a suitable cellular access point for its network carrier. But under some circumstances you may need to specify which access point to use. This is a specialized and relatively unusual move you perform from the APN Settings screen in the Settings app. APN, short for Access Point Name, is the name of a particular gateway between a cellular network and the Internet. Only some cellular iPads and carriers enable you to do this.

Specify Your iPad's Cellular Access Point

1. Press **Home**.

   The Home screen appears.

2. Tap **Settings** (⚙).

   The Settings screen appears.

3. Tap **Cellular Data** (📶).

   The Cellular Data screen appears.

4. Tap **Cellular Data Options**.

   The Cellular Data Options screen appears.

5. Tap **APN Settings**.

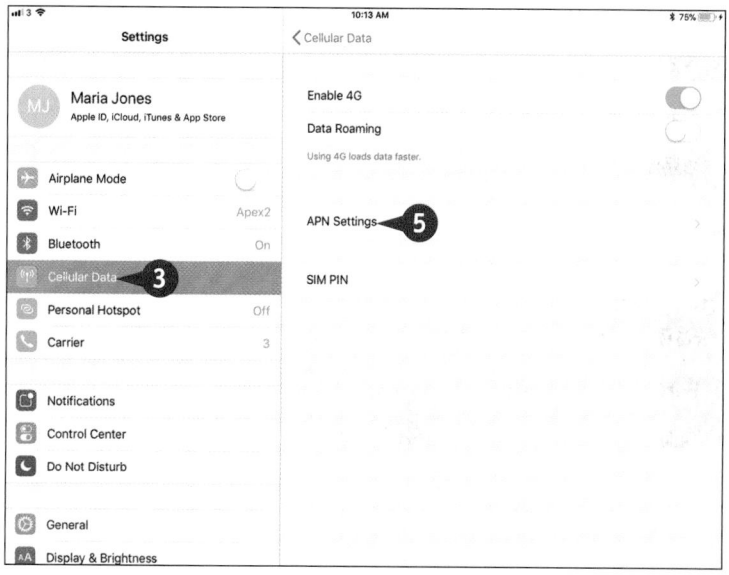

   The APN Settings screen appears.

6. Type the name of the APN.
7. Type the username if you need to provide one.
8. Type the password if applicable.

   A You can tap **Reset Settings** to reset the cellular settings on your iPad to their defaults.

9. Tap **Back** (<).

   The Cellular Data Options screen appears again.

10. Tap **Cellular Data** (<).

    The Cellular Data screen appears again.

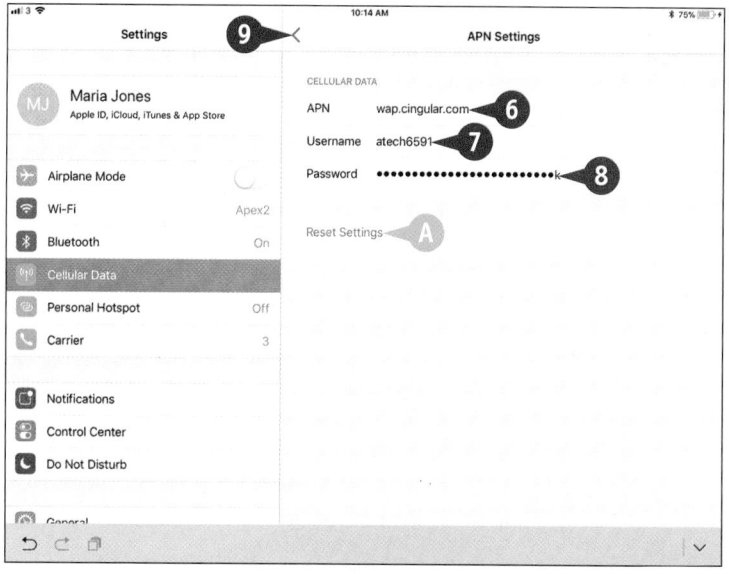

Share Items via AirDrop

AirDrop is a technology for sharing files swiftly and easily with iOS devices and Macs near your iPad via Wi-Fi or Bluetooth. For example, you can use AirDrop to share a photo or a contact record. You can use AirDrop in any app that displays a Share button ( ).

You can turn AirDrop on and off, as needed. When AirDrop is on, you can choose between accepting items only from your contacts or from everyone.

Share Items via AirDrop

Turn AirDrop On or Off

1. Swipe up from the bottom of the screen.

   Control Center opens.

2. Tap and hold the **Connections** box.

   The Connections panel opens.

   A The readout shows the AirDrop status: *Receiving Off*, indicating the feature is off; *Contacts Only;* or *Everyone*.

3. Tap **AirDrop** ( ).

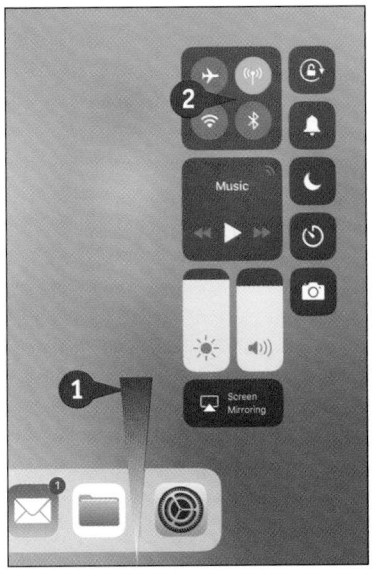

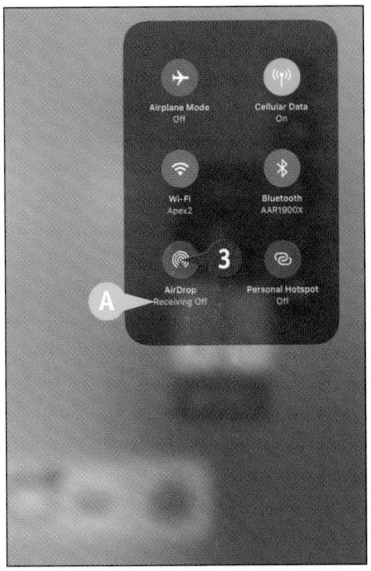

   The AirDrop dialog opens.

4. Tap **Receiving Off**, **Contacts Only**, or **Everyone**, as needed.

   The AirDrop dialog closes.

   The AirDrop readout shows the AirDrop setting you chose.

5. Tap the screen outside the Connections panel.

   The Connections panel closes.

6. Tap the screen outside Control Center.

   Control Center closes.

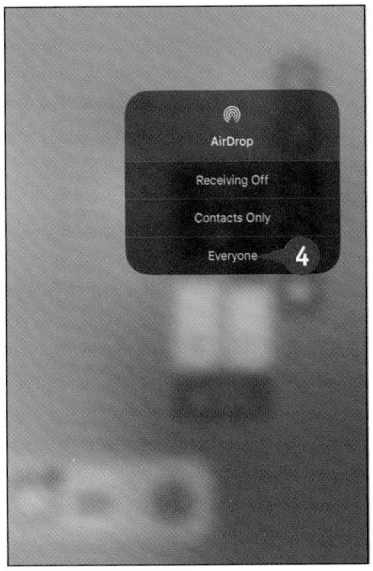

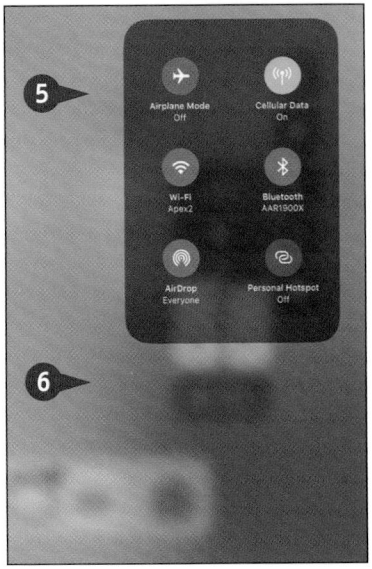

B The Wi-Fi network your iPad has connected to appears at the top of the screen with a check mark to its left.

C The Wi-Fi signal icon (📶) in the status bar and on the Wi-Fi screen shows the strength of the Wi-Fi signal. The more bars that appear, the stronger the signal is.

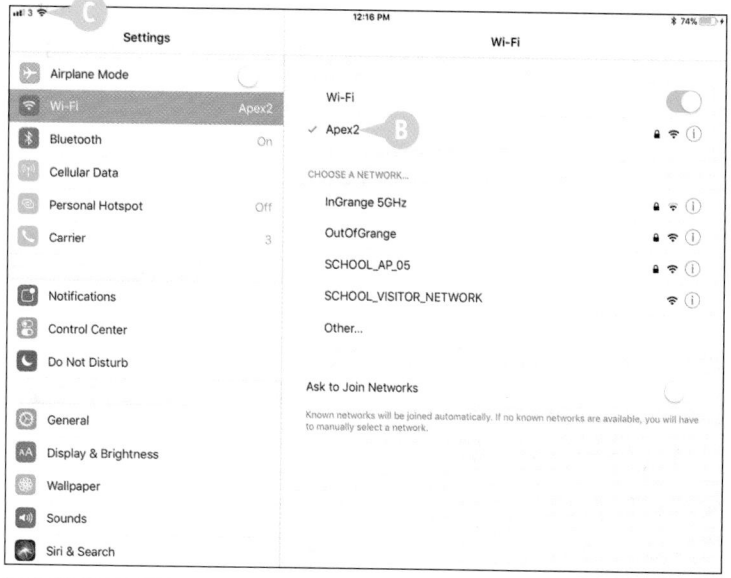

Connect to a Network Not Listed on the Wi-Fi Screen

Note: A wireless network configured not to broadcast its network name does not appear on the Wi-Fi screen.

1. On the Wi-Fi screen, tap **Other**.

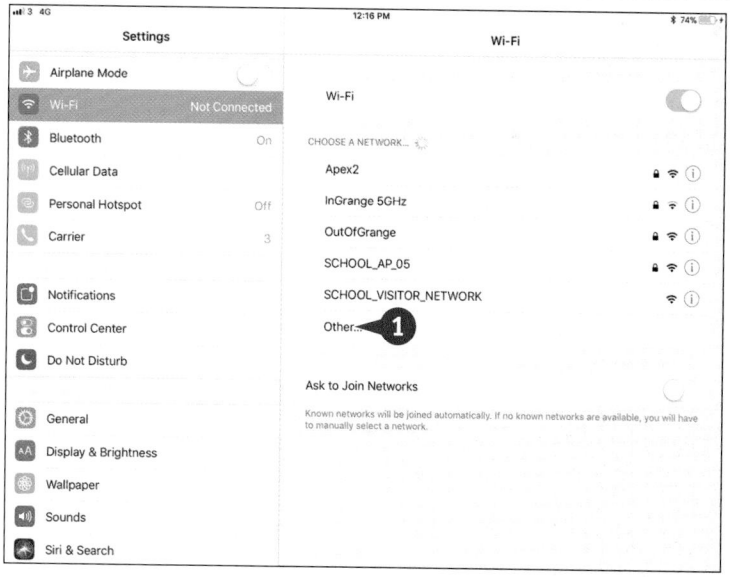

TIPS

What does the Ask to Join Networks switch control?
Your iPad automatically connects to networks it has connected to before. Set the **Ask to Join Networks** switch to On (◐) if you want your iPad to prompt you when wireless networks are available that your iPad has never used.

How do I stop using a particular wireless network?
Tap **Information** (ⓘ) to the right of the network's name on the Wi-Fi screen. On the network's screen, tap **Forget This Network**. In the dialog that opens, tap **Forget**.

continued ▶

When you are in town or on the road, you can log in to Wi-Fi hotspots to enjoy fast Internet access.

You can find Wi-Fi hotspots at many locations, including coffee shops and restaurants, hotels, and airports. Some municipal areas, and even some parks and highway rest stops, also provide public Wi-Fi. Some Wi-Fi hotspots charge for access, whereas others are free to use. For security, it is a good idea to encrypt your communications with a virtual private network — VPN — when using a hotspot.

Connect to Wi-Fi Networks and Hotspots (continued)

Connect to a Network Not Listed on the Wi-Fi Screen (continued)

The Other Network dialog opens.

2. Type the network name.
3. Tap **Security**.

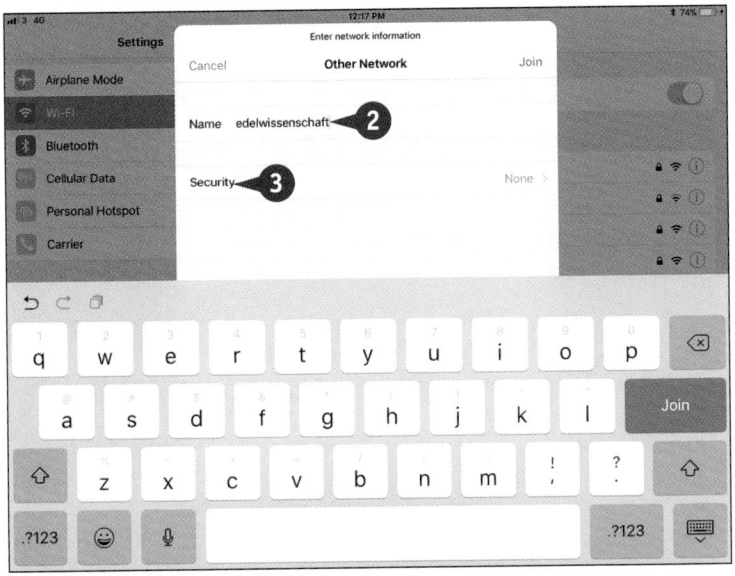

The Security dialog opens.

4. Tap the security type — for example, **WPA2**.
5. Tap **Other Network** (<).

The Other Network dialog opens again.

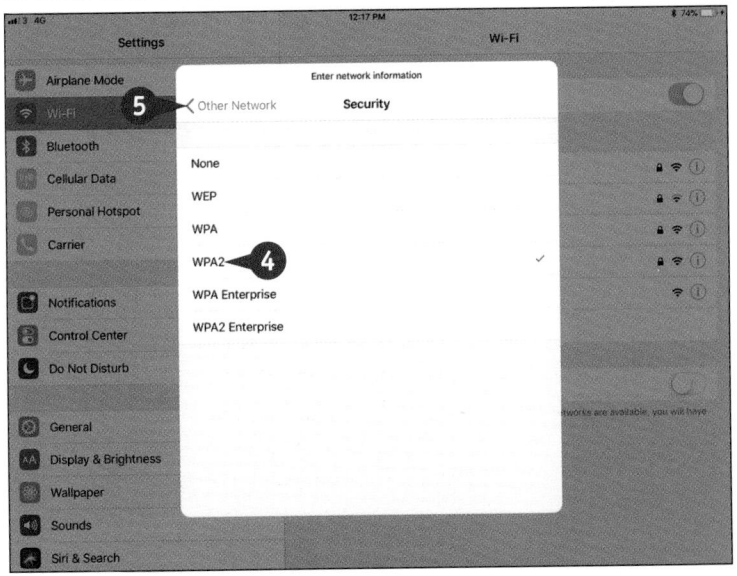

6. Type the password in the Password field.
7. Tap **Join**.

   Your iPad joins the Wi-Fi network.

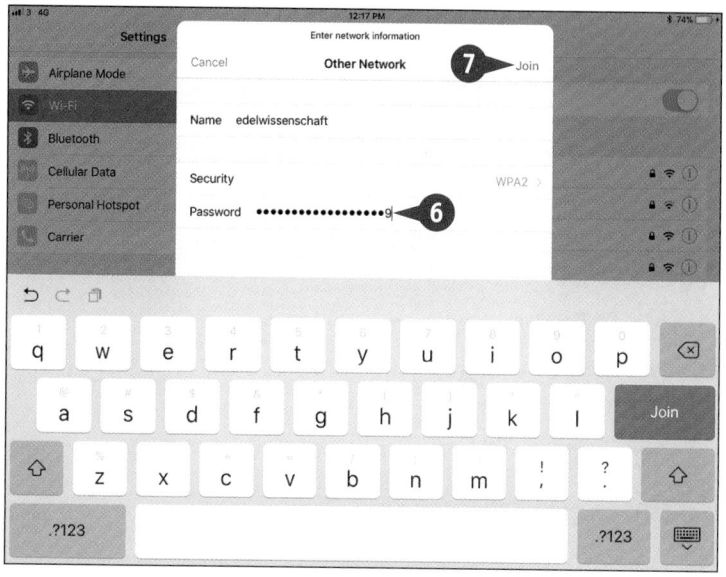

Use a Wi-Fi Hotspot

1. On the Wi-Fi screen, tap the entry for the Wi-Fi hotspot.

   Your iPad connects to the hotspot.
2. Press **Home**.

   The Home screen appears.
3. Tap **Safari** ( ).

   Safari opens.

   The login screen for the Wi-Fi hotspot appears.
4. Type your login details.
5. Tap **Login** or an equivalent button.

   After connecting to the hotspot, you can use the Internet. For example, you can browse the web using Safari or send and receive e-mail using the Mail app.

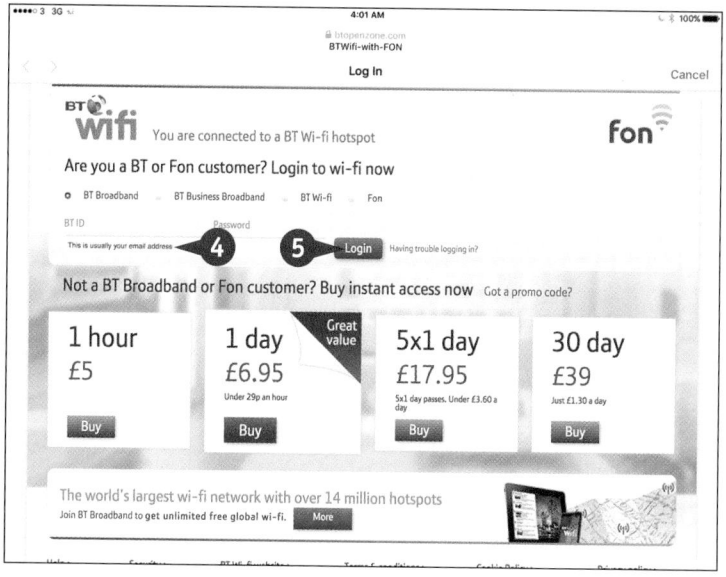

TIP

What precautions should I take when using Wi-Fi hotspots?

The main danger is that you may connect to a malevolent network. To stay safe, connect only to hotspots provided by reputable establishments — for example, national hotel chains or restaurant chains — instead of hotspots run by unknown operators. When you finish using a Wi-Fi hotspot you will not use again, tell the iPad to forget the network by tapping **Information** (ⓘ) next to the network's name, tapping **Forget This Network**, and then tapping **Forget** in the confirmation dialog. Forgetting the network ensures that the iPad does not connect to another network that has the same name, security type, and password — but is in fact a malevolent hotspot set up to trap traffic from the genuine hotspot.

Connect to a Network via VPN

If you use your iPad for work, you may need to connect it to your work network via virtual private networking, or VPN, across the Internet. You can also use VPN to change your iPad's apparent geographical location — for example, to use a U.S.-restricted media service when you are located in another country.

VPN uses encryption to create a secure connection across the Internet. By using VPN, you can connect securely from anywhere you have an Internet connection.

Connect to a Network via VPN

Set Up the VPN Connection on the iPad

1. Press **Home**.

   The Home screen appears.

2. Tap **Settings** ( ).

   The Settings screen appears.

3. Tap **General** ( ).

   The General screen appears.

4. Tap **VPN**.

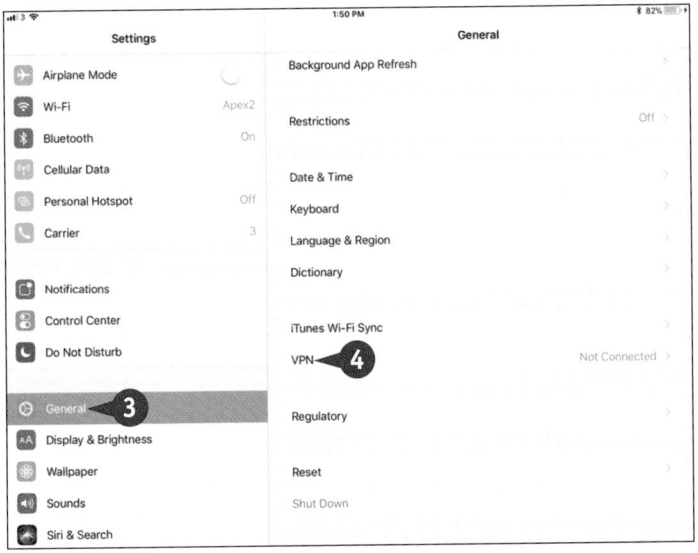

   The VPN screen appears.

5. Tap **Add VPN Configuration**.

Note: If your iPad already has a VPN you want to use, tap it, and then go to step **1** of the next set of steps, "Connect to the VPN."

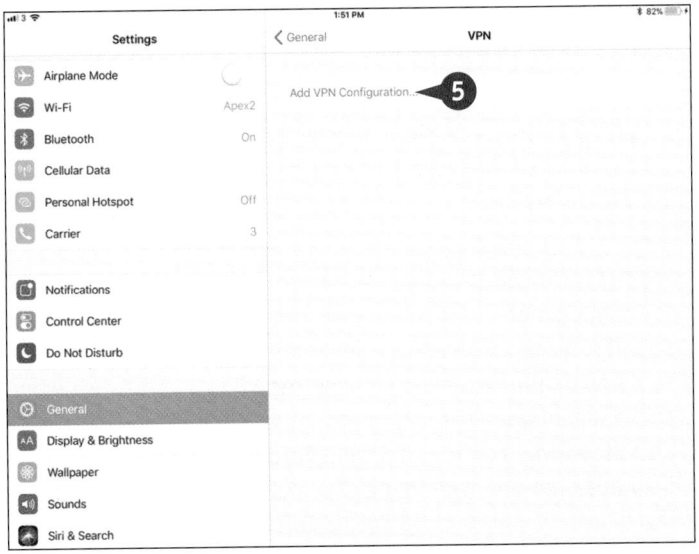

The Add Configuration dialog opens.

6 Tap **Type**; select the VPN type, such as **L2TP**, in the Type dialog that opens; and then tap **Back** (<).

7 Fill in the details of the VPN.

8 Set the **Send All Traffic** switch to On ( ) if you want all your Internet traffic to go via the VPN.

9 Tap **Done**.

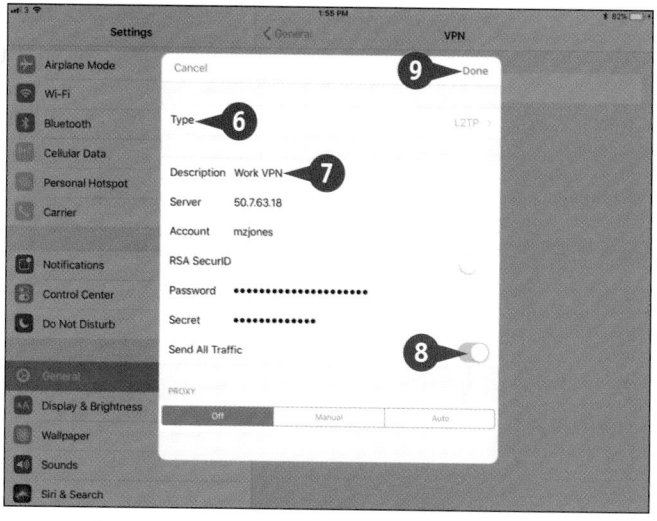

Connect to the VPN

1 On the VPN screen, set the **Status** switch to On ( ).

The iPad connects to the VPN.

A The Status readout shows *Connected*.

B The VPN indicator appears in the status bar.

2 Work across the network connection as if you were connected directly to the network.

C You can tap **Information** (ⓘ) to display information about the connection, including the assigned IP address and the connection time.

3 When you are ready to disconnect from the VPN, set the **Status** switch on the VPN screen to Off ( ).

D You can turn the VPN on and off by setting the **VPN** switch in the left column to On ( ) or Off ( ).

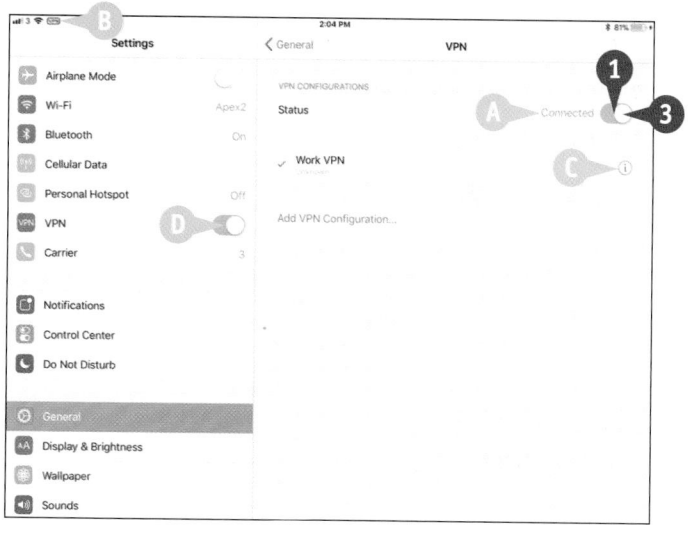

TIPS

Is there an easier way to set up a VPN connection?
Yes. An administrator can provide the VPN details in a file called a *configuration profile*, either via e-mail or via a web page. When you install the configuration profile, your iPad adds the VPN automatically. You can then connect to the VPN.

How can I connect to a VPN type that iOS does not support?
Look for an app designed to connect to this type of VPN. Ask the VPN's administrator for details of the VPN and suggestions on which app to use.

Send Text and Multimedia Messages

When you need to communicate quickly with another person, but do not need to speak to him or her, you can send an instant message using the Messages app.

The Messages app runs on Macs and on the iPad, the iPhone, and the iPod touch. You can use Messages to send instant messages to other users of Messages on these devices. You can send text, multimedia content, emoji, animations, handwriting, and other items — even payments.

Send Text and Multimedia Messages

1. Press **Home**.
2. Tap **Messages** ( ).

   The Messages screen appears.
3. Tap **New Message** ( ).

   The New Message screen appears.
4. Start typing the contact's name, address, or phone number.

   A Alternatively, you can tap **Add Contact** (⊕) and then tap the contact in the Contacts dialog.

   A list of matches appears.
5. Tap the appropriate contact.

   Messages starts a new message to the contact.
6. Tap in the text field, and then type your message.
7. To add a photo, tap **Expand** ( ).

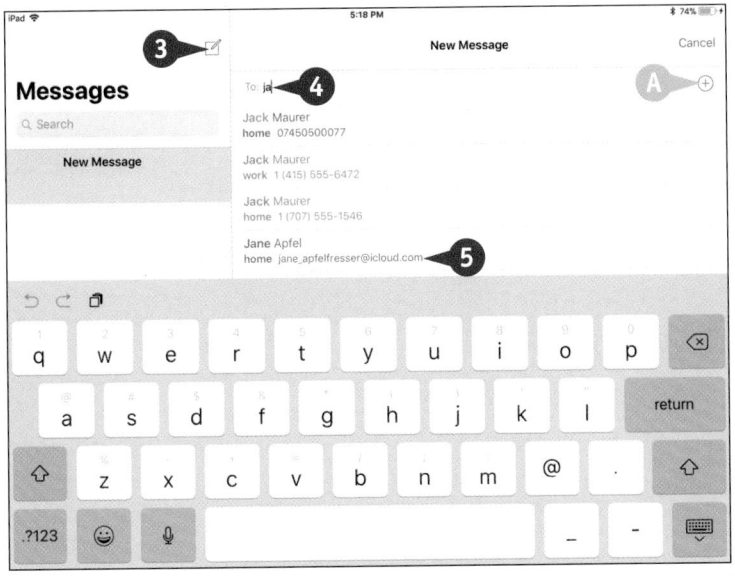

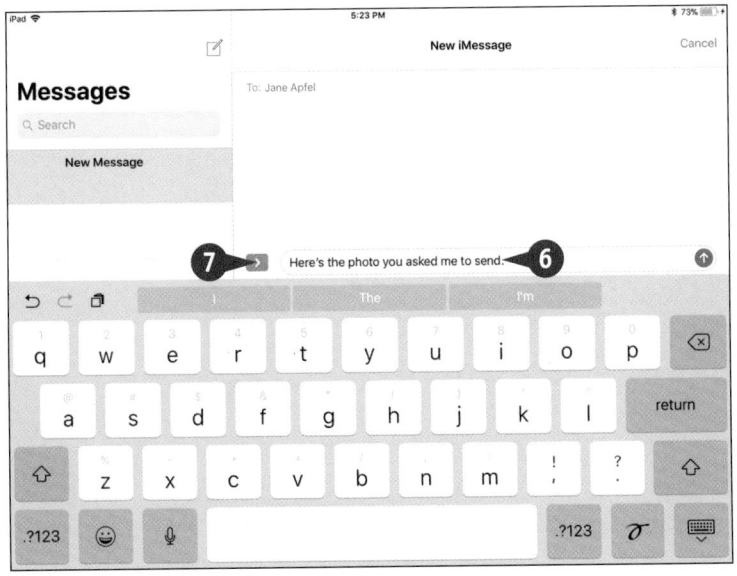

The other buttons appear.

8 Tap **Photo** (📷).

The Photo pane appears.

B The right side shows recent photos.

C You can tap **Take Photo** (◯) to take a photo using the iPad's rear camera.

D You can tap **Switch Cameras** (📷) to switch to the front camera.

E You can tap **Photos** (▬) to open the Photos dialog, and then browse for a photo.

9 Tap the photo you want to use, either in the Photo pane or in the Photos dialog.

F The photo appears in the message.

Note: You can attach another photo or video by repeating steps **7** to **9**.

10 Tap **Send** (↑).

Messages sends the message.

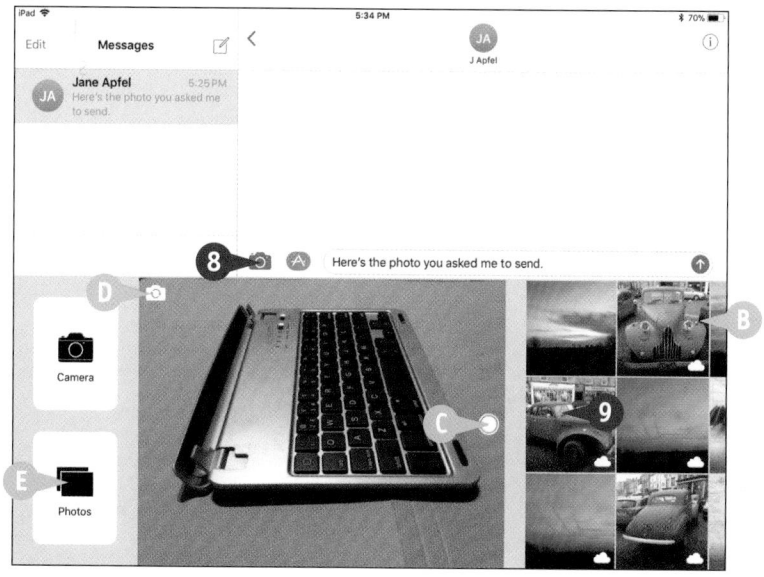

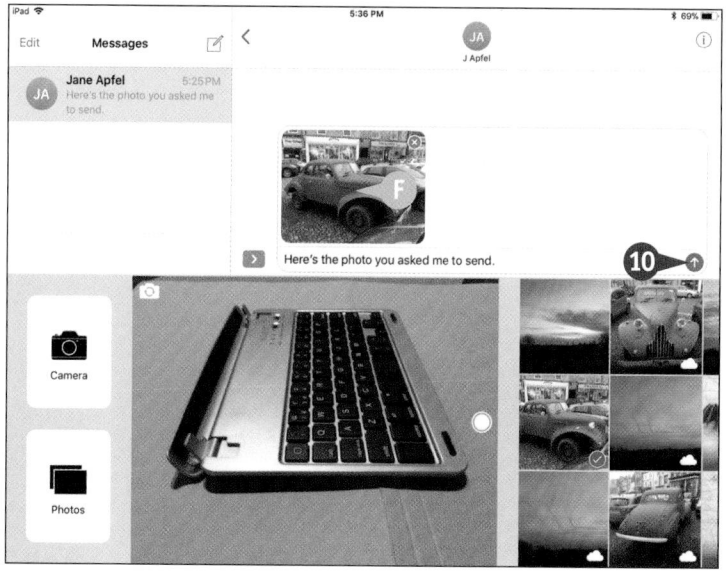

TIP

Is there another way to send a photo or video?

Yes. You can start from the Camera app or the Photos app. This way of sending a photo or video is handy when you are taking photos or videos or when you are browsing your photos or videos. Tap the photo or video you want to share, and then tap **Share** (⬆). On the Share sheet, tap **Message** (💬). Your iPad starts a message containing the photo or video in Messages. You can then address and send the message.

Using Emoji and Other iMessage Features

The Messages app makes it easy to include emoji — graphical characters — in your messages. Apple's iMessage service also lets you enhance your messages with features including stickers, handwriting and sketches, animations, and Digital Touch, which can send a pattern of taps or your heartbeat. You can also respond quickly to a message by using the Tapback feature and send a payment by using the Payment feature.

Add Emoji to Messages

The Messages app makes it easy to add emoji to your messages. After typing your text, tap **Emoji** (☺) on the keyboard. Messages highlights with color any words in the message that you can replace with emoji; tap a word to insert the corresponding emoji icon, such as 👍 for "great!"

You can also insert other emoji manually by tapping them on the emoji keyboard. Tap the buttons at the bottom of the screen, or simply scroll the emoji panel left or right to browse the available emoji.

Send a Handwritten Message or Sketch

To send a handwritten message or sketch, tap **New** (✎) to begin a new message. Address the message to an iMessage user, and then tap **Digital Touch** (●) to display the Digital Touch controls.

Tap **Expand** (⌃) to expand the panel to full screen, tap the color you want, and then write or draw what you want to send. Tap **Send** (↑) to send the message.

Send a Message with Effect

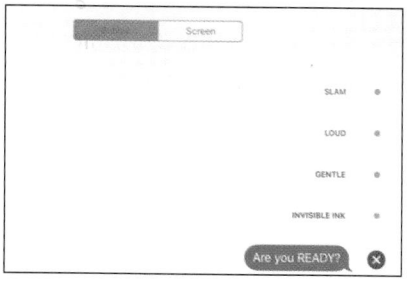

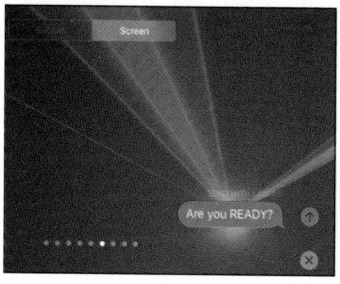

To send a message with effect, write the text for the message, and then tap and hold **Send** (). The Send with Effect pane appears. At the top of the pane, tap **Bubble** if you want to send a bubble with an effect such as Slam or Invisible Ink, and then tap the button for the effect; a preview then appears. To send text with a full-screen effect, tap **Screen** at the top of the pane, and then swipe left or right to find the effect you want; again, a preview appears. When you are ready to send the message, tap **Send** ().

Send Heartbeats or Taps

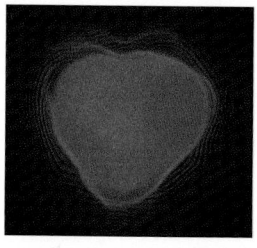

To send Digital Touch animations such as heartbeats or taps, tap **New Message** () to begin a new message. Address the message to an iMessage user, and then tap **Digital Touch** () to display the Digital Touch controls.

To send a kiss, tap with two fingers. To send a heartbeat, tap and hold with two fingers on the screen. To send a heartbreak, tap and hold with two fingers, then drag down. To send a tap, tap with one finger. To send a fireball, press with one finger.

Messages displays the appropriate animation on your iPad and sends it to the recipient. You do not need to tap **Send** ().

Respond Quickly Using the Tapback Feature

iMessage enables you to respond quickly to an incoming message by tapping and holding it. The Tapback panel opens, and you can tap the icon you want to send as an instant response.

Send a Payment to a Contact

With iMessage, you can send a payment to a contact. Tap **New** () to begin a new message, and then address the message to an iMessage user. Tap **Apps** () to display the Apps panel. Swipe left or right if necessary to display the Apple Pay button, and then tap **Apple Pay** (). Use the controls to specify the amount, and then tap **Pay**. The payment ticket appears in the message box. Tap **Send** () to send it.

Manage Your Instant Messages

If you send and receive many messages, the Messages interface may get so full that it becomes hard to navigate. To keep your messages under control, you can forward messages to others and delete messages you do not need to keep. You can either delete messages from a conversation, leaving the conversation's other messages, or delete the entire conversation.

Manage Your Instant Messages

Forward or Delete One or More Messages from a Conversation

1. Press **Home**.

   The Home screen appears.

2. Tap **Messages** ( ).

   The Messages screen appears.

3. In the Messages column, tap the appropriate conversation.

   The messages in the conversation appear.

4. Tap and hold the first of the messages you want to forward or delete.

5. Tap **More**.

   A selection button ( ) appears to the left of each message.

   A Messages selects the message you tapped ( ).

   B You can tap another selection button (changes to) to select that message.

6. Tap **Forward** ( ).

   Messages starts a new message containing the forwarded messages.

   C Instead of forwarding the selected messages, you can tap **Delete** ( ) to delete them from the conversation.

   D You can tap **Delete All** to delete all the messages.

7. Address the message and tap **Send** to send it.

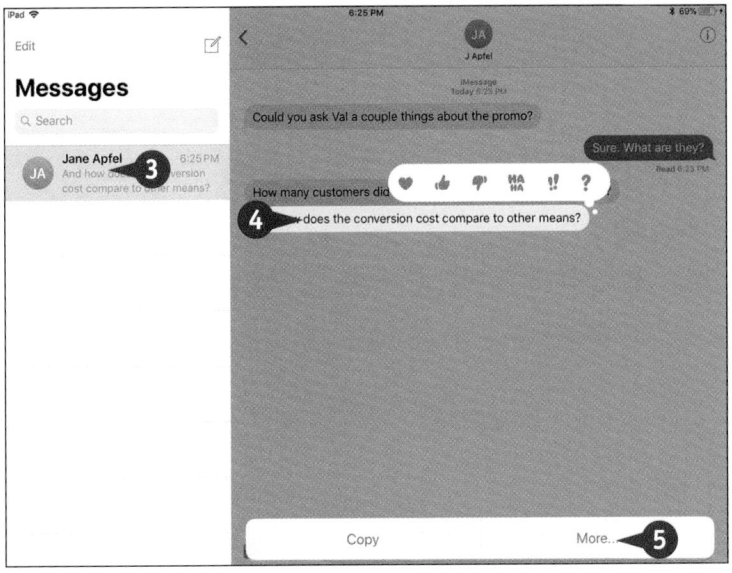

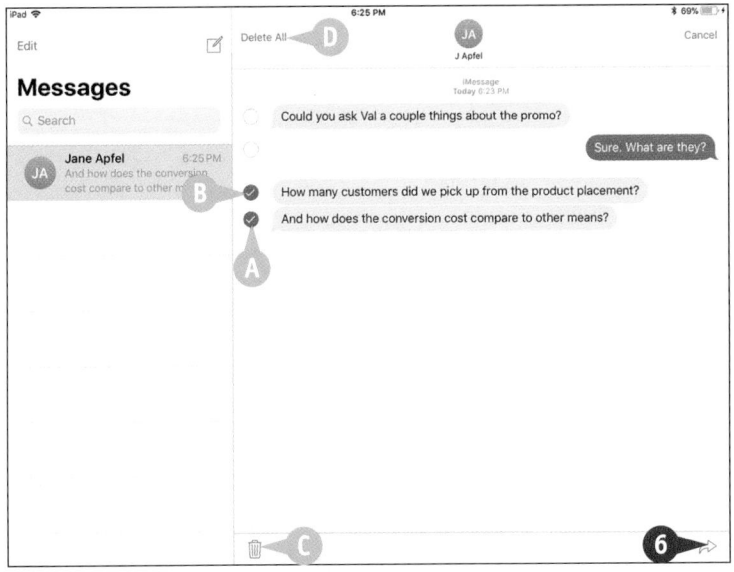

Delete a Conversation

1. Press **Home**.

   The Home screen appears.

2. Tap **Messages** ( ).

   The Messages screen appears.

3. Tap **Edit**.

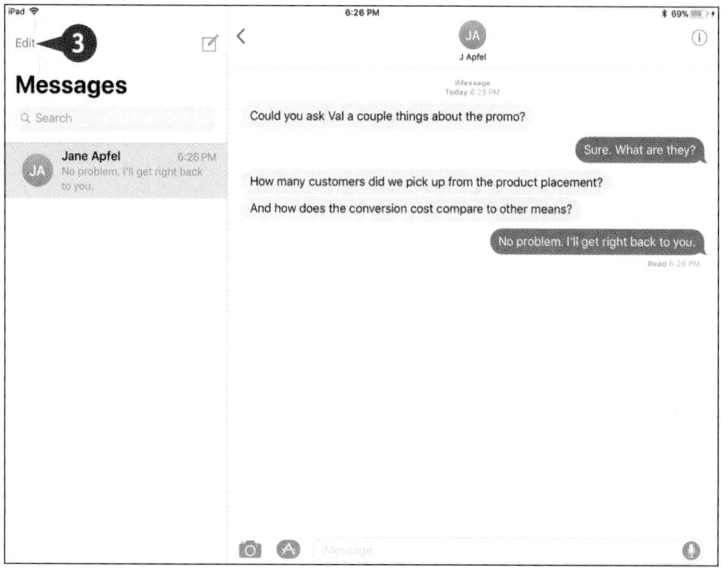

   The Messages column switches to Edit Mode.

4. Tap the selection button ( ) for the conversation you want to delete (changes to).

   The Delete button appears.

5. Tap **Delete**.

   Messages deletes the conversation and turns off Edit Mode.

Note: You can also delete a conversation by tapping it in the conversation list, swiping to the left, and then tapping **Delete**.

TIP

Can I resend a message?

Yes. You can resend a message in either of these ways:

- If a red icon with an exclamation point appears next to the message, the message has not been sent. Tap the icon and then tap **Try Again** to attempt to send the message again.
- If the message has been sent, tap and hold the message text, and then tap **Copy** to copy it. Tap and hold in the message text field, and then tap **Paste** to paste in the text. Tap **Send** to send the message.

Mute a Conversation or Share Your Location

You may need to mute a Messages conversation temporarily while you focus on other things. You can mute a conversation by displaying the Details screen for the conversation and setting the Hide Alerts switch to On.

From the Details screen for a conversation, you can also share your current location by sending an embedded link for the Maps app, enabling the recipient to see exactly where you are. You can also share your location for a specific length of time with all your contacts.

Mute a Conversation or Share Your Location

Open Messages and Display the Details Screen for the Conversation

1. Press **Home**.

   The Home screen appears.

2. Tap **Messages** ( ).

   The Messages screen appears.

3. Tap the conversation you want to view.

   The conversation appears.

4. Tap **Details** (ⓘ).

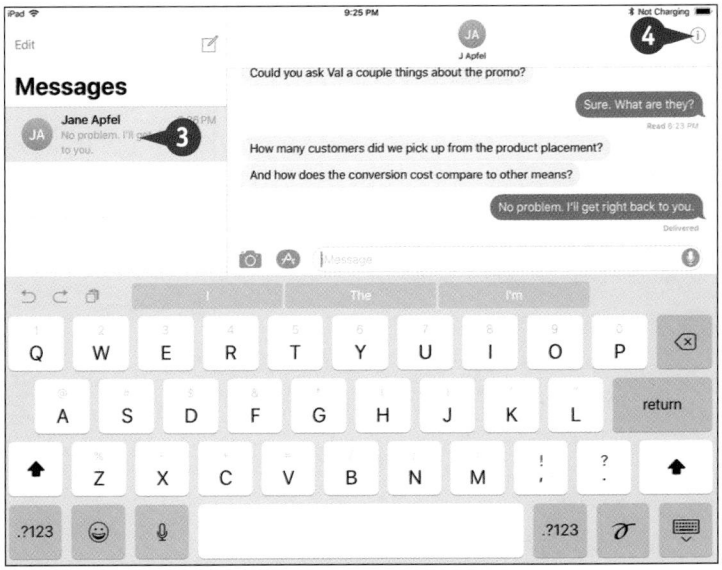

Turn On Hide Alerts for the Conversation

1. On the Details screen, set the **Hide Alerts** switch to On ( ).

Note: After you turn on Hide Alerts for a conversation, your iPad does not display notifications for that conversation.

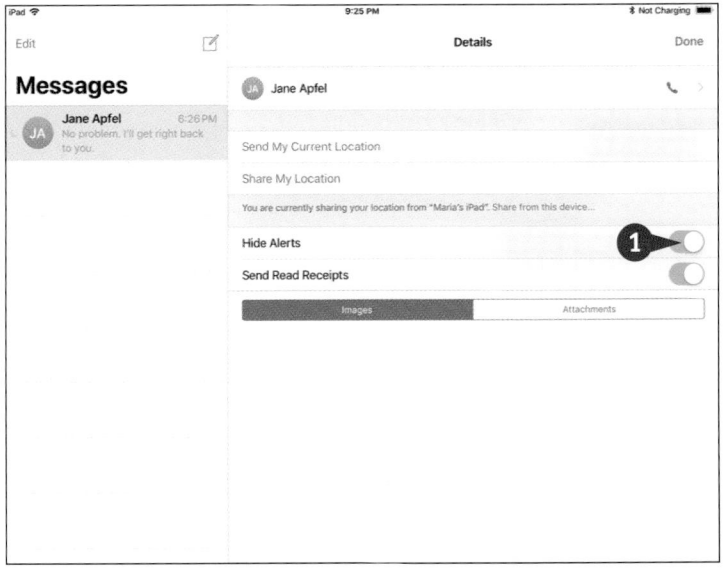

The iPad starts a FaceTime call, showing your video preview.

7. When your contact answers, smile and speak.

Note: Tap to display the on-screen controls. They disappear automatically if you do not use them for a few seconds.

When the connection is established, your iPad displays the caller full-screen, with your video inset.

8. If you need to mute your microphone, tap **Mute** (). Tap **Mute** () when you want to turn muting off.

9. If you need to show your contact something using the rear-facing camera, tap **Switch Cameras** (). Your inset video then shows the picture that is being sent to your contact. Tap **Switch Cameras** () again when you are ready to switch back.

B. You can tap **Take Photo** () to take a photo during the call.

10. When you are ready to end the call, tap **End** ().

Note: When your iPad receives a FaceTime request and the screen shows who is calling, aim the camera at your face, and then tap **Accept** to answer.

TIP

Are there other ways of starting a FaceTime call?

Yes. Here are three other ways of starting a FaceTime call:

- In the Contacts app, tap the contact to display the contact record, and then tap **FaceTime** ().
- In a Messages conversation, tap **Details** (), and then tap **FaceTime** ().
- Ask Siri to call a contact via FaceTime. For example, press and hold **Home** to summon Siri, and then say "FaceTime John Smith."

CHAPTER 6

Working with Apps and Files

You can customize the Home screen to optimize the layout of the icons you need most and to organize them into folders. You can switch quickly among open apps, use the iPad's multitasking features, and manage your apps by installing apps, updating apps to the latest versions, and removing apps you do not use. You can also manage files; apply formatting; and use Cut, Copy, and Paste.

Customize the Home Screen and the Dock 152
Organize Apps with Folders 154
Switch Quickly from One App to Another 156
Multitask with Split-Screen Views 158
Find the Apps You Need 164
Update and Remove Apps 166
Manage Automatic Downloads and Your Apple ID 168
Manage Files with the Files App 170
Enter Text Quickly in Apps 174
Cut, Copy, and Paste Text 176
Bold, Italicize, Underline, and Replace Text 178
Take Screenshots and Use Instant Markup 180

Customize the Home Screen and the Dock

You can customize the Home screen to put the apps you use most frequently within easy reach. When the existing Home screens fill up with icons, the iPad adds more Home screens automatically, as needed. You can also create more Home screens — up to 11 screens total — manually and move the app icons among them.

You can customize the Dock by adding icons to it, rearranging icons on it, and removing icons from it.

Customize the Home Screen and the Dock

Move an Icon

1. Press **Home**.

   The Home screen appears.

2. Swipe left or right to display the Home screen you want to customize.

   A You can also tap the dot for the Home screen you want to display.

3. Tap and hold the icon you want to move until the icon expands momentarily, indicating that it is movable.

4. Drag the icon to where you want it.

   Any other icons move out of the way.

5. When the icon is in the right place, drop it by lifting your finger from the screen.

   The icon stays in its new position.

Note: To move the icon to a different Home screen, drag it to the left edge or right edge of the current Home screen, wait until the previous or next Home screen appears, and then drag the icon to where you want to place it.

Note: To create a new Home screen, drag an icon to the right edge of the last current Home screen.

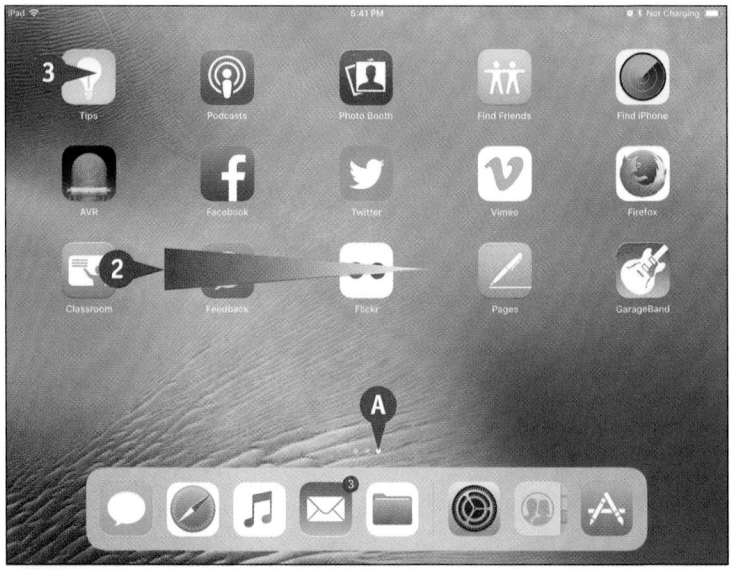

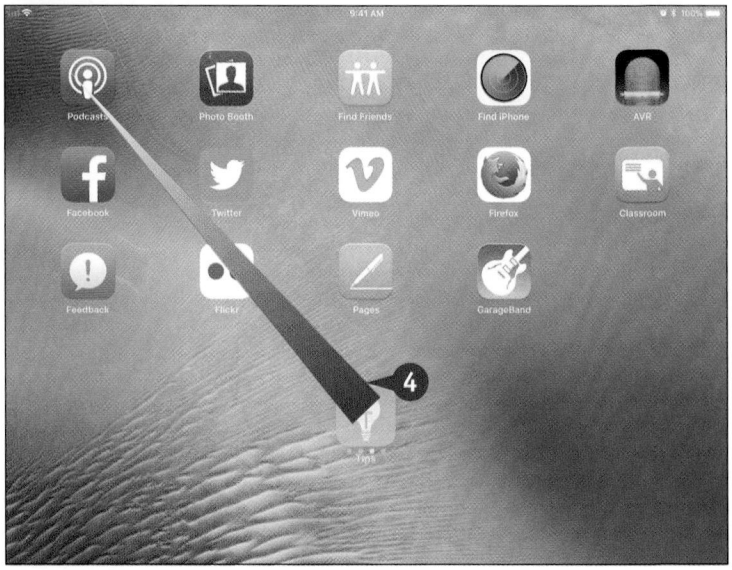

Customize the Dock

1. Tap and hold the icon you want to move until the icon expands momentarily, indicating that it is movable.
2. Drag an icon from the Home screen to the Dock.

   The existing Dock icons move out of the way.
3. Drop the icon.

Note: To remove a Dock icon, drag the icon from the Dock to the Home screen.

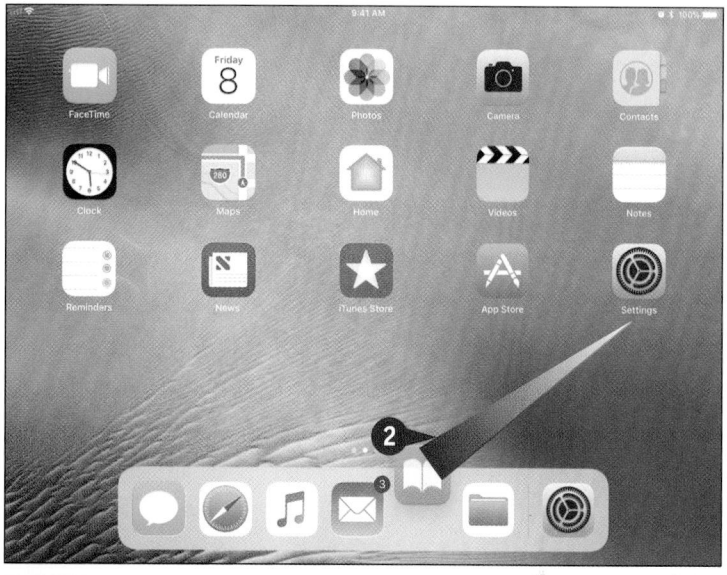

4. Tap and hold the Dock icon you want to move until the icon expands momentarily, indicating that it is movable.
5. Drag the icon from its existing position to where you want it.
6. Drop the icon.

Note: If you synchronize your iPad with a computer, you can use iTunes to customize the Home screens and the Dock. You may find this an easier way to make extensive changes.

TIP

How can I put the default apps back on the first Home screen?
Press **Home**, tap **Settings** (), and then tap **General** (). At the bottom of the General screen, tap **Reset**. On the Reset screen, tap **Reset Home Screen Layout**, and then tap **Reset** in the dialog that opens. Press **Home** to return to the Home screen.

When you reset the Home screen, iOS arranges the icons for third-party apps in alphabetical order, starting after the last of the default apps.

Organize Apps with Folders

You can organize the Home screen by arranging the icons into folders. The default Home screen layout on your iPad does not include any folders, but you can create as many as you need.

You create a folder by dragging one icon onto another icon. Doing this creates a folder containing both items. You can then rename the folder and add other items to it. To run an app stored in a folder, you open the folder to reveal its contents, and then tap the app.

Organize Apps with Folders

Create a Folder

1. Display the Home screen that contains the item you want to put into a folder.
2. Tap and hold an icon until the icons start to jiggle.

Note: When creating a folder, you may find it easiest to first put at least the first two items you will add to the folder on the same screen.

3. Drag one of the app icons you want to place in the folder and hold it over the icon of another app destined for the folder.

   The iPad creates a folder, puts both icons in it, and assigns a default name based on the genre.

4. Tap **Delete** (⊗) in the folder name field.

   The keyboard appears.

5. Type the name for the folder.
6. Tap outside the folder.

Note: You can also tap **Done** on the keyboard.

   The iPad applies the name to the folder.

7. Press **Home**.

   The icons stop jiggling.

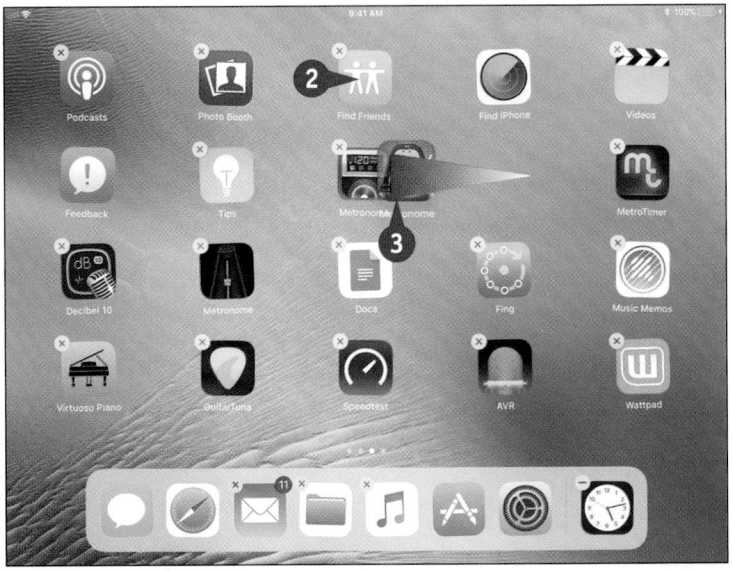

Open an Item in a Folder

1. Display the Home screen that contains the folder.
2. Tap the folder's icon.

   The folder's contents appear, and the items outside the folder fade.

   A If necessary, tap a dot to display a different screen in the folder. You can also swipe left or right to change screens in the folder.

3. Tap the item you want to open.

   The item opens.

Add an Item to a Folder

1. Display the Home screen that contains the item.
2. Drag the icon on top of the folder, hold it there for a moment, and drop it there.

Note: If the folder is on a different Home screen from the icon, drag the icon to the left edge to display the previous Home screen or to the right edge to display the next Home screen.

The item goes into the folder.

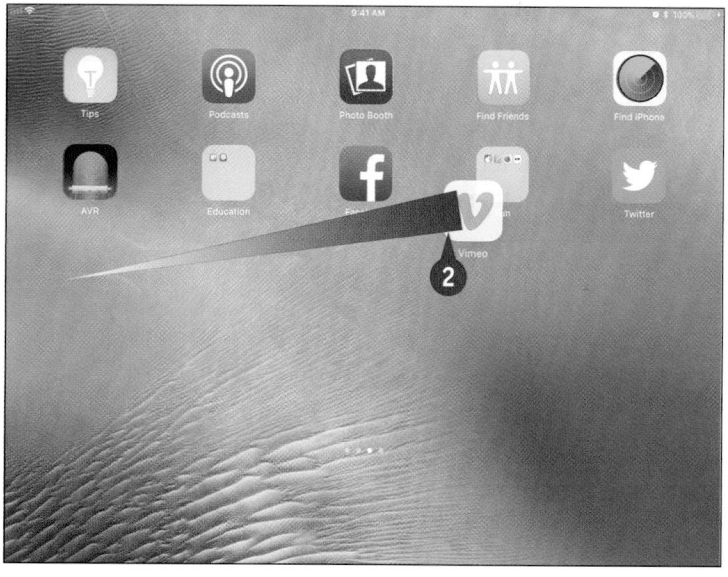

TIP

How do I take an item out of a folder?

1. Tap the folder to display its contents.
2. Drag the item out of the folder. The folder closes and the Home screen appears.
3. Drag the item to where you want it, and then drop it.

Switch Quickly from One App to Another

You can run many apps on your iPad at the same time, switching from one app to another as needed. The most straightforward way to switch among apps is to press **Home** to display the Home screen and then tap the icon for the app you want to start using.

For faster switching among apps that are already running, use the App Switcher. The App Switcher also enables you to close running apps.

Switch Quickly from One App to Another

1. While using an app, swipe up from the bottom of the screen.

Note: If swiping up displays only the Dock, swipe up farther to display the App Switcher.

Note: You can also press **Home** twice in quick succession to display the App Switcher.

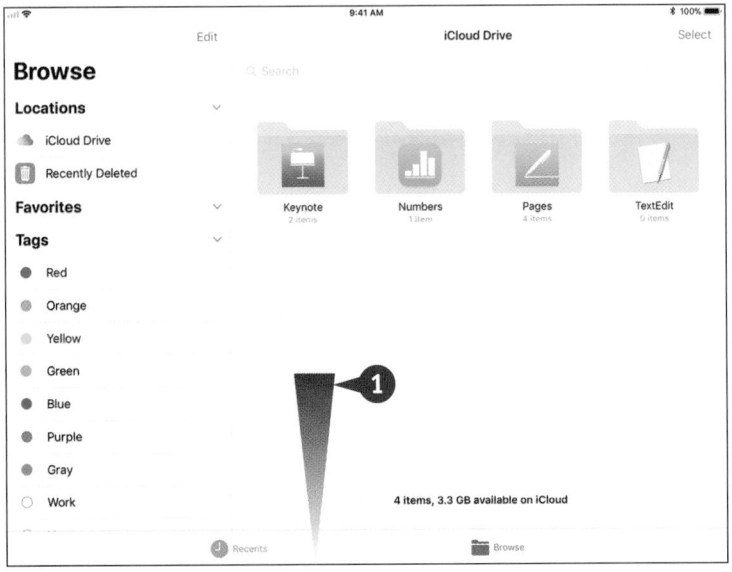

The App Switcher appears, showing a thumbnail for each open app.

- **A** The app you were using appears in the upper-right position.
- **B** The previous app appears in the lower-right position.
- **C** Other apps appear farther to the left in the order you last used them.

Note: If necessary, swipe right until you can see the app you want.

2. Tap the thumbnail of the app you want to use.

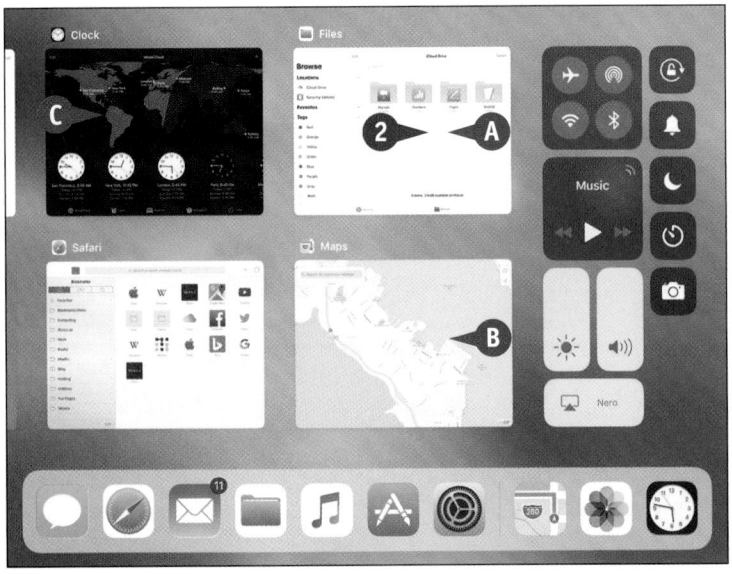

The app appears, and you can work in it as usual. For example, in the Maps app, navigate to the area you want to view.

3. When you are ready to switch back, swipe up from the bottom of the screen or press **Home** twice in quick succession.

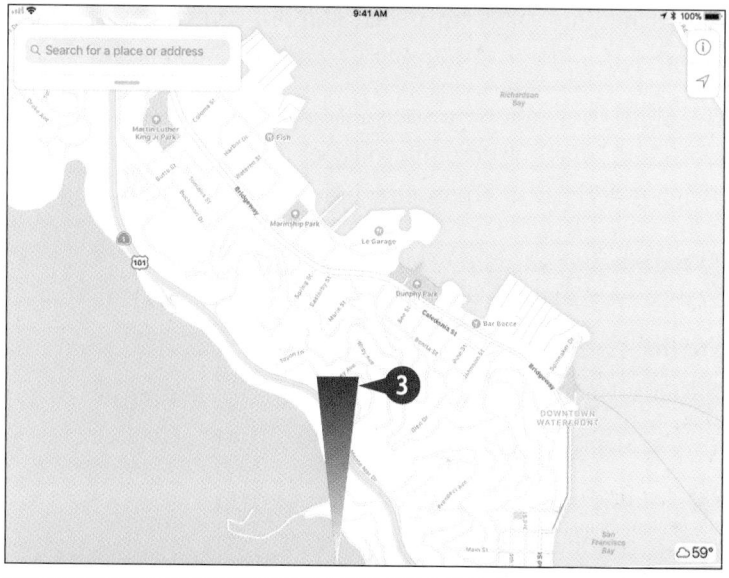

The App Switcher appears.

4. Tap the app to which you want to return.

The app appears, ready to resume from where you stopped using it.

Note: You can also tap another app's thumbnail to switch to that app instead.

TIP

How do I stop an app that is not responding?

If an app stops responding, you can quickly close it from the App Switcher. Swipe up from the bottom of the screen or press **Home** twice to open the App Switcher. Scroll right if necessary until you can see the problem app, and then swipe it upward so it disappears off the screen. You can then either tap the app you want to use or press **Home** to return to the Home screen.

You can use this move to close any app that you no longer want to use, whether or not it has stopped responding.

Multitask with Split-Screen Views

Your iPad normally runs each app full-screen, so you see a single app at a time. But on recent iPad models you can also split the screen between two apps in any of three ways.

The Slide Over feature displays a second app in the rightmost third of the screen. The Split View feature divides the screen evenly or unevenly between the two apps. The Picture-in-Picture feature displays a video in a pop-up window over another app or the Home screen.

Multitask with Split-Screen Views

Enable and Configure Multitasking

1. Press **Home**.

   The Home screen appears.

2. Tap **Settings** ( ).

   The Settings screen appears.

3. Tap **General** ( ).

   The General screen appears.

4. Tap **Multitasking & Dock**.

   The Multitasking & Dock screen appears.

5. Set the **Allow Multiple Apps** switch to On ( ) to enable multitasking.

6. Set the **Persistent Video Overlay** switch to On ( ) if you want to be able to overlay a playing video on other screens.

7. Set the **Gestures** switch to On ( ) if you want to be able to give multitasking gestures with four or five fingers. See the tip for details on the gestures.

8. Set the **Show Suggested and Recent Apps** switch to On ( ) if you want to display suggested apps and recent apps on the right side of the Dock.

9. Tap **General** ( ).

   The General screen appears.

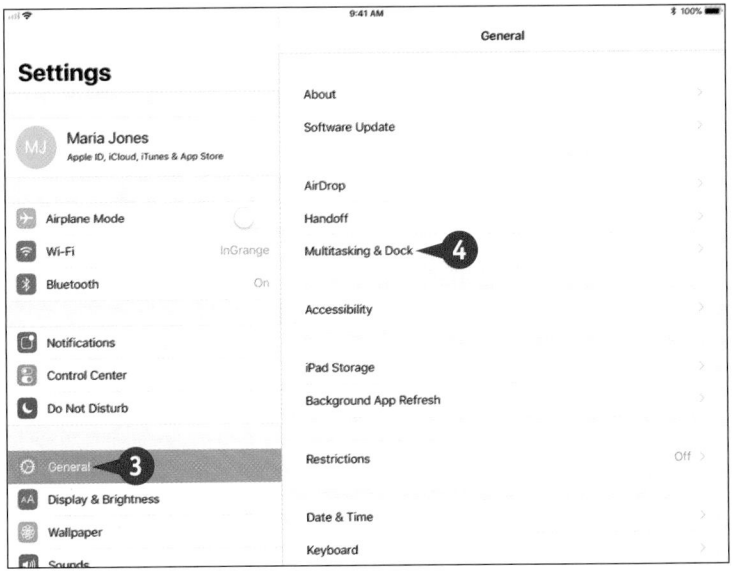

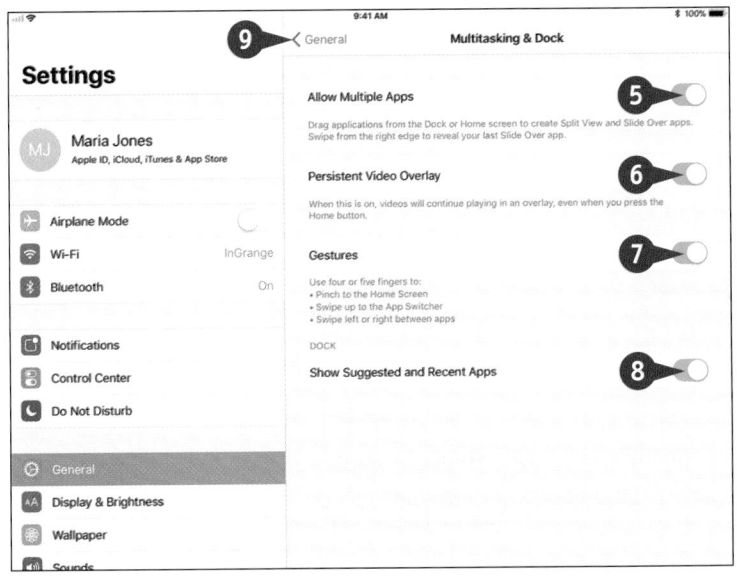

Use Two Apps with Slide Over and Split View

1. With an app open that you want to use, swipe up a short way from the bottom of the screen.

Note: You can use the multitasking views in either landscape orientation or portrait orientation.

The Dock appears.

2. Tap and hold the icon for the app you want to display, and then drag upward from the Dock.

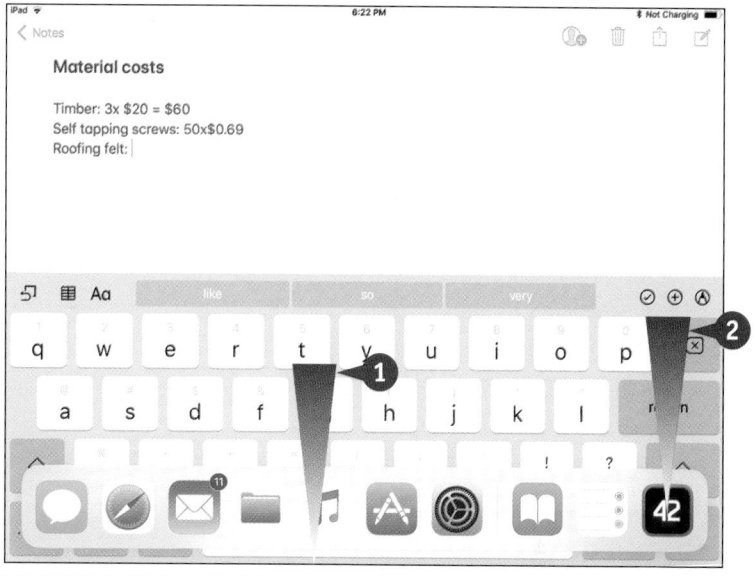

A thumbnail for the app appears.

3. Release the app's icon.

TIP

What multitasking gestures can I use on my iPad?

To display the Home screen, place four or five fingers apart on the screen and pinch them together.

To display the App Switcher, swipe up from the bottom of the screen with four or five fingers.

To switch among running apps, swipe left or right with four or five fingers.

continued ▶

You can multitask with many of the apps that come with your iPad and with many third-party apps. But some apps cannot run in either Slide Over or Split View. For example, the Settings app can run only full-screen, so you cannot multitask with it. Other apps can run in Slide Over but not in Split View.

Multitask with Split-Screen Views (continued)

The app appears in Slide Over view on the right side of the screen.

You can start using the app.

Note: You can also open other apps in Slide Over view. Each app you open appears over the previous Slide Over app.

A You can drag the app's handle to the left to move the Slide Over app to the left side of the screen.

4 Drag the app's handle down a short way.

iOS switches the app to Slide Over view.

The app appears in a separate pane, taking up the right-hand third of the screen.

The other app occupies the left-hand two-thirds of the screen.

5 Drag the handle on the divider bar between the apps to the left.

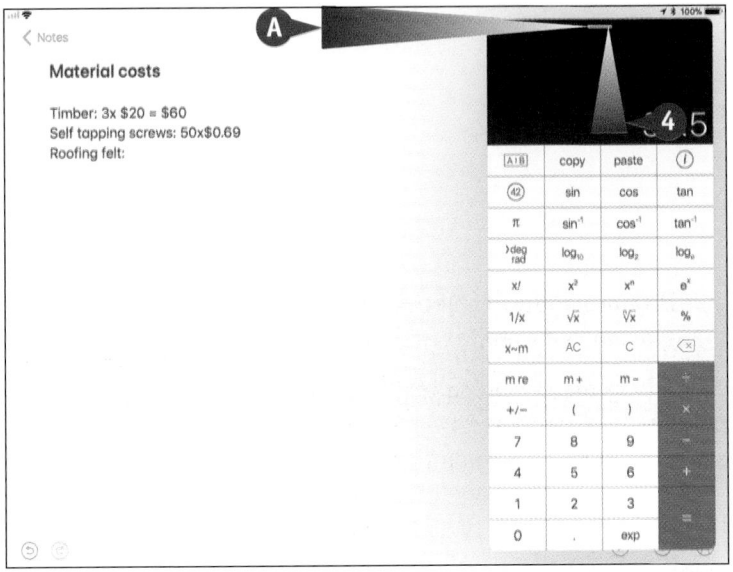

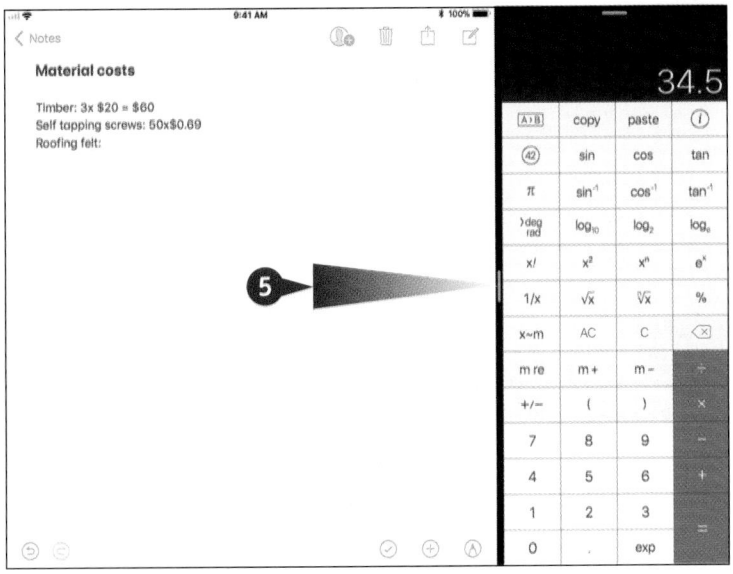

iOS changes the division of the screen between the apps.

6 When the division is where you want it, lift your finger.

The apps appear in the panes, and you can work in either app.

Note: Drag the handle on the divider bar all the way to the left to switch the right-hand app to full-screen. Drag the handle all the way to the right to switch the left-hand app to full-screen.

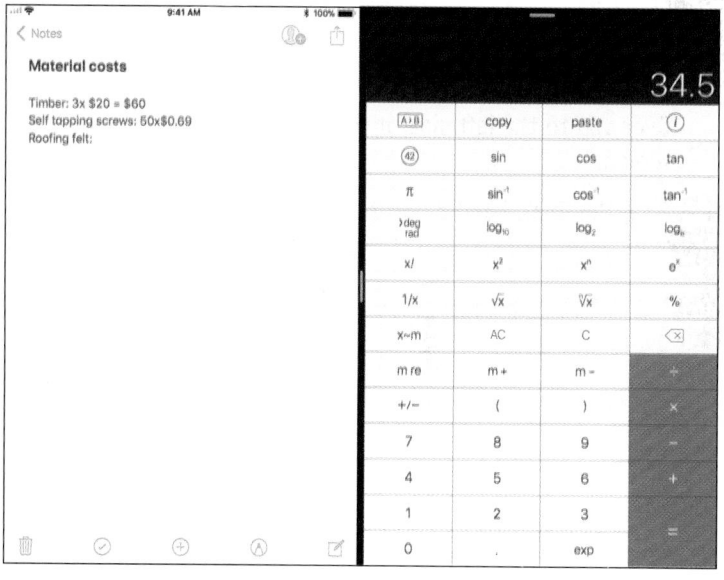

TIP

Do the split-screen and pop-up features work with all iPad models?

The Split View feature requires an iPad Air 2 or later model, such as an iPad mini 4 or an iPad Pro.

The Slide Over feature and the Picture-in-Picture feature both require an iPad mini 2, an iPad Air, an iPad Pro, or a later model.

continued ▶

The Picture-in-Picture feature enables you to switch a video you are playing from full-screen to a small floating window. You can reposition the floating window in any of the four quadrants of the screen so that you can continue to watch the video while working in another app — or in two other apps using Slide Over or Split View.

The Picture-in-Picture feature works only on recent iPad models, such as the iPad mini 2, iPad mini 4, iPad Air 2, the iPad Pro, and later models.

Multitask with Split-Screen Views (continued)

Use the Picture-in-Picture Feature

1. Press **Home**.

   The Home screen appears.

2. Tap **TV** ( ).

Note: You can also use Picture-in-Picture with other apps, such as YouTube and Safari.

   The TV app opens.

3. Navigate to and tap the video you want to view, and then tap **Play** ( ).

   The video starts playing.

B You can tap **Picture-in-Picture** ( ) to shrink the video to a floating window without displaying the Home screen.

4. Press **Home**.

   The video shrinks down to a floating window and continues playing unless you pause it.

   The Home screen appears, with the video window floating above it.

5. Tap the app you want to launch. This example uses **Notes** ( ).

The app opens.

Note: If you last used the app in Slide Over or in Split View with another app, the app appears in that view with that app next to it.

6. Tap the video window and drag it to the quadrant where you want it.
7. Work in the app you have launched.
8. Tap the video window.

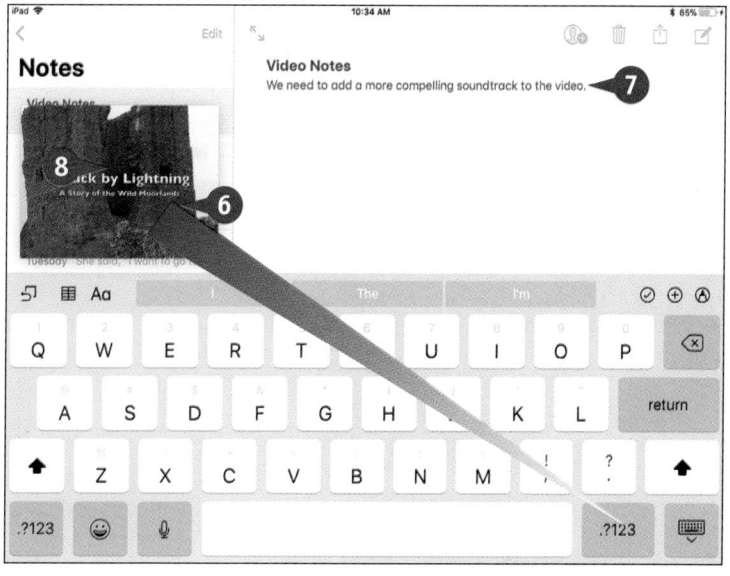

The video controls appear.

Note: The video controls disappear after a few seconds if you do not use them.

C. You can tap **Pause** ( ) to pause playback.
D. You can tap **Full Screen** ( ) to switch the video back to full-screen.
E. You can tap **Close** ( ) to close the video window.

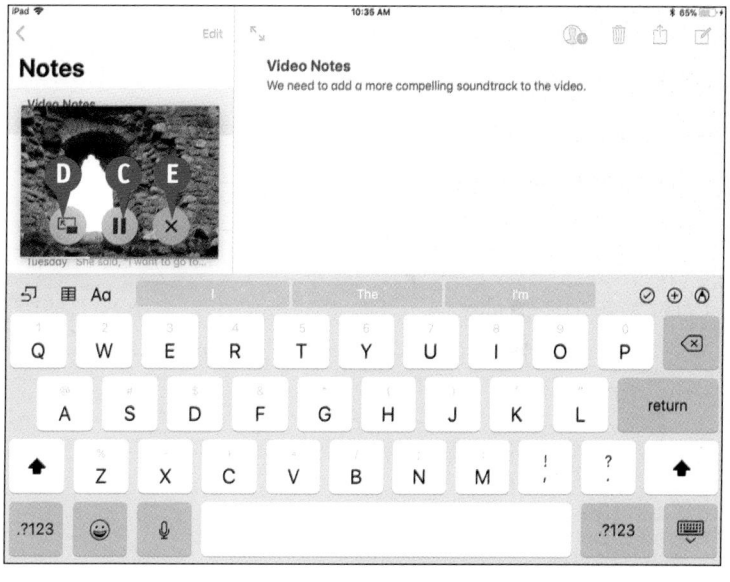

TIP

How do I resize the video window?
As of this writing, you cannot resize the video window. The video window size and aspect ratio vary somewhat depending on the resolution of the video you are playing.

Find the Apps You Need

The iPad comes with essential apps, such as Safari for surfing the web, Mail for e-mail, and Calendar for keeping your schedule. But to get the most out of your iPad, you will likely need to add other apps.

To get apps, you use the App Store, which provides apps that Apple has approved as correctly programmed, suitable for their intended purpose, and free of malevolent code. Before you can download any apps, including free apps, you must create an App Store account.

Find the Apps You Need

1. Press **Home**.

   The Home screen appears.

2. Tap **App Store** ( ).

   The App Store app opens.

3. Tap **Apps** (changes to).

   The Apps screen appears.

4. Swipe up to scroll down.

   A If you need to change the Apple ID for the App Store, tap **Account** ( ). In the Account dialog that opens, tap **Sign Out**. Then tap **Sign In** and specify the other Apple ID.

   Further lists on the Apps screen appear.

5. Tap **See All** or the category or group you want to see.

Note: Apple ties each app you buy or get for free from the App Store to the Apple ID you use. To avoid confusion, use the same Apple ID for each app you get. When setting up the Apple ID, use an e-mail address you plan to use for the long term. If you change your Apple ID or e-mail address, you will need to re-authenticate your apps.

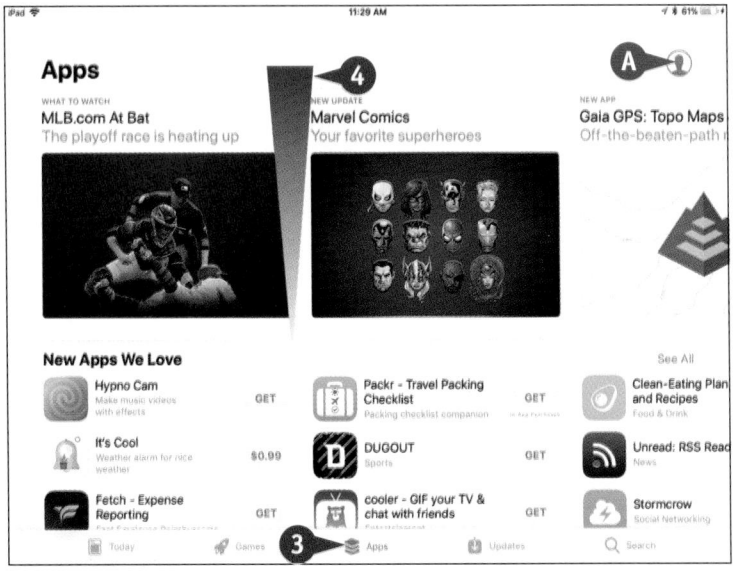

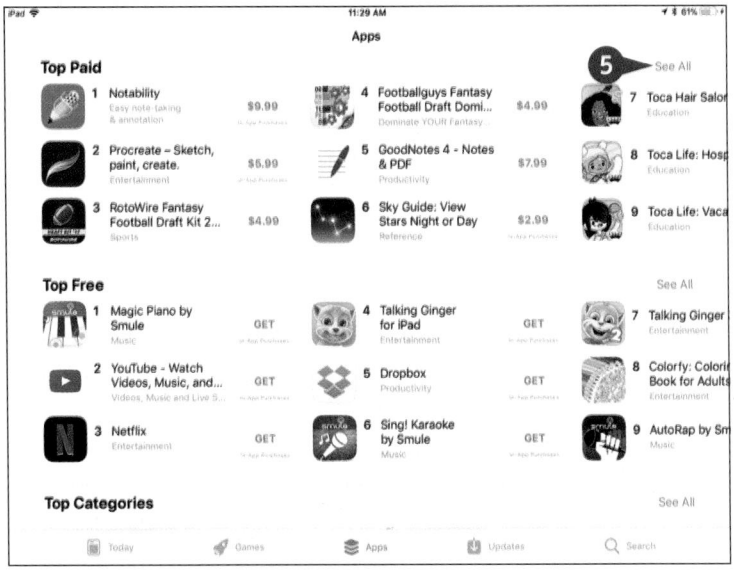

The linked screen appears, showing its lists of apps.

Note: Swipe up to see more apps in a list.

6 Tap the app you want to view.

The app's screen appears.

Note: To understand what an app does and how well it does it, look at the app's rating, read the description, and look through the user reviews.

B You can tap **More** (•••) to share the app's details with others via e-mail, messaging, AirDrop, or other means.

7 Tap the price button or the **Get** button.

The price button or Get button changes to an Install App button.

8 Tap **Install App**.

9 If the iPad prompts you to sign in, type your password and then tap **OK**.

Note: If you have not created an App Store account already, the iPad prompts you to create one now.

The iPad downloads and installs the app.

10 Tap **Open** to launch the app.

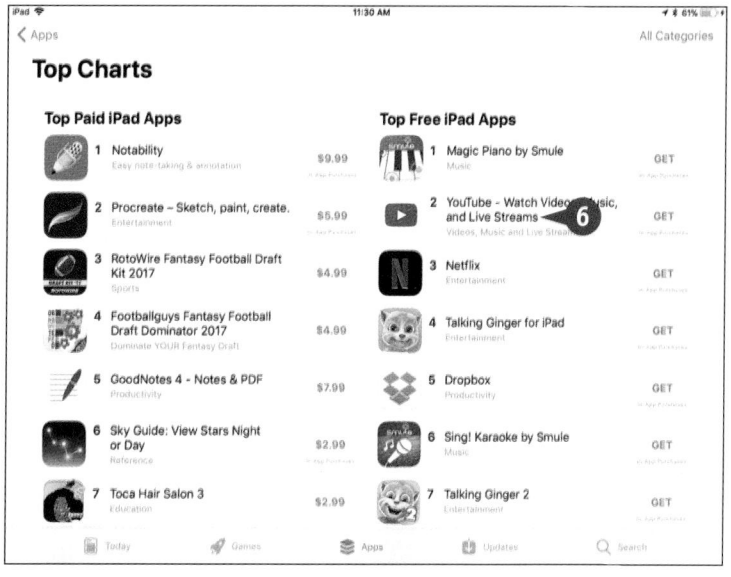

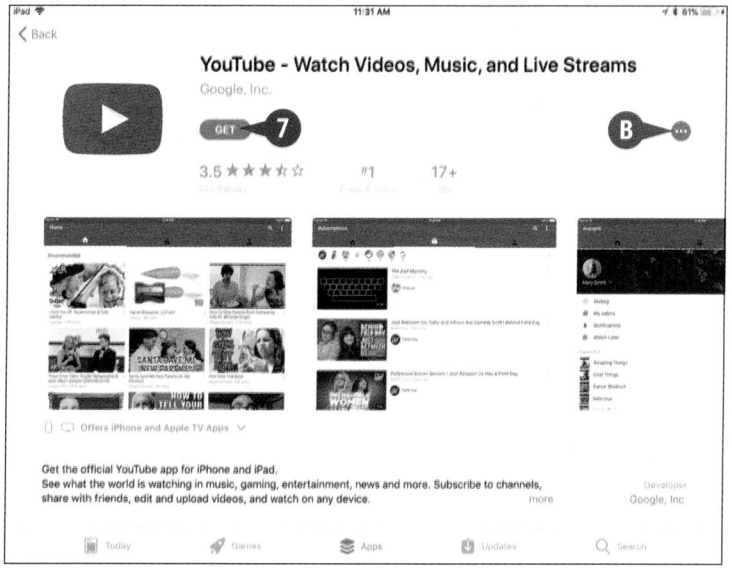

TIP

Why does the App Store not appear on the Home screen or when I search?

If the App Store does not appear on the Home screen, and if searching for it does not show a result, the iPad has restrictions applied that prevent you from installing apps. You can remove these restrictions if you know the restrictions passcode. Press **Home**, tap **Settings** (⚙), and then tap **General** (⚙). Scroll down, and then tap **Restrictions**. Type the passcode in the Enter Passcode dialog, and then set the **Installing Apps** switch to On (changes to).

Update and Remove Apps

To keep the apps running smoothly on your iPad, you should install app updates when they become available. Most updates for paid apps are free, but you must usually pay to upgrade to a new version of the app. You can download and install updates using the App Store app on your iPad.

When you no longer need an app, you can remove it from the iPad and recover the space it was occupying.

Update and Remove Apps

Update an App

1. Press **Home**.

   The Home screen appears.

   A The badge on the App Store icon shows the number of available updates.

2. Tap **App Store** ( ).

   The App Store app opens.

   The Updates screen appears.

3. Tap **Updates** (changes to).

   B You can tap **Update** to update a single app.

4. Tap **Update All**.

Note: If the Apple ID Password dialog opens, type your password and then tap **OK**.

   Your iPad downloads and installs the updates.

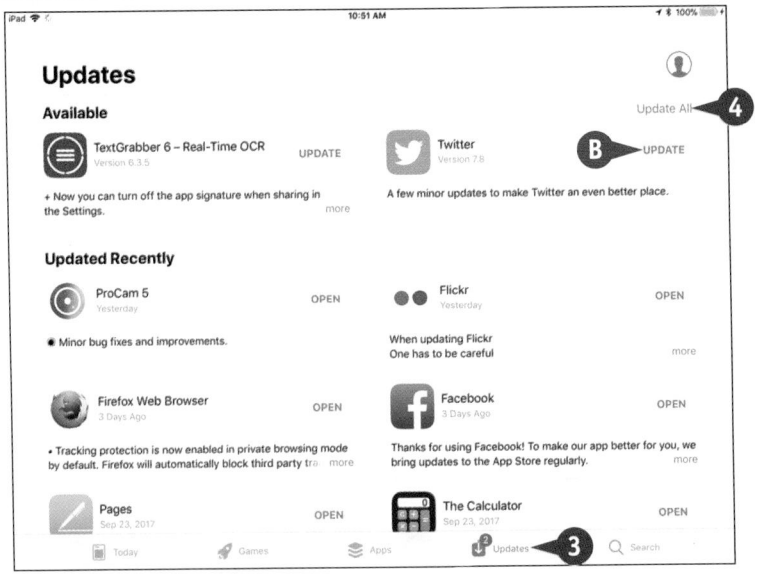

Remove an App from the iPad

1. Press **Home**.

   The Home screen appears.

2. Display the Home screen that contains the app you want to delete.

3. Tap and hold the item until the icons start to jiggle.

4. Tap **Delete** (⊗) on the icon.

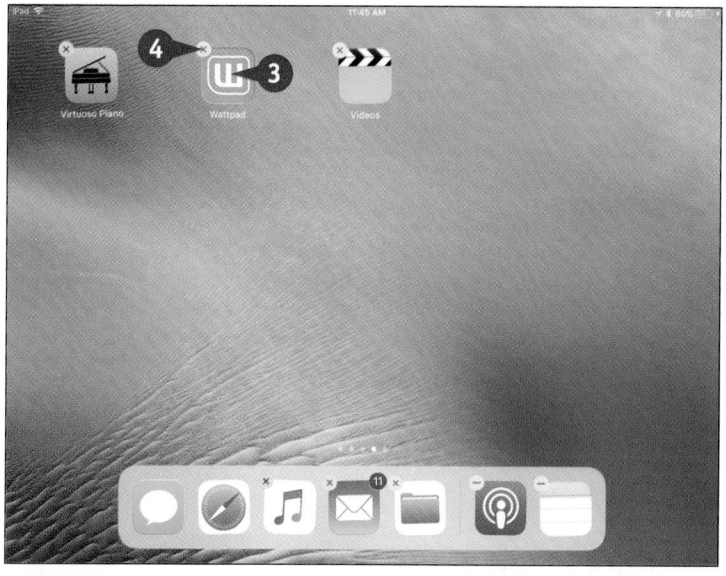

   The Delete dialog appears.

5. Tap **Delete**.

   The iPad deletes the app, and the app's icon disappears.

6. Press **Home**.

   The icons stop jiggling.

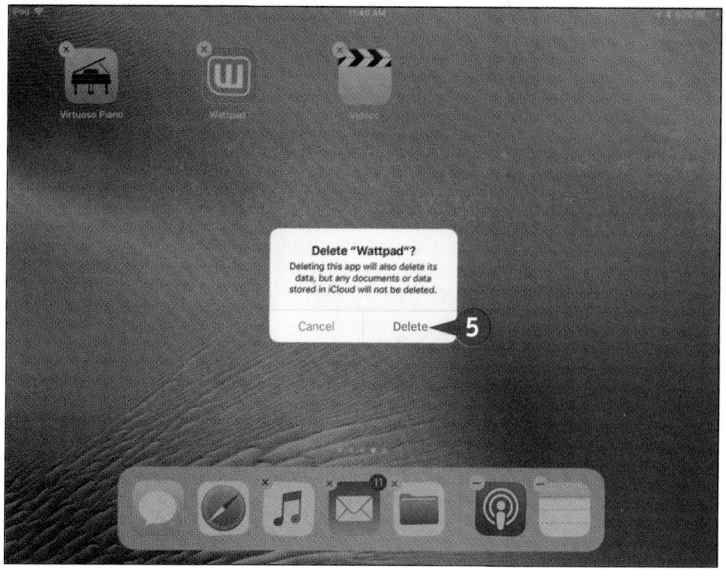

TIP

Can I reinstall an app after removing it?

Yes, you can easily reinstall an app. Press **Home**, tap **App Store** (Ⓐ), and then tap Updates (⬇). Tap Account (👤) to open the Account dialog, and then tap **Purchased** to open the All Purchases dialog. Tap the **Not on This iPad** tab at the top and locate the app; you can then tap **Search Purchased Apps** and search by keyword if necessary. Then tap **Install** (☁) to install the app.

Manage Automatic Downloads and Your Apple ID

The App Store and iTunes Store can automatically download apps, music, and other content for you. You can turn off automatic downloads if you prefer to keep manual control, and on a cellular iPad, you can control whether downloads can use the cellular network.

From the iTunes & App Store screen in the Settings app, you can also view the details of your current Apple ID and switch from one Apple ID to another.

Manage Automatic Downloads and Your Apple ID

Choose Which Items to Download Automatically

1. Press **Home**.

   The Home screen appears.

2. Tap **Settings** ( ).

   The Settings screen appears.

3. Tap **iTunes & App Store** ( ).

   The iTunes & App Stores screen appears.

4. Set the **Music** switch, **Apps** switch, **Books & Audiobooks** switch, and **Updates** switch to On ( ) or Off ( ), as needed, to specify which items to download automatically.

5. Tap **Video Autoplay** to display the Video Autoplay screen; tap **On**, **Wi-Fi Only**, or **Off**, as needed; and then tap **iTunes & App Stores** ( ).

6. Set the **In-App Ratings & Reviews** switch to On ( ) if you agree to allow apps to prompt you for feedback.

7. Set the **Offload Unused Apps** switch to On ( ) if you want iOS to automatically remove unused apps.

8. Tap **Password Settings**.

   The Password Settings screen appears.

9. In the Purchases and In-App Purchases box, tap **Always Require** or **Require After 15 Minutes**, as needed.

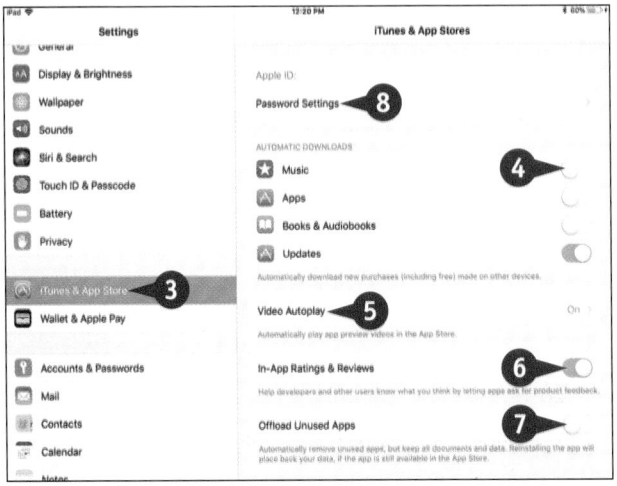

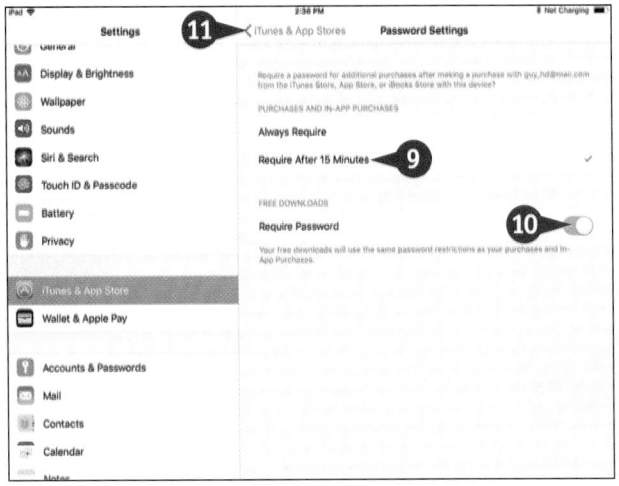

10. If you choose Require After 15 Minutes, set the **Require Password** switch to On ( ) or Off ( ), as needed.

11. Tap **iTunes & App Stores** ( ).

Switch Apple ID or View Its Details

1. On the iTunes & App Stores screen in the Settings app, tap **Apple ID**.

   The Apple ID dialog opens.

2. To switch the Apple ID, tap **Sign Out**.
3. Tap **Apple ID** and type the e-mail address for the Apple ID you want to use.
4. Tap **Password** and type the password.
5. Tap **Sign In**.

   Your iPad signs in using the Apple ID.

6. To view the details of your current Apple ID, tap **View Apple ID**.

   The Account dialog opens.

7. Examine the Apple ID as needed:

   A. Tap **Apple ID** to display the My Apple ID web page in Safari.

   B. Tap **Family Sharing** to view Family Sharing information.

   C. Tap **Payment Information** to display an Account dialog that contains your credit- or debit-card details.

   D. Tap **Country/Region** to change your country or region.

8. Tap **Done** when you finish reviewing your Apple ID.

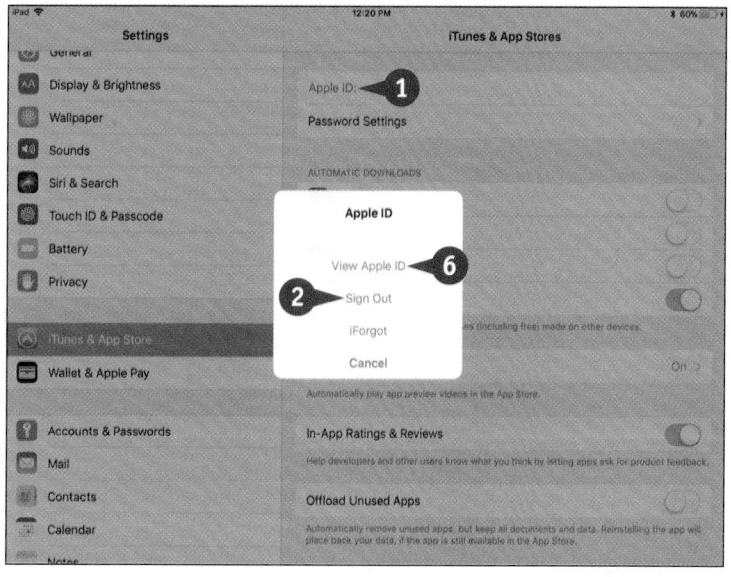

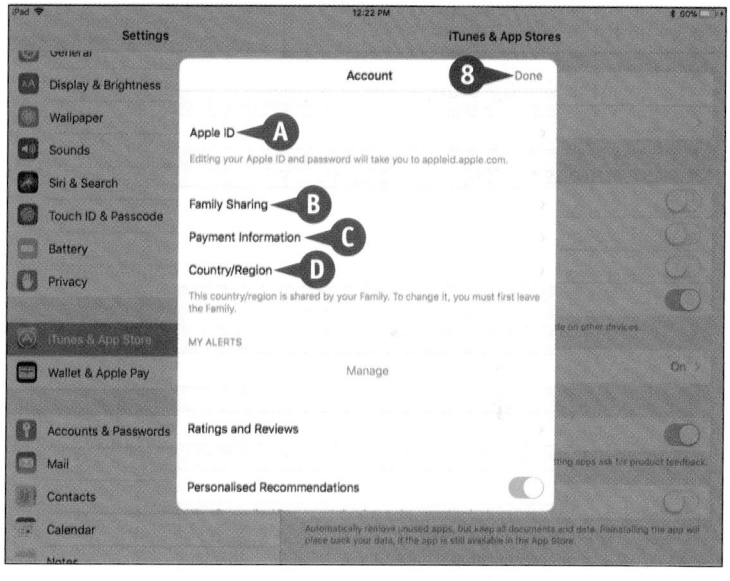

TIP

Is it a good idea to download items automatically?

Whether you download items automatically is up to you, but having the items appear on your iPad without your intervention is often helpful. If your iPad has cellular capability and you set the **App Store** switch to On (◐) on the Cellular Data screen in Settings, monitor your data usage carefully. Most e-book files are small, but music and video files can go through your cellular allowance quickly. Be especially careful about downloading apps automatically, because some of them are huge. You may prefer to allow automatic downloads but set the **App Store** switch to Off ( ), restricting automatic downloads to Wi-Fi.

Manage Files with the Files App

The Files app enables you to work with files stored on your iPad; files stored on network servers, such as macOS Server; and files stored on online storage services, such as iCloud Drive. You can quickly locate files by using the Recents screen, by using the Browse screen, or by searching by keyword. You can also recover recently deleted files by using the Recently Deleted Location. You navigate the Files app using similar techniques to those for navigating file-opening and file-saving features within apps.

Manage Files with the Files App

Open the Files App

1. Press **Home**.

   The Home screen appears.

2. Tap **Files** ( ).

   The Files app opens.

3. Tap **Browse** (changes to).

   The Browse screen appears.

A The Recently Deleted location contains files that you have deleted recently, somewhat like the Trash on macOS or the Recycle Bin on Windows. To retrieve a deleted file, tap **Recently Deleted**, tap and hold the file, and then tap **Recover** on the command bar that appears.

Browse Files and Open Files

1. Tap **Recents** (changes to).

   The Recents screen appears.

B You can search your recent files by tapping **Search** ( ) and then typing a search term.

C Some of your most recent files appear at the top.

D Older files appear listed by their tags, such as the Health tag and the Important tag in this example.

2. Tap **Browse** (changes to).

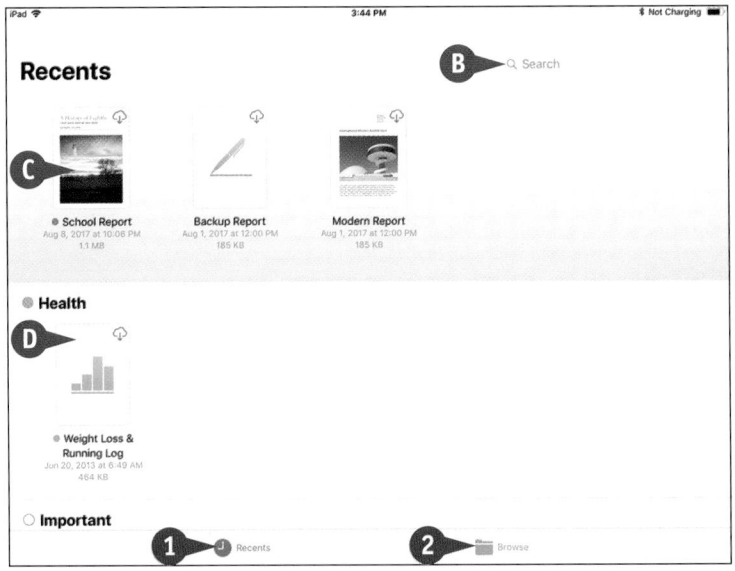

The Browse screen appears.

E You can search all your files by tapping **Search** (🔍) and then typing a search term.

3 Tap the location you want to browse. This example uses iCloud Drive.

The screen for the location appears.

4 Tap the folder you want to open.

The folder opens and its contents appear.

F You can tap **Download** (☁) to download a file stored online to your iPad.

5 Tap the file you want to open.

The file opens in the default app for the file type, assuming your iPad has such an app.

The app appears, and you can work on the file.

Note: You can open only those files for which your iPad contains a suitable app. If there is no suitable app, Files displays the file for viewing if it has a suitable viewer, but you cannot change the file.

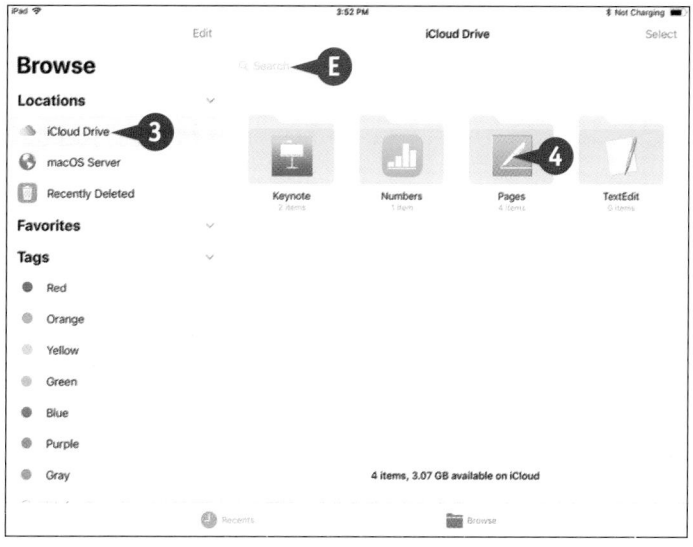

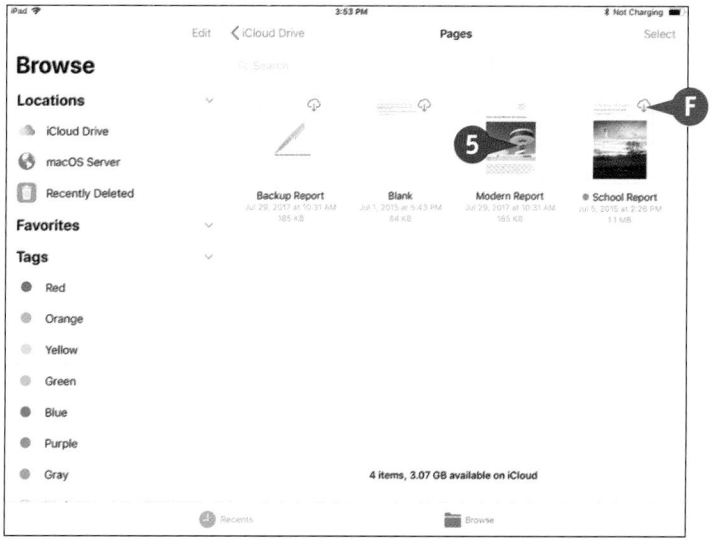

TIP

How do I add locations to the Locations list?

You add locations — such as OneDrive, Google Drive, or Dropbox — by adding accounts for those locations in the Settings app. Press **Home** to display the Home screen, and then tap **Settings** (⚙) to display the Settings screen. Tap **Accounts & Passwords** (🔑) to display the Accounts & Passwords screen, and then tap **Add Account**. On the Add Account screen, tap the account type. To add an account type that does not appear on the Add Account screen, tap **Other** to display the Other screen, and then tap the button for the account type, such as **Add macOS Server Account**.

continued ▶

As well as opening a file, the Files app enables you to take other actions with a file, such as renaming it, copying it and pasting a copy, duplicating it in the same location, or moving it to another location.

The Files app also enables you to use tags to group and sort your files. The Files app comes with default tags with color names, such as Red and Orange, but you can customize the names and create new tags as needed.

Manage Files with the Files App (continued)

Take Other Actions with a File

1. Tap and hold the file you want to affect.

   The control bar appears.

   - G Tap **Copy** to copy the file. Navigate to where you want to paste the copy, tap and hold open space, and then tap **Paste** on the control bar.
   - H Tap **Duplicate** to create a duplicate file in the same folder.
   - I Tap **Rename** to display the Rename Document screen. Type the new name, and then tap **Done**.
   - J Tap **Move** to display a screen for moving the file. Tap the location, and then tap **Move**.
   - K Tap **Delete** to delete the file.
   - L Tap **Share** to open the Share sheet for sharing the file.
   - M Tap **Info** to display information about the file.

2. Tap **Tags**.

   The Tags panel opens.

3. Tap each tag you want to apply to the file. Also tap any applied tag that you want to remove.

4. Tap outside the Tags panel.

   The Tags panel closes.

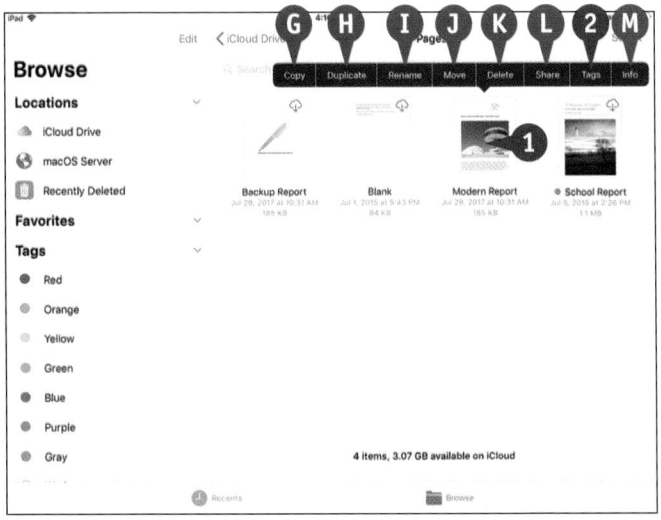

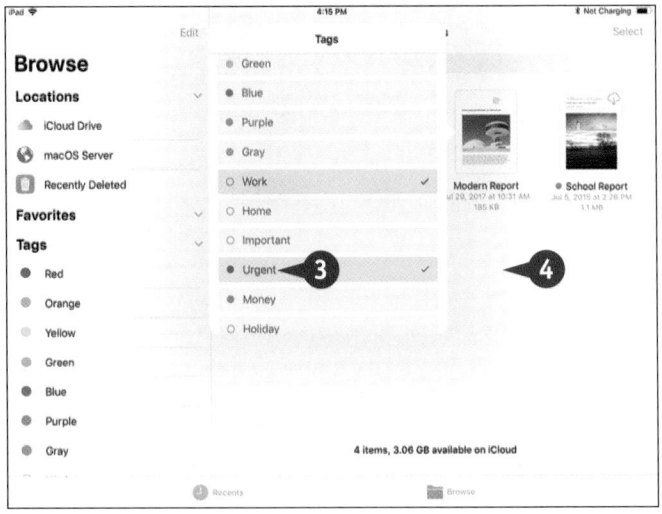

Organize Your Locations and Tags

1. Tap **Browse** (changes to).

   The Browse screen appears.

2. Tap **Edit**.

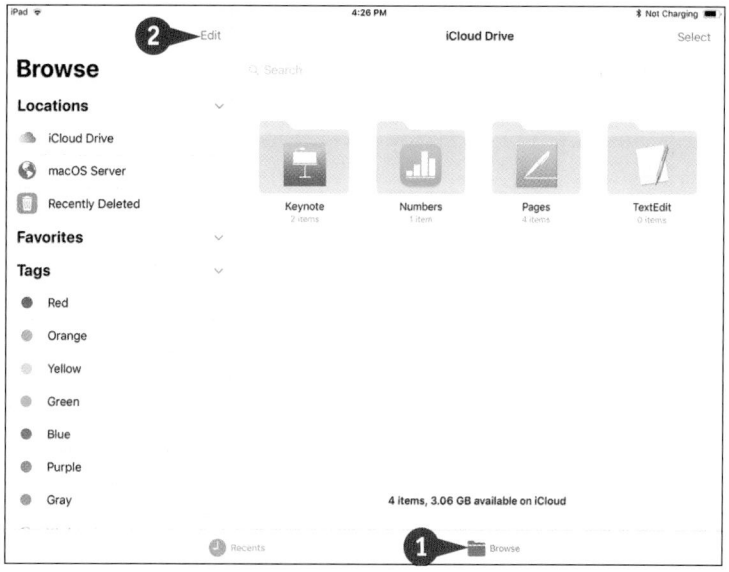

   The Browse screen switches to Edit Mode.

3. In the Locations list, set a switch to Off (changes to) if you want to hide the location.

4. Tap a handle and drag a location up or down, as needed.

5. In the Tags list, tap **Delete** ( ) and then tap **Delete** to delete a tag.

6. To change the tag order, tap the handle ( ) and drag the tag up or down the list.

7. To rename a tag, tap it, and then type the new name.

8. When you finish editing the Browse screen, tap **Done**.

   The Browse screen switches off Edit Mode.

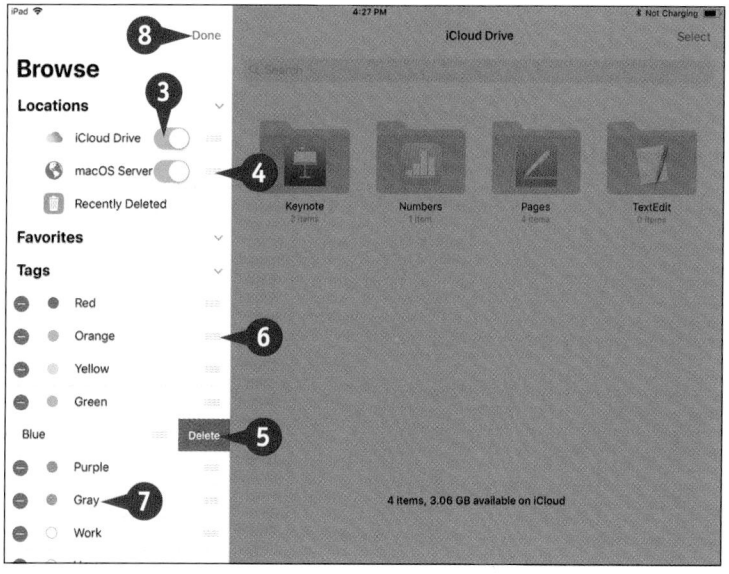

TIP

Can I move or delete multiple files at once?

Yes, you can take several actions with multiple files in the same folder — but only on iCloud Drive and On My iPad as of this writing. First, navigate to that folder, and then tap **Select** to switch to Selection Mode. Tap each item to select it (changes to). After selecting the items, tap the appropriate button at the bottom of the screen — **Share, Duplicate**, **Move**, or **Delete** — and then follow the prompts to complete the action.

Enter Text Quickly in Apps

Even though your iPad does not come with a physical keyboard, it offers powerful time-saving features that enable you to enter text quickly in the apps you use. You can split and reposition the on-screen keyboard to make it easier to use, or keep it in its standard docked position. You can enter words more quickly by accepting predictive text suggestions. And you can configure keyboard settings and create your own shortcuts to enter boilerplate text quickly.

Enter Text Quickly in Apps

Undock and Split the Keyboard and Use Predictions

1. In an app that supports text input, tap a text field.

   The keyboard appears in its docked position at the bottom of the screen.

2. Tap and hold **Hide Keyboard** ( ).

   The keyboard pop-up menu opens.

3. Tap **Undock**.

   The keyboard moves up the screen.

4. Start typing a word.

   Suggested words or phrases appear.

5. Tap the word or phrase you want to insert.

6. Tap and hold **Hide Keyboard** ( ).

7. Tap **Split**.

   The keyboard splits.

Note: With the keyboard split, you can type using "ghost" keys on the opposite side of the keyboard. For example, tap to the right of the T key to type **Y**, and tap to the left of the Y key to type **T**.

Note: Tap and drag **Hide Keyboard** ( ) to move the undocked or split keyboard up or down.

8. Tap and hold **Hide Keyboard** ( ).

9. Tap **Merge** or **Dock and Merge**, as needed.

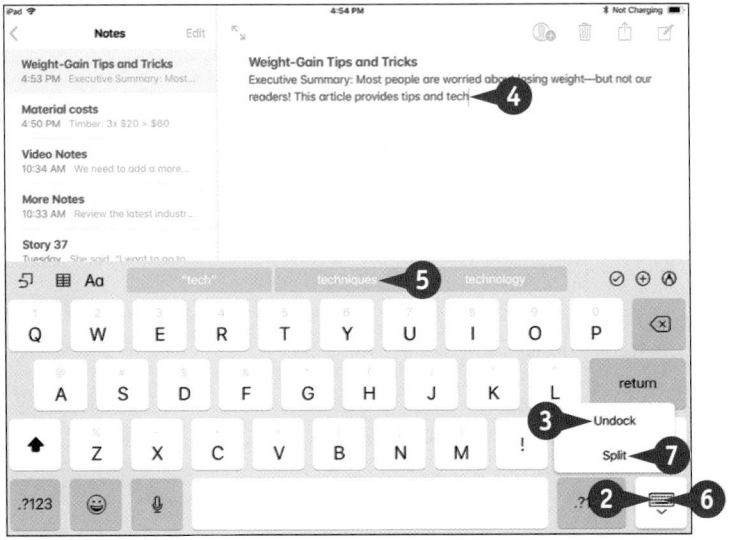

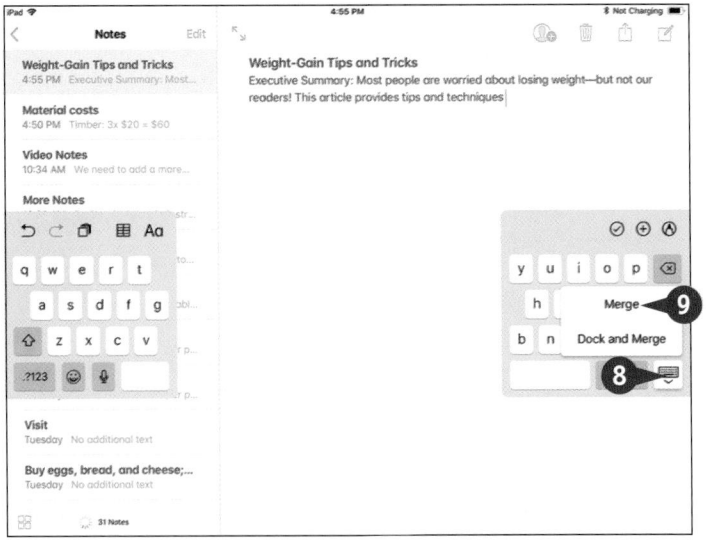

Configure Keyboard Settings and Create Shortcuts

1. Press **Home**.
2. Tap **Settings** ( ).

   The Settings screen appears.
3. Tap **General** ( ).

   The General screen appears.
4. Tap **Keyboard**.

   The Keyboards screen appears.
5. Set the **Auto-Capitalization** switch, **Auto-Correction** switch, **Check Spelling** switch, **Enable Caps Lock** switch, **Shortcuts** switch, **Predictive** switch, **Smart Punctuation** switch, **Split Keyboard** switch, **Enable Key Flicks** switch, and **"." Shortcut** switch to On ( ) or Off ( ), as needed.

Note: The "." Shortcut switch enables you to type a period by pressing Spacebar twice in quick succession.

6. Tap **Text Replacement**.

   The Text Replacement screen appears.
7. Tap **Add** (+).
8. Type the word or phrase.
9. Type the shortcut to use for entering the word or phrase.
10. Tap **Save**.

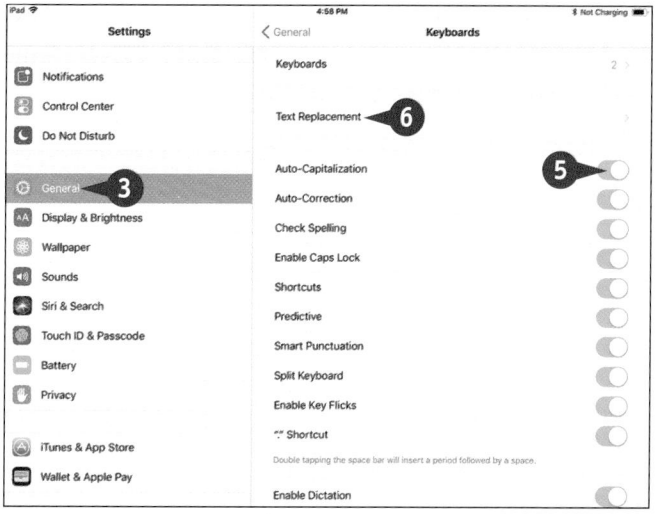

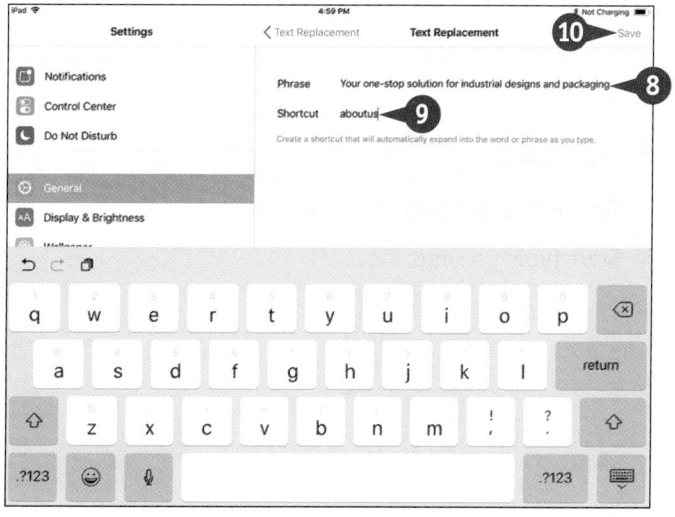

Note: To prevent the spell checker from querying a word, create a shortcut with the word as the phrase text but with no shortcut. The spell checker then accepts the word as correct.

TIP

How do I type characters — such as accents — that do not appear on the keyboard?
Tap and hold a key on the on-screen keyboard to display a pop-up panel of related characters, slide your finger to the character you want to enter, and then lift your finger. For example, tap and hold A to enter characters such as á, à, or ä. Only some characters have these pop-up panels.

Cut, Copy, and Paste Text

Your iPad enables you to copy existing text and paste it elsewhere. For example, you can copy text from a note and paste it into an e-mail message you are composing.

If the text is in a document you can edit, you can cut — remove — the text from the document instead of copying it. If the text is in a document you cannot edit, you can copy the text but not cut it.

Cut, Copy, and Paste Text

Select and Copy Text

1. Tap and hold a word in the text you want to copy.

Note: If the text is editable, either double-tap a word to select it, or tap the word to position the insertion point and then tap **Select** on the command bar to display the selection handles.

- A A selection highlight with handles appears around the word.
- B The command bar appears above the selection.

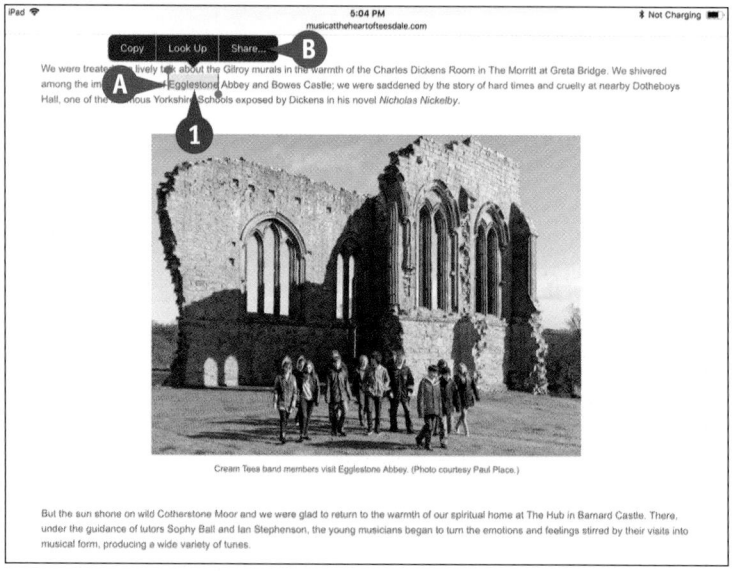

2. Drag the handles of the selection highlight around the text that you want.
3. Tap **Copy**.

Note: If the text is editable, you can tap **Cut** on the command bar to cut the text from the document, placing it on the Clipboard.

Your iPad places the text on the Clipboard, a hidden storage area.

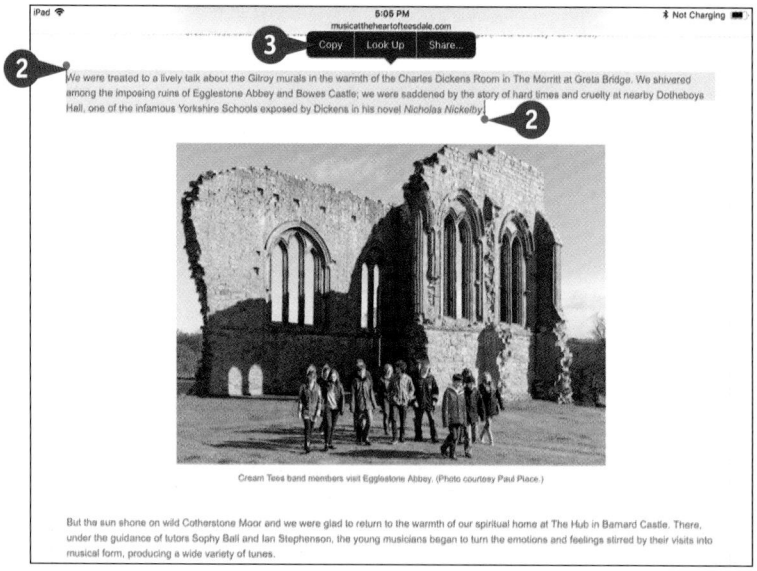

Paste the Content You Have Copied or Cut

1. Open the app in which you want to paste the text.

Note: This example shows text being pasted into a new message in the Mail app.

2. Tap where you want to paste the text.

C In some apps, you can also tap **Paste** (⧉) on the bar above the keyboard to paste.

3. Tap **Paste**.

D The pasted text appears in the document.

Note: You can store only one item on the Clipboard at a time. Each item you cut or copy replaces the existing item on the Clipboard. But until you replace the existing item on the Clipboard, you can paste it as many times as needed.

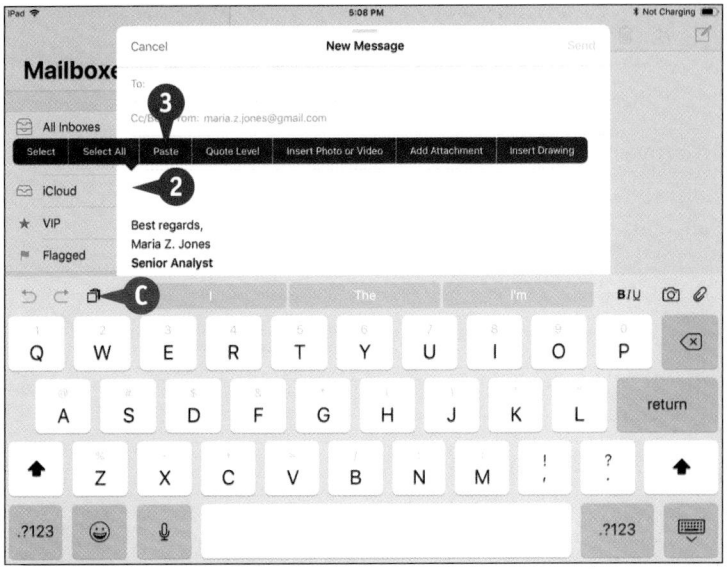

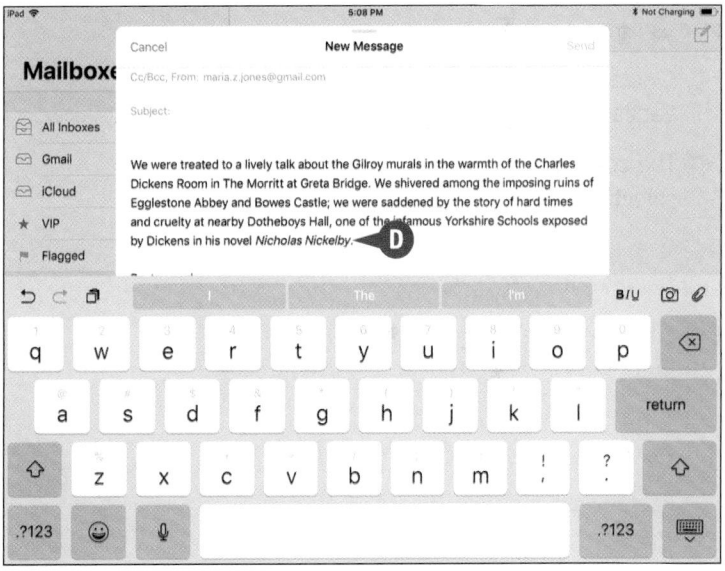

TIP

Can I transfer the contents of the Clipboard to my computer?
If you log in to a Mac running macOS Sierra, macOS High Sierra, or a later version, using the same iCloud account as the iPad, you may be able to use the Universal Clipboard feature. Try copying an item on the iPad and then giving the Paste command on the Mac, or vice versa. Otherwise, transfer the Clipboard's contents indirectly — for example, paste content into an e-mail message and send it to yourself.

Bold, Italicize, Underline, and Replace Text

Some apps enable you to add formatting such as boldface, underline, and italics to text to make parts of it stand out. For example, you can apply formatting in e-mail messages you create using the Mail app and in various apps for creating word-processing documents.

To apply formatting, you first select the text, and then choose options from the pop-up command bar. Some apps also offer other text commands, such as replacing a word or phrase from a menu of suggestions.

Bold, Italicize, Underline, and Replace Text

Apply Bold, Italics, and Underline

1. Tap and hold the text to which you want to apply bold, italics, or underline.

   A command bar appears.

2. Tap **Select**.

Note: Some apps have their own formatting tools, many of which are more extensive than the standard formatting tools shown here.

Note: Some e-mail services and notes services do not support formatting.

   Part of the text is highlighted and handles appear.

3. Drag the handles to select the text that you want to bold, italicize, or underline.

4. Tap the **BIU** button in the command bar.

   A In some apps, you can also tap **BIU** on the bar above the keyboard to display a formatting bar.

   The command bar displays formatting options.

5. Tap **Bold**, **Italics**, or **Underline**, as needed.

   The text takes on the formatting you chose.

6. Tap outside the selected text to deselect it.

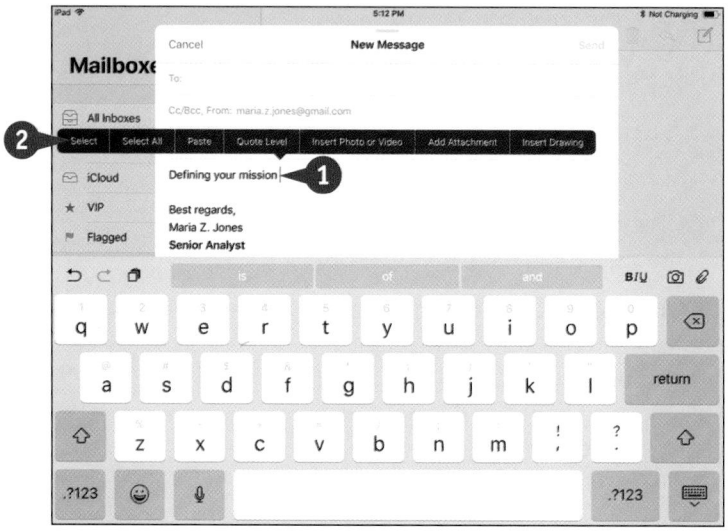

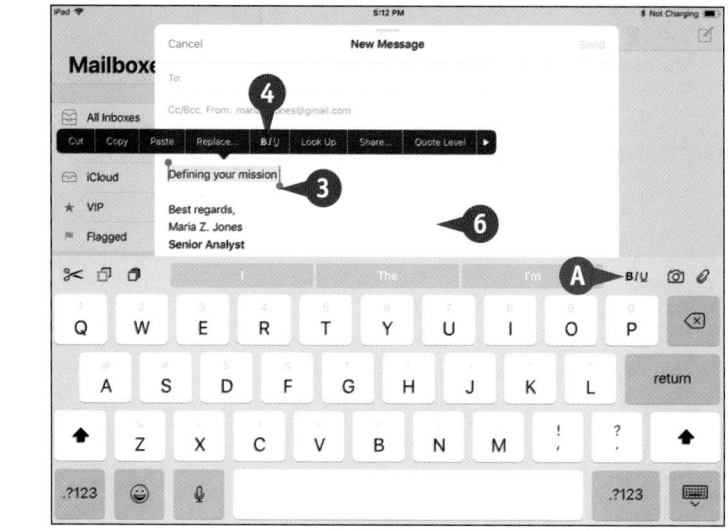

Replace Text with Suggested Words

1. Double-tap the word you want to replace.

Note: You can tap and hold in the word, and then tap **Select** on the command bar to select the word.

Selection handles appear around the word.

The command bar appears.

2. Tap **Replace**.

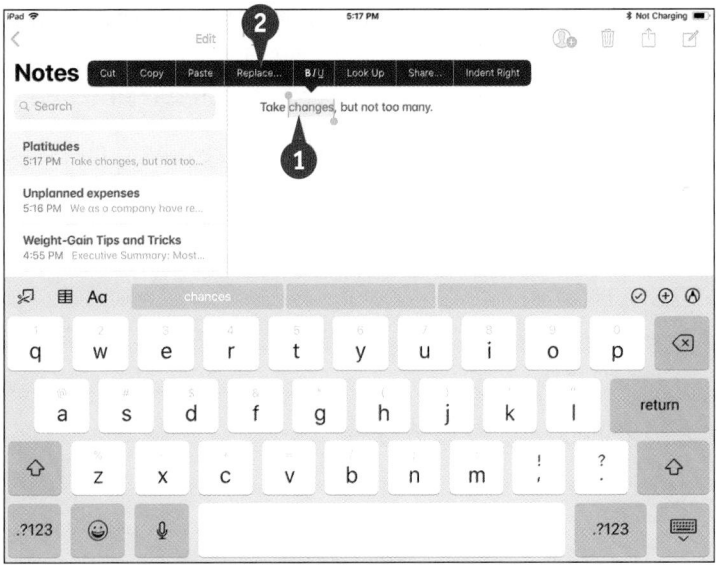

The command bar displays suggested replacement words.

3. Tap the word with which you want to replace the selected word.

Your iPad replaces the word.

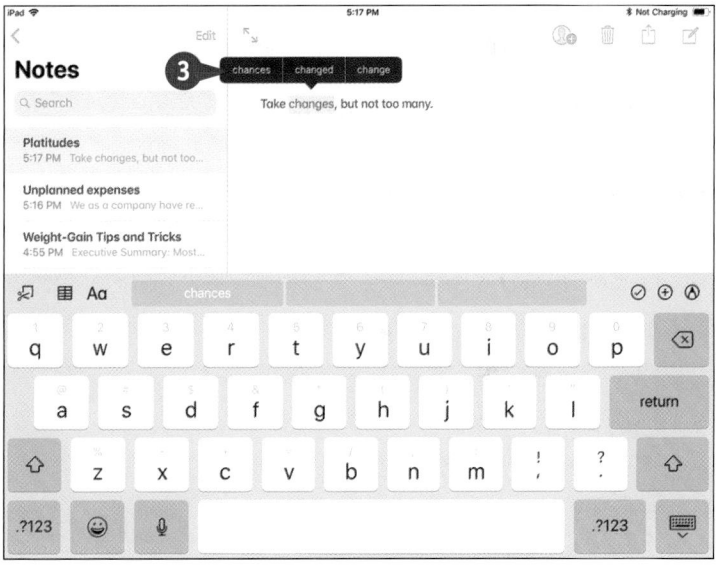

TIP

What does the Quote Level button on the command bar in Mail do?

Tap the **Quote Level** button when you need to increase or decrease the quote level of your selected text. When you tap Quote Level, the command bar displays an Increase button and a Decrease button. Tap **Increase** to increase the quote level, indenting the text more, or **Decrease** to decrease the quote level, reducing the existing indent.

Take Screenshots and Use Instant Markup

iOS includes an easy shortcut for taking a screenshot, a picture that captures whatever currently appears on the screen. Screenshots can be useful for recording items you want to remember or for capturing the details of a problem so that you can report it to tech support.

iOS also provides an Instant Markup feature that you can use to annotate screenshots or other pictures. Instant Markup can include pen drawings, text, and signatures.

Take Screenshots and Use Instant Markup

1. Set up the screen to show the content you want to capture.
2. Press **Sleep/Wake** and **Home** at the same time.

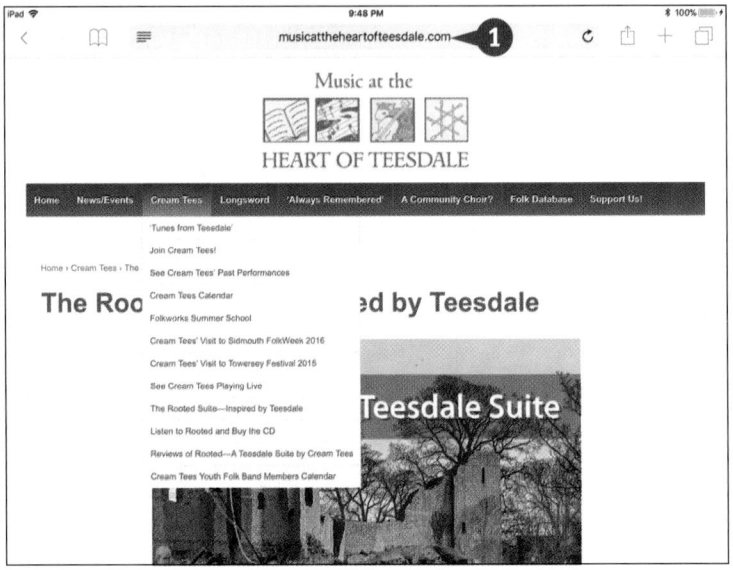

iOS captures the screen.

A A thumbnail of the screenshot appears.

Note: If you do not want to annotate the screenshot, wait a few seconds, and iOS removes the thumbnail from the screen automatically. Alternatively, swipe the thumbnail left off the screen.

Note: The thumbnail does not appear in screenshots, so if you want to take another screenshot immediately, you do not need to remove the thumbnail from the screen first.

3. Tap the thumbnail.

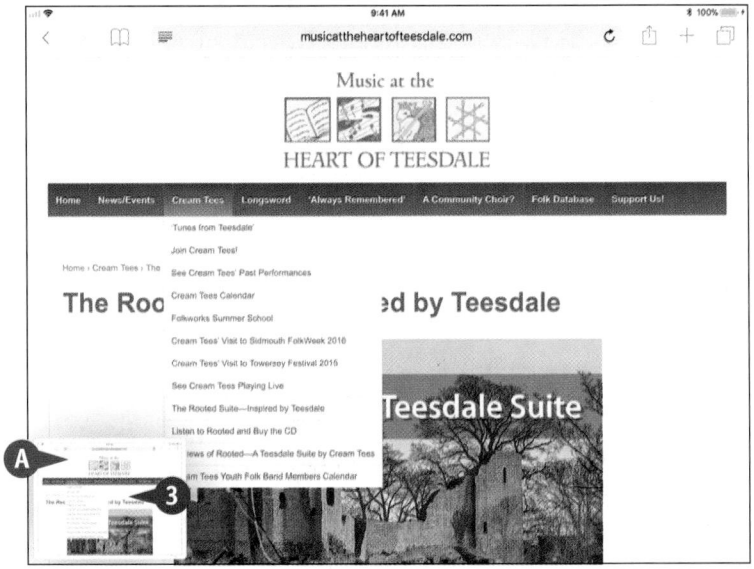

The screenshot opens.

The Instant Markup tools appear.

4. Tap the pen style you want to use.
5. Tap the pen color you want to use.
6. Annotate the screenshot as needed.

   B. You can tap **Eraser** and then tap pen input to erase it.

7. To add other markup, tap **Add** (⊕).

   A pop-up panel opens.

8. Tap **Text** (T), **Signature** (✍), **Magnifier** (🔍), **Rectangle** (□), **Circle** (○), **Caption** (💬), or **Arrow** (↗), and then position the item, following any prompts provided.
9. Tap **Done**.

   A pop-up panel opens.

10. Tap **Save to Photos**.

    iOS saves the marked-up screenshot to the Photos app.

Note: If you do not want to save the screenshot and markup, tap **Done** and then tap **Delete Screenshot** on the pop-up panel to delete the screenshot.

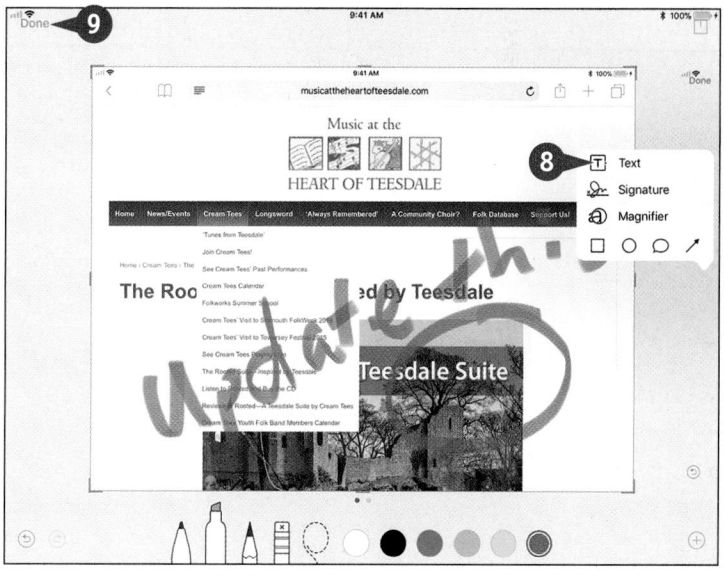

TIP

How can I access my screenshots later?

To access your screenshots, open the Screenshots album in the Photos app. Press **Home** to display the Home screen, and then tap **Photos** (🌸) to open the Photos app. Tap **Albums** (▭ changes to ▭) to display the Albums screen, and then tap **Screenshots**. Your screenshots also appear in the All Photos album along with all the other photos you have taken with the Camera app or otherwise saved on your iPad.

CHAPTER 7

Browsing the Web and Sending E-Mail

Your iPad is fully equipped to browse the web and send e-mail via a Wi-Fi connection or cellular network.

The Share sheet opens.

Note: The options on the Share sheet vary depending on the file type and the apps installed on your iPad.

7 Tap the app in which you want to open the document. For example, tap **Copy to iBooks** (📖).

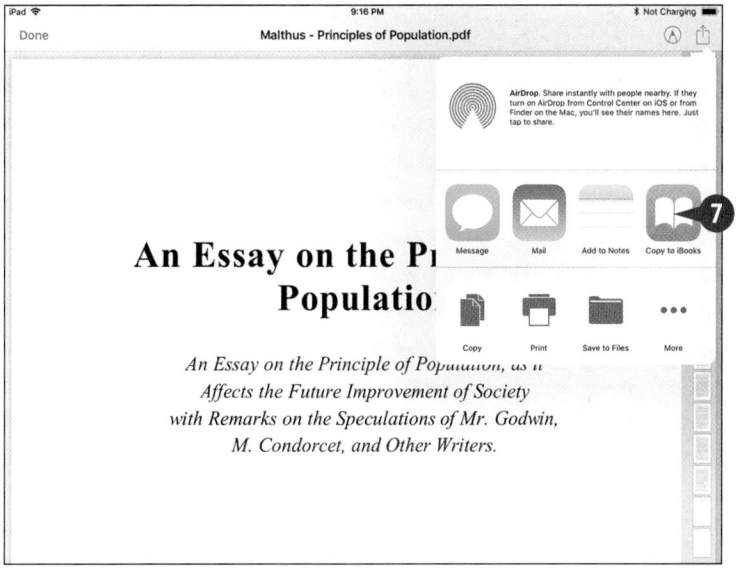

C The file opens in the app you chose.

Note: After you open an attached file in an app, your iPad stores a copy of the file in that app's storage. You can then open the file again directly from that app.

8 Tap **Mail** (❮) when you want to return to the Mail app.

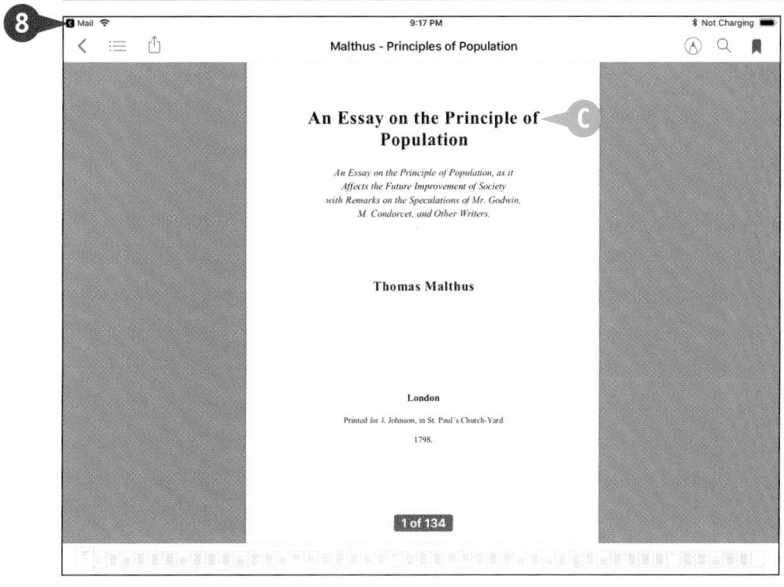

TIP

How can I delete an attached file from an e-mail message I have received?

As of this writing, you cannot directly delete an attached file from an e-mail message you have received in Mail on the iPad. You can delete only the message along with its attached file. If you use an e-mail app such as Mail on the Mac or web-based e-mail such as iCloud.com to manage the same e-mail account, you can remove the attached file using that app. When you update your mailbox on your iPad, the iPad deletes the attached file but leaves the message.

CHAPTER 8

Keeping Your Life Organized

Your iPad comes with the Contacts app for managing your contacts, the Calendars app for organizing your schedule, the Reminders app for tracking tasks, the Maps app for directions, and the Clock app for timekeeping.

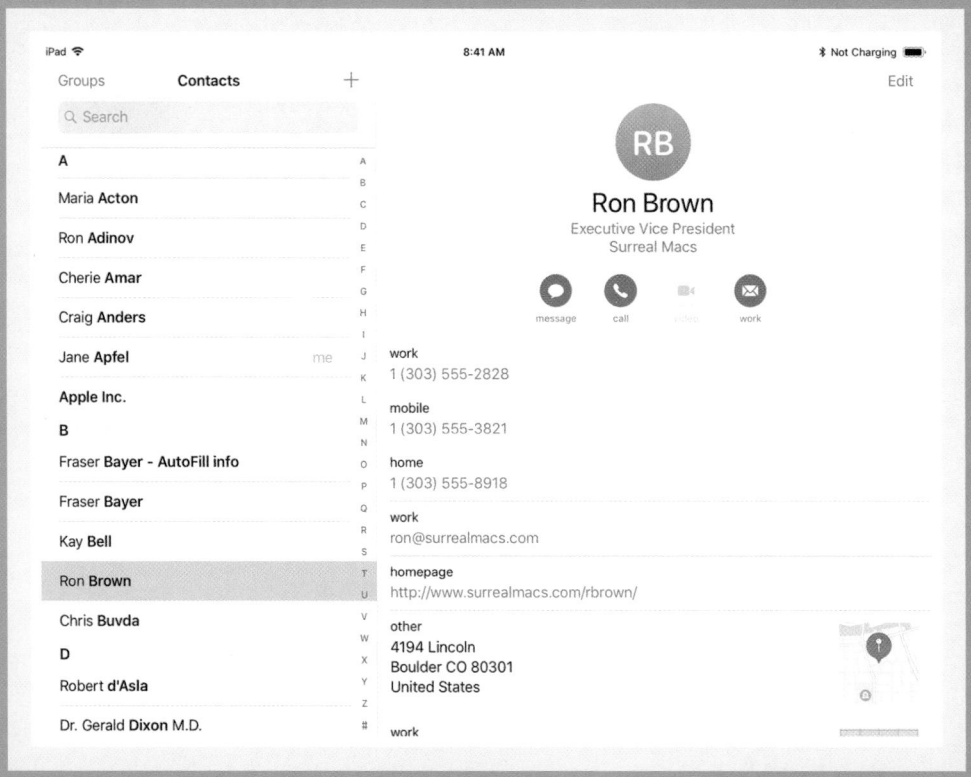

Browse or Search for Contacts 208
Create a New Contact. 210
Share Contacts via E-Mail and Messages 212
Browse Existing Events in Your Calendars 214
Create New Events in Your Calendars 216
Work with Calendar Invitations 218
Track Your Commitments with Reminders 220
Take Notes. 224
Find Your Location with the Maps App 230
Find Directions with the Maps App 232
Using the Maps App's Favorites and Contacts 234
Using the Clock App 236
Using Apple Pay 238

Browse or Search for Contacts

The Contacts app displays the contacts you have synced to your iPad from an online service, such as iCloud, or created directly on the iPad. You can browse your contacts, viewing either the full list of contacts or only particular groups, or search for particular contacts.

Typically, each of your accounts that includes contacts appears as a group, but you can also create groups on your Mac in your iCloud account. You cannot create or edit groups on the iPad.

Browse or Search for Contacts

Browse Your Contacts

1. Press **Home**.

   The Home screen appears.

2. Tap **Contacts** ( ).

   The Contacts list appears.

   A If All Contacts appears, you are viewing all contacts. If Contacts appears, you are viewing only some groups of contacts.

   B To navigate the screen of contacts quickly, tap the letter that you want to jump to. To navigate more slowly, scroll up or down.

3. Tap the contact whose information you want to view.

   The contact's details appear.

4. If necessary, tap and drag up to scroll down the screen to display more information.

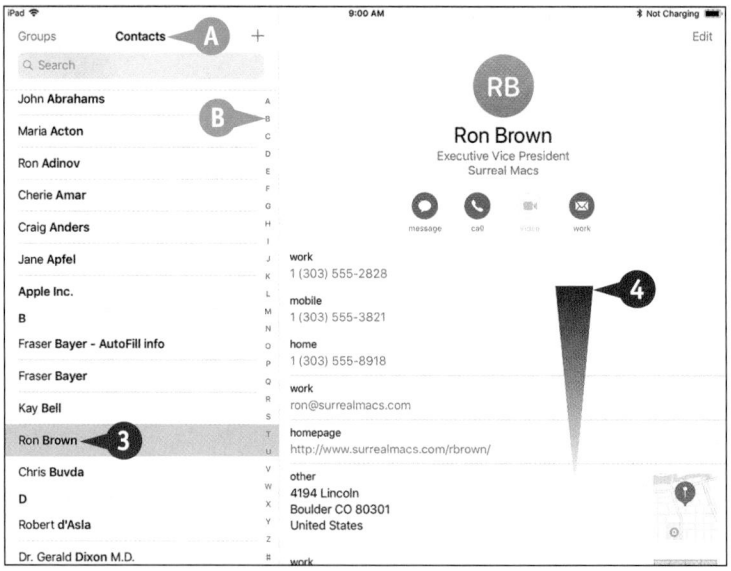

Choose Which Groups of Contacts to Display

1. From the Contacts list, tap **Groups**.

   The Groups panel appears.

2. Tap **Show All Contacts**.

   Contacts displays a check mark next to each group.

Note: When you tap **Show All Contacts**, the Hide All Contacts button appears in place of the Show All Contacts button. You can tap **Hide All Contacts** to remove all the check marks.

3. Tap a group to remove its existing check mark or apply a check mark.

4. Tap **Done**.

   The Contacts list appears, showing the contacts in the groups you selected.

Search for Contacts

1. In the Contacts list, tap **Search** (🔍).

   The Search screen appears.

2. In the Search box, type the name you want to search for.

3. From the list of matches, tap the contact you want to view.

   The contact's information appears.

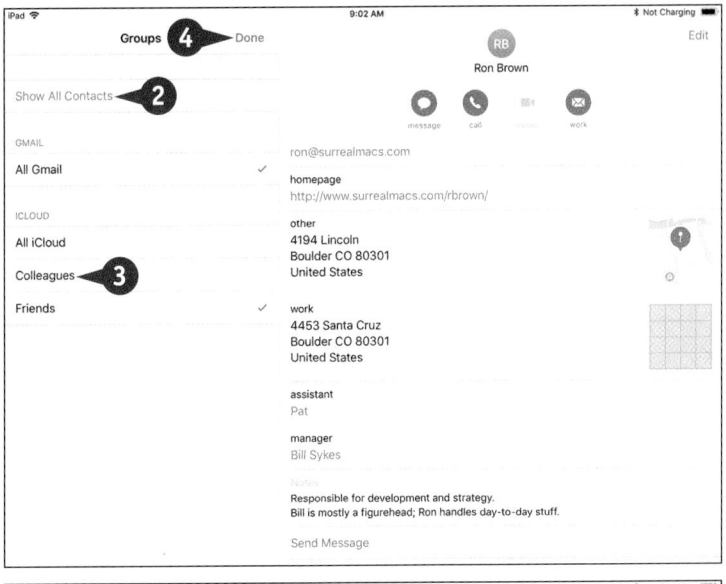

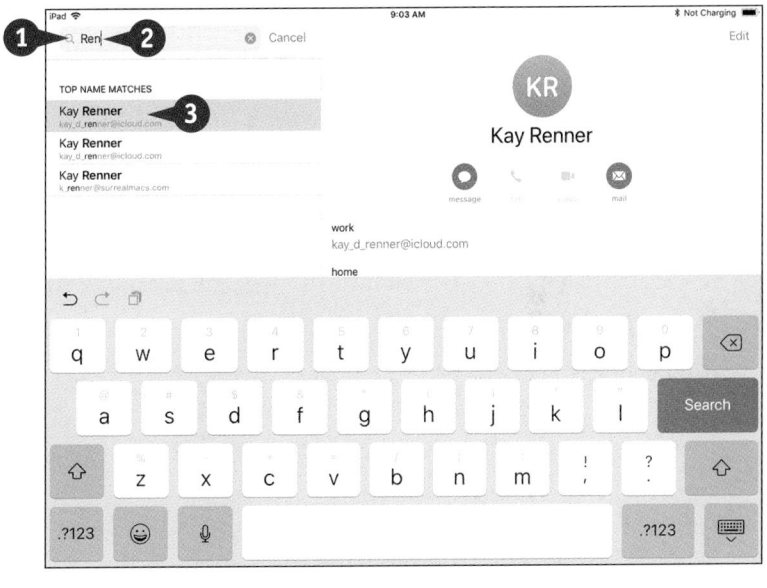

TIPS

How do I make my iPad sort my contacts by first names instead of last names?
Press **Home**. Tap **Settings** (⚙) and then tap **Contacts** (). In the Contacts section, tap **Sort Order**, then tap **First, Last**.

How do I combine two contact records for the same person?
Tap one of the contact records to open it, and then tap **Edit** to switch to Edit Mode. At the bottom of the screen, tap **link contacts**. In the dialog that opens, tap the contact record you want to link, and then tap **Link**. Tap **Done** to switch off Edit Mode.

Create a New Contact

Normally, you put contacts on your iPad by syncing them from existing records on your computer or on an online service such as iCloud. But when necessary, you can create a new contact directly on your iPad — for example, when you meet someone you want to remember.

You can then sync the contact record back to your computer, adding the new contact to your existing contacts.

Create a New Contact

1. Press **Home**.

   The Home screen appears.

2. Tap **Contacts** ( ).

   The Contacts list appears.

3. Tap **Add** (+).

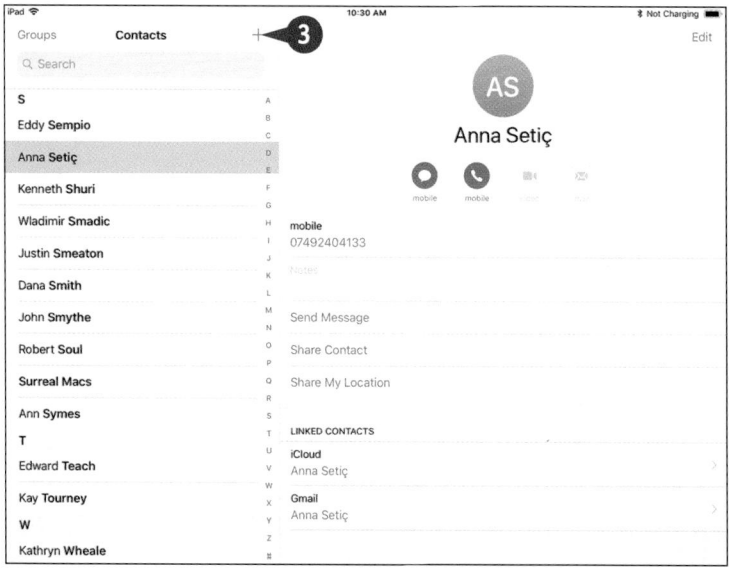

   The New Contact screen appears, with the on-screen keyboard displayed.

4. Type the first name.

5. Type the last name.

6. Add other information as needed by tapping each field and then typing the information.

7. To add a photo of the contact, tap **add photo**.

   The Photo dialog opens.

8. To use an existing photo, tap **Choose Photo** and follow this example. To take a new photo, tap **Take Photo** and see the tip.

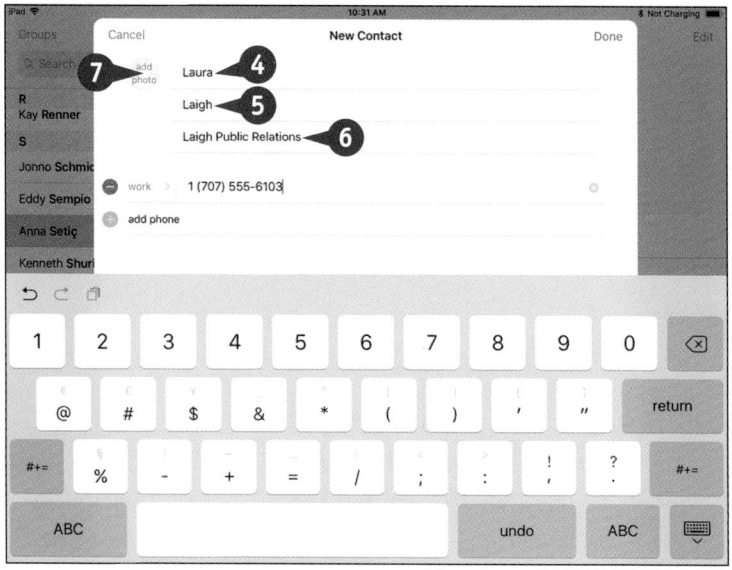

The Photos dialog opens.

9. Tap the album that contains the photo you want to use.

   The album's contents appear.

10. Tap the appropriate photo.

The Move and Scale screen appears.

11. Position the part of the photo you want to use in the middle.

Note: Pinch in with two fingers to zoom the photo out. Pinch out with two fingers to zoom the photo in.

12. Tap **Choose**.

    The photo appears in the contact record.

13. Tap **Done** when you finish editing the contact record.

    The contact appears in your Contacts list.

TIP

How do I take a new photo of my contact?
In the Photo dialog, tap **Take Photo**. The screen shows the image from the rear camera on the iPad. Compose the photo, and then tap **Take Photo** (◉). The Move and Scale screen appears. Position the photo as needed, scale it if necessary, and then tap **Use Photo**.

Share Contacts via E-Mail and Messages

Often in business or your personal life, you will need to share your contacts with other people. Your iPad makes it easy to share a contact record either via e-mail or via iMessage, the instant-messaging service offered by Apple.

The iPad shares the contact record as a virtual business card in the widely used vCard format. Most phones and personal-organizer software can easily import vCard files.

Share Contacts via E-Mail and Messages

Open the Contact You Want to Share

1. Press **Home**.

   The Home screen appears.

2. Tap **Contacts** ( ).

   The Contacts list appears.

3. Tap the contact you want to share.

   The contact's details appear.

4. Tap **Share Contact**.

   The Share sheet opens.

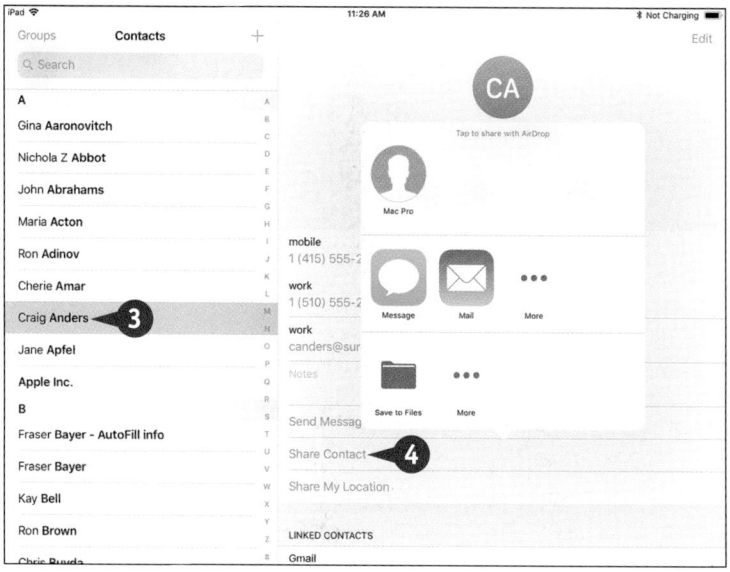

Share a Contact via E-Mail

1. On the Share sheet, tap **Mail** (✉).

   A A new message with the contact's name as the subject appears in the Mail app, with the contact record attached as a vCard file.

2. Address the message by typing the address or by tapping **Add Contact** (⊕) and choosing a contact as the recipient.
3. Edit the default subject line if necessary.
4. Type a message if necessary.
5. Tap **Send** to send the message.

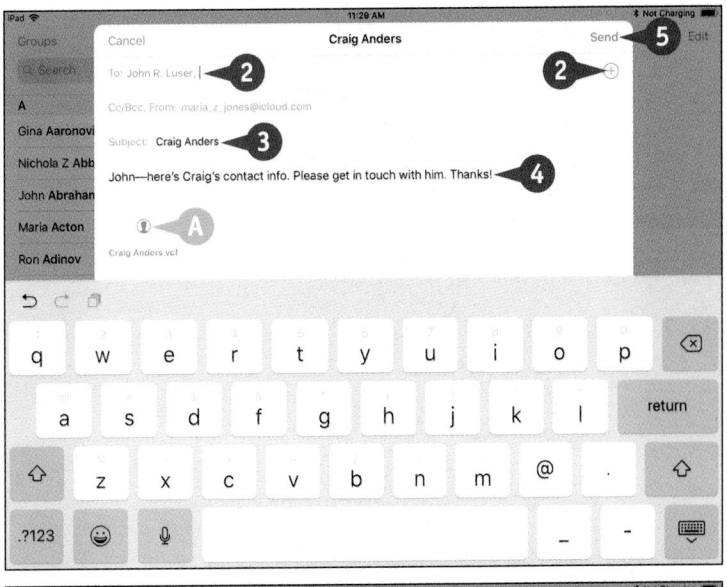

Share a Contact via Messages

1. On the Share sheet, tap **Message** (💬).

   B The New iMessage screen appears, with the contact record attached to the message.

2. Address the message by typing the name or number or by tapping **Add Contact** (⊕) and choosing a contact as the recipient.
3. Type a message if necessary.
4. Tap **Send** (↑) to send the message.

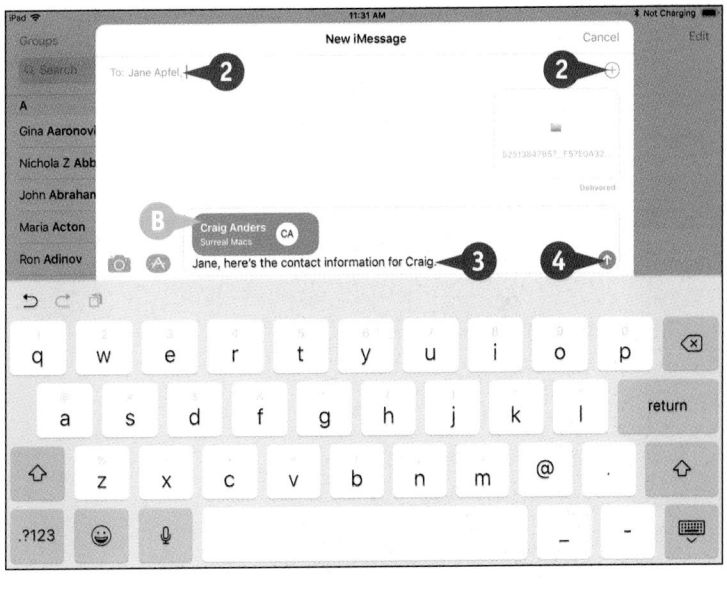

TIPS

Why is the recipient's address on the New Message screen red instead of blue?
The address appears in red if the recipient's address is not registered with the iMessage service. Tap and hold the recipient's name until a dialog opens, and then tap **Remove**.

How do I add a vCard I receive in an e-mail message to my contacts?
In the Mail app, tap the button for the vCard file. Toward the bottom of the dialog that opens, tap **Create New Contact**. If the vCard contains extra information about an existing contact, tap **Add to Existing Contact**, and then tap the contact.

Browse Existing Events in Your Calendars

The Calendar app gives you a great way of managing your schedule and making sure you never miss an appointment.

After setting up your calendars to sync using iCloud, as described in Chapter 1, or another calendar service, you can take your calendars with you everywhere and consult them whenever you need to. You can view all your calendars or only the ones you choose.

Browse Existing Events in Your Calendars

1. Press **Home**.

   The Home screen appears.

2. Tap **Calendar** (22).

   The Calendar screen appears.

3. Tap **Month** to see Month view, in which each day appears in a box on a calendar chart.

   A Month view shows a one-line entry with the time of each event that will fit in the box.

4. Tap an event.

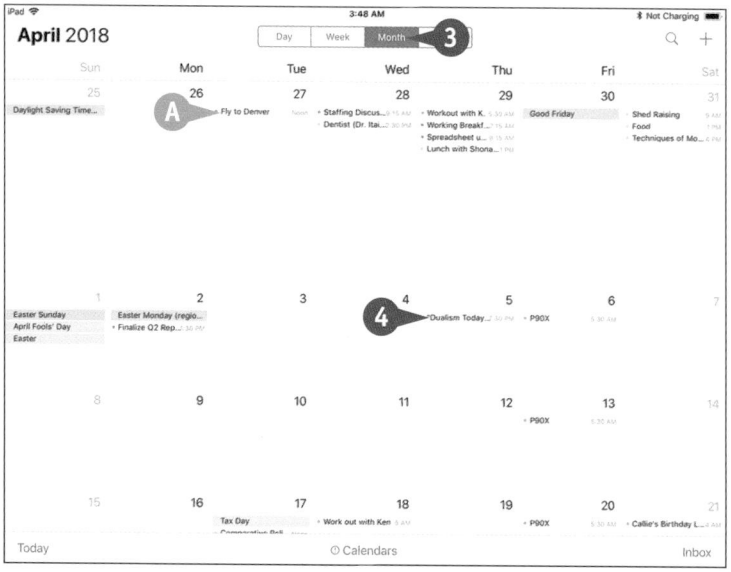

   A dialog opens, showing the event's details.

   B You can tap **Edit** to open the event so you can change its details.

Note: You can drag up and down to change the month that appears.

5. Tap outside the dialog to close it.

6. Tap **Week**.

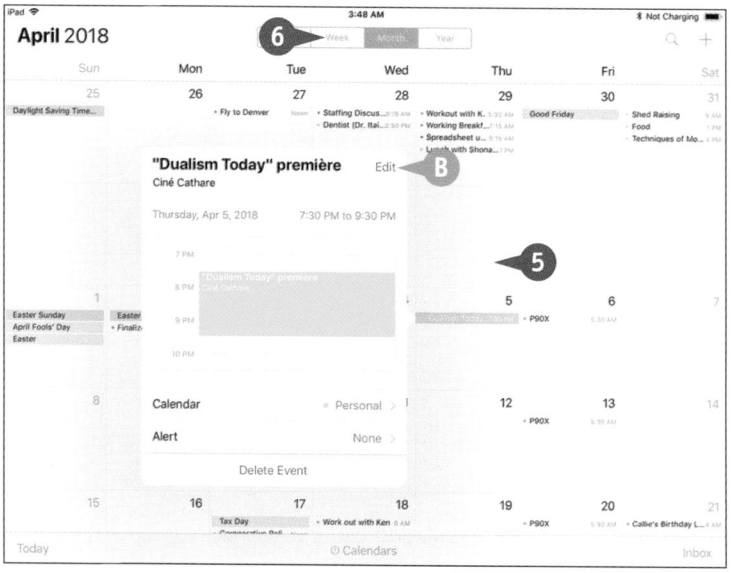

The Calendar switches to Week view.

C Your events appear on a grid that shows the days as columns and the hours as rows.

Note: In Week view, you can scroll left, right, up, or down to change the days and hours shown.

Note: In Week view and Day view, you can move an event by tapping and holding it until its color darkens, and then dragging it to where you want it.

7 Tap **Day**.

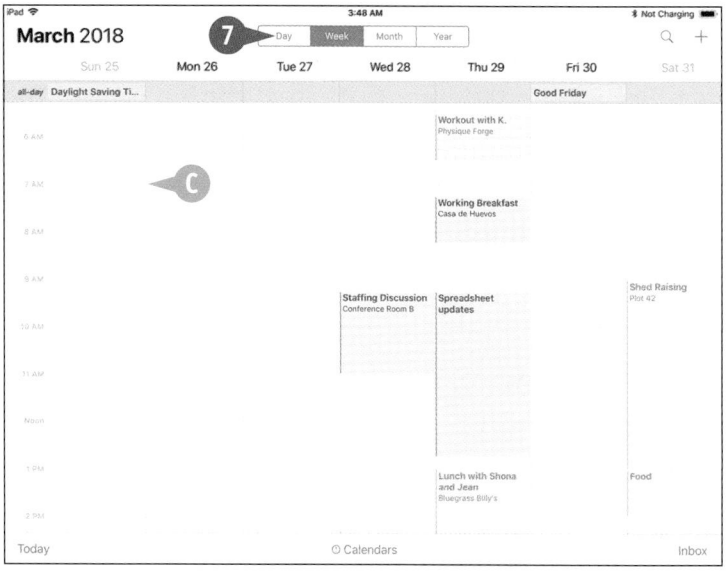

The Calendar switches to Day view.

D You can tap another day to display that day.

E The left pane shows a vertical timeline for the day.

F The right pane shows the details of the selected event.

G You can tap **Edit** to edit the event.

8 Tap **Today**.

Calendar displays the events for the current day.

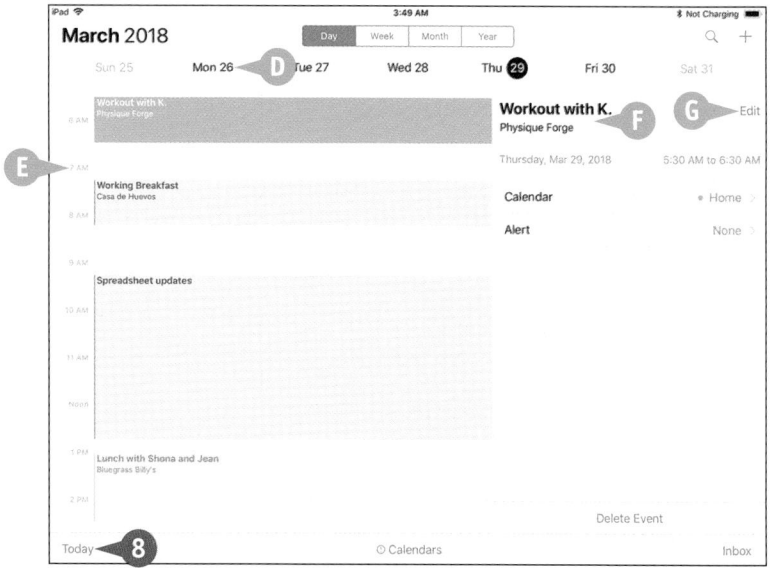

TIPS

How can I quickly find an event?
Tap **Search** (🔍) in the upper-right corner of the Calendar screen, and then type your search term. When Calendar displays a list of matches, tap the event you want to view.

How do I control which calendars' events appear?
Tap **Calendars** at the bottom of the screen. In the Show Calendars dialog, tap to place a check mark next to each calendar you want to see, or tap **Show All Calendars** or **Hide All Calendars**. After making your choices, tap **Done**.

Create New Events in Your Calendars

The Calendar app enables you to both sync events that you have created on other devices to your iPad and to create new events directly on the iPad. You can create either a straightforward, one-time event or an event that repeats on a schedule. You can also choose which calendar the event belongs to.

You can create a new event from any view, but Week view is usually the easiest view to use.

Create New Events in Your Calendars

1. Press **Home**.

   The Home screen appears.

2. Tap **Calendar** (22).

   The Calendar app opens.

3. Tap **Week** to switch to Week view.

4. Tap and hold the appropriate time slot.

   The New Event dialog opens.

5. Type the title of the event.

6. Tap **Location**.

   The Location dialog opens.

7. Type or tap the location of the event.

   The location appears.

   A For an all-day event, set the **All-day** switch to On ( ).

8. Tap **Alert**.

   The Alert dialog opens.

9. Tap the timing for the alert — for example, **30 minutes before**.

   B You can tap **None** to remove the alert that is currently set.

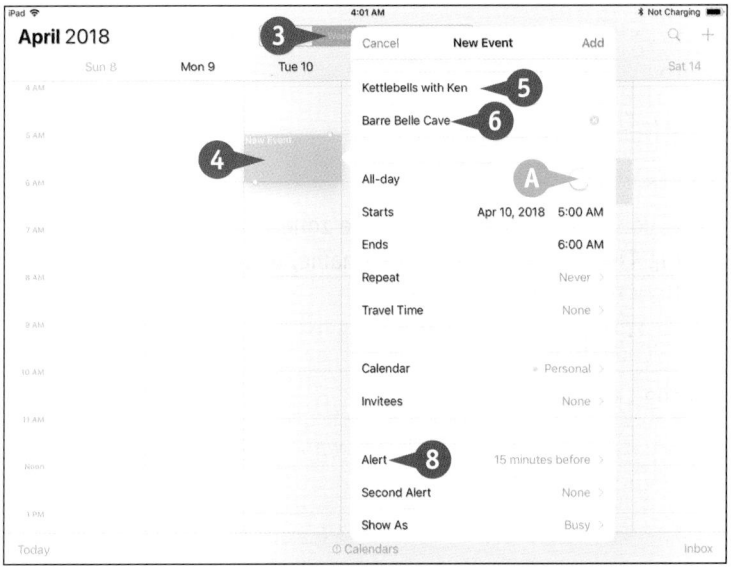

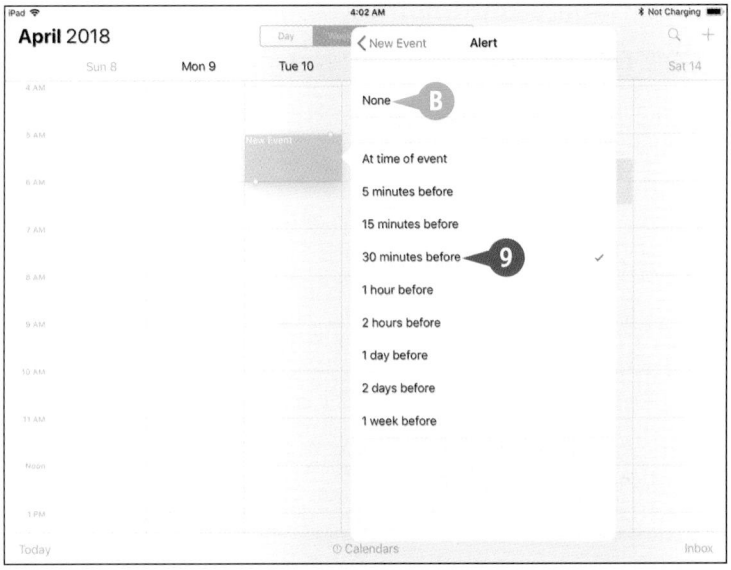

The New Event dialog appears again.

Note: You can assign a second alert to the event by tapping **Second Alert** after choosing the first alert. A second alert can be a useful safety net for events you must not miss.

10. Tap **Starts**.

    The time controls appear.

11. Drag the date and time controls to set the start time.

12. Tap **Ends**.

13. Set the end time.

    C. If you need to change the time zone, tap **Time Zone**, type the city name, and then tap the time zone.

14. Tap **Calendar**.

    The Calendar dialog opens.

15. Tap the calendar to which you want to assign the event.

    The New Event dialog appears again.

16. Tap **Add**.

    The event appears on your calendar.

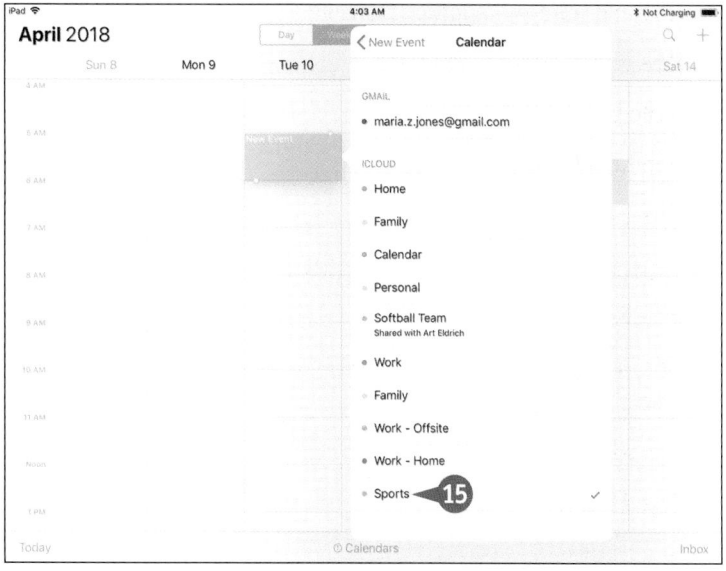

TIP

How do I set up an event that repeats, say, every 2 weeks?
In the New Event dialog, tap **Repeat**. In the Repeat dialog, tap **Every 2 Weeks** to place a check mark next to it, and then tap **Done**.

Work with Calendar Invitations

Most likely, you will receive invitations to events that others create. When you receive an event invitation attached to an e-mail message, you can choose whether to accept the invitation or decline it. If you accept the invitation, you can add the event automatically to a calendar of your choice and set an alert for it.

Work with Calendar Invitations

Deal with an Invitation from an Alert

1. When an invitation alert appears, tap the alert.

Note: To control whether you receive alerts for invitations, press **Home**, and then tap **Settings** (). In the Settings app, tap **Notifications** (), and then tap **Calendar** (). Tap **Invitations** to display the Invitations screen. Set the **Show on Cover Sheet** switch to On () if you want to receive invitation alerts on Cover Sheet. If you want to receive invitation alerts as banners, set the **Show as Banners** switch to On (), and then tap **Temporary** or **Permanent** to specify the banner type.

The Calendar app appears.

A The invitation's event appears in gray.

2. Tap the invitation's event.

A pop-up panel appears showing the details of the invitation.

B Depending on the account type, you may be able to tap **Propose New Time** to propose a different time.

3. Tap **Calendar** and choose which calendar to assign the invitation to.

C You can tap **Alert** and set alert timing.

4. Tap **Accept**, **Maybe**, or **Decline** to give your response.

The pop-up panel closes.

The event takes on the color of the calendar you chose.

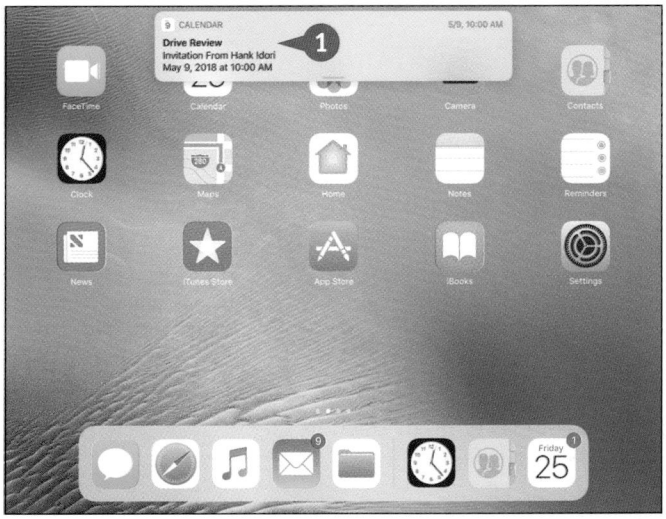

Deal with Invitations from the Inbox

D The number in parentheses on the right of the Inbox button shows the number of invitations.

1 Tap **Inbox**.

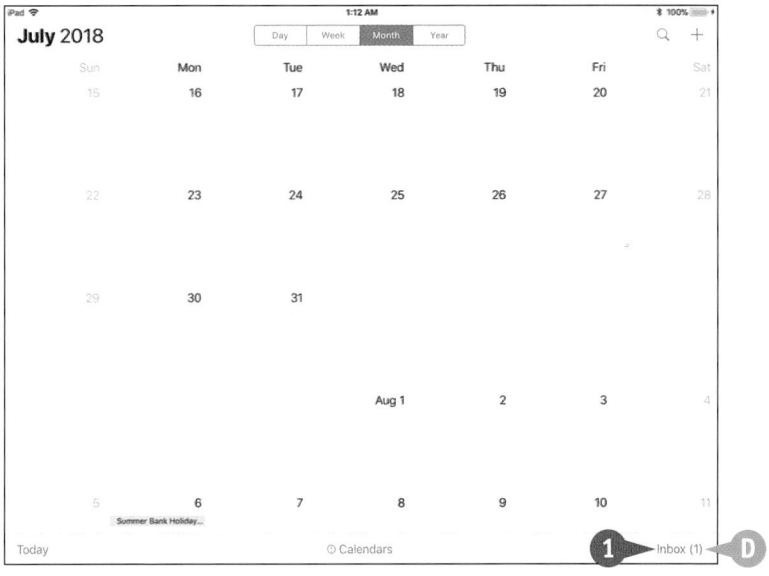

The Inbox panel opens.

E You can tap the invitation to display all its details.

2 Tap **Accept**, **Maybe**, or **Decline** to give your response.

The invitation disappears from the New tab.

F You can tap **Replied** to display the Replied tab, which contains a list of the invitations you have received, including your responses.

3 Tap outside the Inbox panel.

The Inbox panel closes.

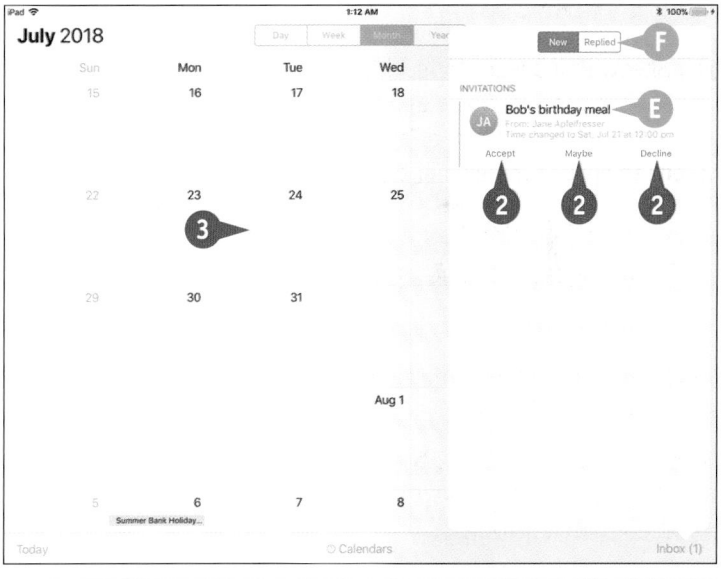

TIP

How do I set the Travel Time item for an event?

Tap the event to open it, tap **Edit** to switch to Edit Mode, and then tap **Travel Time** to display the Travel Time panel. You can then set the **Travel Time** switch to On (◐) to have Calendar automatically add travel time for you to get to the event. Calendar blocks off the travel time so that you will not create or accept other events when you should be traveling to or from the event.

If your work calendar is on an Exchange server, be aware that Exchange ignores travel time. You will see the travel time you set, but others trying to schedule meetings with you via Exchange and Outlook will not see your travel time.

Track Your Commitments with Reminders

The Reminders app gives you an easy way to note and track your commitments. Reminders comes with a built-in list called Reminders, but you can create as many other lists as you need — for example, Errands, Shopping, or Household. You can create a reminder with no due time. Alternatively, you can tie each reminder to a due time, arriving at or leaving a location, or both, and have your iPad remind you of each reminder at the appropriate time or place.

Track Your Commitments with Reminders

Open the Reminders App

1. Press **Home**.

   The Home screen appears.

2. Tap **Reminders** ( ).

   The Reminders screen appears.

Note: When you complete a task, tap the circle (◯) to the left of the reminder (◯ changes to ◉). If you need to reinstate the task, tap the circle again (◉ changes to ◯).

Create a New Reminder

1. In the Reminders app, tap **Add** (+) on the first blank line below the last reminder in the list. You can also simply tap the blank line.

   Reminders starts a new reminder and displays the on-screen keyboard.

2. Type the text of the reminder.

   A If you do not want to set any further details for the reminder, tap **Done**.

3. Tap **Information** (ⓘ).

Note: To create a reminder using Siri, press **Home** for a couple of seconds until Siri beeps, and then say the reminder aloud. For example, say "Remind me at 8AM tomorrow to take the project files to the office."

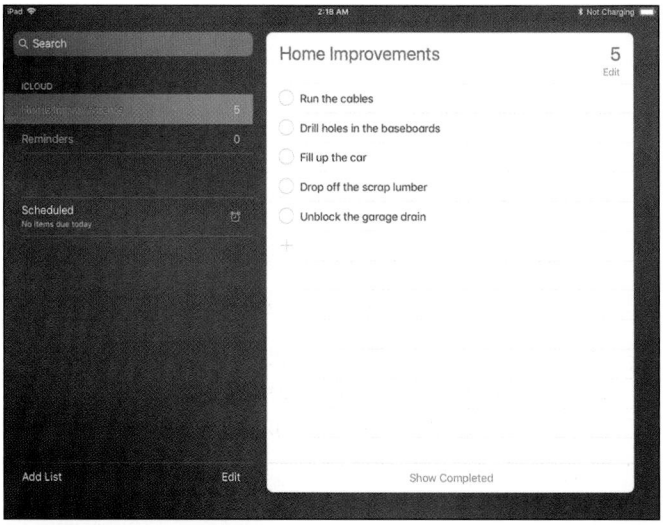

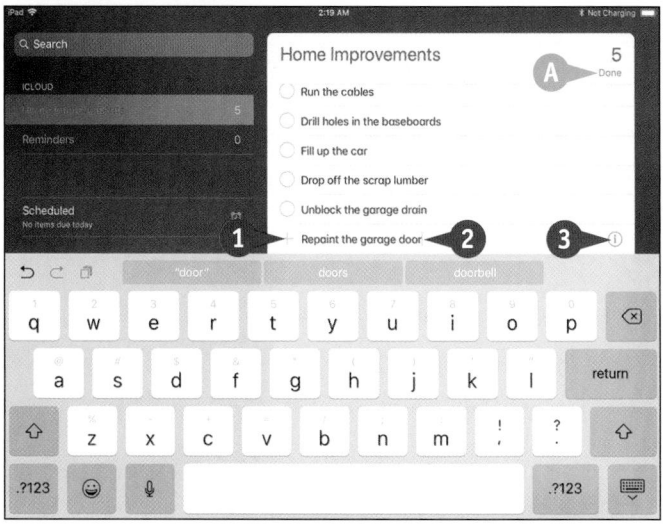

The Details dialog opens.

4. Set the **Remind me on a day** switch to On ( ).

The Alarm button appears.

5. Tap **Alarm**.

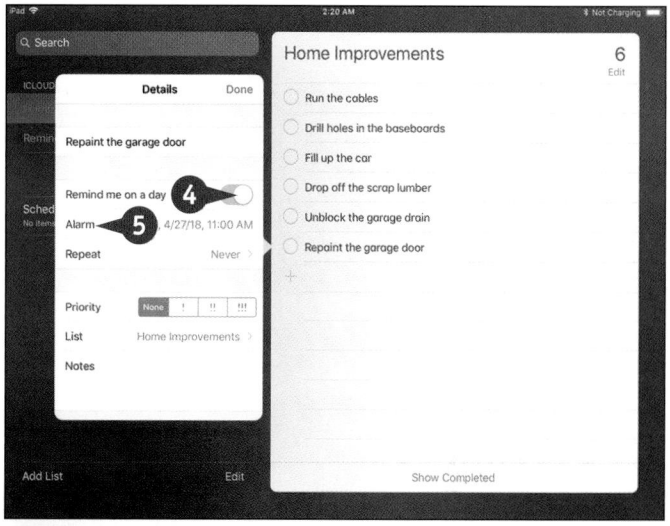

Date and time controls appear.

6. Select the date and time for the reminder.
7. If you need to create a repeating reminder, tap **Repeat** and choose the repeat schedule in the Repeat dialog. For example, touch **Every Day** or **Every Week**.
8. To assign a priority, tap **!**, **!!**, or **!!!**. To remove the priority, tap **None**.
9. To add notes, tap **Notes** and type the text.
10. Tap **Done**.

The Details dialog closes.

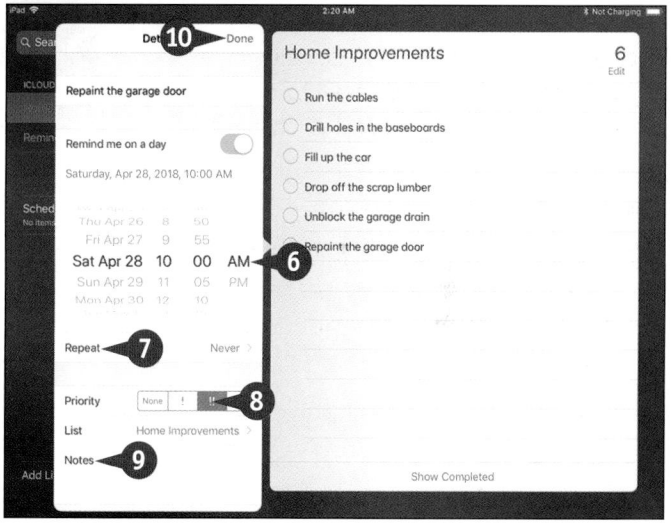

TIP

How do I sync the reminders on my iPad with the ones on my Mac?

Use your iCloud account to sync your iPad reminders with your Mac reminders.

On your iPad, press **Home**, tap **Settings** ( ), tap **Apple ID**, tap **iCloud** ( ), and then set the **Reminders** switch to On ( ).

On your Mac, click **Apple** ( ), click **System Preferences**, click **iCloud** ( ), and then click the **Reminders** check box (changes to).

You can also sync reminders via Exchange, which calls them *tasks*. Press **Home**, tap **Settings** ( ), tap **Accounts & Passwords** ( ), tap the Exchange account, and then set the **Reminders** switch to On ( ).

continued ▶

You can organize your reminders into different lists so that you can look at a single category of reminders at a time. For example, you may find it useful to create a Work list that enables you to focus on your work-related reminders.

After creating lists, you can easily switch among them. You can also move a reminder from one list to another as needed. And when you no longer need a particular reminder, you can delete it.

Track Your Commitments with Reminders (continued)

Create Different Lists of Reminders

1. On the Reminders screen, tap **Add List**.

Note: If you have set up multiple Reminders accounts, the Select Account dialog opens. Tap the account in which to create the list.

2. Type the name for the new list.
3. Tap the color button for the list.
4. Tap **Done**.

   Reminders adds the new list.

Note: To delete a Reminders list quickly, tap it in the lists pane and swipe left; then tap **Delete** and tap **Delete** again in the confirmation dialog. Alternatively, tap **Edit** at the bottom of the lists pane, tap **Delete**, and then tap **Delete** again.

Note: Deleting a Reminders list also deletes all the reminders it contains.

Switch Among Your Reminders Lists

1. On the Reminders screen, tap the list you want to display.

B The list appears.

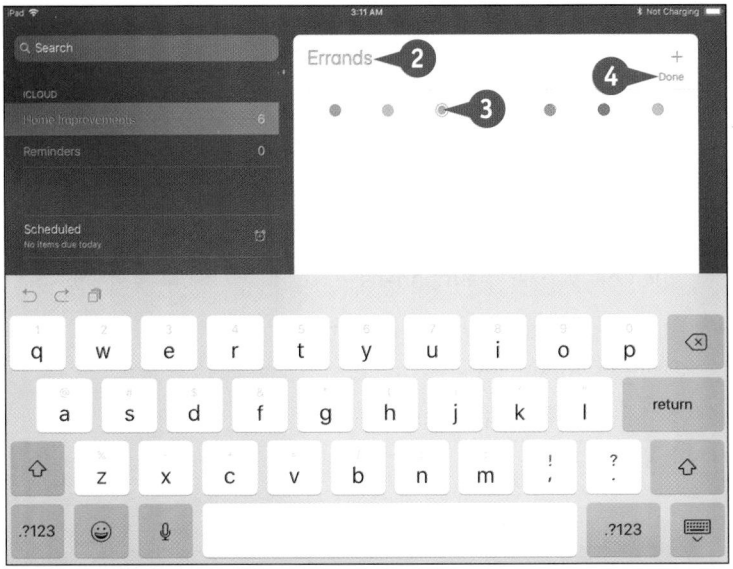

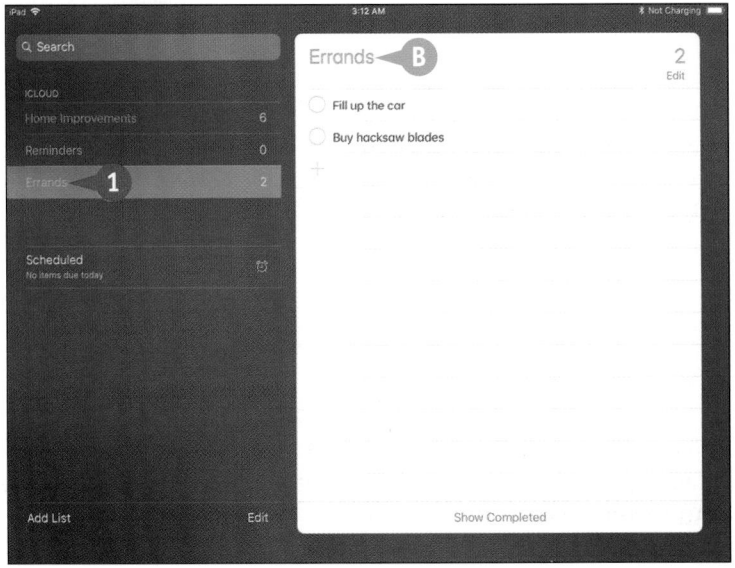

Change the List to Which a Reminder Is Assigned

1. In a Reminders list, tap the reminder.

   The Information button (ⓘ) appears.

2. Tap **Information** (ⓘ).

   The Details dialog opens.

3. Tap **List**.

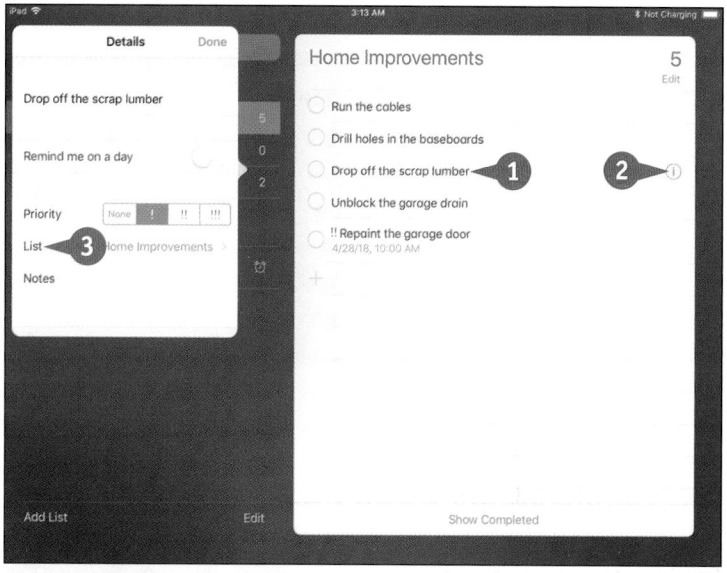

   The Change List dialog opens.

4. Tap the list to which you want to assign the reminder.

   The Details dialog opens.

5. Tap **Done**.

   The Details dialog closes.

   The reminder moves to the list you chose.

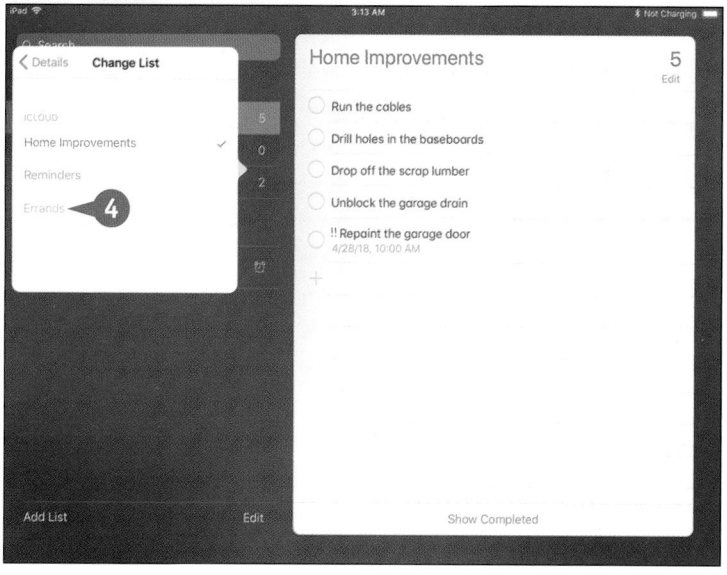

Note: You can delete a reminder by tapping **Edit** on its list page, tapping next to the reminder, and then tapping **Delete**. Alternatively, tap the reminder in its list, swipe left, and then tap **Delete**.

TIP

Can I change the default list that Reminders puts my reminders in?

Yes. Press **Home** to display the Home screen, and then tap **Settings** (⚙) to display the Settings screen. Tap **Reminders** ( ) in the left column to display the Reminders screen, tap **Default List** to display the Default List screen, and then tap the list you want to make the default. On the Reminders screen, you can also tap **Sync** and choose how many reminders to sync — for example, **Reminders 2 Weeks Back** or **All Reminders**.

Take Notes

Your iPad is a great device for taking notes wherever you go. The Notes app enables you to create notes stored in an online account, such as your iCloud account, and sync them across your devices. Alternatively, you can store notes on your iPad itself, which is useful for private notes you do not want to sync with other devices.

Take Notes

Open the Notes App, Choose the Account, and Create a Note

1. Press **Home**.

   The Home screen appears.

2. Tap **Notes** ( ).

Note: If you want to be able to continue work on your latest note quickly, add the Notes widget to Today View. You can then tap the widget to go straight to the latest note in the Notes app.

Note: On an iPad Pro, you can start a note quickly from the lock screen by tapping the screen with the Apple Pencil.

The Notes app opens.

- (A) The Notes pane shows the notes in the account you are currently using.
- (B) The note on which you were last working appears.
- (C) You can tap **Full Screen** ( ) to expand the current note to full-screen, hiding the Notes pane. Tap **Back** ( ) or **Notes** to display the Notes pane again.

3. Tap **Back** ( ).

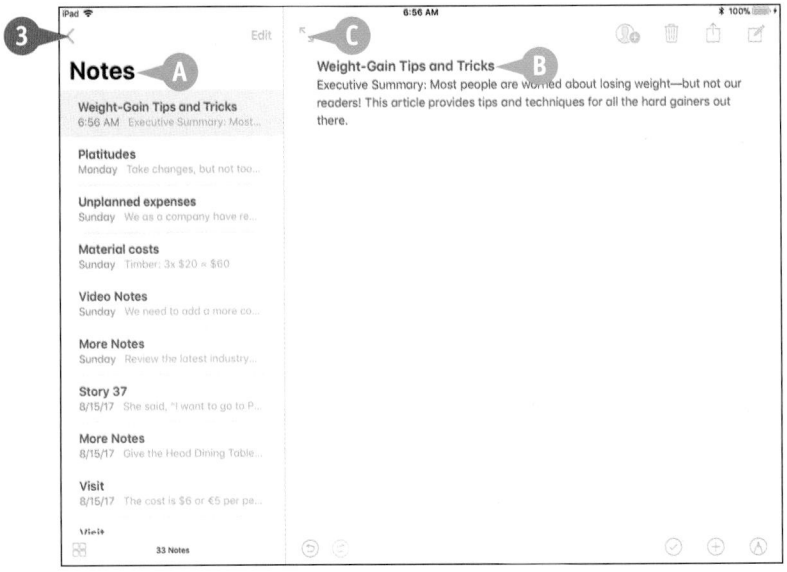

The Folders pane appears.

D The Recently Deleted folder contains notes you have recently deleted. Notes remain here for 30 days and then are deleted.

E You can create a new folder in your iCloud account by tapping **New Folder**.

4 Tap the account or folder in which you want to create the new note.

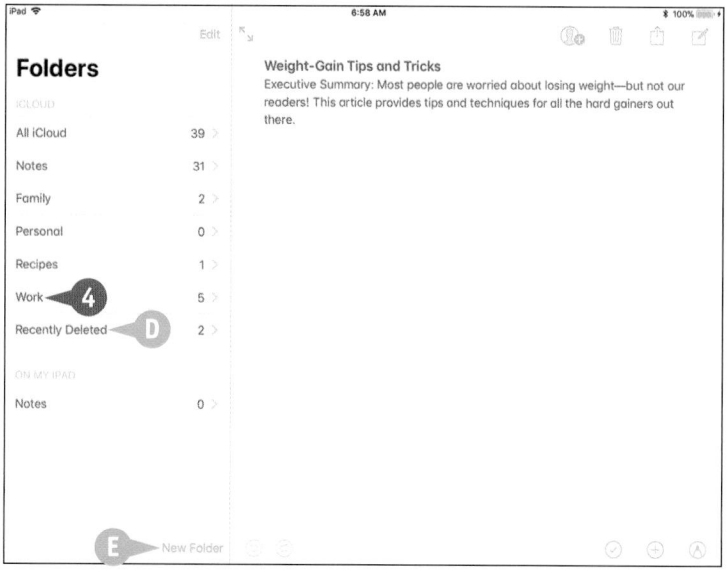

The Notes pane appears, showing the notes in that account or folder.

5 Tap **New** ( ).

A new note opens.

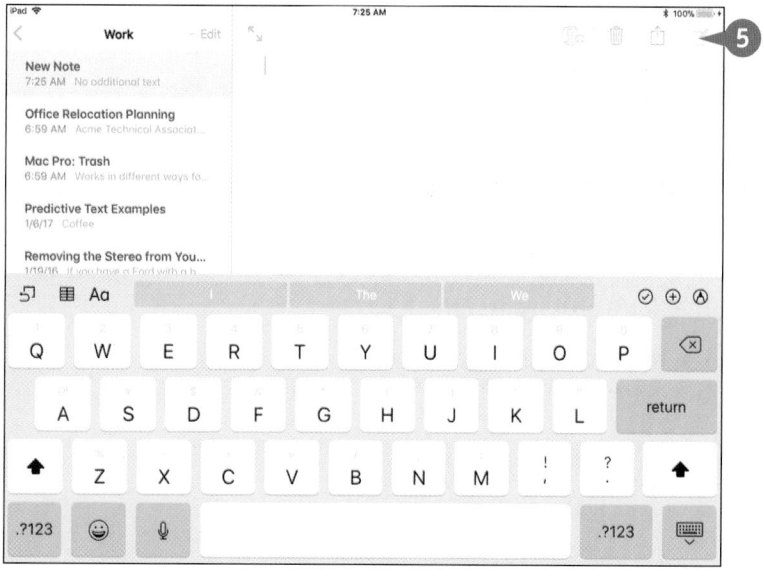

TIPS

What does the button with the curved arrow do?
Tap this button, **More Actions** ( ), to display a pop-up command bar with three buttons. Tap **Undo** ( ) to undo an action. Tap **Redo** ( ) to redo an action you have undone. Tap **Paste** ( ) to paste the Clipboard's contents into the document.

Can I use styles and formatting in all my notes?
Styles are available only in notes you store on your iPad or in iCloud. Basic formatting — boldface, italic, and underline — works for notes on Google, Exchange, and IMAP accounts as well as notes in iCloud.

continued ▶

The Notes app includes built-in styles that enable you to format your notes with a title, headings, body text, bulleted lists, dashed lists, and numbered lists. By using these styles to format notes, you can create structured notes that you can easily use in a word processing app. You can also apply direct formatting, such as bold, italic, underline, and strikethrough.

You can also insert round check boxes to create lists from which you can check off completed items.

Take Notes (continued)

Enter Text and Apply Formatting

1. After starting a note, type the title or first paragraph of the note.

Note: The first paragraph of the new note receives the style specified by the New Notes Start With setting. To change this setting, press **Home**, tap **Settings** (), and then tap **Notes** ( ).

2. Tap **return** and continue typing the note.

   F The note's entry in the Notes pane shows the first line and part of the next line.

3. To apply a style to the current paragraph, tap **Formatting** (Aa).

   The Formatting panel opens.

4. Tap the style or formatting you want to apply.

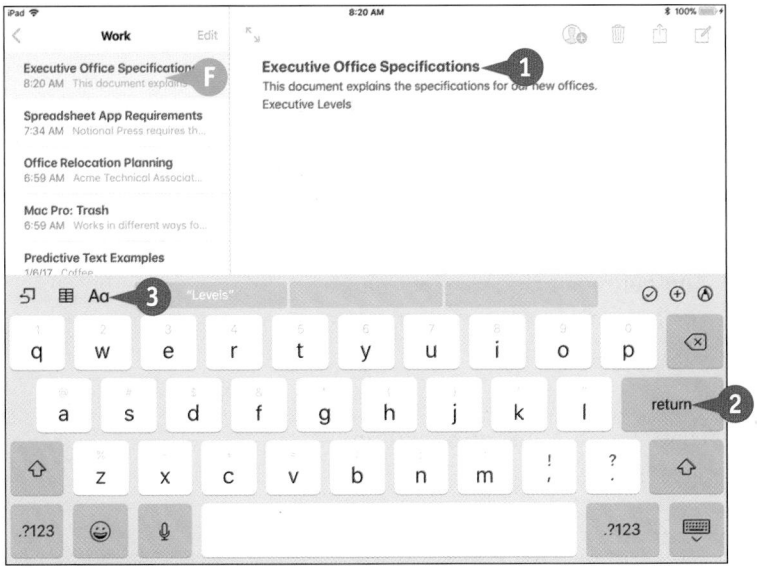

The Formatting panel closes.

G The paragraph takes on the style or formatting.

5 Tap **Check Box** (⊘).

H A round check box appears in the text.

6 Type the text to accompany the check box.

7 Tap **return**.

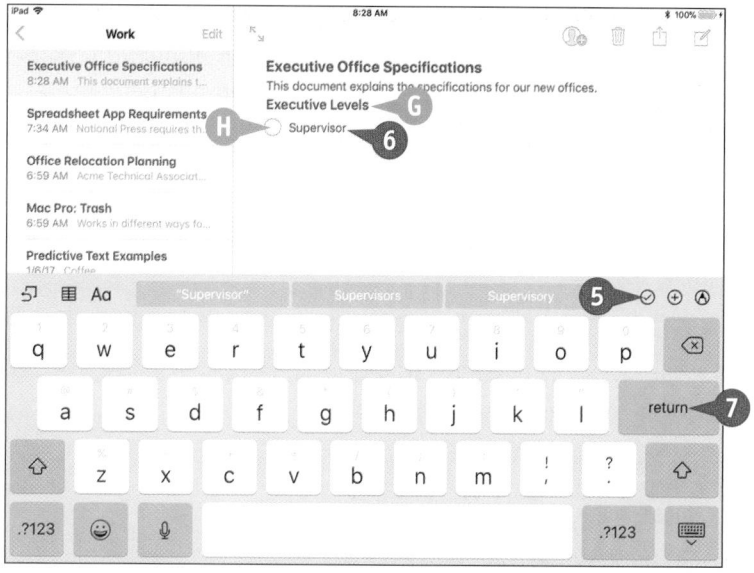

Another round check box appears at the beginning of the next paragraph, continuing the list.

8 When you want to stop using check boxes, tap **return** twice in succession.

Note: You can also stop using check boxes by tapping **Check Box** (⊘) on a paragraph that contains a check box.

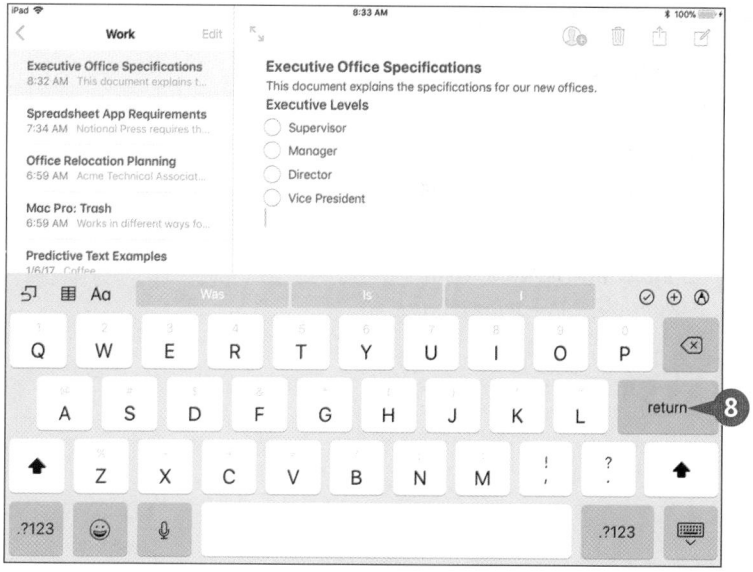

TIP

How do I move a note from one account or folder to another?

In the Notes pane, swipe left on the note you want to move. The Lock button (🔒), Move button (▭), and Delete button (🗑) appear to the right of the note. Tap **Move** (▭) to display the Folders pane. You can then tap the folder to which you want to move the note. You can tap **New Folder** and create a new folder to which you want to move the note.

continued ▶

The Notes app enables you to add tables for laying out data regularly in rows and columns. You can customize each table with the number of rows and columns needed.

You can also add graphical objects to notes. You can use the iPad's camera to scan a hardcopy document into a note, capture a new photo or video with the camera or insert an existing photo or video, or draw a sketch with your finger or with the Apple Pencil.

Take Notes (continued)

Insert a Table

1. Position the insertion point where you want the table to appear.
2. Tap **Table** (▦).

   Notes inserts a table with two columns and two rows.

   The insertion point appears in the first cell.
3. Type the content for the first cell.
4. Tap **Next** on the keyboard.

   The focus moves to the next cell.
5. Type the content for the next cell.
6. Tap **Column Commands** ( ).

   The command bar appears.
7. Tap **Add Column**.

   I You can tap **Delete Column** to delete the current column.

   Notes adds a new column.
8. Continue typing the cell entries, tapping **Next** on the keyboard to move to the next cell.

Note: If the current cell is the last cell in the table, tapping **Next** automatically adds a row to the table.

J You can add a new row below the current row by tapping **Row Commands** ( ) and then tapping **Add Row** on the command bar that appears.

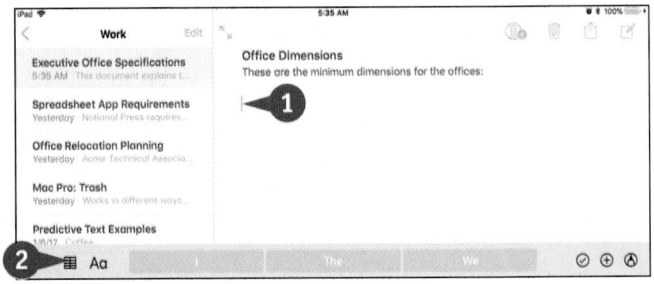

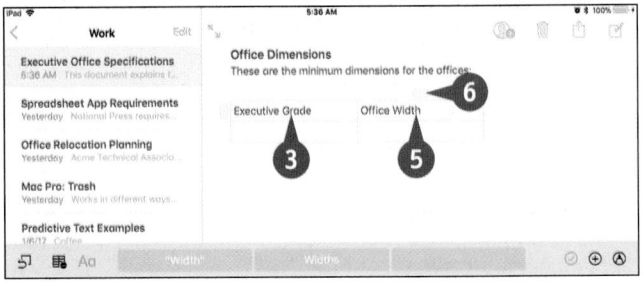

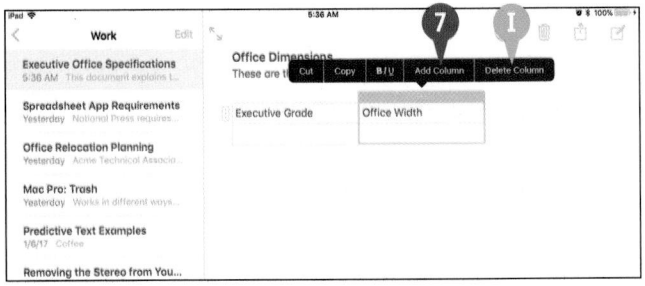

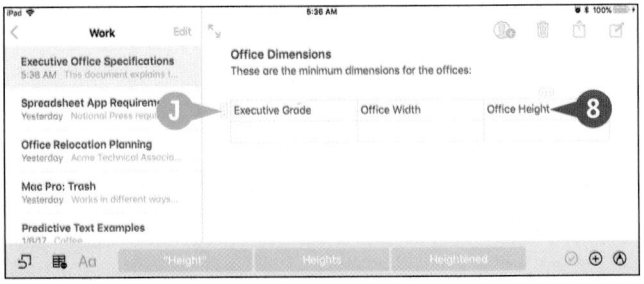

Add a Document, Photo, Video, or Sketch

1. Place the insertion point where you want the item to appear.
2. Tap **Add** (⊕).

   The Add pop-up panel opens.
3. Tap **Scan Documents**, **Take Photo or Video**, **Photo Library**, or **Add Sketch** to specify what you want to add. This example uses Scan Documents.

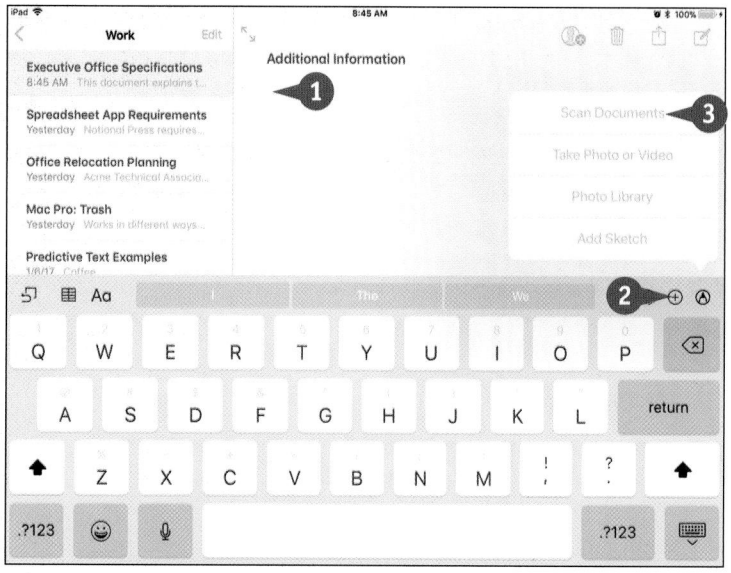

   The appropriate screen appears, such as the screen for scanning documents.
4. Aim the camera at the relevant part of the document.
5. Tap **Take Photo** (◯).

   A crop area appears.
6. Drag the corner handles to select the area you want to keep.
7. Tap **Keep Scan**.

   The item appears in the note.

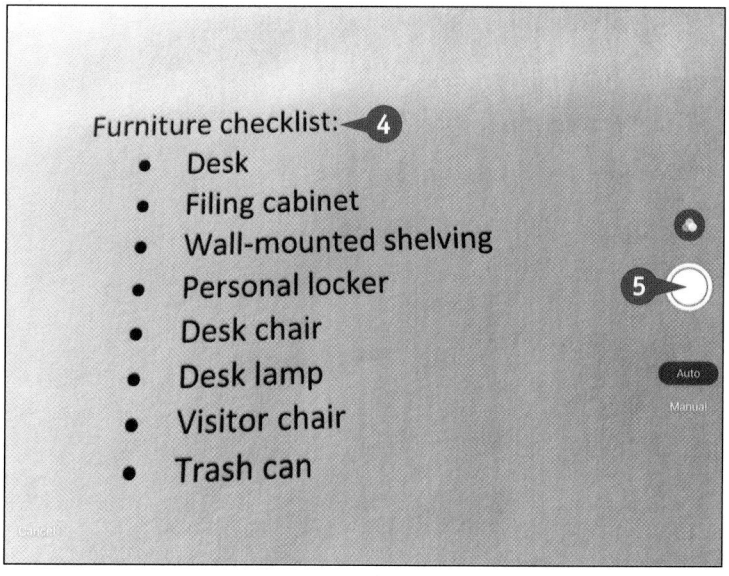

TIP

What does the Table Commands button do?

Tap **Table Commands** (▦) to display a pop-up panel of commands for working with tables. Tap **Copy Table** to copy the table so you can paste it elsewhere. Tap **Share Table** to open the Share sheet so you can share the table. Tap **Convert to Text** to convert the table to text within the note. Tap **Delete Table** to delete the table.

Find Your Location with the Maps App

The Maps app can pinpoint your location by using known Wi-Fi networks or — on cellular iPads — by using GPS (Global Positioning System) satellites or cellular towers. You can view your location on a road map or a satellite picture, either with or without place names. You can switch among map types to find the most useful one. To help you get your bearings, the Tracking feature in the Maps app can show you which direction you are facing.

Find Your Location with the Maps App

1. Press **Home**.

   The Home screen appears.

2. Tap **Maps** ( ).

   The Maps screen appears.

   A A blue dot shows your current location. The expanding circle around the blue dot shows that Maps is determining your location.

Note: It may take a minute for Maps to work out your location accurately. While Maps determines the location, the blue dot moves, even though the iPad remains stationary.

3. Tap and pinch in with two fingers.

Note: You can tap and pinch out with two fingers to zoom in.

   The map zooms out, showing a larger area.

4. Tap **Information** (ⓘ).

   The Maps Settings dialog opens.

5. Tap **Satellite**.

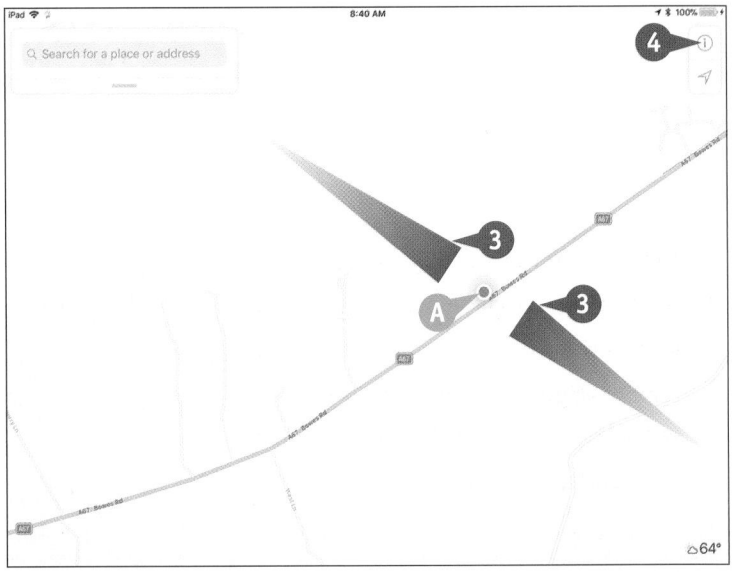

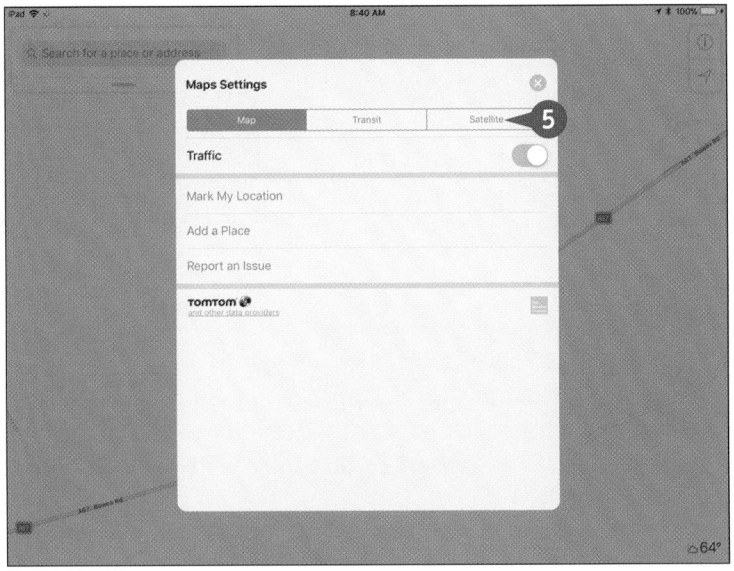

The Satellite view appears.

The Maps Settings dialog changes to a darker theme.

B You can set the **Labels** switch to Off (◘) to hide the place names.

6 Set the **Traffic** switch to On (◘).

7 Tap **Close** (⊗).

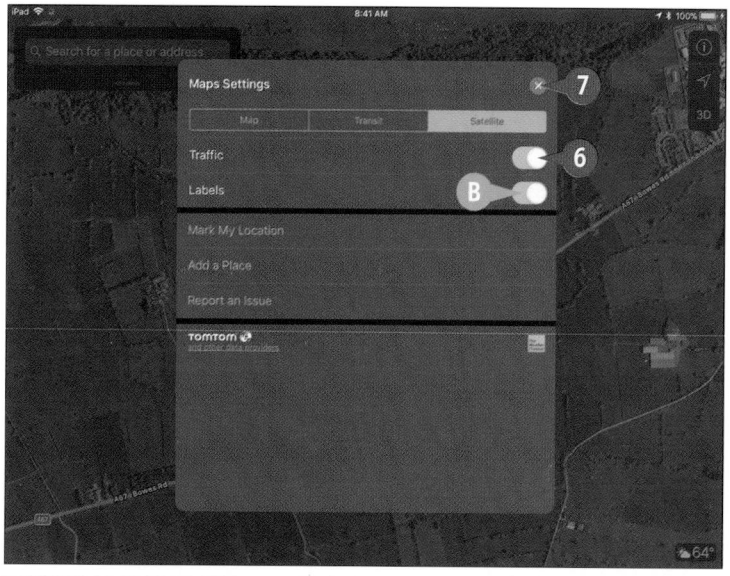

The Maps Settings dialog closes.

C Traffic information appears where it is available.

8 Tap **Location** (➢ changes to ➢) to turn on the Location service.

9 Tap **Location** (➢ changes to ⅄).

D The Compass arrow appears (◉). The red arrow indicates north.

E The map turns to show the direction the iPad is facing, so that you can orient yourself.

F You can tap **3D** to switch to a three-dimensional view.

TIP

What does the blue sector in the location circle mean?

The blue sector shows the direction the iPad is facing. Use this sector to help yourself align the map with the landscape.

Find Directions with the Maps App

The Maps app on your iPad can give you directions to where you want to go. Maps can also show you current traffic congestion to help you identify the most viable route for a journey. Maps displays driving directions by default, but you can also display walking and, in some cities, mass transit directions.

Following map directions requires an Internet connection. If your iPad is not a cellular model and you have an iPhone, share the directions to your iPhone before you leave so that you can follow the route.

Find Directions with the Maps App

1. Press **Home**.

   The Home screen appears.

2. Tap **Maps** ( ).

   The Maps app opens.

3. Tap **Search for a place or address** ( ).

4. Type your search term.

   The Search panel expands and displays search results.

5. Tap the appropriate search result.

   A map of the place appears.

   A panel containing information about the place appears.

6. Tap **Directions**.

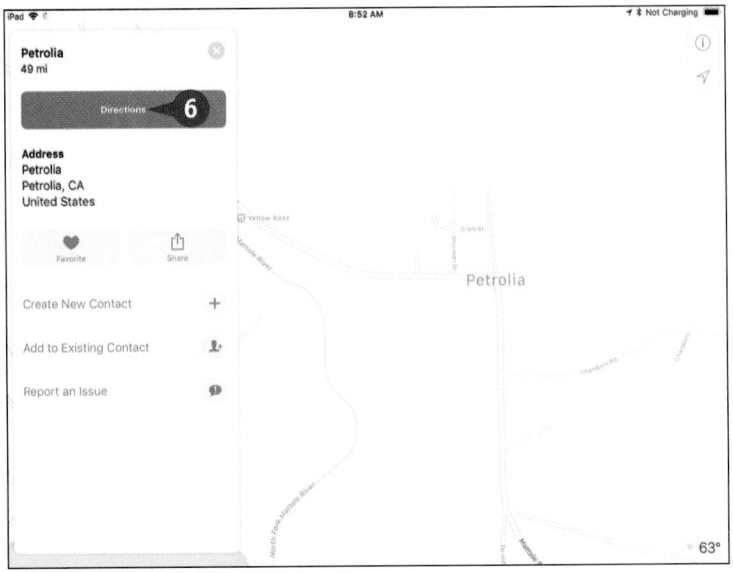

The Directions panel appears, showing possible routes.

A You can change the starting point by tapping the current location, typing the new location in the Change Route dialog, and then tapping **Route**.

Note: In the Change Route dialog, you can tap **Switch Places** (⇅) to switch the start location and end location.

B Red pins mark the start and end points.

C You can tap a time button to view a different route. The time button changes to blue to indicate it is active.

D You can tap **Go** to start following that route.

7 Tap **Details** for the route you want to view.

Maps displays the details for the route.

E You can tap a direction to view that stage of the journey.

F The map shows the detail of that stage.

8 Tap **Done** to return to the overview of the route.

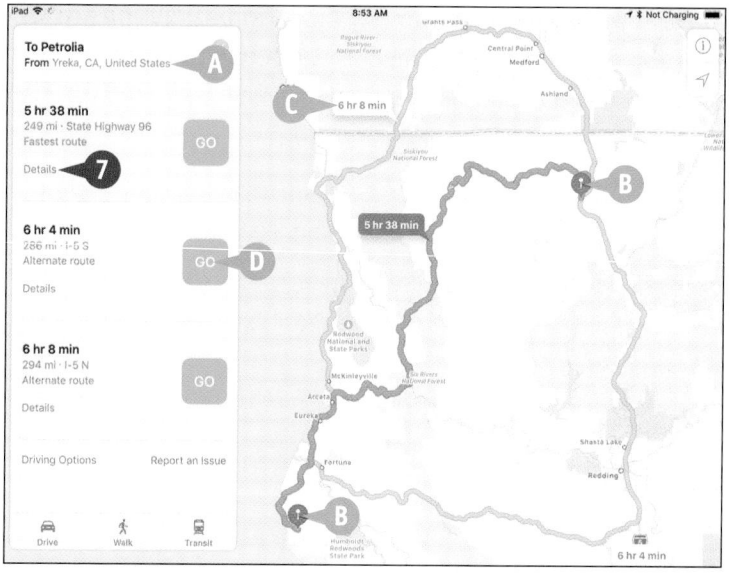

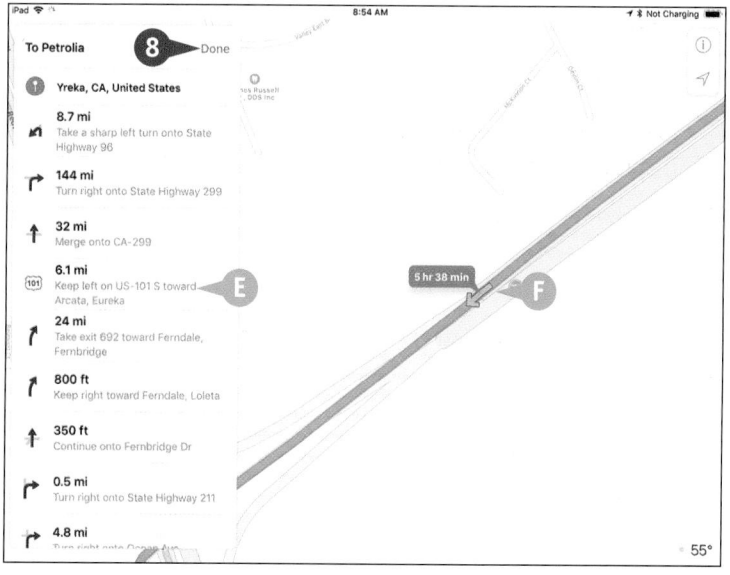

TIPS

How do I get directions for walking?

After getting the directions, tap **Walk** at the bottom of the Directions panel to display the distance and time for walking the route. Be aware that walking directions may be inaccurate. Before walking the route, check that it does not send you across pedestrian-free bridges or through rail tunnels.

How do I get transit directions?

After getting the directions, tap **Transit** at the bottom of the Directions panel to display public transit options. Tap **Details** for the route you would like to view. You can then tap a step in the route to zoom in on it. You can tap **Transit Options** and choose your preferred method or methods of transit.

Using the Maps App's Favorites and Contacts

When you want to return to a location easily in the Maps app, you can create a favorite for the location. Similarly, you can add a location to your contacts, so that you can access it either from the Contacts app or from the Maps app. You can either create a new contact or add the location to an existing contact. You can also return quickly to locations you have visited recently but not marked with a favorite or a contact.

Using the Maps App's Favorites and Contacts

1. Press **Home**.

   The Home screen appears.

2. Tap **Maps** ( ).

   The Maps screen appears.

3. Find the place for which you want to create a favorite. For example, tap and drag the map, or search for the location you want.

4. Tap and hold the place.

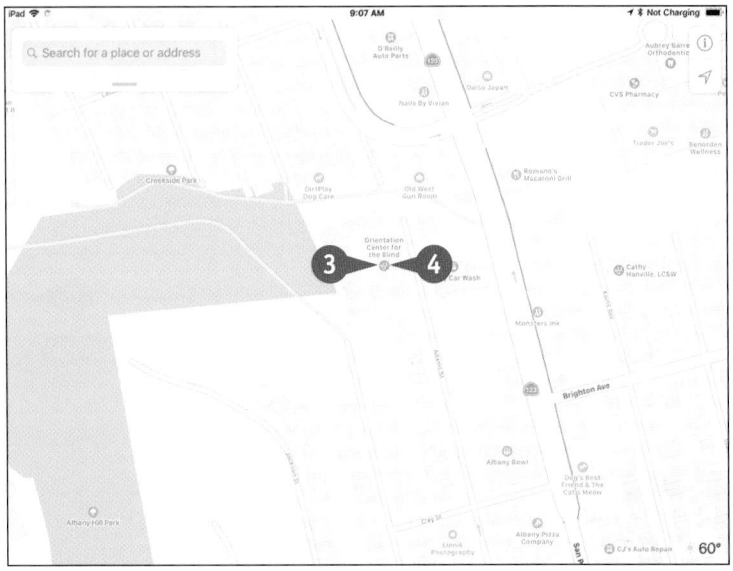

   The Information panel opens, showing details for the place. If the place has a name in Apple Maps, the name appears at the top of the Information panel. Otherwise, the Information panel shows Marked Location.

   A You can quickly get directions to or from this place by tapping **Directions**.

5. Tap **Favorite** ( ).

The Add to Favorites dialog opens.

6 Type the name for the favorite. Alternatively, you can accept the default name, if there is one.

7 Tap **Save**.

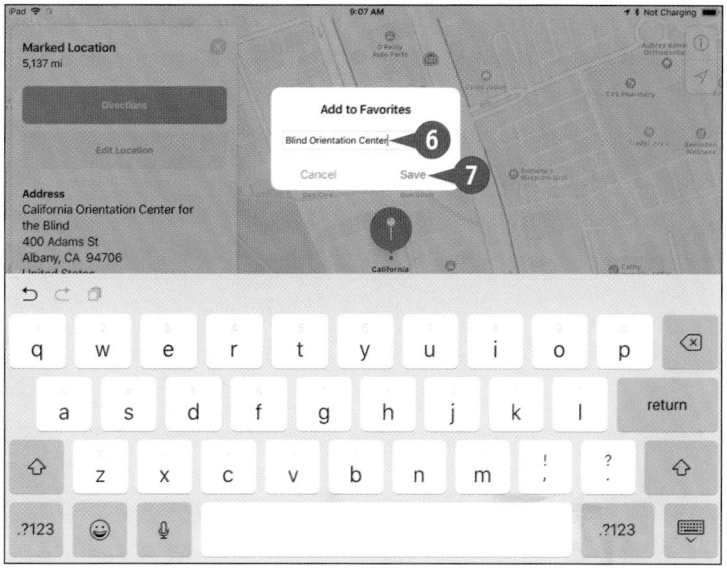

The Add to Favorites dialog closes.

The Information panel remains open.

B Favorite (♥) changes to Favorited (♥).

8 To create a new contact record for this location, tap **Create New Contact** (+). In the New Contact dialog that opens, type the details for the contact, and then tap **Done**.

9 To add this location to an existing contact record, tap **Add to Existing Contact** (👤). On the Contacts screen that appears, tap the contact to which you want to add the location.

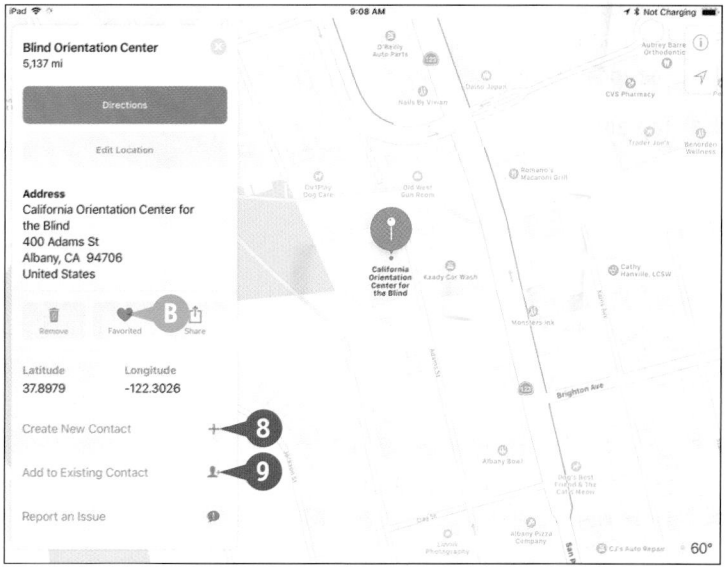

TIP

How do I go to a location for which I have created a favorite or a contact?

In the Maps app, tap **Search for a place or address** and start typing the name of the favorite or contact you want to search for. Matching results appear in the Search panel. Tap the result you want to display.

Using the Clock App

The Clock app on your iPad provides five helpful time-keeping features. The World Clock feature enables you to easily keep track of the time in different cities. The Alarm feature lets you set as many alarms as you need, each with its own schedule and your choice of sound. The Bedtime feature encourages you to follow consistent times for going to bed and waking; it also provides sleep analysis. The Stopwatch feature allows you to time events to the hundredth of a second. The Timer feature counts down a set amount of time and plays a sound when the timer ends.

Open the Clock App and Set Up the World Clock

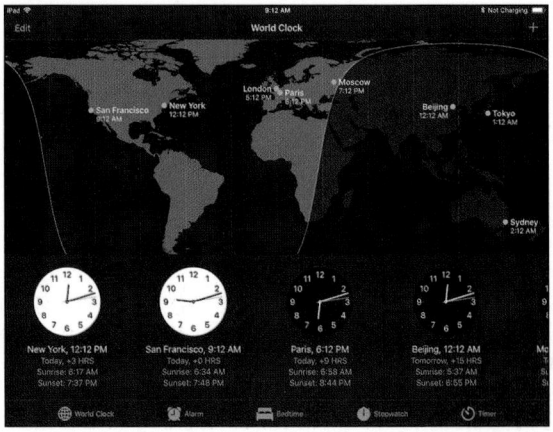

To open the Clock app, press **Home** and then tap **Clock** (🕒) on the Home screen. The app displays the screen for the feature you last used. You can switch among the five features by tapping **World Clock**, **Alarm**, **Bedtime**, **Stopwatch**, or **Timer** at the bottom of the screen.

Tap **World Clock** (🌐 changes to 🌐) at the bottom of the screen to display the World Clock screen. The World Clock shows a dark face for a clock where the local time is between 6:00PM and 5:59AM and a white face for a clock where the local time is between 6:00AM and 5:59PM.

To add cities, tap **Add** (+) and then either type the start of the city name or simply browse the list. Tap the city you want to add, and it appears at the bottom of the list on the World Clock screen.

To rearrange the cities, tap and hold a clock, and then drag it to its new position. To remove a city, tap **Edit**, tap **Delete** (⊖), and then tap **Delete**; tap **Done** when you finish.

Set Alarms

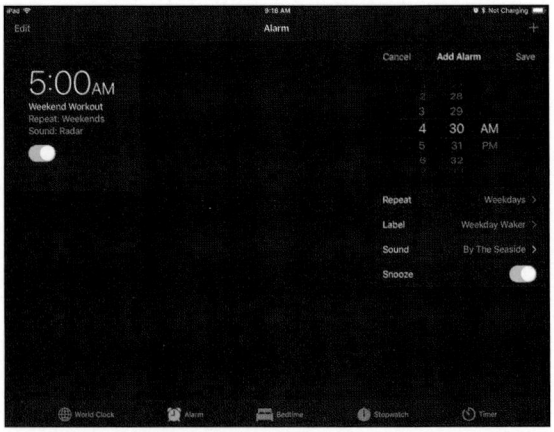

Tap **Alarm** (🕒 changes to 🕒) at the bottom of the screen to display the Alarm screen, which shows the current alarms with switches for enabling and disabling them.

Tap **Add** (+) to start creating a new alarm. In the Add Alarm dialog, spin the dials to set the time. To create a repeating alarm, tap **Repeat** and then tap the days in the Repeat dialog. Tap **Back** (◀) to return to the Add Alarm dialog, tap **Label**, type a descriptive name for the alarm, and then tap **Done**. Tap **Sound** and choose the sound to play, and set the **Snooze** switch to On (◯) or Off ( ), as needed. Tap **Save** to save the new alarm.

Use the Bedtime Feature

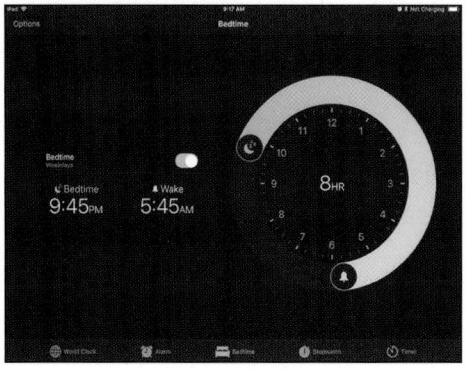

Tap **Bedtime** (changes to) at the bottom of the screen to display the Bedtime screen. To set up the Bedtime feature, tap **Get Started** to open the first Bedtime dialog, in which you specify the time you want to wake up. Tap **Next** to move through the subsequent Bedtime dialogs, in which you choose the days on which the Bedtime alarm should run, specify how many hours of sleep you need each night, choose the timing of your bedtime reminder, and decide what to hear as the alarm. Tap **Save** on the final screen. The Bedtime screen then shows your selections. You can enable or disable Bedtime by setting the **Bedtime** switch to On ( ) or Off ( ). Tap **Options** to change your Bedtime settings.

Time Events with the Stopwatch

Tap **Stopwatch** (changes to) at the bottom of the screen to display the Stopwatch screen. You can then tap **Start** to start the stopwatch running.

If you need to mark lap times, tap **Lap** at the appropriate points. The elapsed lap times appear at the bottom of the screen. The current lap time appears below the main time readout.

Tap **Stop** to stop the stopwatch. You can then tap **Start** to restart the stopwatch or tap **Reset** to reset it so it is ready for its next use.

Use the Timer

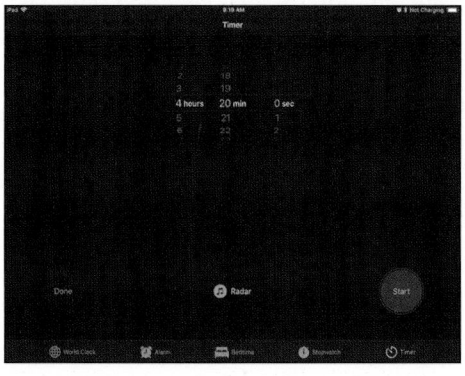

Tap **Timer** (changes to) at the bottom of the screen to display the Timer screen. Spin the **Hours** dial, the **Minutes** dial, and the **Seconds** dial to set the amount of time you want to count down. Tap the current sound name below the dials to display the When Timer Ends dialog, tap the sound you want to play or the **Stop Playing** action, and then tap **Set**. You can then tap **Start** to start the timer.

If you need to interrupt the timer, tap **Cancel** or **Pause**. Otherwise, when the timer sound plays, tap the prompt to stop it.

The Stop Playing action enables you to play music for a period of time and have it stop automatically — for example, to lull you to sleep.

Using Apple Pay

If your iPad has the Touch ID feature for unlocking the screen with a fingerprint, you can use Apple's payment service to make payments online using your iPad. All current iPad models and those from the last several years have Touch ID, but older models do not.

Apple's payment service is called Apple Pay. You can use it at a wide variety of online stores for convenience and security. If you have an iPhone 6 or a later model, such as an iPhone 8 or iPhone X, you can also use Apple Pay to make contactless payments at payment terminals.

Understand How Apple Pay Works

The Apple Pay service links with the four major payment networks — Visa, MasterCard, American Express, and Discover — and enables you to use debit cards and credit cards issued on these networks by a wide variety of banks.

The iPhone 6 and later iPhone models can use Apple Pay to make contactless payments at physical sales terminals in retail locations, thanks to the built-in Near Field Communications, or NFC, chip. At this writing, no iPad has an NFC chip, but iPads that have Touch ID can still use Apple Pay to make payments in compatible apps and websites.

Set Up Your Means of Payment

Before you can make a payment with Apple Pay, you must set up your means of payment. To do so, you add the details of your debit card or credit card to Apple Pay.

When you first set up your iPad, iOS prompts you to add a credit card or debit card to Apple Pay. You can add other cards by using the Settings app. Press **Home** to display the Home screen, and then tap **Settings** (⚙) to display the Settings screen. Tap **Wallet & Apple Pay** (▭) to display the Wallet & Apple Pay screen, tap **Add Credit or Debit Card**, and then follow the prompts. You can either use the iPad's rear camera to recognize the card's details or tap **Enter Card Details Manually** and type in the details.

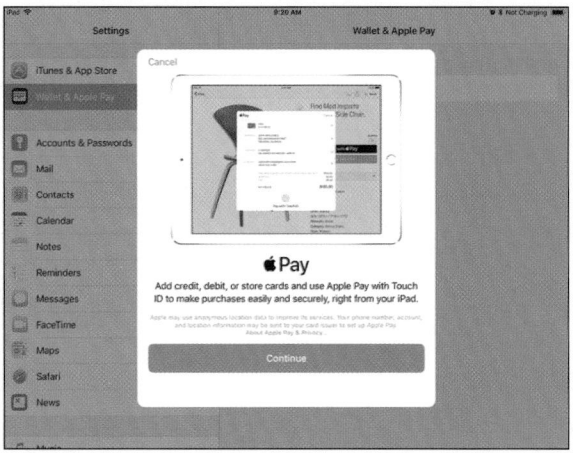

The iPad may also prompt you to add the credit card or debit card associated with your iTunes account to Apple Pay.

Make a Payment Online with Your iPad

After setting up Apple Pay, you can use it to make payments online using your iPad. You can make payments in various apps, including the Safari web browser. You can make payments to any retailer that accepts Apple Pay.

When an app displays a button with the Apple Pay logo on a payment screen, you can tap that button to use Apple Pay. On the subsequent screen, you use one of the fingers you have registered for Touch ID on **Home** to confirm the purchase and authenticate your identity.

Make a Payment at a Payment Terminal with an iPhone or Apple Watch

If you have an iPhone 6 or a later model, such as an iPhone 8 or iPhone X, you can use Apple Pay to make payments easily at payment terminals located in retailers, cafés and restaurants, and places such as stations or airports.

Before you can make a payment, you must set up your means of payment on the iPhone. Apple Pay does not sync credit and debit cards from one iOS device to another, so you must add to Apple Pay on the iPhone each card you want to use for Apple Pay. Press **Home** to display the Home screen, and then tap **Settings** ( ) to display the Settings screen. Tap **Wallet & Apple Pay** ( ) to display the Wallet & Apple Pay screen, tap **Add Credit or Debit Card**, and then follow the prompts.

To make a payment, you simply bring your iPhone up to the payment terminal, verify the amount displayed on-screen, and place one of the fingers you have registered with Touch ID on **Home** to approve the transaction and authenticate your identity.

If you have an Apple Watch, you can use it to make payments at payment terminals. Because your Apple Watch is an accessory to your iPhone, Apple Watch picks up the cards you have added to your iPhone; you do not need to add them to Apple Watch separately.

CHAPTER 9

Playing Music and Videos

In addition to being a powerful handheld computer, your iPad is a full-scale music and video player.

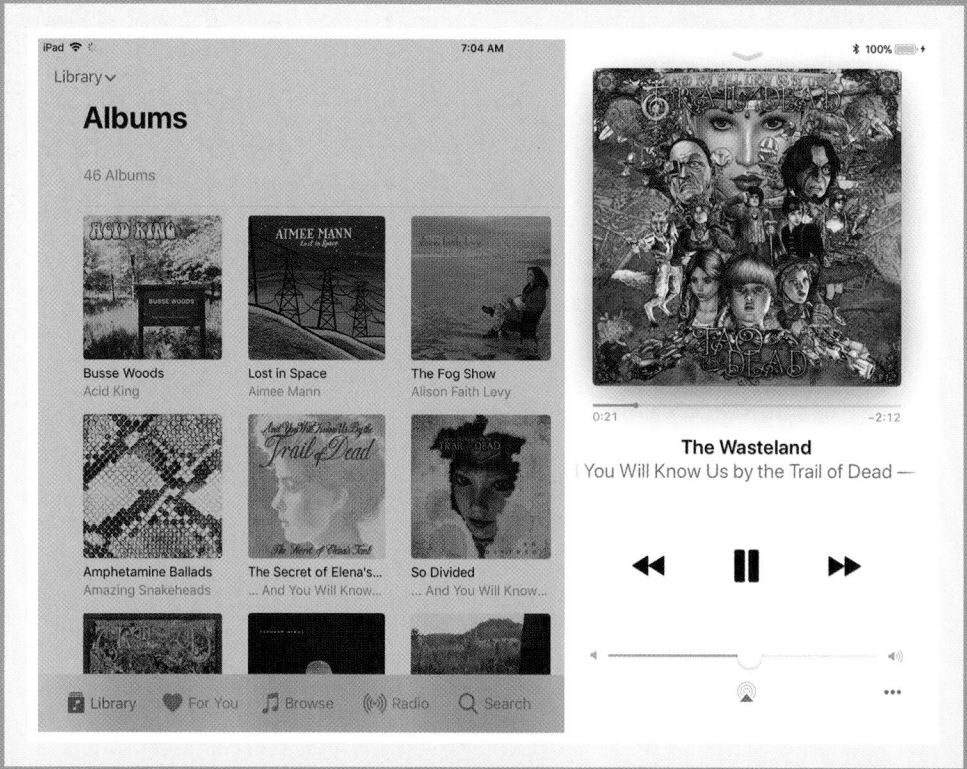

Navigate the Music App and Set Preferences 242
Play Music Using the Music App 246
Play Videos Using the TV App 248
Play Music and Videos Using AirPlay 250
Create a Music Playlist 254
Configure iPad Audio Settings 256
Listen to Apple Music Radio 258

Navigate the Music App and Set Preferences

The Music app enables you to enjoy music you have loaded on your iPad, music you have stored on Apple's iTunes Match service, and music on Apple's Beats 1 Radio and Apple Music services. This chapter shows the Music app with an Apple Music subscription.

The Music app packs a wide range of functionality into its interface. This section shows you how to navigate the Music app and set your musical preferences.

Navigate the Music App and Set Preferences

1. Press **Home**.

   The Home screen appears.

2. Tap **Music** ( ).

   The Music app opens.

3. If Library is not selected, tap **Library** (changes to).

   The Library screen appears, showing your music library.

   A The Recently Added section shows items added recently to your library.

4. Tap **Library** ( ).

   The Library panel opens.

   B You can tap an item, such as **Playlists** or **Artists**, to browse the library by that item.

   C You can tap **Downloaded Music** to see all the music stored on your iPad.

   D You can tap **Home Sharing** to view music that others are sharing on your local network via the Home Sharing feature in iTunes.

5. Tap **Edit**.

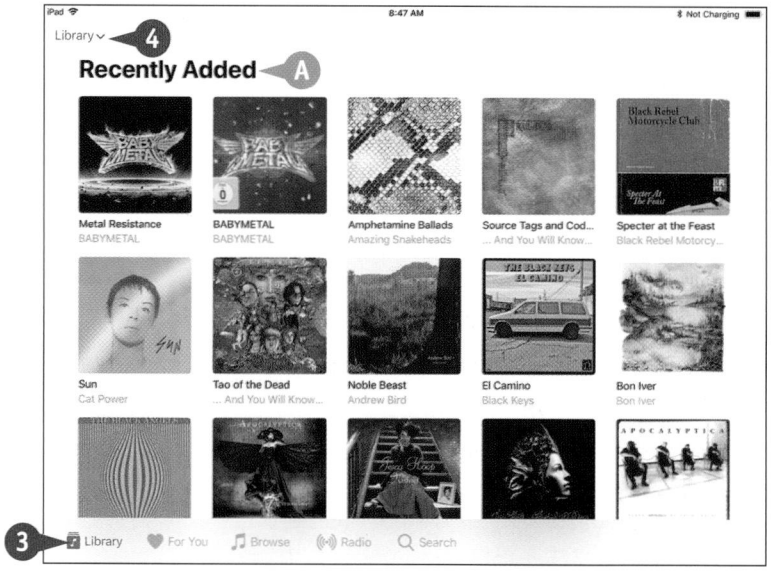

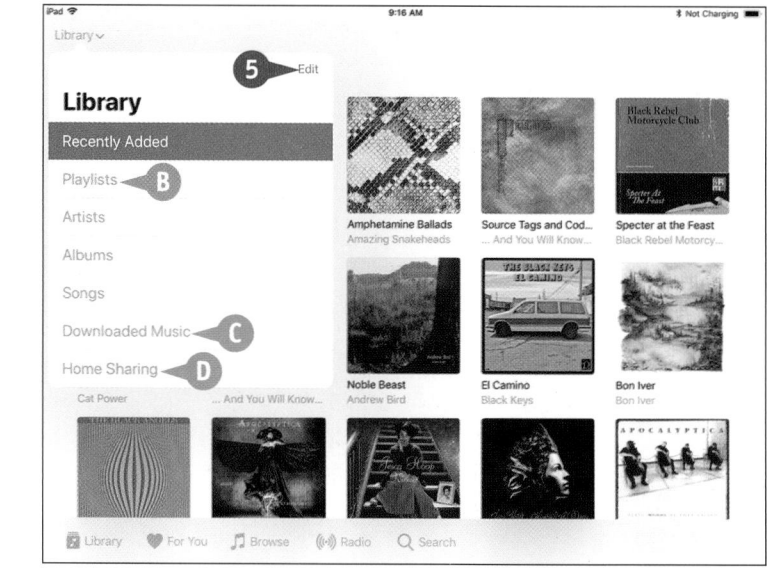

The Library panel opens for editing.

6. Tap an empty selection circle to select it (changes to), adding that item to the Library list.

7. Tap a selected selection circle to deselect it (changes to), removing that item from the Library list.

8. Drag a selection handle ( ) up or down to move an item in the list.

9. Tap **Done**.

   The Library panel displays your customized list.

10. Tap outside the Library panel.

    The Library panel closes.

11. Tap **For You** (changes to).

    The For You screen appears, showing music suggestions for you.

Note: On the For You screen, you can scroll down to see different categories of items, such as Artist Spotlight Playlists and New Releases. Scroll a category left to see more items in it.

E You can tap your avatar icon to display the Account dialog. From here, you can specify which music you like. See the tip for details.

12. Tap **Browse** (changes to).

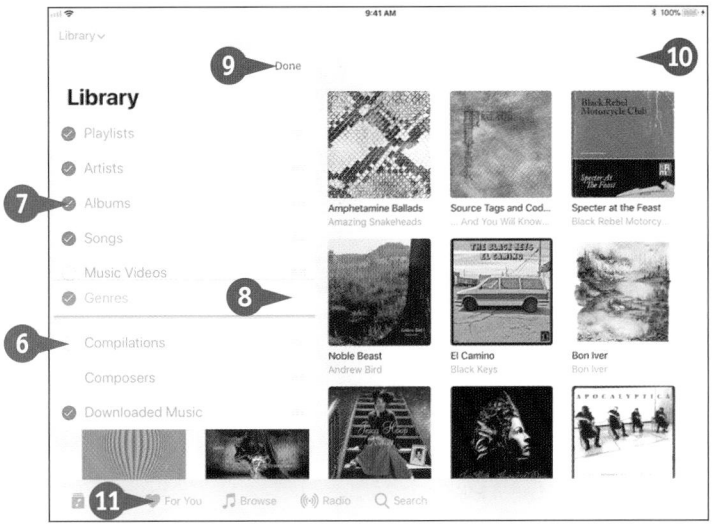

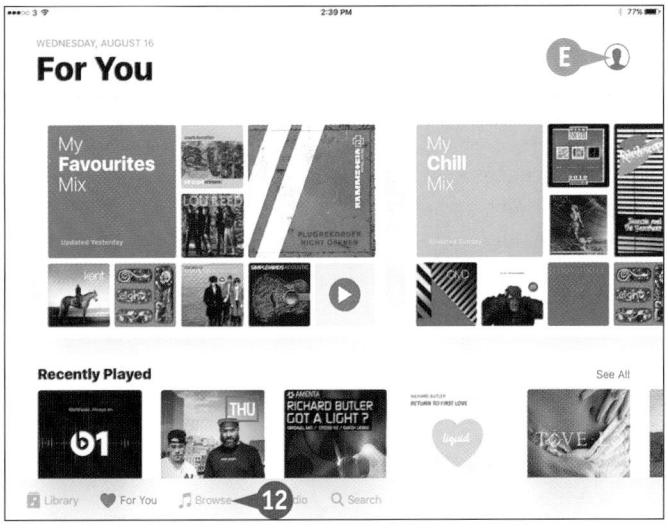

TIP

How do I specify which music genres and artists I like?

Tap **For You** (changes to) to display the For You screen, then tap **Account** ( ) to display the Account dialog. Tap **Choose Artists for You** to display the Tell Us What You're Into screen, which shows circles for genres such as Classic Rock, Metal, and Blues. Tap a circle to indicate you like it; double-tap a circle to indicate you love it; or tap and hold to remove a circle. Tap **Next** to display circles containing artists. Make selections by tapping, double-tapping, or tapping and holding, or tap **More Artists** to change those displayed. Tap **Done** when you finish.

continued ▶

The Radio feature allows you to listen to Apple's Beats 1 Radio station and a wide variety of other stations, while the Connect feature lets you connect to artists — or their social-media representatives — online.

From the Playlists screen, you can quickly access the playlists that come built into the Music app. You can also create and edit your own playlists. From the My Music screen, you can explore and play your own music.

Navigate the Music App and Set Preferences (continued)

The Browse screen appears, providing ways to browse music.

Note: On the Browse screen, scroll down to see categories such as Hot Tracks, New Releases, and Videos. Scroll a category right to see more items in it, or tap **See All** to go to the screen for the category.

13 Tap **Radio** (changes to).

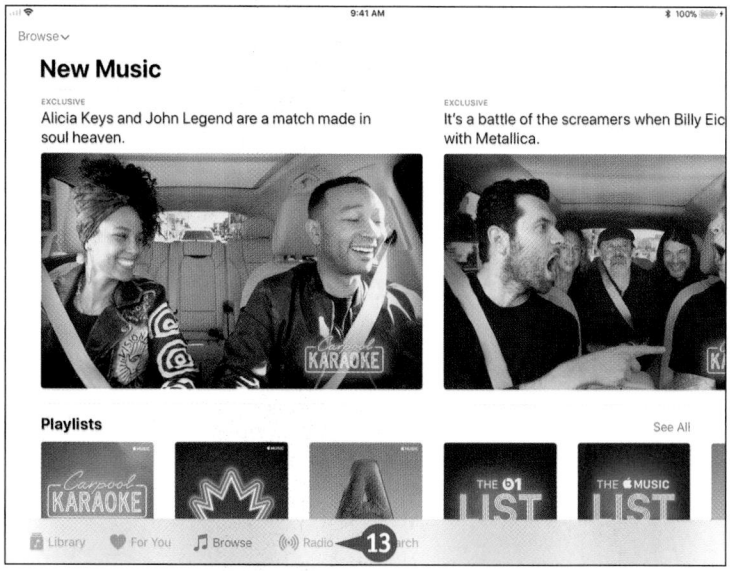

The Radio screen appears.

F You can tap a station to start it playing.

Note: See the section "Listen to Apple Music Radio" later in this chapter for more information on the Radio feature.

14 Tap **Search** (changes to).

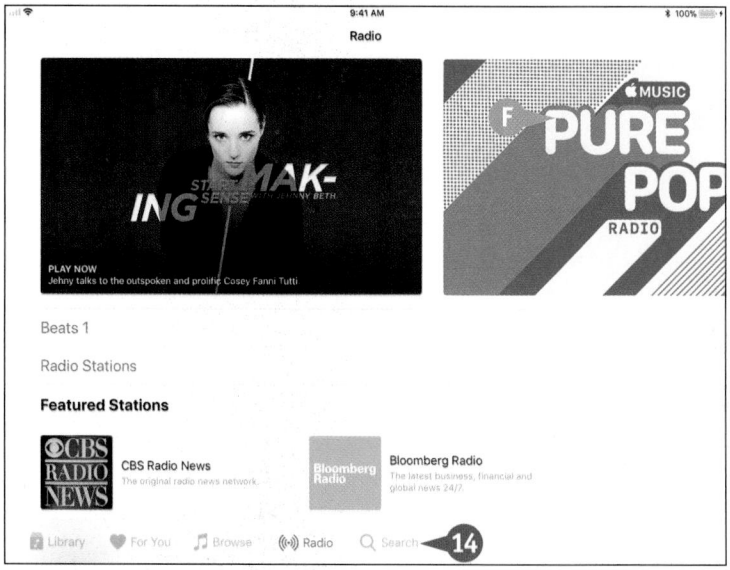

The Search screen appears.

G You can tap one of your recent searches to repeat it.

H You can tap one of the trending searches to perform it. Trending searches are searches that other people are performing on Apple Music.

15 Tap the **Search** box.

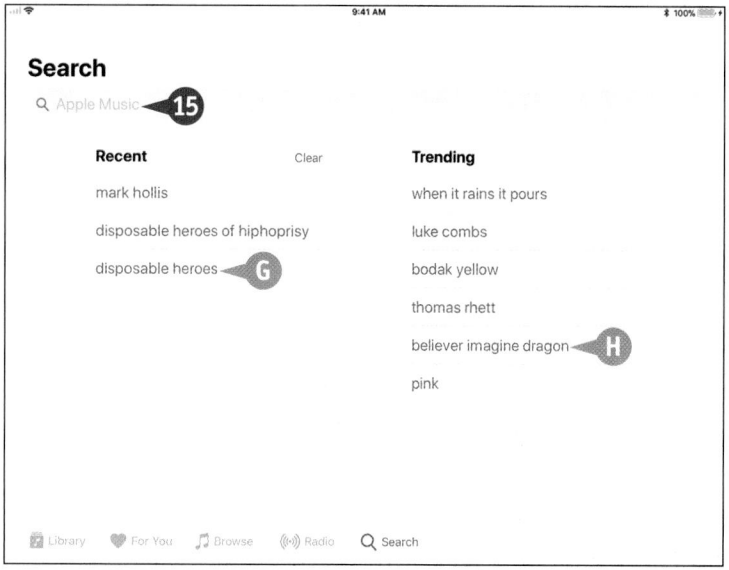

The keyboard and search controls appear.

16 Start typing your search terms.

I Search results appear.

17 Tap **Apple Music** to view results on Apple Music, or tap **Your Library** to view results in your library.

18 Tap the result you want to view.

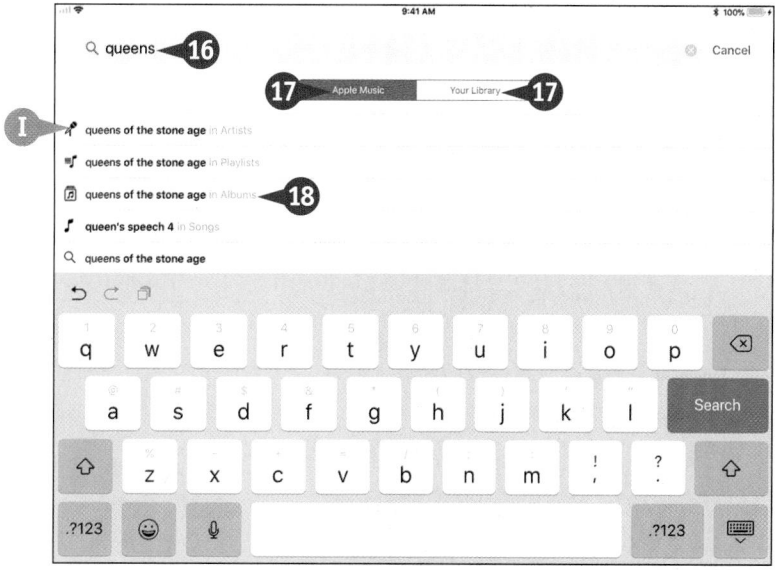

TIP

How do I put my music on my iPad from my computer?

To copy music from your computer to your iPad, use iTunes. See the section "Choose Which Items to Sync from Your Computer" in Chapter 1 for details.

Play Music Using the Music App

After loading music on your iPad, you can play it back using the Music app. If you have an iTunes Match subscription or Apple Music subscription, you can also play music by streaming it across the Internet.

You can play music by song or by album, as described in this section; create custom playlists to play songs in your preferred order, as described in the section "Create a Music Playlist" later in this chapter; or play by artist, genre, or composer.

Play Music Using the Music App

1. Press **Home**.

   The Home screen appears.

2. Tap **Music** (♫).

   The Music app opens.

3. Tap **Library** (changes to).

   The Library screen appears.

4. Tap **Library** (⌄).

   The Library panel opens.

5. Tap the button by which to browse. This example uses **Songs**.

   The associated screen appears. In this example, the Songs screen appears.

   A You can set the sort order by tapping **Sort** and then tapping **Title** or **Artist** on the pop-up panel.

Note: Scroll up or down the screen as needed to reach the song you want to play.

   B You can tap the letter that starts the name of the item you want to play. That section of the list appears.

   C You can tap above the letter A in the navigation list to go back to the top of the screen.

6. Tap the song you want to play.

   D The song starts playing.

7. Tap **Now Playing**, the song's button.

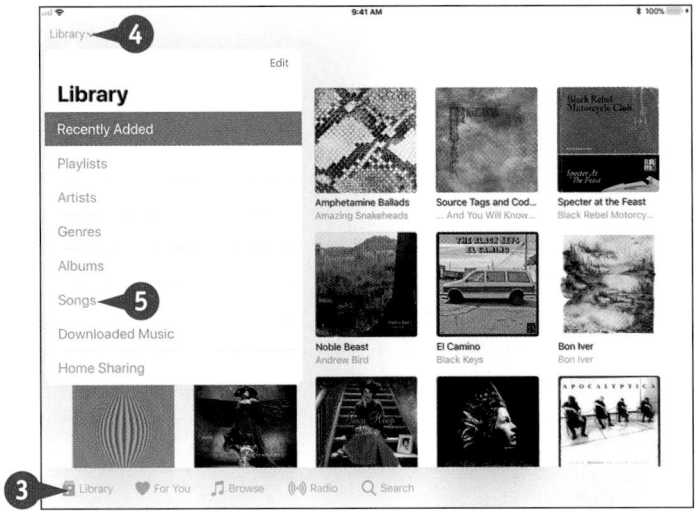

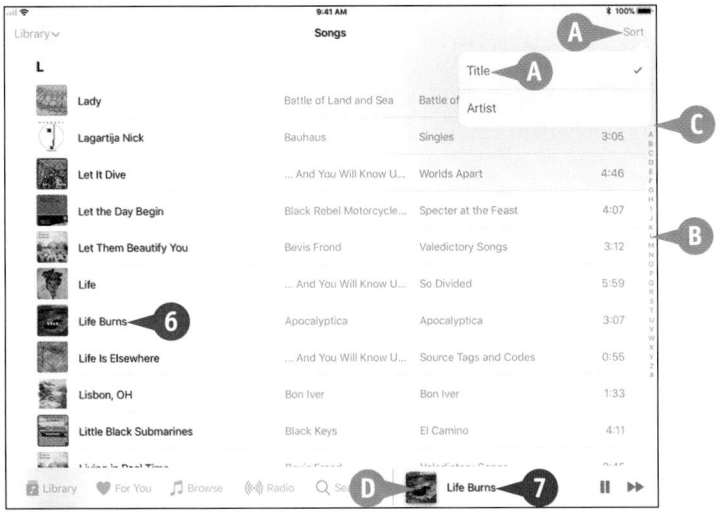

The Now Playing panel appears, showing the album cover and playback controls.

E You can drag the playhead — the circle on the progress bar — to move through the song.

F You can tap **AirPlay** ( ) to open the AirPlay dialog, which lets you play music through an AirPlay device or Apple TV.

G You can tap **Minimize** ( ) to shrink the Now Playing panel down to a button again.

8 Swipe up to display the lower part of the Now Playing panel.

H You can tap **Shuffle** to turn shuffling on (changes to) or off (changes to).

I You can tap **Repeat** (changes to) to repeat the current list. To repeat the current song only, tap **Repeat** (or changes to).

J The Up Next list shows upcoming songs.

K You can tap a song to start it playing.

L You can tap **More** ( ) to display a panel of other actions, such as Love ( ), Dislike ( ), and Add to a Playlist ( ).

9 Tap outside the Now Playing panel.

The Now Playing panel shrinks to a button again.

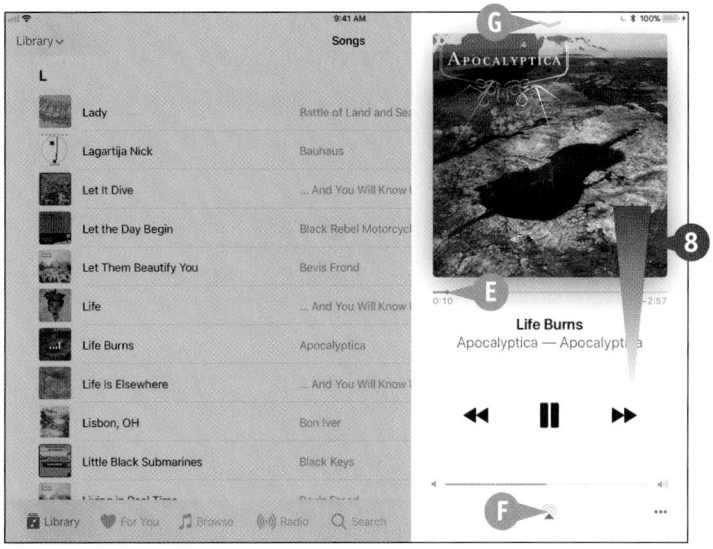

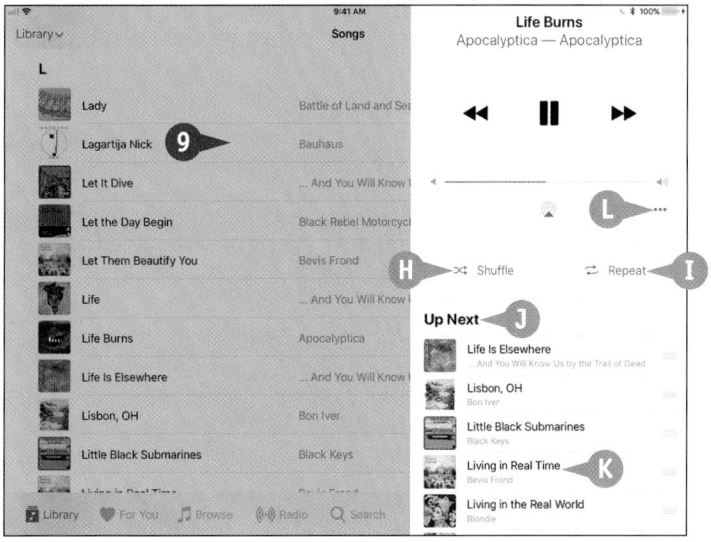

TIP

How can I control the Music app's playback when I am using another app?

You can quickly control the Music app from Control Center. Swipe up from the bottom of the screen to open Control Center, and then use the controls in the Music box. To access further controls, tap and hold the Music box until it expands.

Play Videos Using the TV App

To play videos — such as movies, TV shows, or music videos — you use the TV app, which you can set up to use your existing account with a TV provider. You can play back a video on the iPad screen, which is handy when you are traveling; on a TV to which you connect the iPad; or on a TV connected to an Apple TV box. Using a TV is great when you need to share a movie or other video with family, friends, or colleagues.

Play Videos Using the TV App

Set Up the TV App

1. Press **Home**.

   The Home screen appears.

Note: If your iPad does not have the TV app, use the Videos app ( ) instead. This app does not connect to TV providers.

2. Tap **TV** ( ).

   The Welcome to the TV App dialog opens.

3. Tap **Continue.**

   The Sign In to Your TV Provider dialog opens.

4. Tap **Sign In**.

   A If you do not have a TV provider, or you do not want to sign in now, tap **Not Now**.

   The Choose a TV Provider dialog opens.

   B You can tap **Search** ( ) and start typing your TV provider's name to locate the provider.

5. Tap your TV provider.

   A dialog for signing in to your provider appears.

6. Type your credentials.

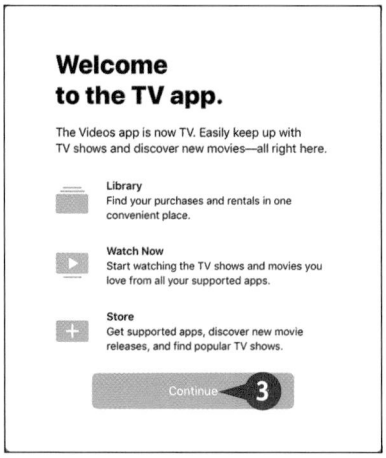

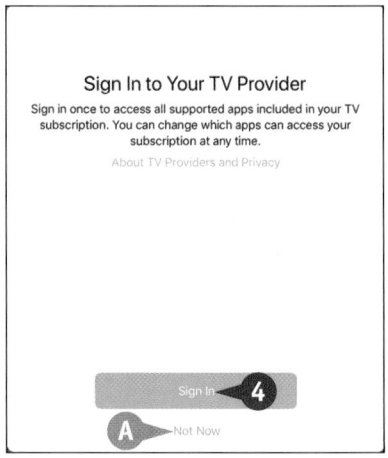

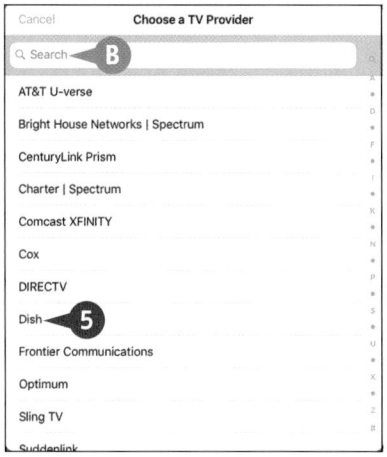

7. Tap **Sign In**.

   The TV app signs in to your TV provider.

   The Watch Now screen appears.

8. Tap **Get Started**, and then follow the prompts to connect any TV-related apps to the TV app.

Watch a Video

1. In the TV app, tap the video source. In this example, tap **Library** (changes to).

   The Library screen appears.

2. Tap the video category, such as **Home Videos**.

   The category screen appears.

3. Tap the video you want to view.

   The details screen for the video appears.

4. Tap **Play** ( ).

   The video starts playing.

5. When you need to control playback, tap the screen.

   The playback controls appear, and you can pause the video, move forward, or take other actions.

C You can drag the playhead to move quickly forward or backward through the movie.

D For some videos, you can tap **Full Screen** (changes to , or changes to) to switch between full-screen and letterboxed views.

E You can drag the **Volume** slider to adjust the volume.

F You can tap **Picture-in-Picture** ( ) to switch to Picture-in-Picture view. Picture-in-Picture ( ) appears only if your iPad supports this feature.

6. Tap **Done** when you want to stop playing the video.

TIPS

How do I play back videos on my television from my iPad?
If you have an Apple TV or AirPlay-compatible device, use AirPlay, as explained in the next section, "Play Music and Videos Using AirPlay." Otherwise, use the Apple Lightning Digital AV Adapter and an HDMI cable to connect your iPad to a TV.

What other videos can I play?
You can also play videos included on web pages. To do so, press **Home**, tap **Safari** ( ), navigate to the appropriate web page, and then tap the video.

Play Music and Videos Using AirPlay

Using the AirPlay feature, you can play music from your iPad on remote speakers connected to an AirPlay-compatible device such as an AirPort Express or Apple TV. Similarly, you can play a video from various apps, such as the TV app, on a TV or monitor connected to an Apple TV. The video appears only on the TV or monitor, not on the iPad's screen.

Play Music and Videos Using AirPlay

Play Music on External Speakers Using AirPlay

1. Press **Home**.

   The Home screen appears.

2. Tap **Music** (♫).

   The Music app opens.

3. Navigate to and tap the song you want to play.

   The song starts playing.

4. Tap **Now Playing**.

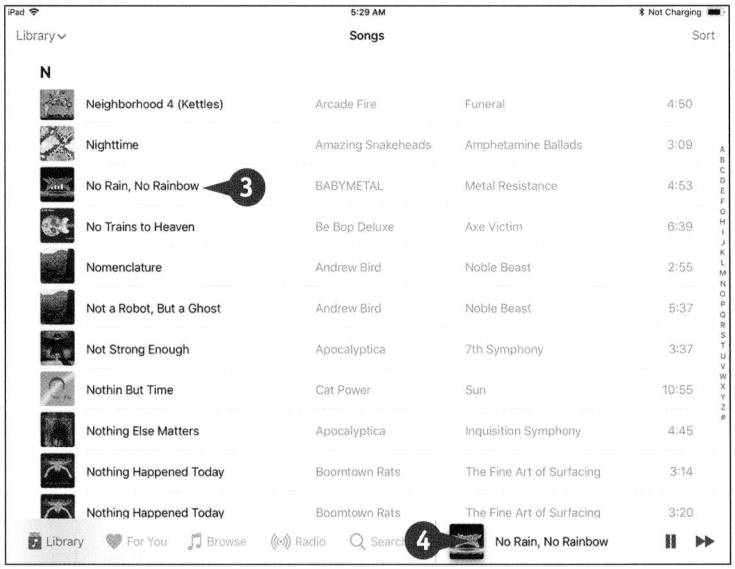

   The Now Playing panel opens.

5. Tap **AirPlay** (◎).

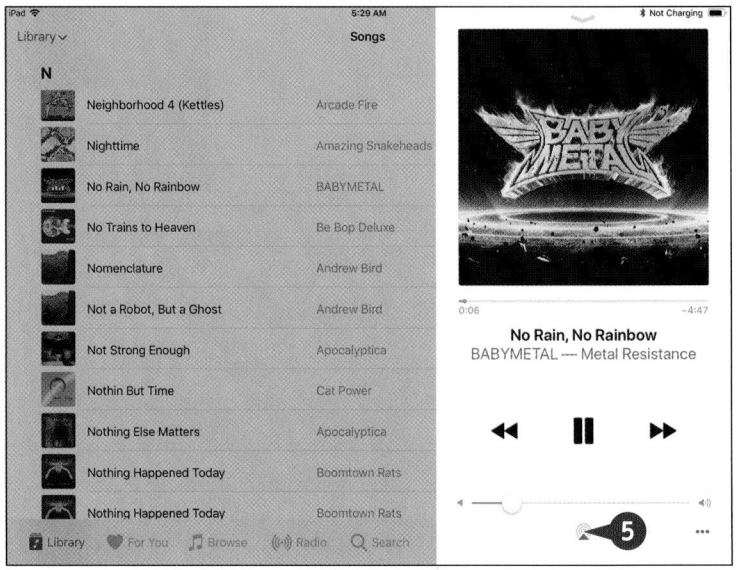

The AirPlay dialog opens.

6. Tap the speakers or Apple TV through which you want to play music.

   The music starts playing through the AirPlay device.

7. Drag the **Volume** slider to adjust the volume as needed.

8. Tap **Done**.

   The AirPlay dialog closes.

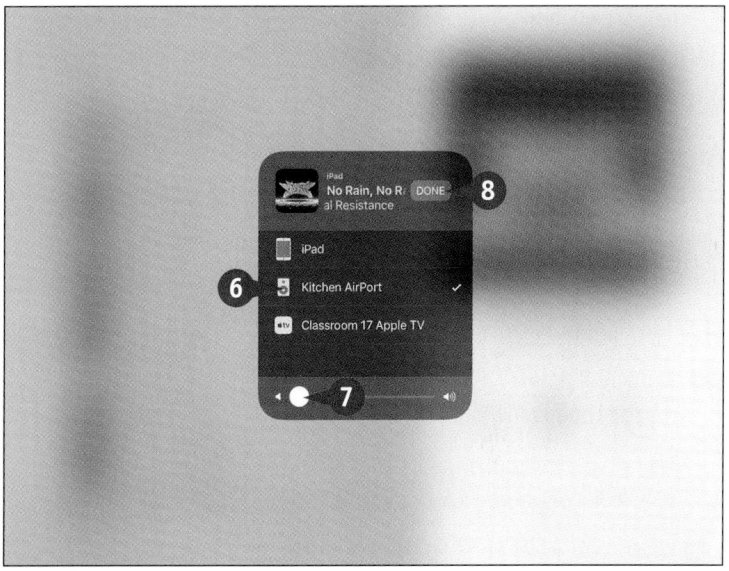

Display Your iPad's Screen on a TV

1. Swipe up from the bottom of the screen.

   Control Center opens.

2. Tap **Screen Mirroring** (▭).

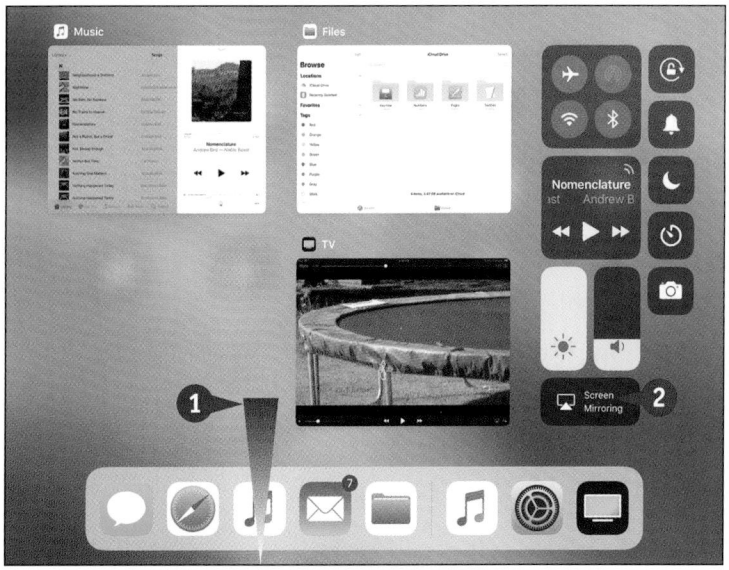

TIP

Why do my devices not appear in the AirPlay dialog?
AirPlay devices appear only when your iPad is connected to the same wireless network as the devices. If you use multiple wireless networks, make sure your iPad is connected to the right network.

continued ▶

The Screen Mirroring feature enables you to display the contents of the iPad's screen on a TV or monitor connected to an Apple TV. Screen Mirroring is great for sharing information, enjoying photos, or working collaboratively.

As well as controlling AirPlay from within the Music app or the TV app, you can control AirPlay from Control Center. This capability is especially convenient for controlling audio playback.

Play Music and Videos Using AirPlay (continued)

The Screen Mirroring dialog opens.

3. Tap the Apple TV to which you want to mirror the screen output.

   The iPad's output appears on the TV or monitor connected to the Apple TV.

A. When you want to stop mirroring the screen, tap **Stop Mirroring**.

4. Tap outside the Screen Mirroring dialog.

   The Screen Mirroring dialog closes.

5. Tap the thumbnail for the app you want to display.

   Control Center closes.

   The app appears full-screen.

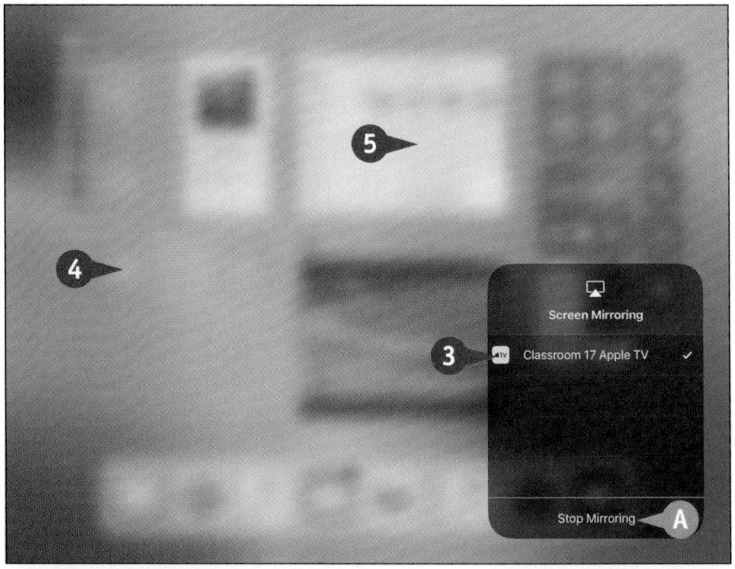

Play Video to an Apple TV via AirPlay

1. Press **Home**.

   The Home screen appears.

2. Tap **TV** ( ).

   The TV app opens.

3. Navigate to and tap the movie or show you want to play.

   The movie or show starts playing.

4. Tap the screen.

   The playback controls appear.

5. Tap **AirPlay** ( ).

The AirPlay dialog opens.

6. Tap the Apple TV you want to use.

   The video starts playing on the TV or monitor connected to the Apple TV.

7. Drag the **Volume** slider to adjust the volume as needed.

8. Tap **Done**.

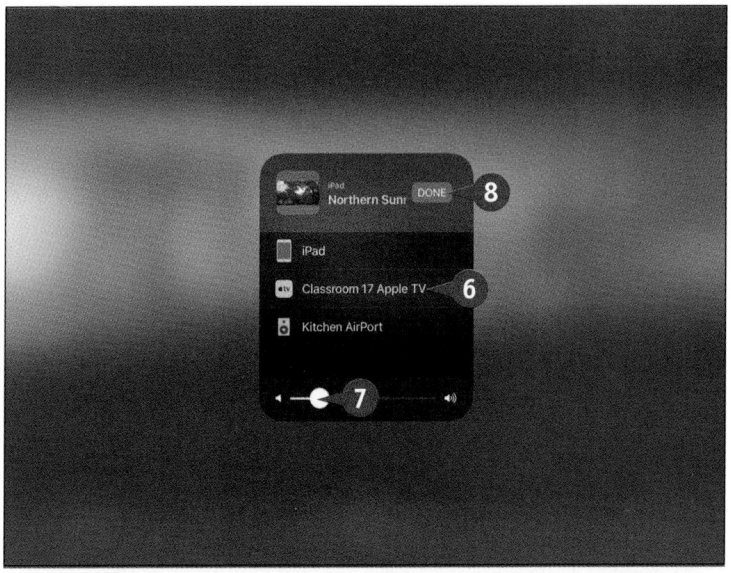

The AirPlay dialog closes.

B. The AirPlay icon (▬) appears in the TV app to indicate that the video is playing via AirPlay.

C. To stop using AirPlay, tap **AirPlay** (▬) to open the AirPlay dialog, tap **iPad**, and then tap **Done**.

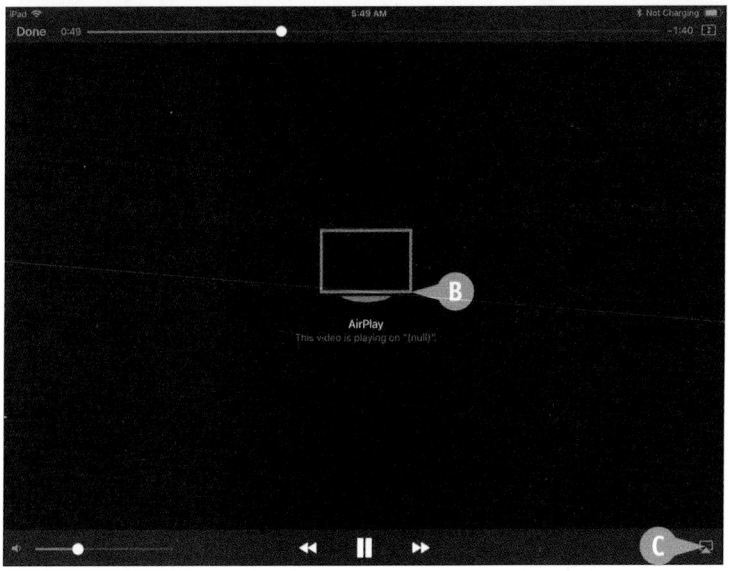

TIPS

How do I use AirPlay for music playback in Control Center?
Swipe up from the bottom of the screen to open Control Center. Tap and hold the Music box to open the Music dialog. You can then tap **AirPlay** (▬) to open the AirPlay dialog, tap the AirPlay device or Apple TV you want to use, and then tap **Done**.

Can I use AirPlay in other apps?
Yes — if an app displays an AirPlay icon, tap that icon to launch AirPlay from within that app.

Create a Music Playlist

Playlists are a great way to enjoy music on your iPad. Instead of playing individual songs or playing a CD's songs from start to finish, you can create a playlist that contains only the songs you want in your preferred order. You can create as many playlists as you need, and you can edit your existing playlists to change the songs and their order.

Create a Music Playlist

1. Press **Home**.

   The Home screen appears.

2. Tap **Music** ( ).

   The Music screen appears.

3. Tap **Library** (changes to).

   The Library screen appears.

4. Tap **Library** ( ).

   The Library panel opens.

5. Tap **Playlists**.

   The Playlists screen appears.

6. Tap **New**.

   The New Playlist screen appears.

7. Type the name for the playlist.

8. Optionally, type a description for the playlist.

   A You can add a photo to the playlist by tapping **Add Photo** ( ) and then tapping either **Take Photo** or **Choose Photo** in the dialog that opens.

9. Tap **Add Music** ( ).

   The Add Music dialog opens.

10. Tap the category by which you want to browse: **Artists**, **Albums**, **Songs**, **Music Videos**, **Genres**, **Composers**, **Compilations**, or **Playlists**. This example uses **Songs**.

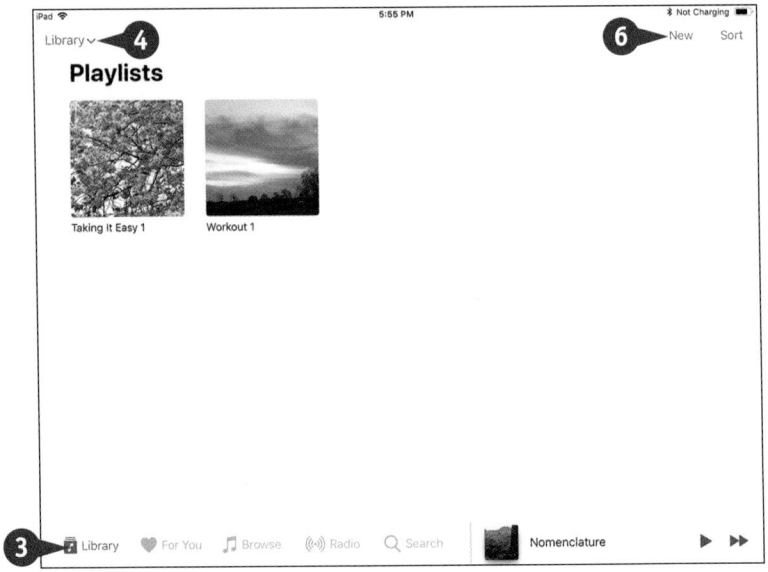

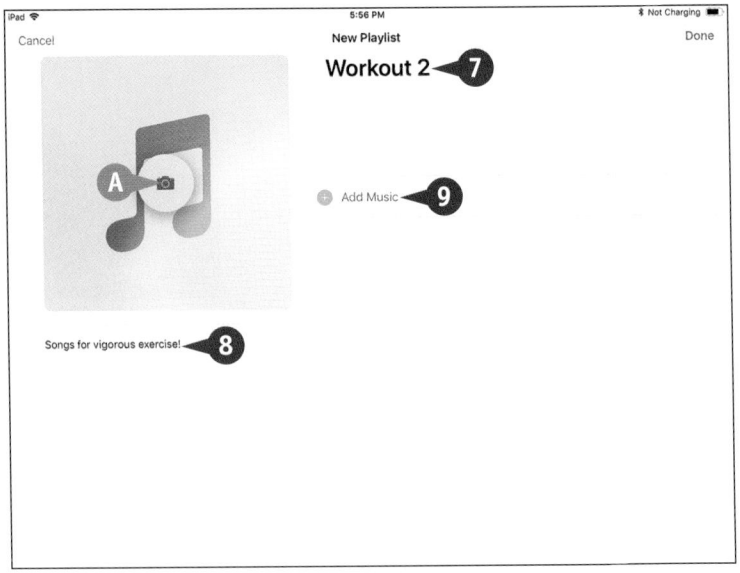

The dialog for that category opens. In this example, the Songs dialog opens.

11 Tap **Add** (+) for each song you want to add, or simply tap the song's button (+ changes to ✓).

12 Tap **Done**.

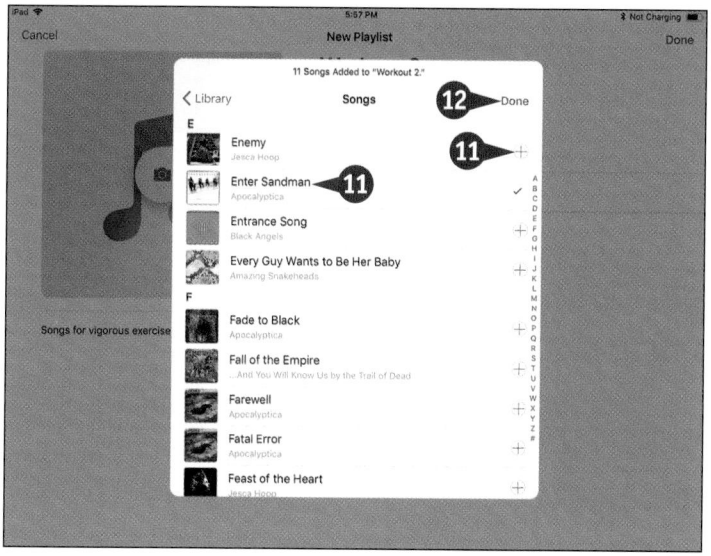

The playlist appears.

13 Tap a handle (≡) and drag a song up or down to move it.

B To remove a song, you can tap **Delete** (⊖) and then tap the textual **Delete** button.

C To add songs, you can tap **Add Music** (⊕).

14 Tap **Done** when you finish editing the playlist.

The playlist appears on the Playlists screen.

You can tap the playlist to open it, and then tap a song to start it playing.

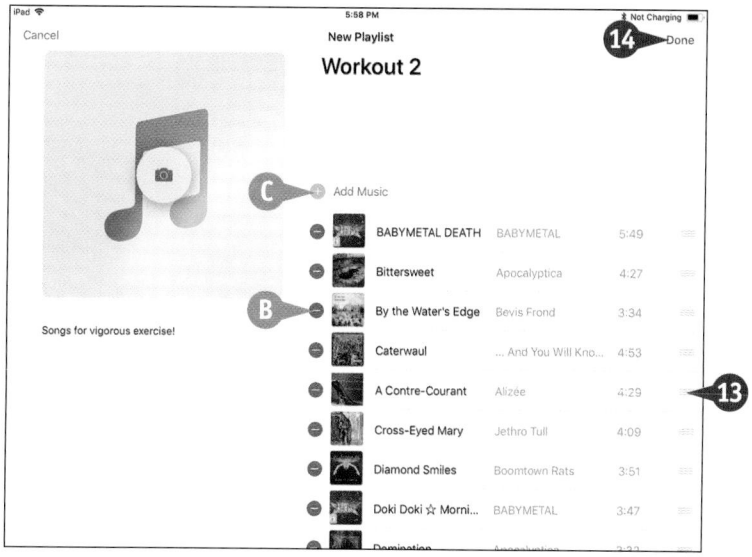

TIP

How do I delete a playlist?

In the Music app, tap **Library** (changes to) to display the Library screen, tap **Library** (⌄) to open the Library panel, and then tap **Playlists** to display the Playlists screen. Tap and hold the playlist you want to delete, tap **Delete from Library** (🗑) in the pop-up panel, and then tap **Delete Playlist** in the confirmation dialog.

You can delete only playlists you have created on your iPad. To remove a playlist you have synced from iTunes, deselect the playlist in iTunes and sync again.

Configure iPad Audio Settings

To make your music sound the way you want, you can apply an Equalizer, or EQ, preset. The EQ offers presets that help to accentuate music, including Rock, Hip Hop, Jazz, Piano, and Vocal Latin. The EQ even includes Spoken Word and Vocal Booster presets.

EQ presets change the sound quality as soon as you apply them. Some settings are more noticeable than others. Which EQ preset is best depends on your music, your speakers or headphones, and your ears.

Configure iPad Audio Settings

1. Press **Home**.

   The Home screen appears.

2. Tap **Settings** ( ).

   The Settings screen appears.

3. Tap **Music** ( ).

   The Music screen appears.

4. Set the **Sound Check** switch to On ( ) to have iTunes play songs at the same volume level, or to Off ( ) to play each song at its own level.

5. Tap **EQ**.

   The EQ screen appears.

Note: The EQ options are audio presets that you can choose to customize audio playback on your iPad.

6. Tap an EQ option to select it.

Note: Playing music with an EQ preset uses a little more battery power than playing without a preset, but not usually enough to worry about.

7. Tap **Music** ( ).

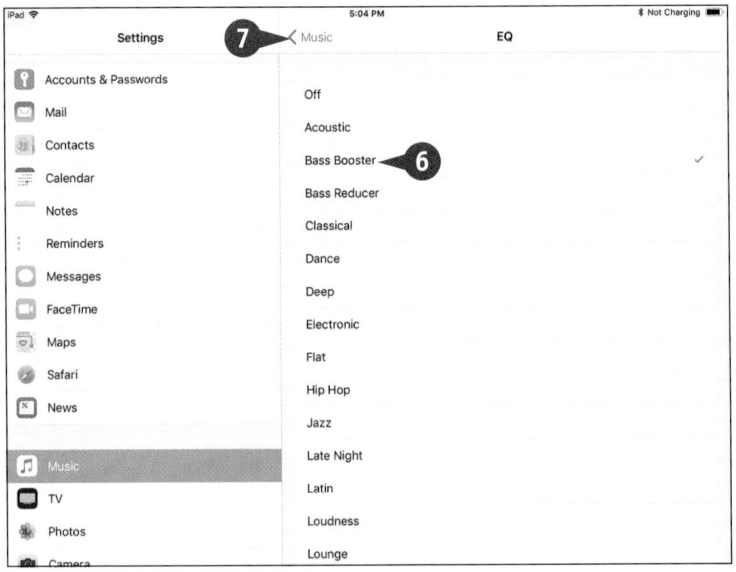

The Music screen appears again.

8 Set the **Show Apple Music** switch to On (◐) if you want the Music app to display Apple Music results.

9 Set the **Show Star Ratings** switch to On (◐) if you want to see star ratings, or to Off ( ) if you do not.

A You can tap **Downloaded Music** to display the Downloaded Music screen, which shows the music stored on your iPad. From here, you can delete an artist, an album, or a song, as needed.

10 Tap **Volume Limit** if you want to set a maximum volume at which audio will play on your iPad.

The Volume Limit screen appears.

11 Drag the slider to the desired level.

12 Tap **Music** (<).

The Music screen appears once more.

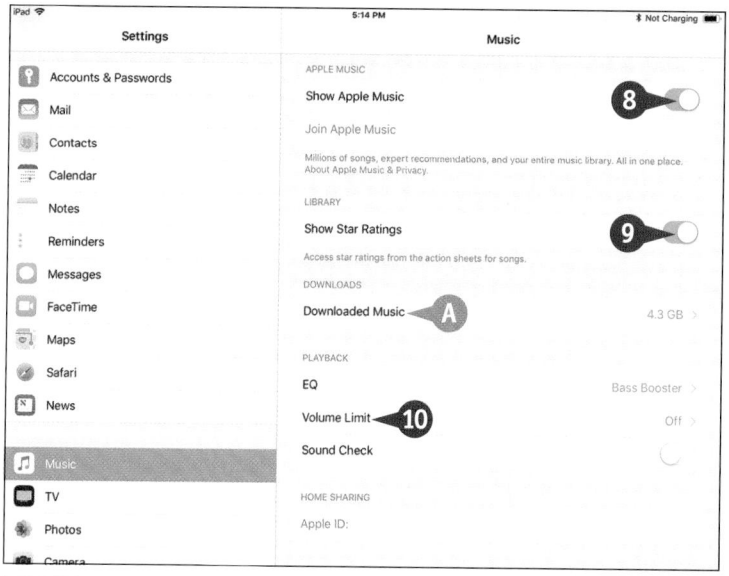

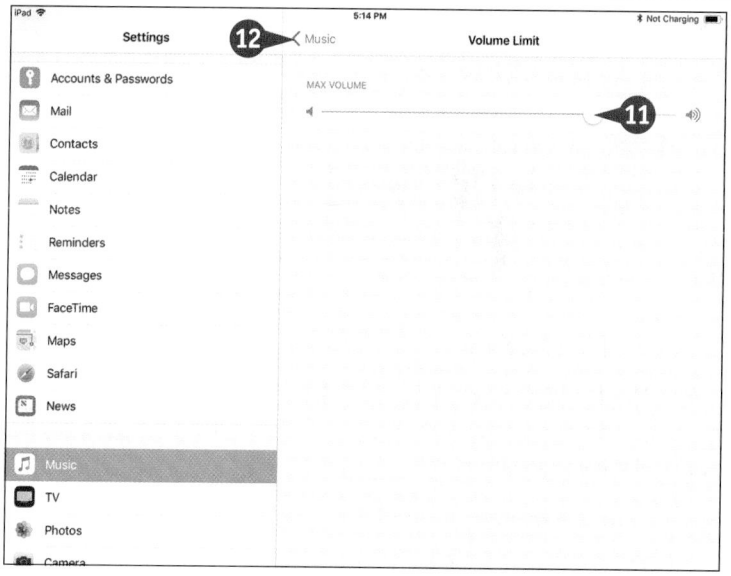

TIPS

Can I keep the volume limit from being changed after I set it?
Yes. Set the volume limit as described in this section, and then apply restrictions. In the Settings app, tap **General** (⚙), and then tap **Restrictions**. Tap **Enable Restrictions**, and then enter a passcode to lock the restrictions. On the Restrictions screen, tap **Volume Limit**. On the Volume Limit screen, tap **Don't Allow Changes**.

Should I use the Sound Check feature?
Try Sound Check and see if it suits you. Sound Check reduces the variations in volume between songs at the expense of dynamic range, so music tends to lose impact when Sound Check is on.

Listen to Apple Music Radio

The Radio feature in the Music app enables you to listen to the Apple Music Radio service. Apple Music Radio has two main parts, one free and one paid. The free part comprises the Beats 1 global radio station and other live radio stations. The paid part is curated, on-demand radio stations and custom radio stations, which require a subscription to the Apple Music service. An individual subscription costs $9.99 per month; a family subscription, which covers up to six people, costs $14.99 per month.

Listen to Apple Music Radio

1. Press **Home**.

   The Home screen appears.

2. Tap **Music** (♫).

   The Music app opens.

3. Tap **Radio** (((•)) changes to ((•))).

   The Radio screen appears.

   - A You can tap the current Beats 1 thumbnail to start the station playing.
   - B You can swipe left to see more shows.
   - C You can tap **Beats 1** to display a screen showing all Beats 1 shows.

4. Swipe up to scroll down.

   The Recently Played list appears.

   - D You can tap a thumbnail to start the station playing.

5. Tap **Radio Stations**.

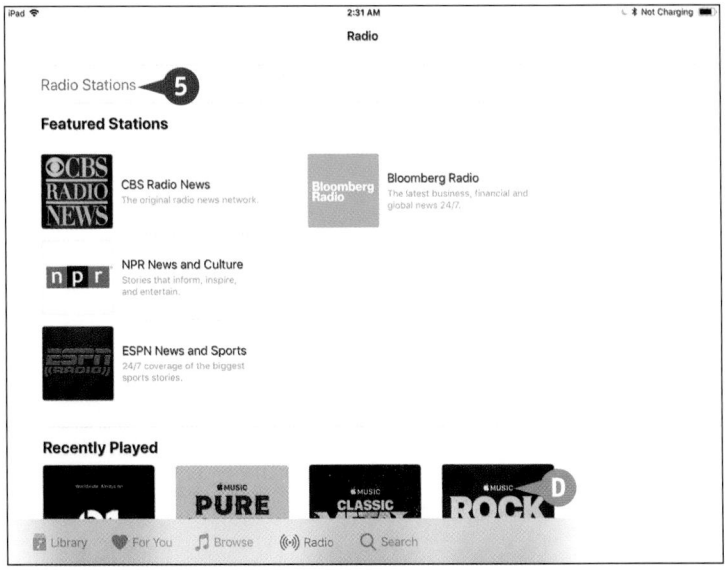

The Radio Stations screen appears.

E You can swipe left on the large thumbnails to see other stations.

F You can swipe left on the Featured Stations thumbnails to see more featured stations.

6 Swipe up to scroll down.

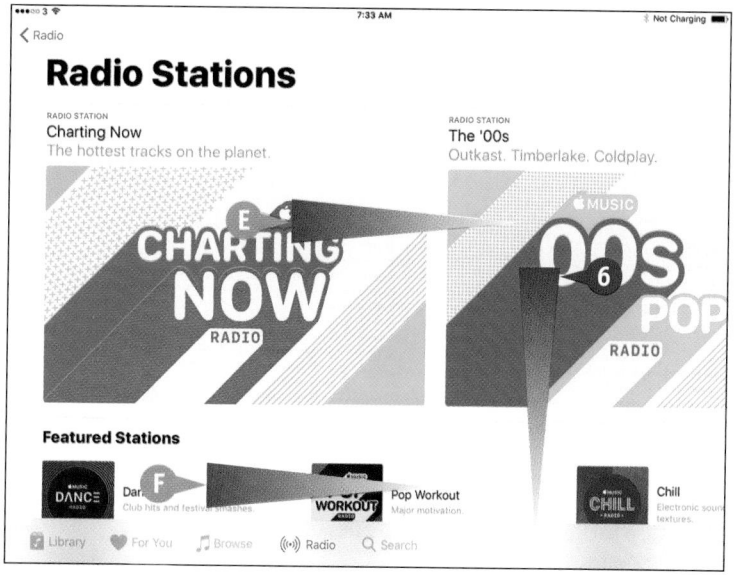

The All Genres list appears.

7 Tap the genre you want to view. This example uses the Alternative & Indie genre.

TIP

Why can I not skip this unlistenable song?
Apple Music Radio lets you skip a maximum of six songs between ads. But if you have a subscription to Apple Music or to the iTunes Match service from Apple, you can skip as many songs as you want.

continued ▶

Beats 1 carries a selection of entertaining shows aimed at relatively large audiences. If your tastes run to particular genres, you may get greater enjoyment from listening to some of the genre-specific stations that Apple Music Radio provides. For music tailored even more closely to your preferences, you can create a custom station based on a particular song.

Listen to Apple Music Radio (continued)

The screen for the genre appears, such as the Alternative screen, showing the list of genre stations.

8 Tap the station you want to play.

The station starts playing.

G The station's current song appears on the Now Playing button.

H You can tap **Pause** (❚❚) to pause playback.

I You can tap **Skip** (▶▶) to skip to the next track.

9 Tap **Now Playing**.

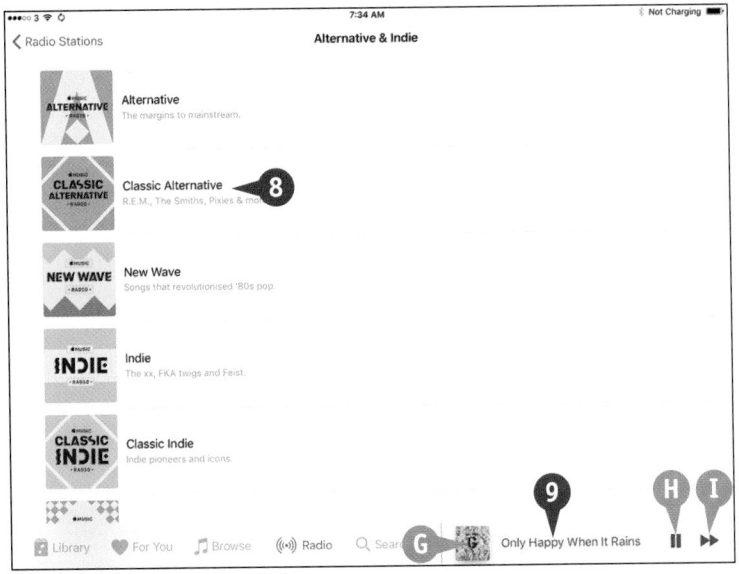

The Now Playing panel appears.

J You can tap **Close** (⌄) when you want to close the Now Playing panel. Alternatively, tap to the left of the Now Playing panel.

K You can drag the playhead to move through the song.

L You can drag the volume control to adjust the volume.

10 To use AirPlay, tap **AirPlay** (◠).

The AirPlay dialog opens.

11 Tap the AirPlay device you want to use.

The AirPlay dialog closes.

Your iPad starts playing through the AirPlay device.

12 To take other actions, tap **More** (⊙).

The More dialog opens.

M You can tap **Add to Library** (+) to add the song to your library.

N You can tap **Add to a Playlist** (⊕≡) to add the song to a playlist.

Note: Both the Add to Library command and the Add to a Playlist command work only if you use iCloud Music Library.

O You can tap **Create Station** (⊕)) to create a station based on the song.

P You can tap **Lyrics** (❝≡) to display the song's lyrics if they are available.

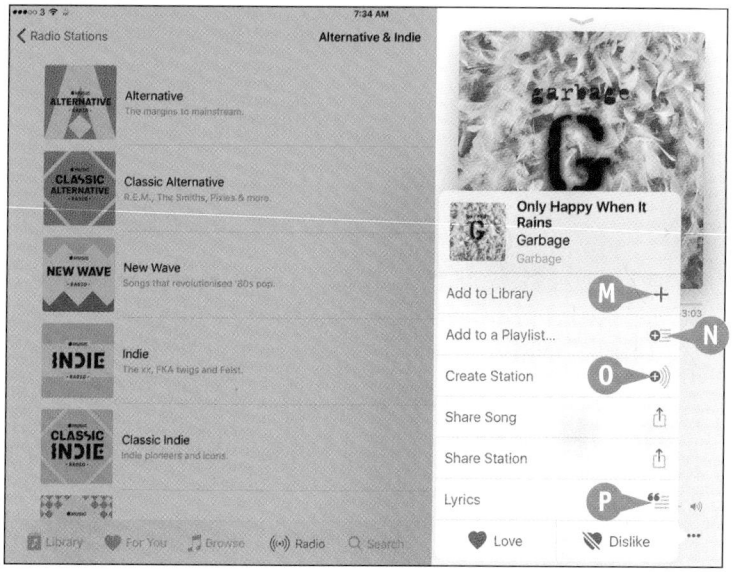

TIP

What do the Share Station button and Share Song do?

The Share Station button (⇧) enables you to share a link to a station on Apple Music Radio. Similarly, the Share Song button (⇧) lets you share a link to a song on the iTunes Store. You can use various means of sharing, such as sending the link via Mail or Messages, posting it to Facebook or Twitter, or simply setting yourself a reminder to listen to — or avoid — the music.

CHAPTER 10

Working with Photos and Books

In this chapter, you learn to use the Photos app to view and share photos. You also learn to use the iBooks app to read e-books and PDF files.

Browse Photos Using Years, Collections, and Moments . . 264
Browse Shared Photos 266
Browse Photos Using Albums 268
Create Albums 270
Share Photos Across Your Devices and Computers 272
Share Photo Albums with Other People via iCloud 274
Share and Use Your Photos 276
Play Slide Shows of Photos 278
Read Digital Books with iBooks 280

Browse Photos Using Years, Collections, and Moments

You can use the Photos app to browse the photos you have taken with the camera in your iPad, photos you have synced using iTunes or via the iCloud Shared Streams feature, and photos you saved from instant messages, e-mail, web pages, and social media.

You can browse your photos by date and locations using the smart groupings that Photos creates. Each Year grouping contains Collections, and the Collections grouping contains Moments, which contain your photos.

Browse Photos Using Years, Collections, and Moments

1. Press **Home**.

   The Home screen appears.

2. Tap **Photos** ( ).

   The Photos app opens.

3. Tap **Photos** (changes to).

   The Photos screen appears, showing the Years list.

   A You can tap **Search** (Q) to search your photos by groups, such as Nearby or Favorites, or by keywords.

4. Tap the year you want to open.

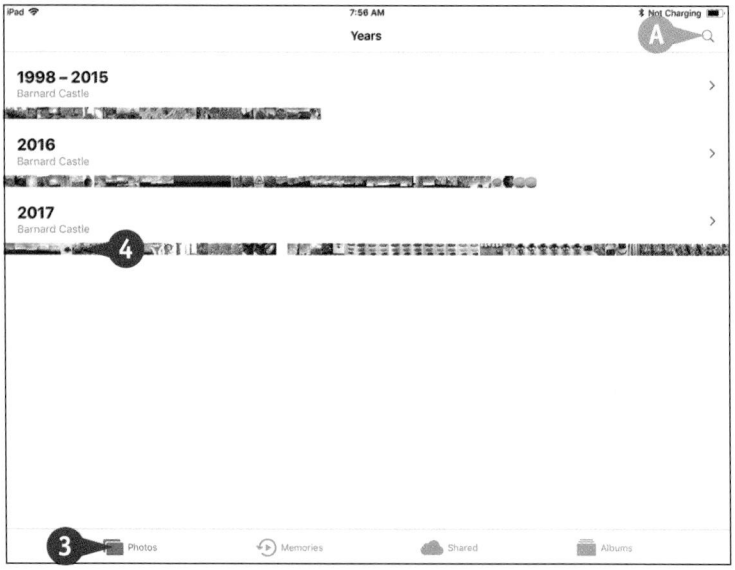

   The Collections screen for the year appears.

Note: Scroll up or down as needed to see other collections. You can scroll from one year to another.

5. Tap the collection you want to open.

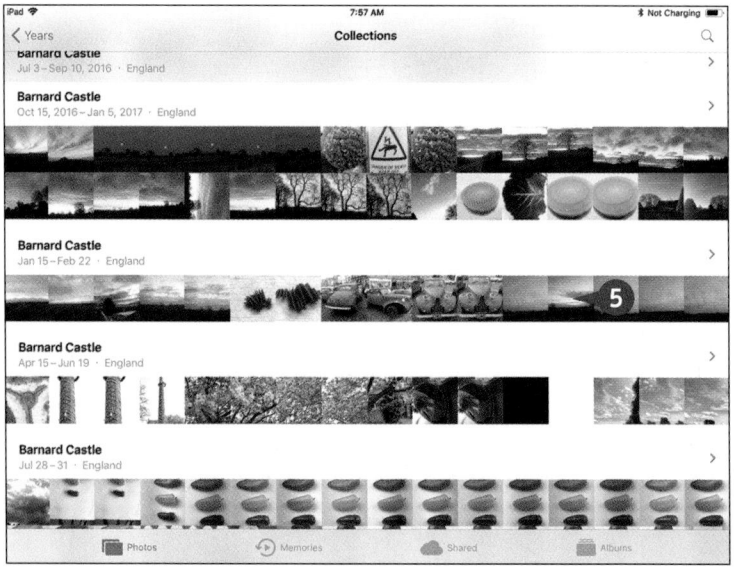

The Moments screen for the collection appears.

B You can tap > to display the overview screen for the moment.

6 Tap the photo you want to view.

The photo opens.

C You can tap **Favorite** (♡ changes to ♥) to make the photo a Favorite.

D You can tap **Share** (⬆) to share the photo, as explained later in this chapter.

E You can tap **Delete** (🗑) to delete the photo.

F You can tap **Edit** to edit the photo, as explained in Chapter 11.

7 Tap and swipe left or right to display other photos in the moment.

G You can also tap another photo in the Thumbnails bar.

Another photo appears.

8 Tap **Moments** (<).

The Moments screen appears.

9 Tap **Collections** (<).

The Collections screen appears.

10 Tap **Years** (<).

The Years screen appears, and you can navigate to another year.

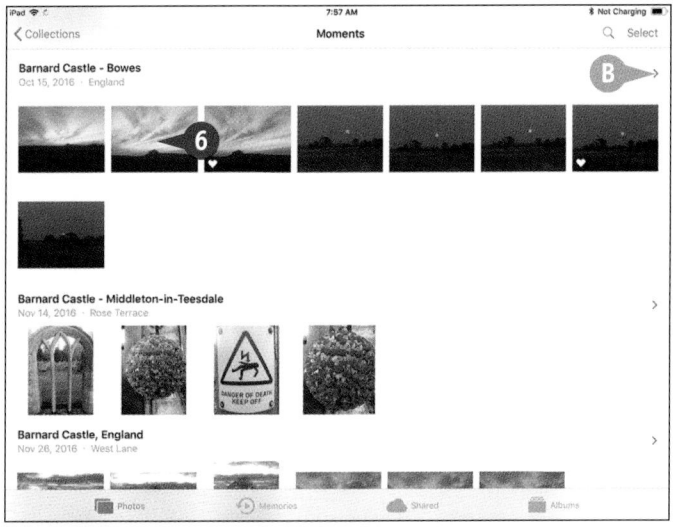

TIP

How can I move a photo to a different year?

To move a photo to a different year, you need to change the date set in the photo's metadata. You cannot do this with the Photos app on the iPad, but you can change the date with a third-party app such as Pixelgarde, which is free from the App Store at this writing. Alternatively, if you sync the photos from your computer, you can change the date in the photo on your computer. For example, in the Photos app on the Mac, select the photo or photos, click **Image** on the menu bar, and then click **Adjust Date and Time**.

Browse Shared Photos

The Photos app on your iPad includes support for sharing photo albums on iCloud. This feature enables you to share photos easily with others and enjoy the photos they are sharing. In this section, you learn how to add other people's shared albums to the Photos app on your iPad by accepting invitations. You also learn how to browse through the photos they are sharing.

Later in this chapter, you learn to share your own photos via shared albums.

Browse Shared Photos

1. When you receive an invitation to a photo stream, open the e-mail message in Mail.
2. Tap **Subscribe**.

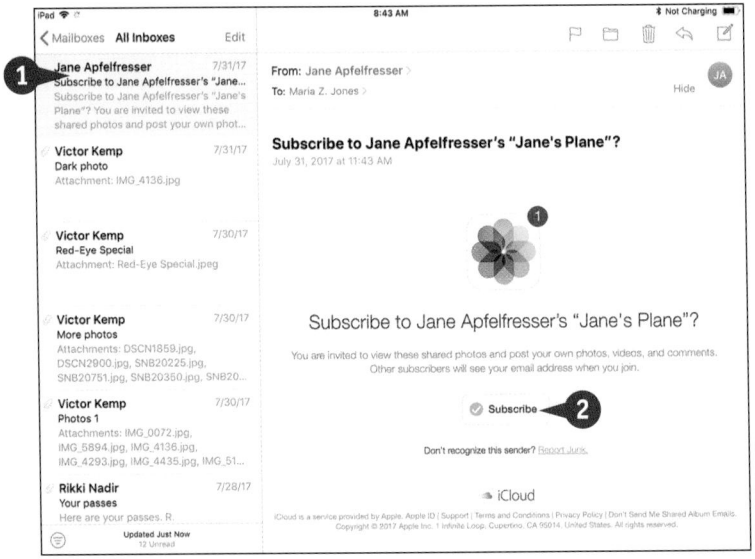

The Photos app becomes active, and the Shared screen appears.

The new album appears on the Shared screen.

Note: The Activity item in the upper-left corner of the Shared screen shows new activity on your shared albums. Tap **Activity** to see the latest photos posted on all your shared albums.

A You can tap **Mail** (<) to return to the Mail app.

3. Tap the new album.

The new album's screen appears.

4 Tap a photo.

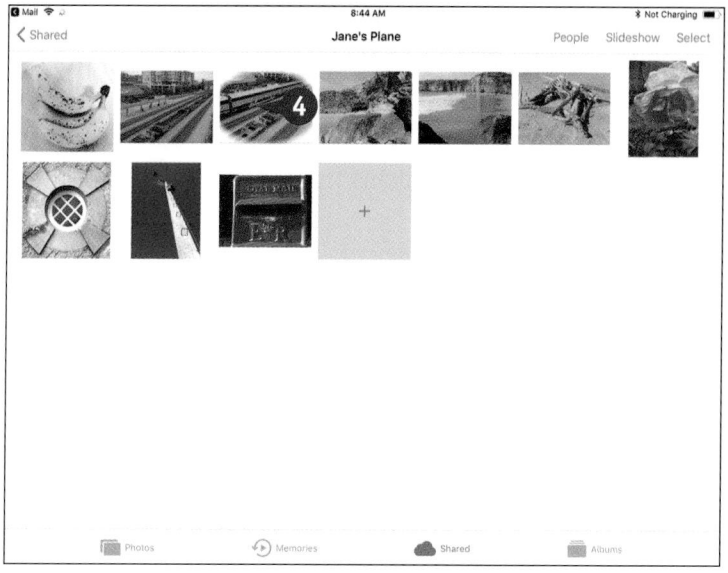

The photo opens.

B You can tap **Add a comment** to add a comment on the photo.

C You can tap **Share** (⬆) to share the photo with others.

D You can tap **Like** to indicate you like the photo.

Note: You can swipe left or right to display other photos.

5 Tap the album's name (<).

The album's screen appears.

6 Tap **Shared** (<).

The Shared screen appears, and you can navigate to another album.

TIP

How do I remove a shared album?

In the Photos app, tap **Shared** (☁ changes to ☁) to display the Shared screen. Tap **Edit** to turn on Editing Mode, and then tap **Remove** (⊖) at the upper-left corner of the album you want to remove. Tap the **Unsubscribe** button in the Unsubscribe dialog that opens. Tap **Done** to turn off Editing Mode.

Browse Photos Using Albums

Along with browsing by collections and browsing shared photo albums, you can browse your photos by albums. The Camera app on your iPad automatically maintains several albums, storing each photo you take in the All Photos album, each video in an album called Videos, and each time-lapse video in an album called Time-Lapse. You can also create other albums manually from your photos or sync existing albums from your computer.

Browse Photos Using Albums

1. Press **Home**.

   The Home screen appears.

2. Tap **Photos** ( ).

   The Photos app opens.

3. Tap **Albums** (changes to).

   The Albums screen appears.

Note: All Photos is the album in which iOS places the photos you take; photos you save from web pages, e-mail messages, instant messages, and social media; and photos you save after opening them from other people's albums and editing them.

4. Tap the album you want to open. This example uses the Favorites album.

   The album's screen appears, showing a thumbnail of each photo.

Note: The Favorites album contains all the photos you mark as Favorites. iOS automatically adds each Favorite to the album.

5. Tap the photo you want to view.

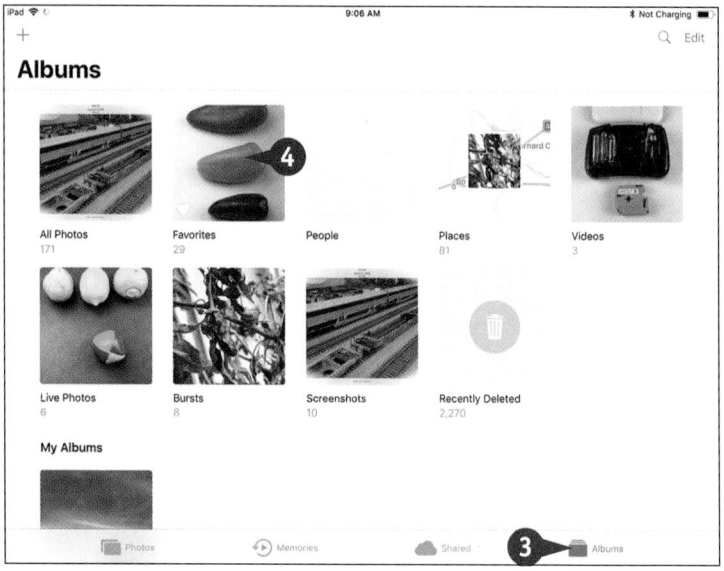

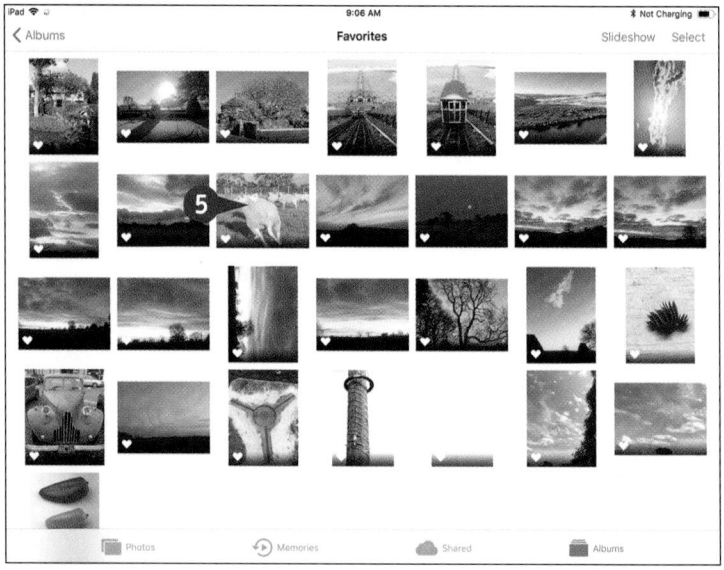

The photo opens.

6 Tap a photo on the Thumbnails bar.

Note: You can also swipe left to display the next photo or swipe right to display the previous photo.

The photo you tapped appears.

7 Tap the album's name (<) in the upper-left corner of the screen.

The album appears.

8 Tap **Albums** (<).

The Albums screen appears, and you can tap another album to display it.

TIP

How can I move through a long list of photos quickly?

You can move through the photos quickly by using momentum scrolling. Tap and flick up with your finger to set the photos scrolling. As the momentum drops, you can tap and flick up again to scroll further. Tap and drag your finger in the opposite direction to stop the scrolling.

Create Albums

Not only can you sync photo albums you have created on your computer to your iPad, but you can also create albums directly on your iPad. The process is similar to creating a playlist within the Music app in that you start a new album, name it, and then select the photos you want to include in it. You can create albums to store a collection of photos with a similar theme and include only the photos that you want to view.

Create Albums

1. Press **Home**.

   The Home screen appears.

2. Tap **Photos** ( ).

   The Photos app opens.

3. Tap **Albums** (changes to).

   The Albums screen appears.

   A The top part of the Albums screen shows albums that iOS maintains for you, such as All Photos, People, and Places.

   B The My Albums section shows albums you create.

4. Tap **New** (+).

   The New Album dialog opens.

5. Type the name for the new album.

6. Tap **Save**.

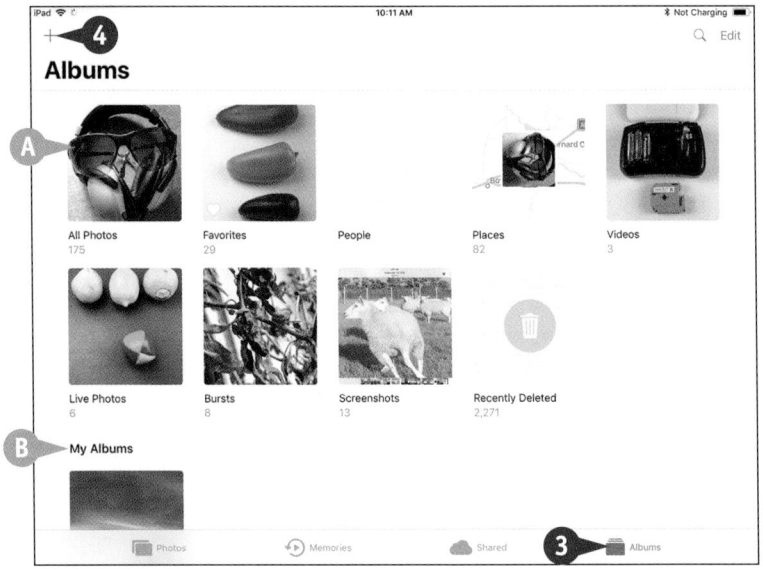

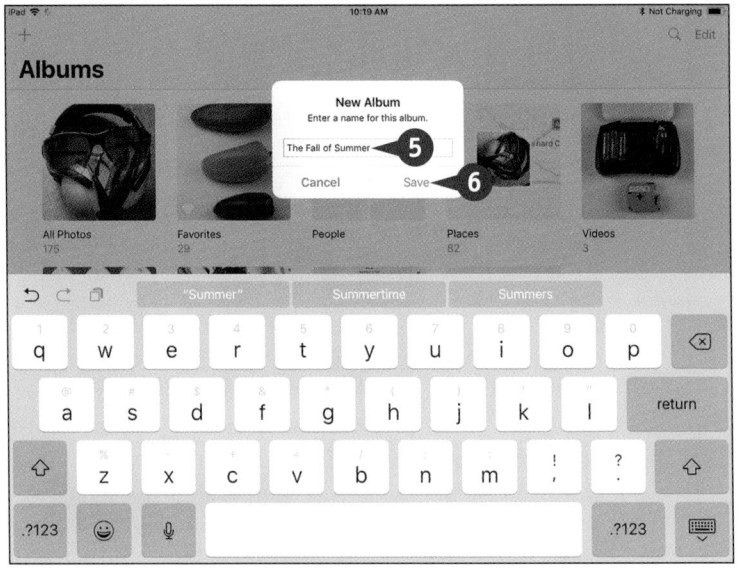

The Photos category automatically opens.

7. Tap each photo that you want to add to the album.

   A check mark appears in the bottom-right corner of each selected photo.

Note: You can select multiple adjacent photos in one move by sliding your finger across them.

C You can tap **Select** to select a whole group of photos, such as a Moment.

D You can tap **Select All** to select all the photos displayed.

8. Tap **Done**.

   Photos adds the selected photos to the album.

E The album appears in the My Albums section of the Albums screen. You can tap the album to open it and view its contents.

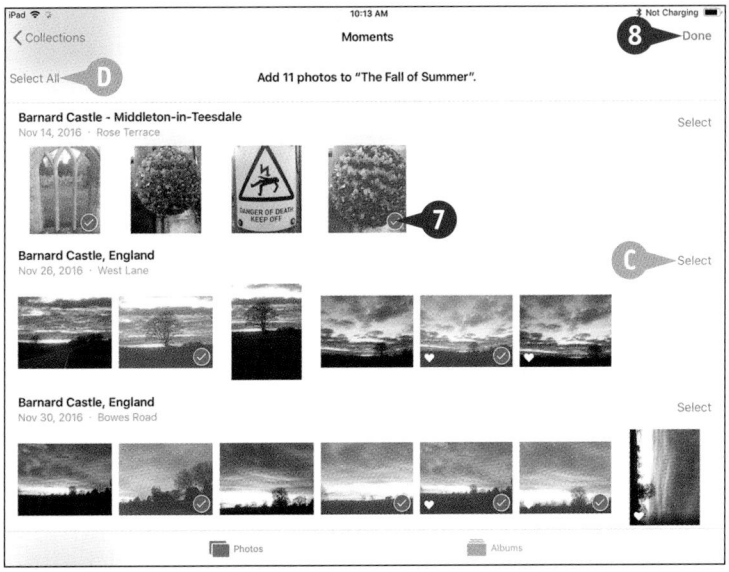

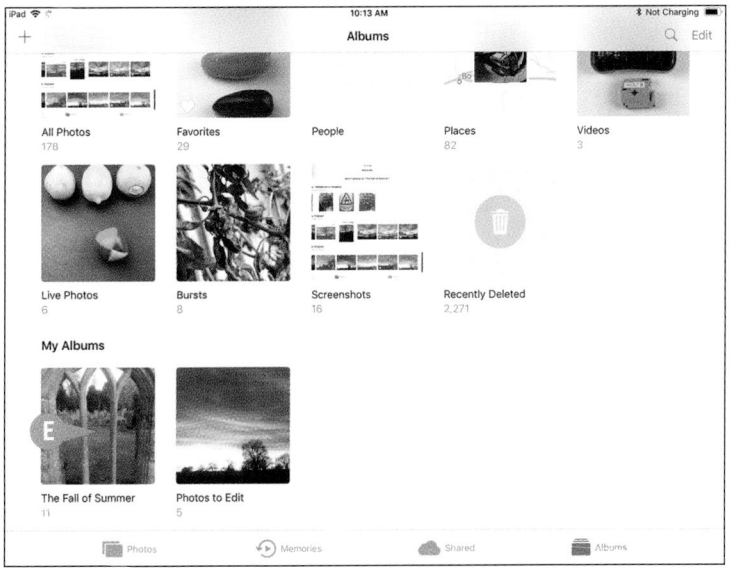

TIP

How do I delete albums from my iPad?

In Photos, tap **Albums** (changes to), and then tap **Edit**. A Delete icon ( ) appears in the upper-left corner of the albums you created on your iPad; to delete the album, tap this icon, and then tap **Delete** in the Delete dialog that opens. Tap **Done** to turn off Edit Mode. You cannot use this method to delete albums that you have synced from your computer. To remove those albums, choose not to sync those albums to your iPad and then run another sync.

Share Photos Across Your Devices and Computers

If you have an iCloud account, you can use the My Photo Stream feature to share your photos among your iOS devices and your computer.

After you turn on My Photo Stream on your iPad, other iOS devices, and your computers, Photo Stream automatically syncs your 1,000 most recent photos among the devices and your computers.

Share Photos Across Your Devices and Computers

Turn On My Photo Stream on Your iPad

1. Press **Home**.

   The Home screen appears.

2. Tap **Settings** ( ).

   The Settings screen appears.

3. Tap **Apple ID**, the button that shows your Apple ID name.

   The Apple ID screen appears.

4. Tap **iCloud** ( ).

   The iCloud screen appears.

5. Tap **Photos** ( ).

   The Photos screen appears.

   A You can set the **iCloud Photo Library** switch to On ( ) to store your entire library in iCloud.

6. Set the **Upload to My Photo Stream** switch to On ( ).

7. Set the **Upload Burst Photos** switch to On ( ) if you want to upload every photo in bursts you shoot.

8. If you want to share photo streams with others, set the **iCloud Photo Sharing** switch to On ( ). See the next section, "Share Photo Albums with Other People via iCloud," for details.

9. Tap **iCloud** ( ).

   The iCloud screen appears again.

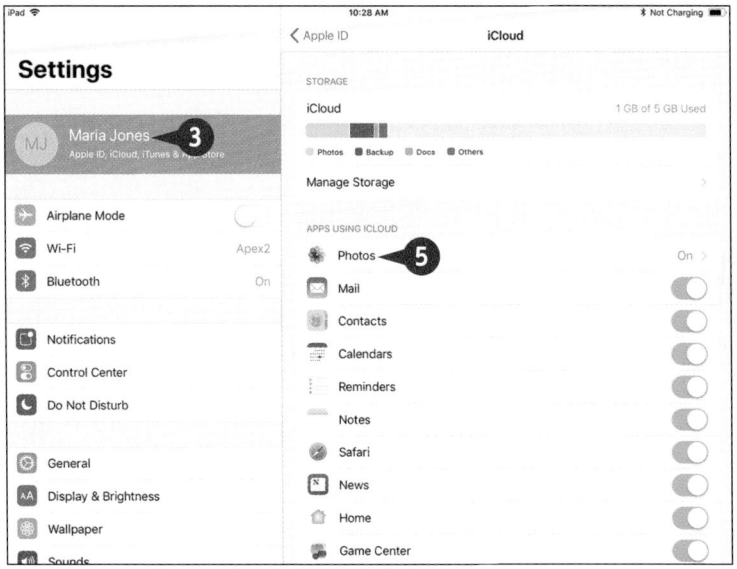

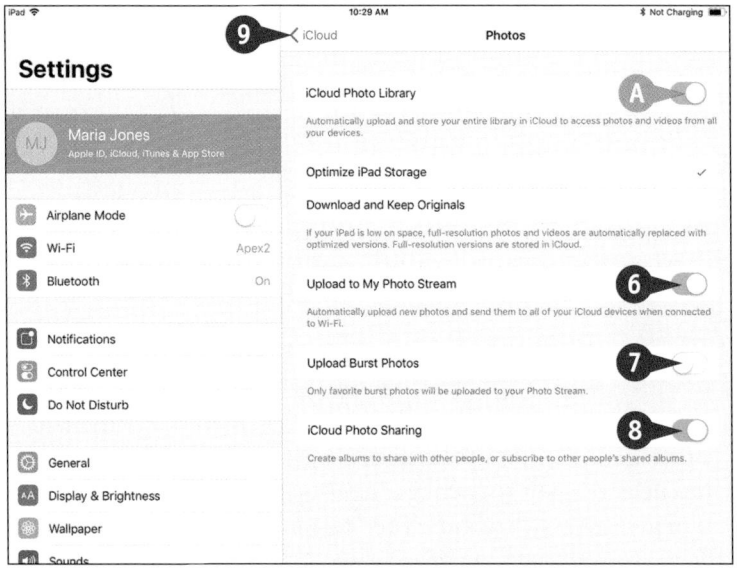

Set Your Mac to Upload Photos to My Photo Stream

1. Right-click or Control+click **System Preferences** (⚙) on the Dock.

   The shortcut menu opens.

2. Click **iCloud**.

   The System Preferences app opens.

   The iCloud pane appears.

3. Click **Photos** (☐ changes to ☑).

4. Click **Options**.

   The iCloud Photo Options dialog opens.

5. Click **iCloud Photo Library** (☐ changes to ☑) to use iCloud Photo Library.

6. Click **My Photo Stream** (☐ changes to ☑).

7. If you want to share photo streams with others, click **iCloud Photo Sharing** (☐ changes to ☑).

8. Click **Done**.

9. Click **System Preferences**.

10. Click **Quit System Preferences**.

    Your Mac is now configured to import your recent photos from your devices that do not use iCloud Photo Library and to send its new photos to the My Photo Stream on those devices.

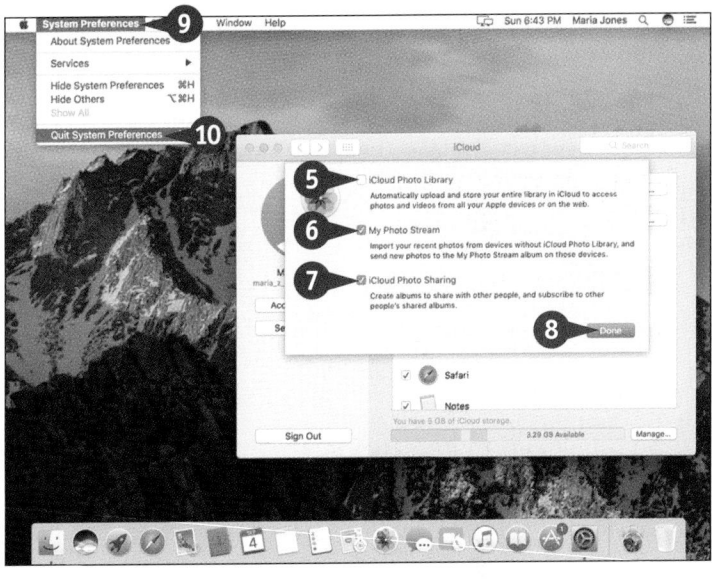

TIP

How do I configure Photo Stream in Windows?

In Windows 10, click **Start** to display the Start menu, click **All Apps**, click the **iCloud** folder, and then click **iCloud** to display iCloud Control Panel. Click **Photos** (☐ changes to ☑). Click **Options** to display the Photos Options dialog. Click **My Photo Stream** (☐ changes to ☑) and **iCloud Photo Sharing** (☐ changes to ☑). Click **Change** and select the folder. Click **OK**, and then click **Apply**.

Share Photo Albums with Other People via iCloud

After turning on the Photo Sharing feature in the Settings app, you can create shared photo albums, invite people to subscribe to them, and add photos. See the previous section, "Share Photos Across Your Devices and Computers," to turn on the Photo Sharing feature.

You can also control whether subscribers can post photos and videos, decide whether to make the album publicly available, and choose whether to receive notifications when subscribers comment on your photos or post their own.

Share Photo Albums with Other People via iCloud

1. Press **Home**.

   The Home screen appears.

2. Tap **Photos** ( ).

   The Photos app opens.

3. Tap **Shared** (changes to).

   The Shared screen appears.

4. Tap **Add** (+).

   The iCloud dialog opens.

5. Type the name for the album.

6. Tap **Next**.

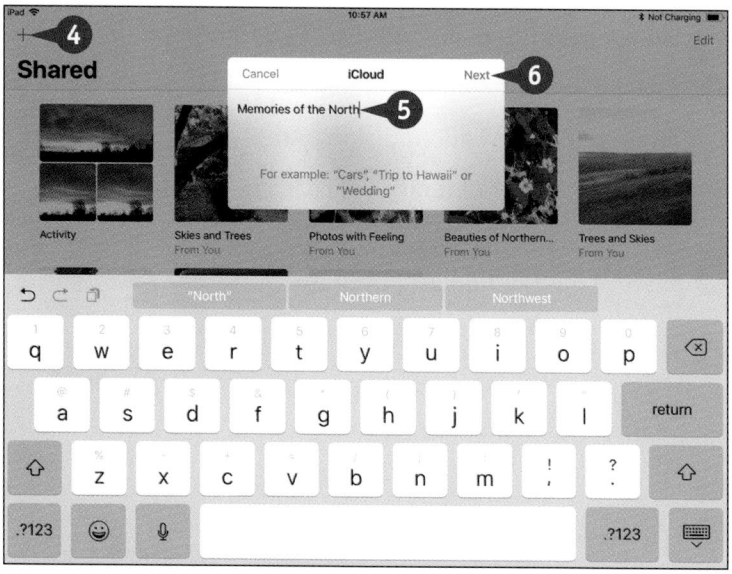

   Another iCloud dialog opens.

7. Tap **Add Contact** (⊕) to display the Contacts screen, and then tap the contact to add.

8. Repeat step **7** to add other contacts as needed. You can also type contact names.

9. Tap **Create**.

   The Shared screen appears.

10. Tap the new stream.

    The stream's screen appears.

11. Tap **Add** (+).

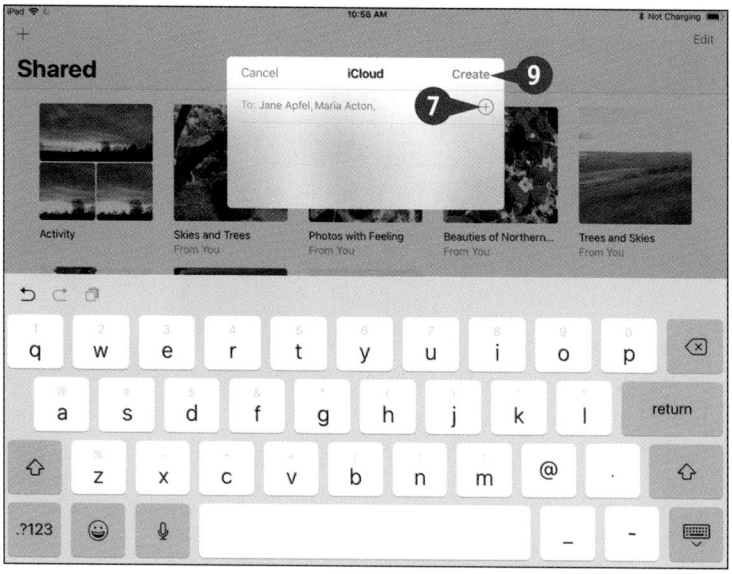

The Moments screen appears, with the selection controls displayed.

Note: You can add photos from other views. For example, tap Albums (changes to) to browse by albums.

12 Tap each photo you want to add.

13 Tap **Done**.

14 In the iCloud dialog that appears, type any text you want to post with the photos.

15 Tap **Post**.

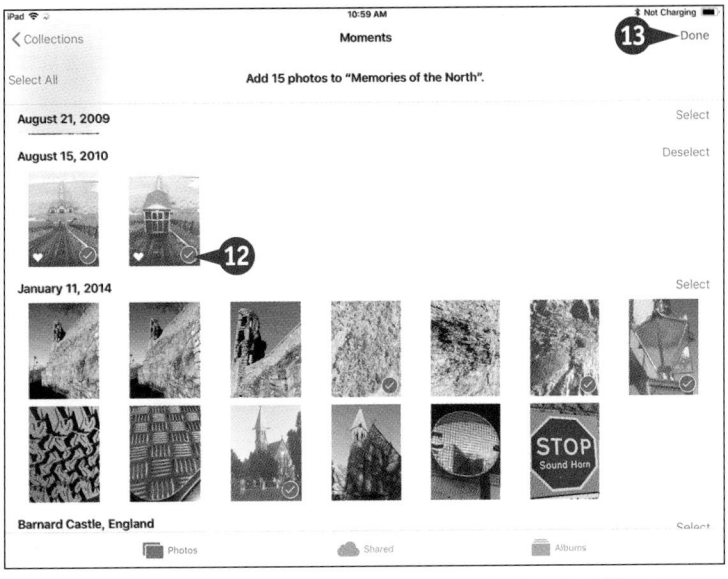

16 On the album's screen, tap **People**.

The Edit Shared Album panel appears.

A To invite others to the stream, tap **Invite People**.

17 Set the **Subscribers Can Post** switch to On ( ) or Off ( ), as needed.

18 Set the **Public Website** switch to On ( ) or Off ( ) to control whether to make the stream publicly accessible on the iCloud.com website.

19 Set the **Notifications** switch to On ( ) or Off ( ), as needed.

20 Tap outside the Edit Shared Album panel to close it.

TIP

If I make a shared album public, how do people find the website?

In the Edit Shared Album panel, when you set the **Public Website** switch for a shared album to On ( ), a Share Link button appears. Tap **Share Link** to display the Share sheet, and then tap the means of sharing you want to use — for example, **Message** ( ), **Mail** ( ), **Twitter** ( ), or **Facebook** ( ).

Share and Use Your Photos

From the Photos app, you can quickly share photos via e-mail, instant messaging, or various other means. Some means of sharing, such as assigning a photo to a contact or setting wallpaper, use only a single message at a time, but you can send either a single photo or multiple photos in an e-mail message or instant message. You access the sharing commands from the Share sheet.

Share and Use Your Photos

Select a Photo and Display the Share Sheet

1. In the Photos app, browse to the photo you want to share.
2. Tap **Share** ( ).

   The Share sheet appears.
3. To include another photo from the same source, tap the photo's selection button (changes to). Scroll left or right as needed to find the photos you want.

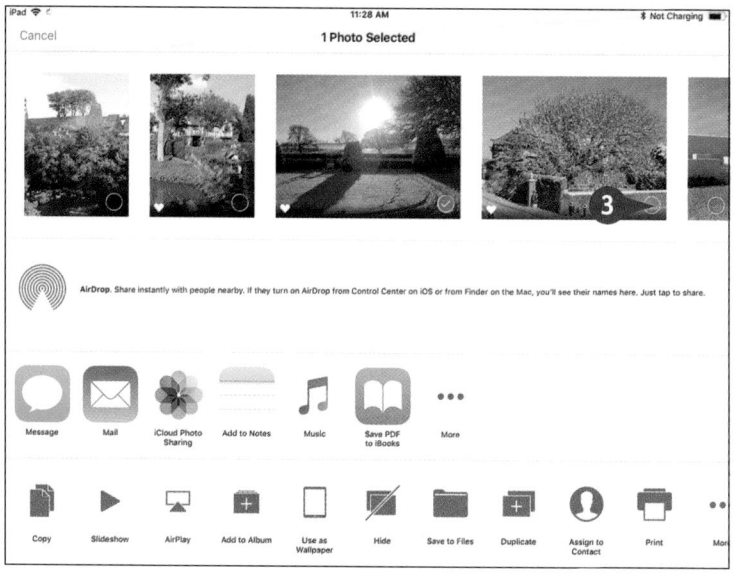

Select Multiple Photos and Display the Share Sheet

1. In the Photos app, display the collection of photos. For example, tap **Albums** (changes to) to display the Albums screen, and then tap the appropriate album.
2. Tap **Select** in the upper-right corner of the screen.

   The Photos app switches to Selection Mode.
3. Tap each photo to include (appears on each photo).
4. Tap **Share** ( ).

   The Share sheet appears.

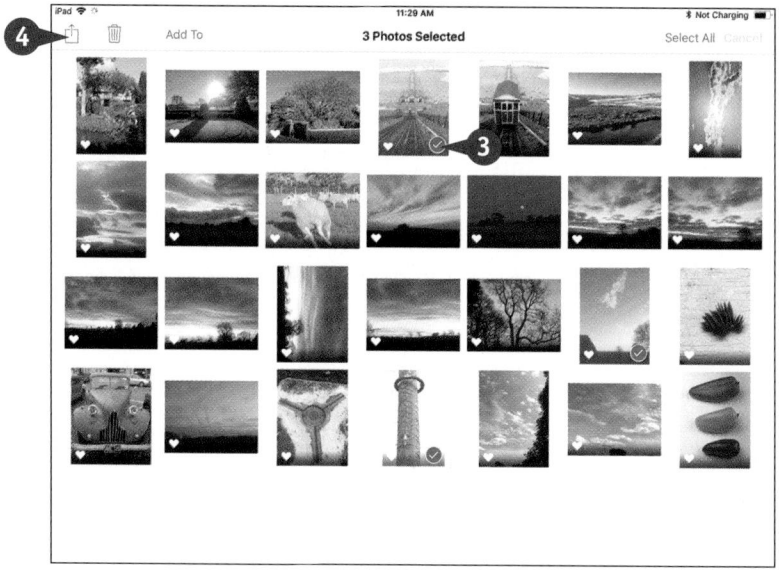

Share the Photo via Messaging

1. On the Share sheet, tap **Message**.

   Your iPad creates a new message in the Messages app with the photo attached to the message.

2. Tap **To** and address the message.
3. Tap in the body area, and then type any text needed.
4. Tap **Send** (↑).

   The Messages app sends the message.

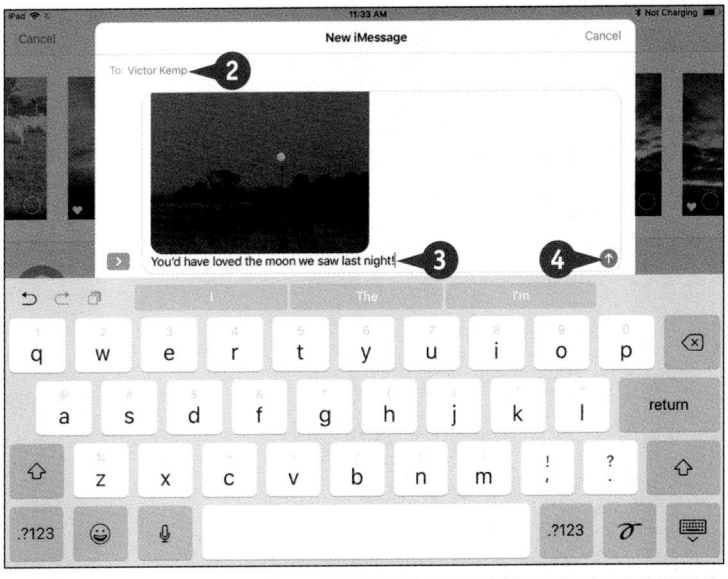

Share the Photo via E-Mail

1. On the Share sheet, tap **Mail**.
2. Tap **To** and address the e-mail message.
3. Tap **Subject** and type the subject for the e-mail message.
4. Tap in the body area, and then type any text needed.
5. Tap **Cc/Bcc, From**.

   The Cc area, Bcc area, From area, and Image Size options appear.

6. Tap **Small**, **Medium**, **Large**, or **Actual Size**, as needed.
7. Tap **Send**.

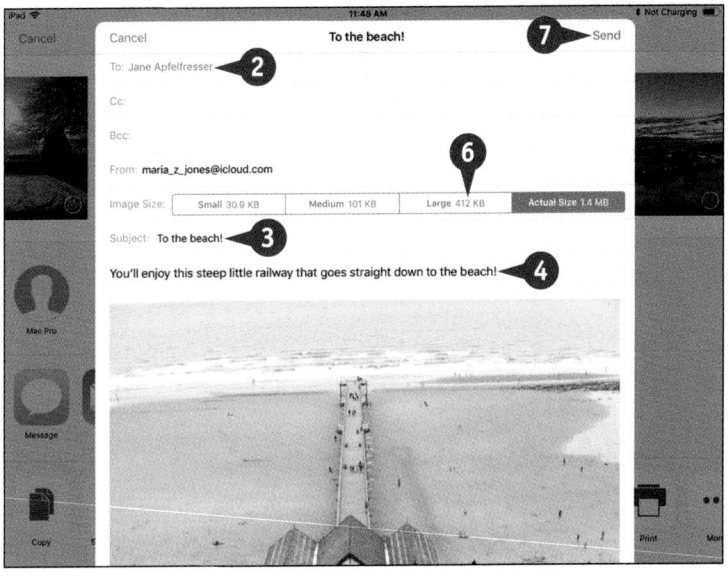

TIP

What is the best size to use when sending photos via e-mail?
This depends on what the recipient will do with the photo. If the recipient needs to edit or print the photo, choose **Actual Size**. If the recipient will merely view the photo on-screen, choose **Large** or **Medium**. The **Small** size works for contact card images, but its picture quality is too low for most other uses.

Play Slide Shows of Photos

Your iPad can not only display your photos, but also play them as a slide show. You can select an existing group of photos, such as an album, or make a custom selection from moments. You can also choose to repeat the slide show or run the photos in random order. Then, when you start the slide show, you can choose which transition to use and add music. To make the most of your slide shows, you can choose the slide timing in the Photos screen in Settings.

Play Slide Shows of Photos

1. Press **Home**.

   The Home screen appears.

2. Tap **Photos** ( ).

   The Photos screen appears.

3. Navigate to the photo with which you want to start the slide show. For example, tap **Albums** (changes to), and then tap the appropriate album to open it.

4. Tap the photo you want to use at the beginning of the slide show.

   The photo opens.

5. Tap **Share** ( ).

   The Share sheet appears.

   A If you want the slide show to include only some of the photos following the one you selected, tap each photo you want to include (changes to). If you want the slide show to include all of the following photos, you do not need to select them.

6. Tap **Slideshow** (▸).

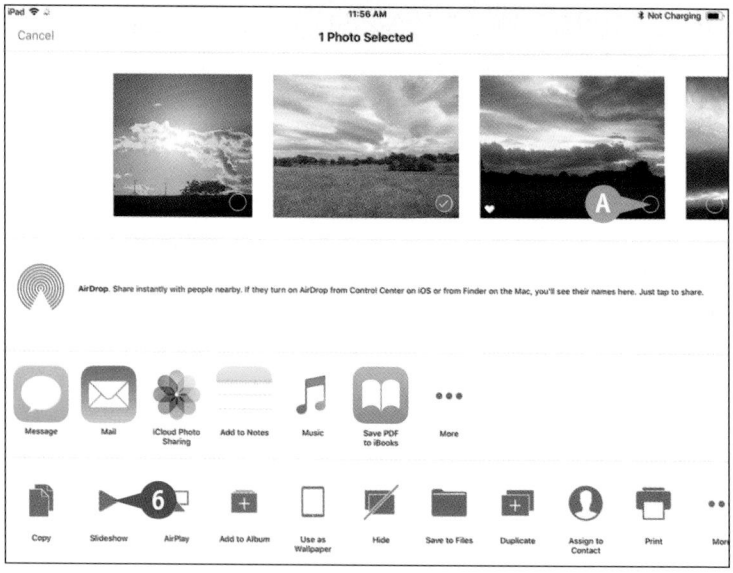

The slide show starts playing with default settings.

7. Tap the screen.

   The controls appear.

   B You can tap **AirPlay** (▣) to play the slide show to an Apple TV.

   C You can tap **Pause** (❚❚) to pause the slide show while you choose options.

8. Tap **Options**.

   The Options dialog opens.

9. Drag the slider to set the playback speed.

10. Set the **Repeat** switch to On (◐) if you want the slide show to repeat.

11. Tap **Theme**.

    The Themes dialog opens.

12. Tap the theme you want to use.

13. Tap **Music**.

    The Music dialog opens.

14. Tap the music you want, or tap **None** if you prefer no music.

    The Music dialog closes, and the Options dialog reappears.

15. Tap the screen.

    The Options dialog closes.

Note: If you paused the slide show, tap **Play** (▶) to resume playback.

TIP

How can I play my photos on a TV or projector?

To play your photos on a bigger screen, you have two options. First, you can use AirPlay to play photos on a TV or monitor connected to an Apple TV. Second, you can use the Apple Lightning Digital AV Adapter and an HDMI cable to connect your iPad to a TV.

Read Digital Books with iBooks

Using the iBooks app, you can read e-books that you load on the iPad from your computer, read e-books that you download for free or purchase from online stores, or read PDF files you transfer from your computer.

If you have already loaded some e-books, you can read them as described in this section. If iBooks contains no books, tap the **Store** button to visit the iBooks Store, which offers both free books and books for which you must pay.

Read Digital Books with iBooks

1. Press **Home**.

   The Home screen appears.

2. Tap **iBooks** (📖).

   The Books screen appears.

   A If Books does not appear in the upper-middle area of the iBooks screen, tap the pop-up menu button (▼). In the Collections dialog that appears, tap **Books** to display the list of books.

   B You can tap **List** (☰) to display the books as a list instead of as a grid.

3. Tap the book you want to open.

   The book opens.

Note: When you open a book, iBooks displays your current page. When you open a book for the first time, iBooks displays the book's cover, first page, or default page.

4. Tap anywhere on the screen to hide the reading controls. Tap again to display them once more.

5. Tap the right side of the page to display the next page.

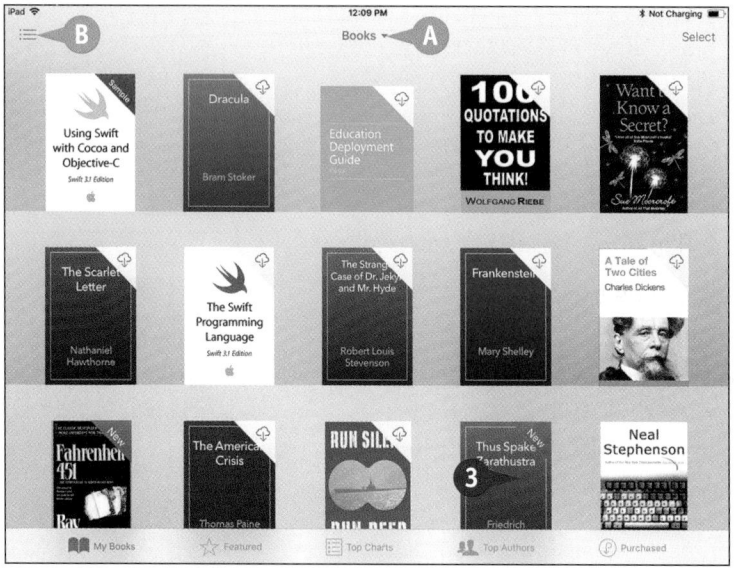

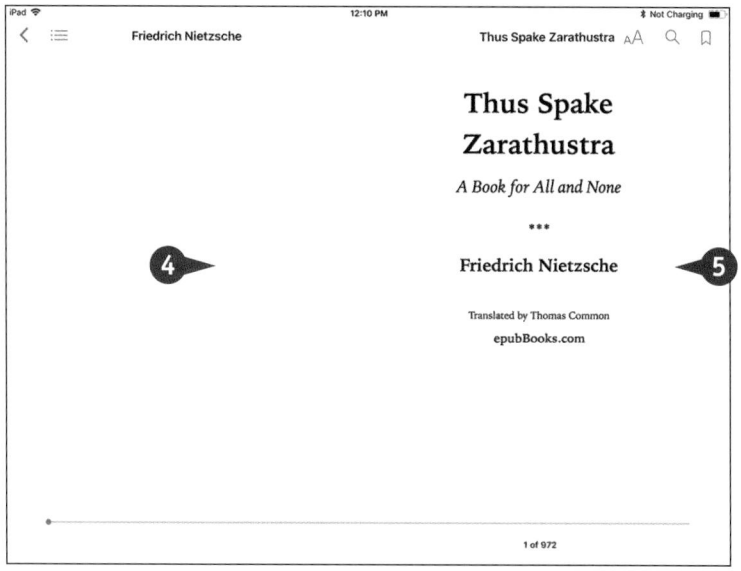

Note: To display the previous page, tap the left side of the page. Alternatively, tap the left side of the page and drag to the right.

6. To look at the next page without fully revealing it, tap the right side and drag to the left. You can then either drag further to turn the page or release the page and let it fall closed.

7. To jump to another part of the book, tap **Table of Contents** (☰).

Note: Alternatively, you can drag the indicator at the bottom of the screen to move quickly through the book.

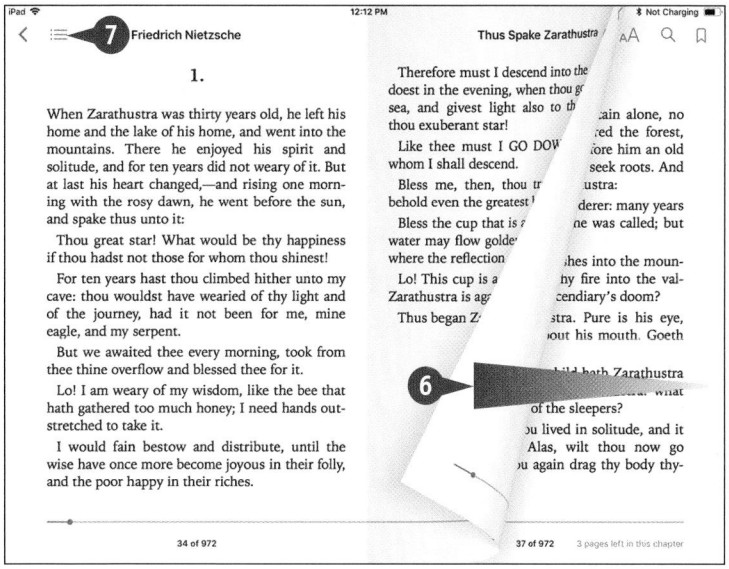

The table of contents appears.

8. Tap the part of the book you want to display.

Note: To search in the book, tap **Search** (🔍). On the Search screen, type the search term, and then tap the match you want to display.

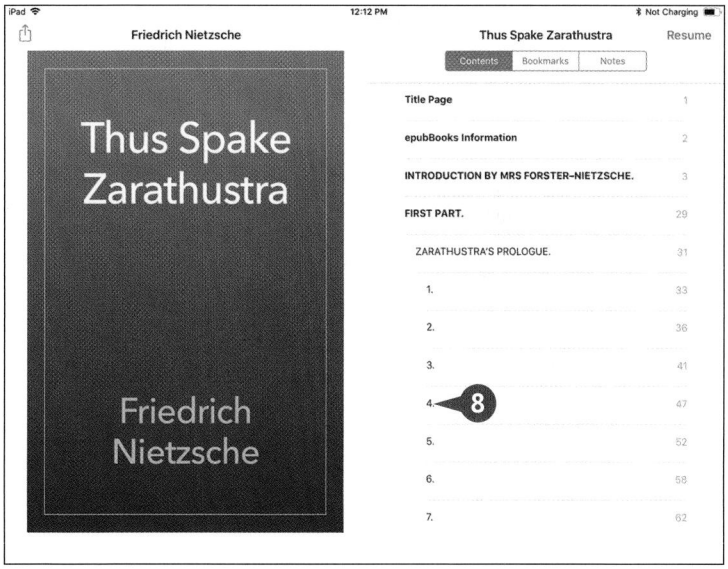

TIP

How do I change the font iBooks uses?

Tap the screen to display the controls, and then tap **Font Settings** (AA). In the Font Settings dialog, tap **Smaller** or **Larger** to change the font size. Tap **Fonts** to display the font list, and then tap the font you want to use.

In the Font Settings dialog, you can also tap one of the colored circles to apply a theme, such as the Sepia theme or the Night theme. You can set the **Auto-Night Theme** switch to On (◐) to have iBooks automatically apply the Night theme when ambient light is low. And you can set the **Scrolling View** switch to On (◐) to display the book as a long scrolling page instead of individual pages that you turn.

CHAPTER 11

Taking Photos and Videos

The Camera app on the iPad enables you to take both still photos and videos, and the Photo Booth app lets you take fun photos. You can also edit your photos on the iPad, improving their colors, cropping unwanted parts, and applying filters to change the look.

Take Photos with the Camera App 284
Take HDR Photos and Square Photos. 286
Using the Self-Timer and the Grid. 288
Take Time-Lapse Movies 290
Take Fun Photos with Photo Booth 292
Crop, Rotate, and Straighten Photos. 294
Enhance Photos 296
Reduce Red-Eye in Photos 297
Adjust the Colors in Photos. 298
Apply Filters to Photos 300
Capture Video 302

Take Photos with the Camera App

Your iPad includes a high-resolution camera on the back for taking still photos and videos, plus a lower-resolution camera on the front for taking photos and videos of yourself and for making video calls.

To take photos using the cameras, you use the Camera app. For the rear camera, this app includes a digital zoom feature for zooming in and out, a feature for taking HDR (high dynamic range) photos, and a grid that you can use for composing your photos.

Take Photos with the Camera App

1. Press **Home**.

   The Home screen appears.

2. Tap **Camera** (📷).

   The Camera app opens, showing whatever is positioned in front of the lens.

3. Aim the iPad so that your subject appears in the middle of the photo area.

Note: If you need to take tightly composed photos, get a tripod and a tripod mount that fits the model of iPad you have. You can find various models on Amazon, eBay, and photography sites.

4. To zoom quickly, place two fingers together on the screen and pinch outward to zoom in or place two fingers apart and pinch together to zoom out.

5. For more precise zoom, tap **Zoom In** (➕) to zoom in or **Zoom Out** (➖) to zoom out. Tap as many times as needed.

   A You can also zoom by tapping and dragging the **Zoom slider** (●).

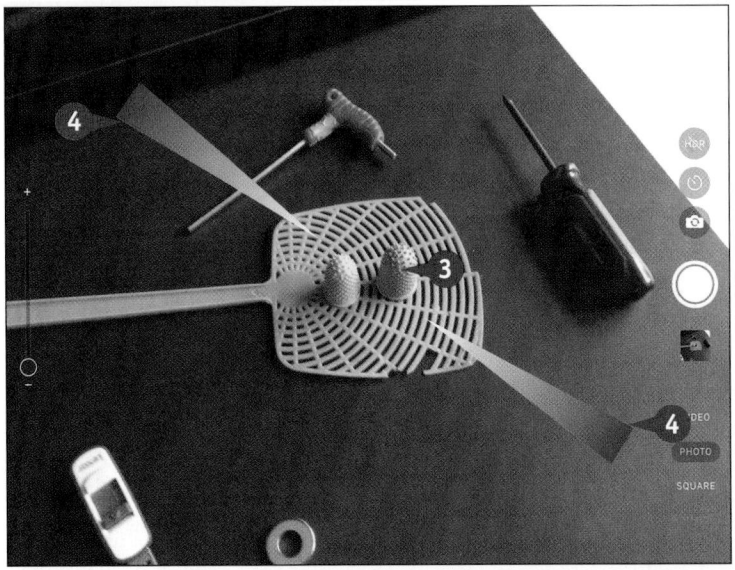

6 Tap where you want to focus.

The focus changes.

Note: By default, the Camera app focuses on the center of the screen because that is where your subject is most likely to be. If what you see on the screen appears blurred, tap the subject to change the focus.

7 Tap **Take Photo** ( ).

Note: On many iPad models, you can tap and hold **Take Photo** ( ) to take a burst of photos.

The Camera app takes the photo and displays a thumbnail.

8 Tap the thumbnail.

The photo appears.

B From the photo screen, you can navigate as discussed in Chapter 10. Tap a thumbnail to display its photo, swipe left to display the next photo, or swipe right to display the previous photo.

C You can tap **Favorite** (changes to) to make the photo a Favorite.

D You can tap **Share** ( ) to share the photo.

E You can tap **Delete** ( ) to delete the photo.

F You can tap **Edit** to open the photo for editing.

9 Tap **Back** ( ) to go back to the Camera app.

TIP

How do I switch to the front-facing camera?

Tap **Switch Cameras** ( ) to switch from the rear-facing camera to the front-facing camera. The image that the front-facing camera is seeing appears on-screen, and you can take pictures as described in this section. Tap **Switch Cameras** ( ) again when you want to switch back to the rear-facing camera.

Take HDR Photos and Square Photos

To help you capture photos with lush, vibrant color, the Camera app includes a feature called *high dynamic range*, or HDR for short. HDR combines several photos into a single photo with adjusted color balance and intensity.

When you need to take a photo that is perfectly square, you can use the Square feature. Some iPad models also have the capability to take panoramic photos.

Take HDR Photos and Square Photos

Take an HDR Photo

1. Press **Home**.

   The Home screen appears.

2. Tap **Camera** ( ).

   The Camera app opens, showing whatever is positioned in front of the lens.

3. Tap **HDR** ( ).

A changes to .

B The HDR flag appears at the top of the screen.

4. Tap **Take Photo** ( ).

   Camera takes a photo.

Note: HDR photos have a larger file size than regular photos because they contain more data, but you can still fit many of them on your iPad.

C You can tap the thumbnail to view the photo.

Take a Square Photo

1. In the Camera app, tap **Square**.

Note: Square photos are useful for adding to contact records and similar needs.

D Camera reduces the frame to a square by displaying black borders at the sides.

2. Tap **Take Photo** (◯).

   Camera takes a photo.

E If Pano appears, your iPad can take panoramic photos. Hold the iPad in portrait orientation rather than landscape orientation, tap **Pano** to switch to Pano Mode, and then tap **Take Photo** (◯). Move the iPad in a clockwise circle following the white arrow on the screen to take the panoramic photo.

TIP

When should I use the HDR feature?

Turn on HDR when you need to get the best color and lighting balance for a stationary subject. The Camera app needs longer to take an HDR photo than to take a regular photo, so HDR is not suitable for subjects that are moving or otherwise changing. For example, use HDR for photographing landscapes or houses, but do not use it for photographing live sports, people, or animals. HDR can be especially useful in bright sunlight, which can make automatic light-metering more difficult.

Using the Self-Timer and the Grid

The Camera app includes a self-timer feature that enables you to set the app to take a burst of photos 3 seconds or 10 seconds after you tap the Take Photo button. By using the self-timer, you can include yourself in group shots or simply minimize camera shake when taking photos of still subjects.

The Camera app also includes a Grid feature that you can turn on to help you compose your pictures. You can display the grid at any point when you find it useful, or simply display the grid all the time.

Using the Self-Timer and the Grid

Open the Camera App and Take a Timed Photo

1. Press **Home**.

   The Home screen appears.

2. Tap **Camera** ( ).

   The Camera app opens.

3. Tap **Timer** ( ).

   The Timer settings appear.

4. Tap **3s** or **10s** to set the number of seconds to delay.

5. Compose the photo.

6. Tap **Take Photo** ( ).

   A The Timer icon shows the delay set.

   B The Camera app displays an on-screen countdown.

   When the countdown ends, the app takes a burst of photos.

Note: The timer remains set until you change it.

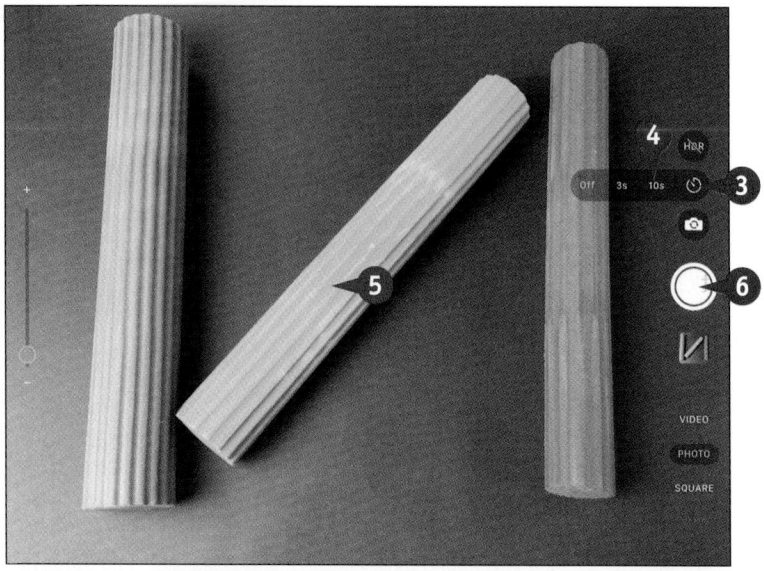

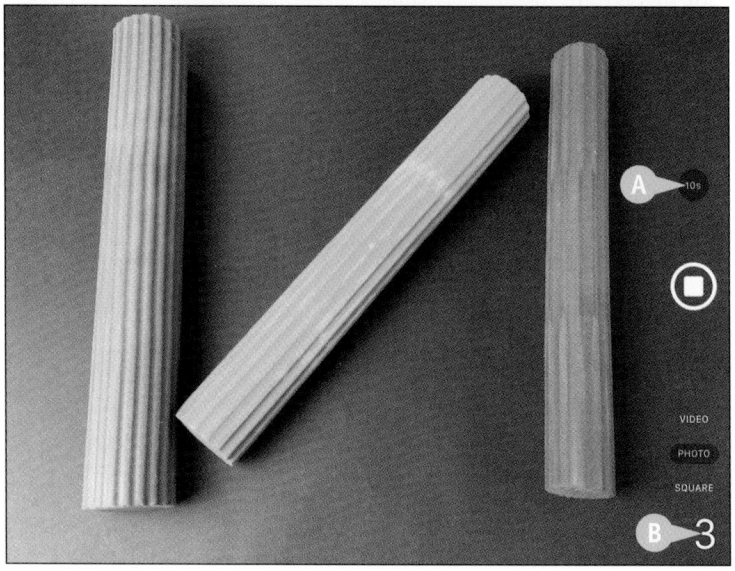

Turn the Grid On or Off

1. Press **Home**.

   The Home screen appears.

2. Tap **Settings** ( ).

   The Settings screen appears.

3. Tap **Camera** ( ).

   The Camera screen appears.

4. Set the **Grid** switch to On ( ) or Off ( ), as needed.

5. To control whether the Camera app keeps the normal photo when taking HDR photos, set the **Keep Normal Photo** switch to On ( ), the default setting, or Off ( ).

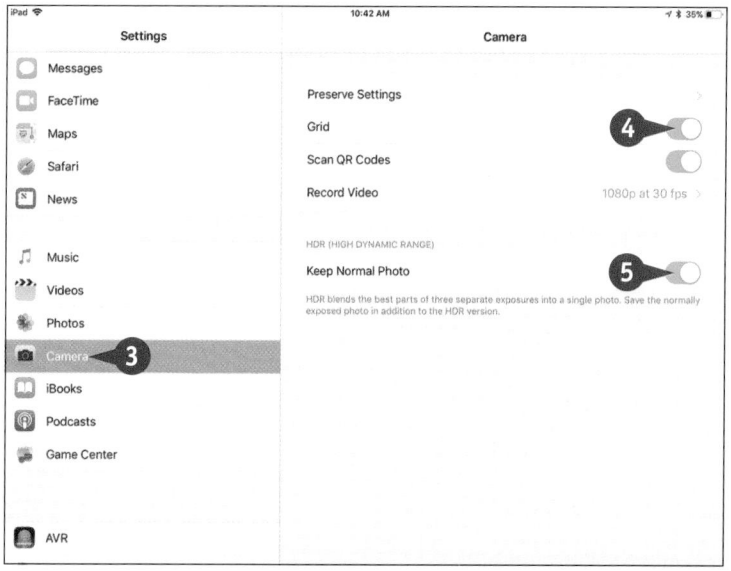

Compose Photos Using the Grid

1. Press **Home**.

   The Home screen appears.

2. Tap **Camera** ( ).

   The Camera app opens.

3. Use the grid to position your subject and align the iPad.

4. Tap **Take Photo** ( ).

   The Camera app takes the photo.

TIP

How does the Grid feature help with photo composition?

Apart from enabling you to align vertical lines and horizontal lines quickly and accurately, the grid can help you implement the Rule of Thirds. This rule suggests placing the major point of interest on one of the dividing lines or intersections in the picture.

Take Time-Lapse Movies

The Camera app's Time-Lapse feature enables you to take time-lapse movies easily: All you need to do is point the camera lens at your subject, select the Time-Lapse feature, start taking the movie, and then stop it at the appropriate point. This feature is great for shooting movies of sunrises and sunsets, changing weather patterns, or wildlife.

To take effective time-lapse movies, use a tripod or another type of holder to keep your iPad still and aimed in the right direction.

Take Time-Lapse Movies

1. Set up the iPad on the tripod or holder.
2. Press **Home**.

   The Home screen appears.
3. Tap **Camera** (📷).

   The Camera app opens.
4. Aim the lens at your subject.

Note: You cannot use zoom for time-lapse movies.

5. Scroll the Camera options down until the Time-Lapse item appears.

6. Tap **Time-Lapse**.

   The view changes to that of the video camera.
7. Tap **Take Time-Lapse Movie** (⬤).

The Camera app starts filming.

8. When the time has elapsed, tap **Stop Recording** (■).
9. Tap the thumbnail for the movie.

The movie opens.

10. Tap **Play** (▶).

The movie starts playing.

Note: The Camera app makes your time-lapse movies available through both the Videos album and the Time-Lapse album. There is only one copy of each time-lapse movie, but it appears in both albums for convenience.

TIPS

How much space do time-lapse movies take up?
Time-lapse movies take around 5MB to 10MB per minute at the 1080p resolution.

How do I control the number of frames the Time-Lapse feature shoots?
At this writing, you cannot control the number of frames beyond choosing when to start and stop shooting the movie. The Time-Lapse feature has no configurable settings. The Camera app automatically adjusts the focus and the exposure as necessary to cope with changing subjects and lighting conditions.

Take Fun Photos with Photo Booth

Your iPad includes the Photo Booth app, which you can use to take photos using special effects such as Thermal Camera, X-Ray, or Kaleidoscope.

On your iPad, you can use Photo Booth with either the front camera — the one on the screen side — or the rear camera, so you can apply the effects to subjects other than yourself if you choose. Photo Booth stores the photos you take in the Camera Roll album, so they appear together with the photos you take with the Camera app.

Take Fun Photos with Photo Booth

1. Press **Home**.

   The Home screen appears.

2. Tap **Photo Booth** (📷).

   Photo Booth opens, showing the front camera on your iPad.

3. Tap the effect you want to use. This example uses Kaleidoscope.

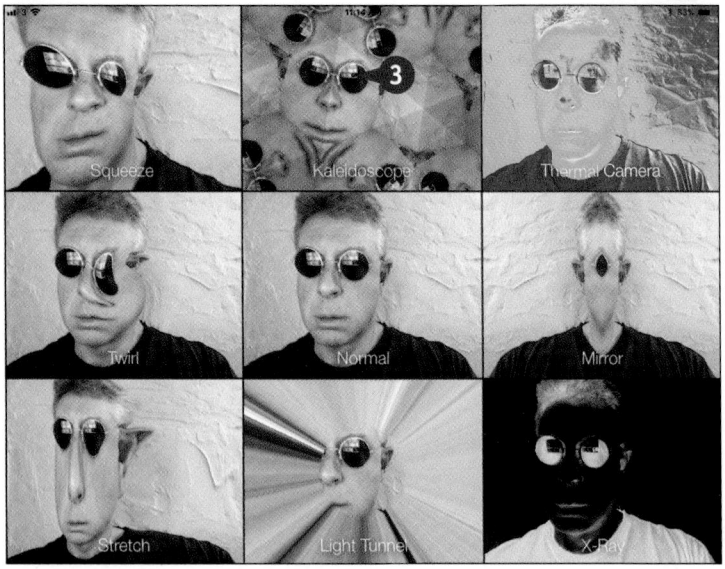

Photo Booth displays the camera's input full screen with the effect applied.

4. Compose your features to suit the effect.
5. Tap **Take Photo** ( ).

   Photo Booth takes the photo.
6. Tap **Switch Cameras** ( ).

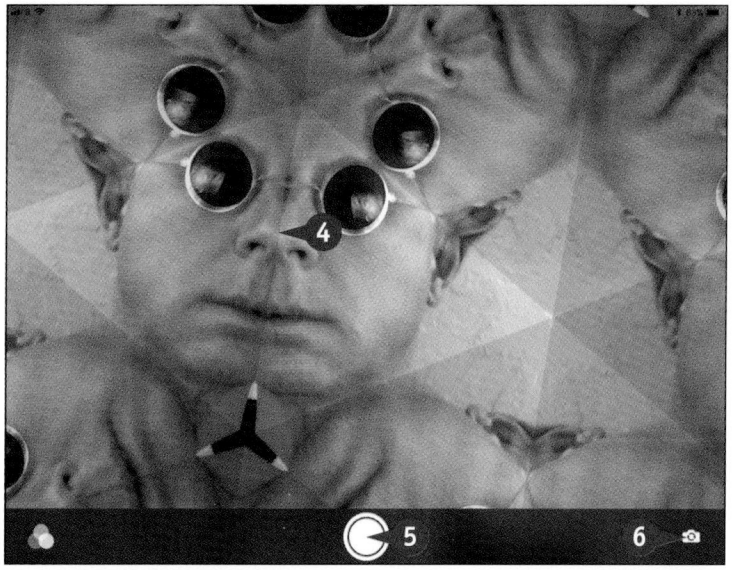

Photo Booth switches to the rear camera.

7. Tap **Filters** ( ).

   The screen for choosing effects appears.
8. Tap the effect you want. This example uses **Thermal Camera.**

   The effect appears on-screen.
9. Tap **Take Photo** ( ).

   Photo Booth takes the photo.

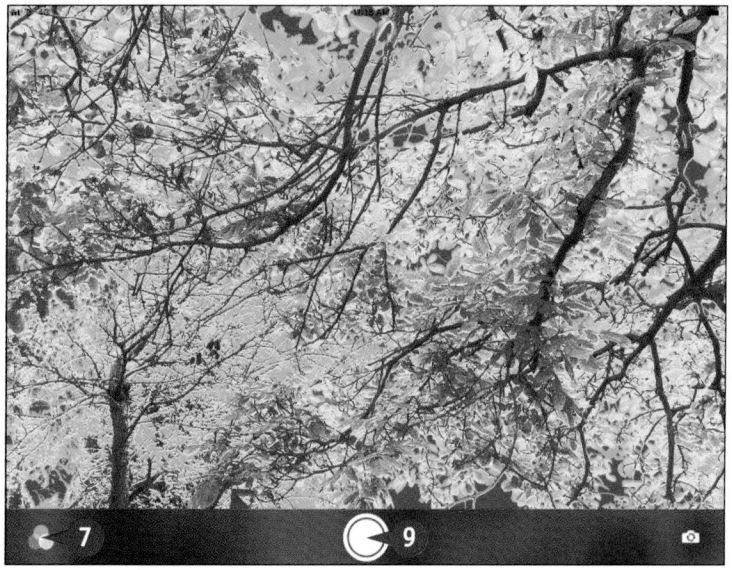

TIP

How do I share the photos I take in Photo Booth?

Photo Booth stores the photos in the Camera Roll album, just as the Camera app does, so you can share them like any other photos. Press **Home** and tap **Photos** ( ) to open the Photos app, and then tap **Albums** and **Camera Roll** to open the Camera Roll album. You can then tap a photo to open it, and tap **Share** ( ) to open the Share sheet.

Crop, Rotate, and Straighten Photos

If you have a photo where the subject is sideways or upside down, you can use the Rotate feature in the Photos app to rotate the photo so it is the right way up. If the photo is the right way up but is not straight, you can straighten it. This works both for photos you take on the iPad and for photos you copy to the iPad.

Crop, Rotate, and Straighten Photos

1. Press **Home**.

   The Home screen appears.

2. Tap **Photos** ( ).

   The Photos app opens.

3. Navigate to and open the photo you want to rotate.

Note: You may need to tap the screen to reveal the controls at the top of the screen. These options disappear after a brief period of inactivity.

4. Tap **Edit**.

Note: If the This Photo Is Not Editable dialog opens when you tap **Edit**, tap **Duplicate and Edit** to create a duplicate photo in your Camera Roll album and open it for editing.

   The editing controls appear.

5. Tap **Crop** ( ).

The Photos app automatically applies any straightening that it detects the photo needs.

A You can tap **Reset** to undo the automatic straightening.

B You can move the rotation dial to adjust the straightening.

C You can tap **Rotate** ( ) to rotate the photo 90 degrees counterclockwise. Tap again to rotate to 180 degrees; tap a third time to rotate to 270 degrees.

Note: You can tap **Cancel** and then tap **Discard Changes** to abandon the edit, restoring the photo to its previous state.

6 Tap and drag a corner crop handle or a border to adjust the cropping.

7 Tap **Done**.

Photos saves your changes to the photo.

TIP

How can I crop a photo to a specific size ratio?
You can crop a photo to a specific aspect ratio, such as 3:2 or Square, by tapping **Aspect Ratio** ( ), and then tapping the appropriate ratio in the dialog that opens.

Enhance Photos

To instantly improve the appearance of a photo, use the Enhance feature. Enhance analyzes the brightness and color balance of the photo and attempts to improve them by lightening or darkening the photo, raising the contrast, and boosting dull colors. If the enhancement does not give the result you want, you can easily remove the changes.

Enhance Photos

1. Press **Home**.

   The Home screen appears.

2. Tap **Photos** ( ).

   The Photos app opens.

3. Navigate to and open the photo that you want to enhance.

4. Tap **Edit**.

Note: You may need to tap the screen to reveal the menu options at the top of the screen. These options disappear after a brief period of inactivity.

   The editing tools appear.

5. Tap **Enhance** ( ).

   Photos enhances the image.

Note: Tap **Enhance** ( ) to toggle Enhance off and on so you can judge the effect.

6. Tap **Done**.

Reduce Red-Eye in Photos

Red-eye is a photographic effect that occurs when the camera's flash reflects off the back of the subject's eyes, causing the eyes to glow red. You can reduce or remove red-eye by using the Red-Eye feature in the Photos app. The Red-Eye feature is designed for human eyes and does not usually work for animal eyes, whose flash-reflection effect is more yellow or green than red.

Reduce Red-Eye in Photos

1. Press **Home**.

   The Home screen appears.

2. Tap **Photos** ( ).

   The Photos app opens.

3. Open the photo for which you want to reduce red-eye.

4. Tap **Edit**.

Note: You may need to tap the screen to display the controls.

The editing tools appear.

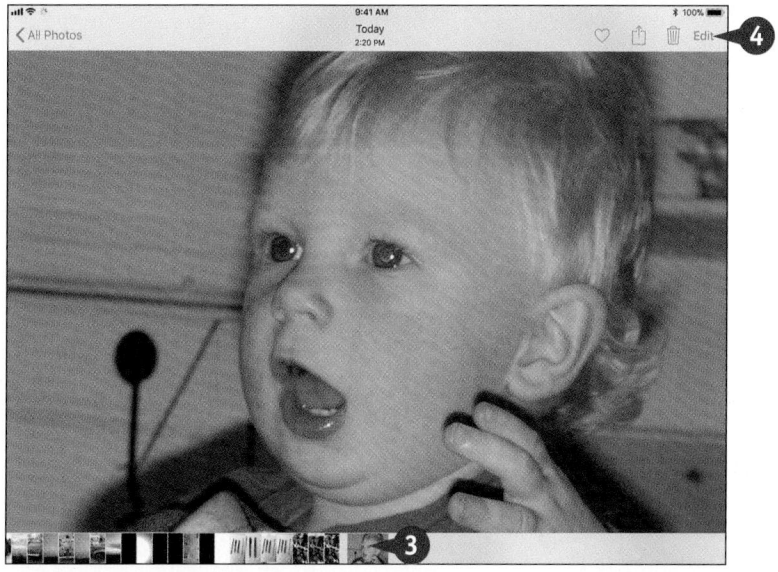

5. Tap **Red-Eye** ( ).

6. Tap each red eye in the photograph.

   Photos tries to remove the red-eye.

Note: You can tap each red eye again to undo your changes.

7. Tap **Done**.

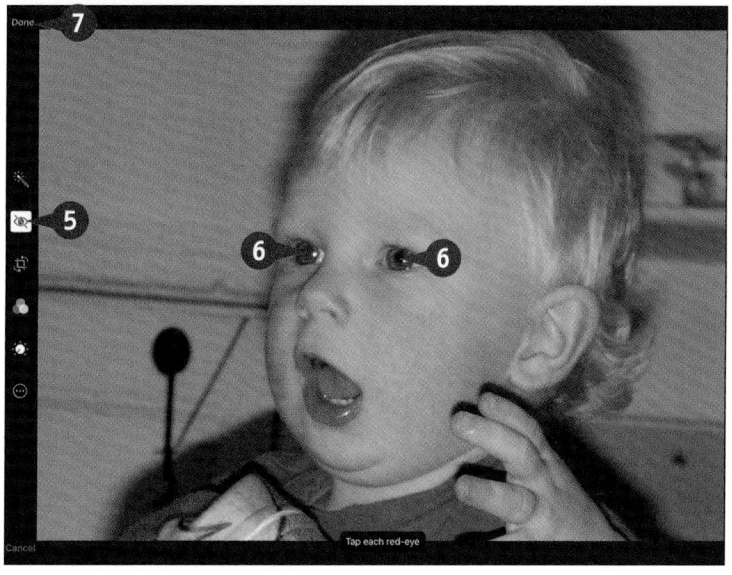

Adjust the Colors in Photos

The Photos app enables you to adjust the colors in your photos. For example, you can increase the exposure or brightness of a photo that is too dark; adjust the saturation, contrast, or color of an anemic photo; or control black-and-white settings such as intensity, tone, and grain.

The Photos app divides the settings into three categories: Light, Color, and B&W. You can adjust all the settings in a category at once or adjust each individual setting as needed.

Adjust the Colors in Photos

1. Press **Home**.

   The Home screen appears.

2. Tap **Photos** ( ).

   The Photos app opens.

3. In the Photos app, open the photo whose colors you want to adjust.

4. Tap **Edit**.

   The editing tools appear.

5. Tap **Adjust** ( ).

   The Adjust controls appear.

6. Tap **Light** ( ).

   The controls for adjusting the Light category of settings using preset algorithms appear.

7. Drag the slider up or down to adjust the Light category's settings. In this example, you would drag the slider down to increase the brightness.

8. Tap **Color** ( ).

   The controls for adjusting the Color category of settings appear.

9. Tap **List** ( ).

The Color list appears.

10 Tap **Saturation**.

The Saturation controls appear.

11 Drag the slider up or down to adjust the color saturation. In this example, you would drag the slider down to increase the color saturation.

A You can tap **List** (☰) to return to the list Color list and change other color settings.

B You can tap **B&W** (◐) to adjust the black-and-white settings. You can adjust these settings either as a category or individually. See the tip for details.

12 When you finish making changes, tap **Done**.

Photos saves the changes to the photo.

TIP

Should I adjust the settings individually or as a category?
This is up to you. The category algorithms work well for many photos, so it is often worth trying the category adjustment first before digging into the individual settings. However, when you want full control of the changes, start with the individual settings instead.

Apply Filters to Photos

You can use the Filter feature in the Photos app to change the look of a photo by applying a filter such as Mono, Tonal, Chrome, Transfer, or Instant. If you like the effect, you can save the photo with the effect applied.

Photos applies the filter as an effect overlaid on the photo rather than by making it an integral part of the photo. This means you can subsequently remove the filter, returning the photo to its previous state. Alternatively, you can apply another filter, giving the photo a different look.

Apply Filters to Photos

1. Press **Home**.

   The Home screen appears.

2. Tap **Photos** ( ).

   The Photos app opens.

3. Navigate to the photo and tap it.

   The photo appears.

4. Tap **Edit**.

   The editing controls appear.

5. Tap **Filters** ( ).

Ⓐ The Filters bar appears.

6 Tap the filter you want to apply.

Photos displays the filter effect on-screen.

7 Tap **Done**.

Photos saves the change to the photo.

TIP

How do I remove a filter from a photo?

Open the photo, and then tap **Edit** to switch to Edit Mode. Tap **Filters** ( ) to display the Filters bar, and then tap **None**. Tap **Done** to apply the change.

After opening an edited photo for further editing, you can also tap **Revert**, and then tap **Revert to Original** to restore the photo to its original state. Reverting to the original photo removes any other edits you have made, as well as removing the filter you have applied.

Capture Video

Along with capturing still photos, the cameras on your iPad can capture high-quality, full-motion video. The rear camera records 1080p video, while the front camera records 720p video. A single video can use only one resolution.

To capture video, you use the Camera app. You launch the Camera app as usual, and then switch it to Video Mode. After taking the video, you can view it on the iPad screen.

Capture Video

1. Press **Home**.

   The Home screen appears.

Note: To change the video resolution, tap **Settings** (), tap **Camera** (), tap **Record Video**, and then tap the resolution.

2. Tap **Camera** ().

   The Camera screen appears, showing the image the lens is seeing.

   A Some iPad models can also shoot video in slow motion. Tap **Slo-Mo** to access this feature.

3. Tap **Video**.

   The video image and video controls appear.

4. Aim the camera at your subject.

5. Tap **Record** ().

   The camera starts recording.

   B The time readout shows the time that has elapsed.

   C You can zoom by tapping **Zoom In** () or **Zoom Out** (), dragging the **Zoom** slider (), or by pinching apart or together, as usual.

6. To finish recording, tap **Stop Recording** ().

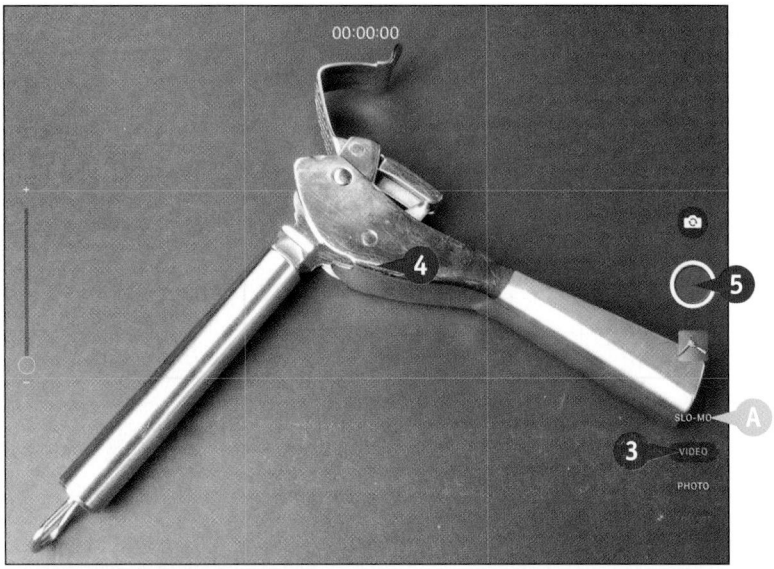

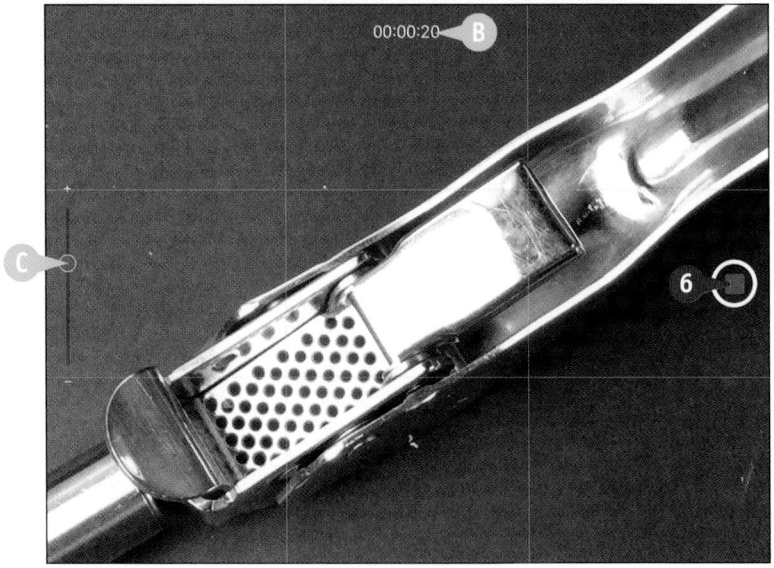

The Camera app stops recording and displays a thumbnail of the video's first frame.

D You can tap **Record** (◉) to start recording another video clip if necessary.

7 Tap the thumbnail.

The video appears.

8 Tap **Play** (▶).

The video starts playing.

Note: Tap anywhere on the screen to display the video controls.

Note: If you want to trim the video, tap **Edit** to switch to Edit Mode. Tap the Thumbnails bar at the bottom of the screen, drag the **Start** handle (❮) to the first frame you want to keep, and then drag the **End** handle (❯) to the last frame you want to keep. Tap **Done** and **Save as New Clip**.

9 When you finish viewing the video, tap **Back** (<).

The Camera app appears again.

Note: Video takes up a lot of space on your iPad, so delete any videos that are not worth keeping.

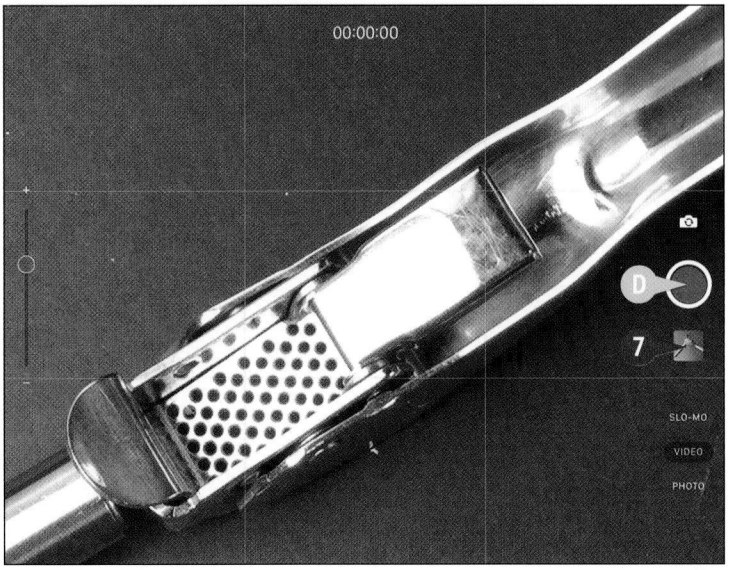

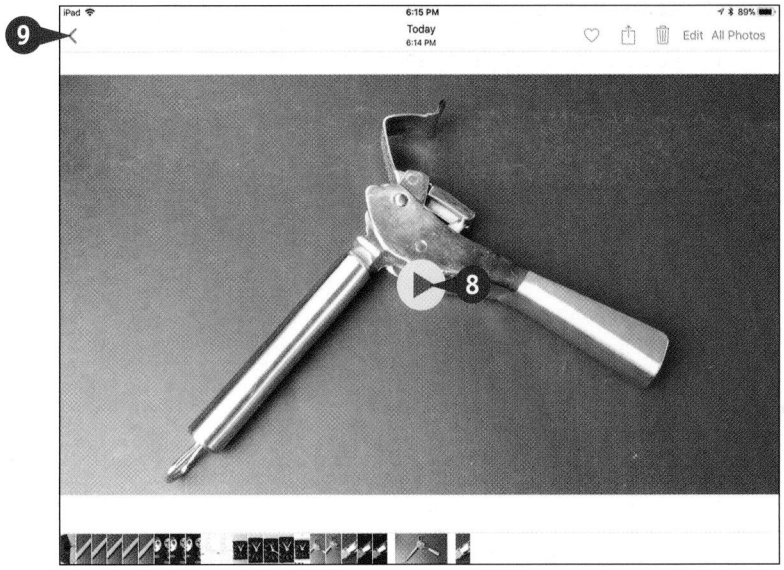

TIPS

Why do the picture and picture shape change when I switch to the video camera?

The picture may appear to zoom in because the video camera uses a longer focal length than the still camera. The picture shape changes because the video camera uses a different aspect ratio, 16:9, than the still camera, which uses 4:3.

What does the bar of miniature pictures at the bottom of the video playback screen do?

The navigation bar gives you a quick way of moving forward and backward through the movie. Tap the vertical playhead bar, and then drag to the right or to the left, either when the movie is playing or when it is paused.

CHAPTER 12

Troubleshooting Your iPad

To keep your iPad running well, you should learn essential troubleshooting moves to use on the iPad itself and in iTunes. You can also update your iPad software and track the device if it goes missing.

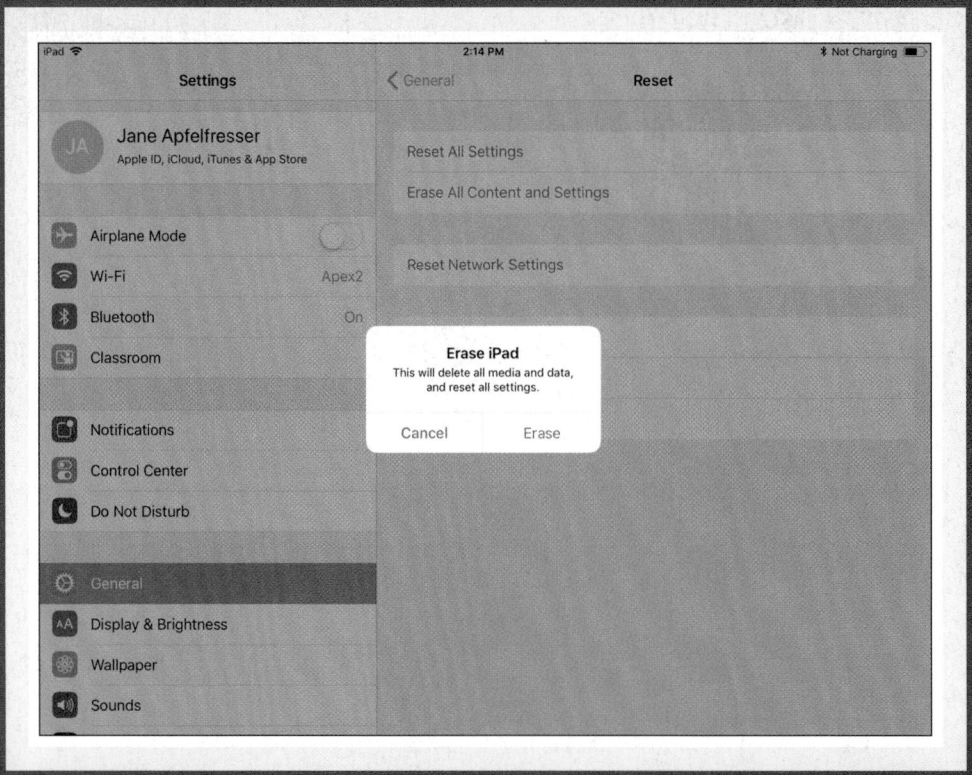

Close an App That Has Stopped Responding 306
Update the Software on Your iPad. 308
Extend Your iPad's Runtime on the Battery 310
Back Up and Restore Your iPad Using iTunes. 312
Back Up and Restore Your iPad Using iCloud. 314
Restore the Operating System Using iTunes 316
Restore Your iPad to Factory Settings 318
Troubleshoot Wi-Fi Connections. 320
Locate Your iPad with Find My iPad 322

Close an App That Has Stopped Responding

Normally, the apps on your iPad run without problems, but if an app stops responding, you can force it to close. Usually, you can easily tell when an app has stopped responding, because the screen does not change and your taps and gestures on the screen get no reaction. But if you are not certain that an app has stopped responding, allow the app a few seconds to recover before you force it to close.

Close an App That Has Stopped Responding

1. When an app stops responding, press **Home** twice in quick succession. The app in this example is Safari.

Note: You can display the app-switching screen by swiping up from the bottom of the screen.

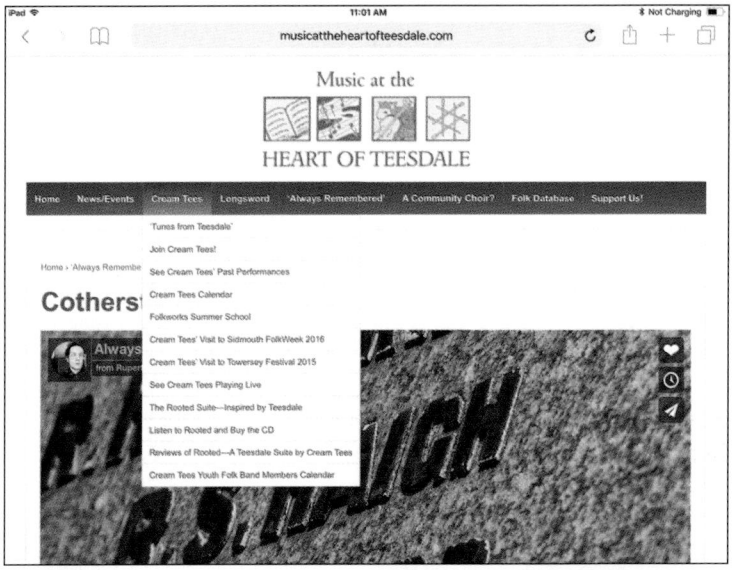

The app-switching screen appears, showing a thumbnail for each running app.

A The latest app — the app that has stopped responding — appears as the upper-right thumbnail.

2. Swipe up on the thumbnail for the app that has stopped responding.

iOS closes the app.

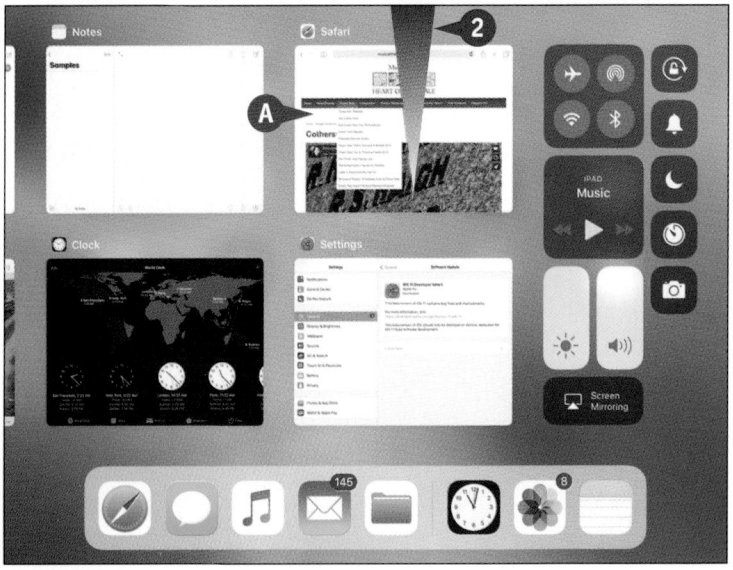

The app disappears from the list.

B If you want to switch to another running app, tap its thumbnail.

3 Press **Home**.

C You can also tap open space to display the Home screen.

D If the Dock contains an icon for the app you closed, you can tap the icon to open the app again.

The Home screen appears.

4 Tap the icon of the app that you closed.

Note: You may need to display another Home screen to reach the app's icon.

The app launches again, and you can resume using it.

TIP

How else can I regain control of my iPad when it will not display the app-switching screen?
If your iPad does not display the app-switching screen when you press **Home** twice in rapid succession, shut down the iPad. Hold down **Sleep/Wake** until the Slide to Power Off prompt appears, and then drag the slider across. If the Slide to Power Off prompt does not appear, continue to hold down **Sleep/Wake** until the iPad shuts down. You can then press **Sleep/Wake** again to restart the iPad.

Update the Software on Your iPad

Apple periodically releases new versions of iOS for the iPad to fix problems, improve performance, and add new features. To keep your iPad running quickly and smoothly, and to add any new features, update the device's software when a new version becomes available.

Your iPad notifies you automatically when a new version of the iPad software is available; if you sync your iPad with a computer, iTunes notifies you, too. You can also check manually for new software versions.

Update the Software on Your iPad

1. Press **Home**.

   The Home screen appears.

   A The badge on the Settings icon indicates that an update is available.

2. Tap **Settings** ( ).

   The Settings screen appears.

3. Tap **General** ( ).

   The General screen appears.

4. Tap **Software Update**.

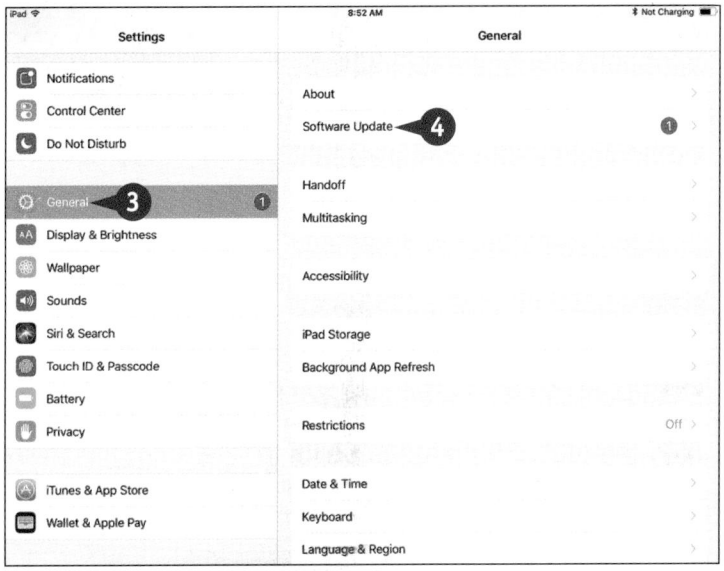

The Software Update screen appears.

5 Tap **Install Now**.

Note: If the iPad has already requested the software update, the Update Requested button appears in place of the Install Now button. If the iPad is already downloading the update, the Downloading button appears. In either case, allow the download to complete, and then tap **Install Now**.

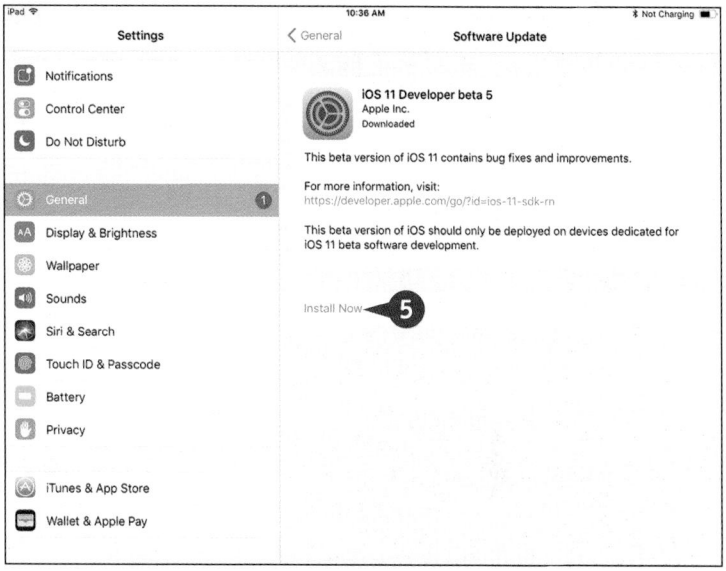

The Enter Passcode dialog opens.

6 Type your passcode.

The Terms and Conditions screen appears.

7 Tap **Agree**.

The Terms and Conditions dialog opens.

8 Tap **Agree** in the dialog.

The installation procedure begins.

Your iPad restarts, and you can resume using it.

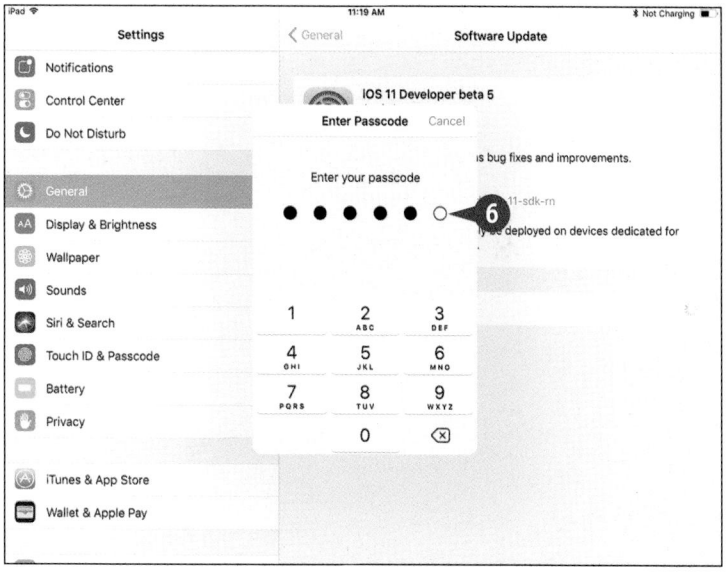

TIP

How do I update my iPad's software using iTunes?

Connect your iPad to your computer via USB. If iTunes displays a dialog prompting you to update your iPad, click **Update**; otherwise, click **iPad** ( ), click **Summary**, and then click **Check for Update**. If the check produces an update, click **Update**, and then follow the prompts that iTunes and your iPad display.

Extend Your iPad's Runtime on the Battery

You can extend the runtime of your iPad on its battery by reducing the demands on the battery. You can dim the screen so that it consumes less power. You can set your iPad to go to sleep quickly. You can turn off Wi-Fi and Bluetooth when you do not need them, and you can turn off the power-hungry GPS feature on a cellular iPad when you do not need it for navigation or other purposes.

Extend Your iPad's Runtime on the Battery

Dim the Screen

1. Press **Home**.

   The Home screen appears.

2. Tap **Settings** ( ).

   The Settings screen appears.

3. Tap **Display & Brightness** ( ).

   The Display & Brightness screen appears.

4. Tap the **Brightness** slider and drag it to the left to dim the screen.

   A Set the **Auto-Brightness** switch to On ( ) if you want the iPad to adjust the brightness automatically to suit the ambient light conditions.

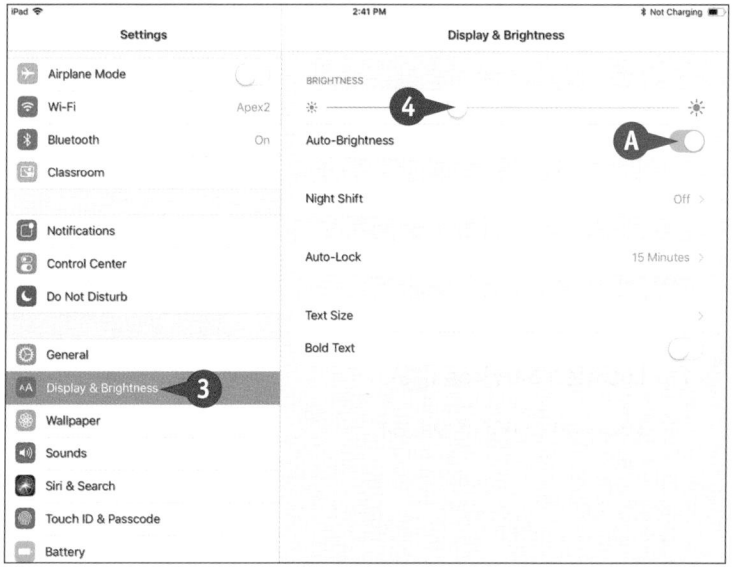

Turn Off Wi-Fi and Bluetooth

1. On the Settings screen, tap **Wi-Fi** ( ).

   The Wi-Fi screen appears.

2. Set the **Wi-Fi** switch to Off ( ).

3. Tap **Bluetooth** ( ).

Note: If you have a cellular iPad, turning off Wi-Fi may cause data transfer over the cellular connection instead of over Wi-Fi.

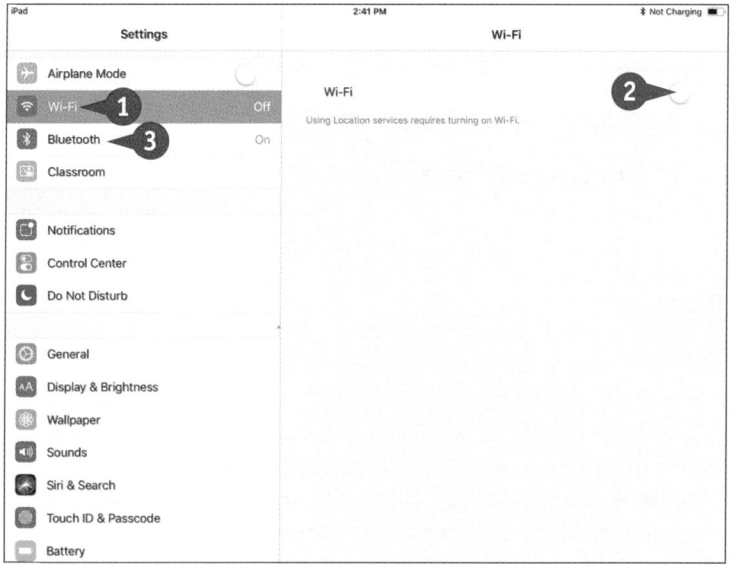

The Bluetooth screen appears.

4. Set the **Bluetooth** switch to Off ( ).

Note: You can enable or disable Wi-Fi and Bluetooth quickly from Control Center. You can also adjust the display brightness, but you cannot control Auto-Brightness.

Note: For a cellular iPad, you can save power by turning off cellular data either from Control Center or from the Cellular Data screen in the Settings app.

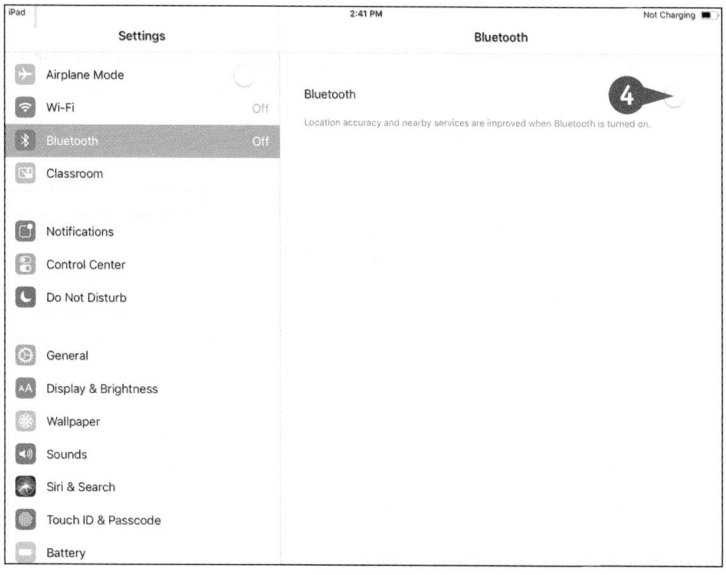

Turn Off the GPS Feature

1. On the Settings screen, tap **Privacy** ( ).

   The Privacy screen appears.

2. Tap **Location Services** ( ).

   The Location Services screen appears.

3. Set the **Location Services** switch to Off ( ).

   The Location Services dialog opens.

4. Tap **Turn Off**.

5. Tap **Privacy** ( ).

   The Privacy screen appears.

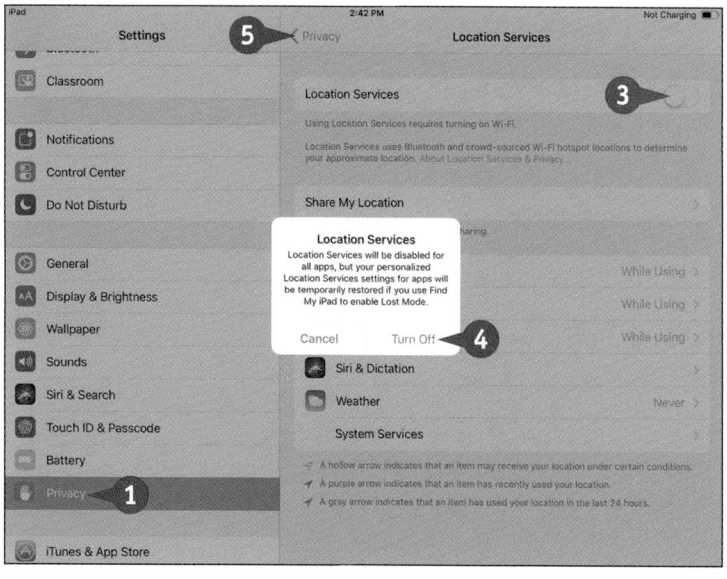

TIPS

How can I make my iPad put itself to sleep quickly?
You can set a short time for the Auto-Lock setting. To do so, press **Home**. Tap **Settings** ( ), tap **Display & Brightness** ( ), and then tap **Auto-Lock**. Tap a short interval — for example, **2 Minutes**.

What is the best way to charge my iPad quickly?
Use the iPad Power Adapter or an Apple-certified equivalent power adapter. These adapters charge your iPad much more quickly than a standard USB port, such as those in a generic charger, computer, or car. Be careful with uncertified third-party power adapters, because these may cause electrical problems.

Back Up and Restore Your iPad Using iTunes

You can back up your iPad either to your computer or to iCloud. Backing up your iPad to your computer using iTunes creates a full backup of the iPad on your computer, enabling you to restore your data and settings to the iPad — or to a new iOS device — if your iPad becomes corrupted or damaged. If you encrypt the backup, iTunes saves your passwords, enabling you to restore them as well.

Back Up and Restore Your iPad Using iTunes

Back Up Your iPad Using iTunes

1. Connect your iPad to your computer via the USB cable.
2. Click **iPad** ( ) on the navigation bar in iTunes.

   The iPad-management screen appears.
3. Click **Summary**.

   The Summary screen appears.
4. Click **This computer** (changes to).
5. Click **Back Up Now**.

A The Latest Backup readout shows the date and time of your most recent backup.

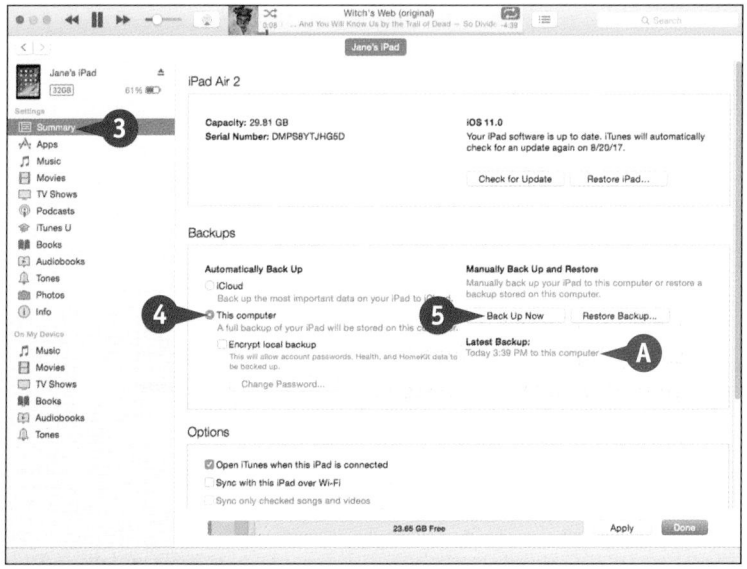

Restore Your iPad Using iTunes

1. Click **Restore Backup**.

Note: If a message appears saying *Find My iPad must be turned off before iPad can be restored*, tap **Settings** ( ) on the iPad, tap **Apple ID**, and then tap **iCloud** ( ). Tap **Find My iPad** ( ), and then set the **Find My iPad** switch to Off (changes to).

2. In the Restore From Backup dialog, click the pop-up menu ( ), and then click the backup to use.
3. Click **Restore**.

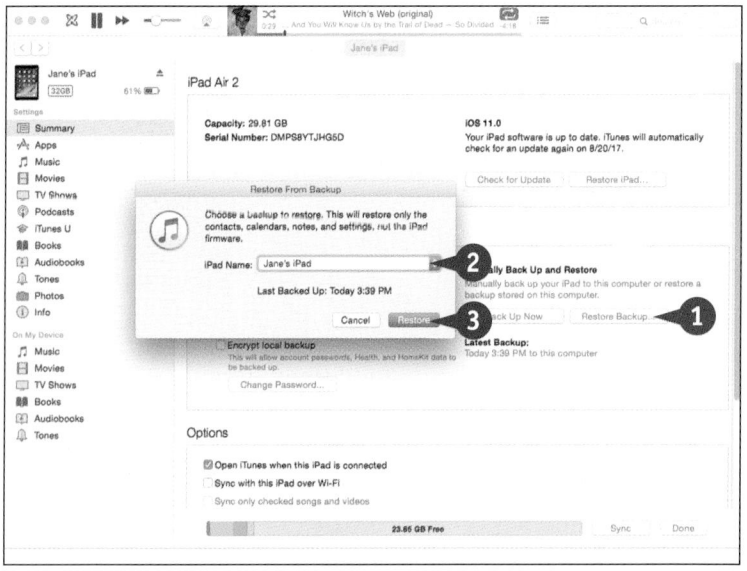

B iTunes restores the data from the backup, showing a progress readout as it does so.

Note: Do not disconnect the iPad during the restore process. Doing so can leave the iPad in an unusable state.

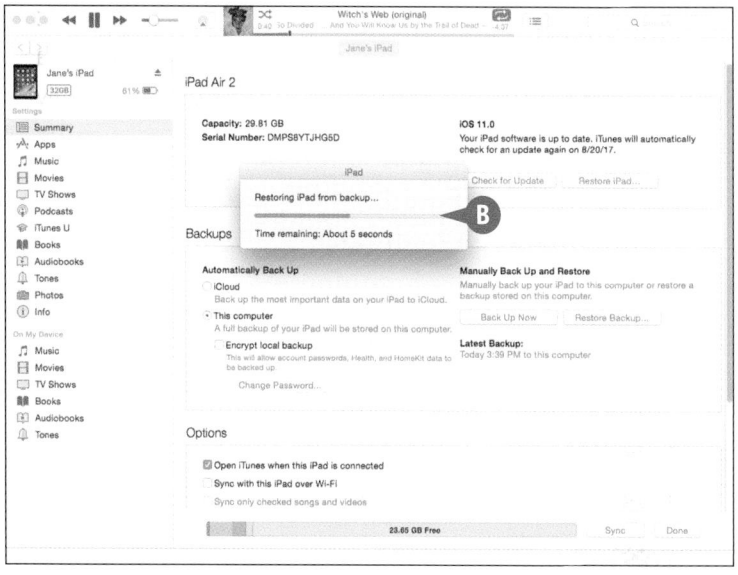

iTunes displays a message saying that the settings for your iPad have been restored.

4 Click **OK** or wait for the countdown timer to close the dialog automatically.

Your iPad restarts.

iTunes automatically syncs your iPad.

5 After the sync completes, disconnect the iPad from your computer.

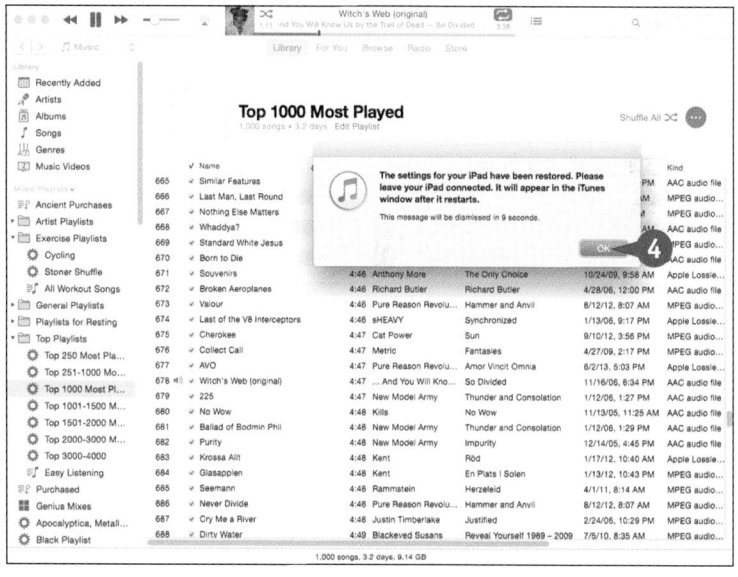

TIP

How can I protect confidential information in my iPad backups?

On the Summary screen in iTunes, click **Encrypt local backup** (☐ changes to ☑). In the Set Password dialog, type the password, and then click **Set Password**. iTunes then encrypts your backups using strong encryption.

In the Set Password dialog on the Mac, you can click **Remember this password in my keychain** (☐ changes to ☑) to store the password securely in your account's keychain.

Back Up and Restore Your iPad Using iCloud

Instead of backing up your iPad to your computer, you can back it up to iCloud. If your iPad suffers a software or hardware failure, you can restore the data and settings that you have backed up. You can choose which items to back up to iCloud.

iCloud Backup is less comprehensive than iTunes' backup: It does not back up apps, media files, or games you have bought from the iTunes Store, because you can download them again. iCloud Backup also does not back up your app data or your passwords.

Back Up and Restore Your iPad Using iCloud

1. Press **Home**.

   The Home screen appears.

2. Tap **Settings** ( ).

   The Settings screen appears.

3. Tap **Apple ID**, the button bearing your Apple ID name.

4. Tap **iCloud** ( ).

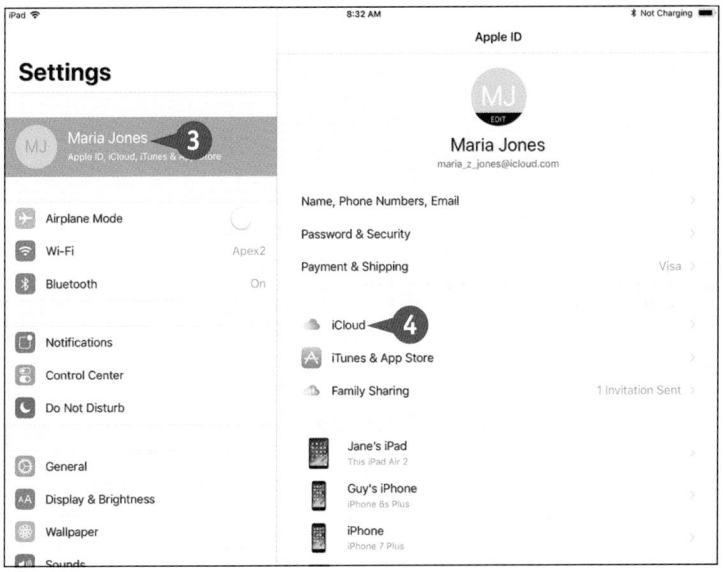

The iCloud screen appears.

5. Look at the Storage readout to verify that you have storage space available.

   A. If you need more space, tap **Manage Storage** to display the iCloud Storage screen, tap **Upgrade**, and then follow the prompts.

6. In the Apps Using iCloud list, choose which apps can store data in iCloud. See the section "Set Up and Configure iCloud" in Chapter 2 for more details.

7. Swipe up to scroll down the screen.

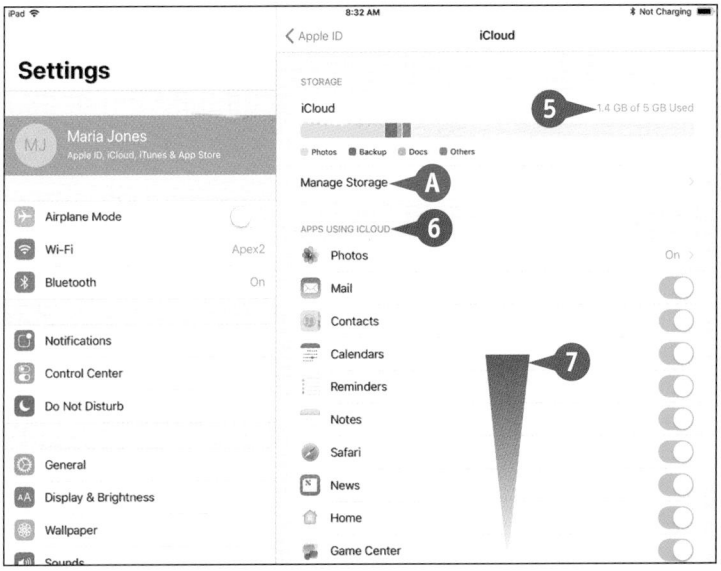

The lower part of the iCloud screen appears.

8 Set the **iCloud Drive** switch to On (◯) if you want to store files on iCloud Drive.

9 Tap **iCloud Backup** (⟲).

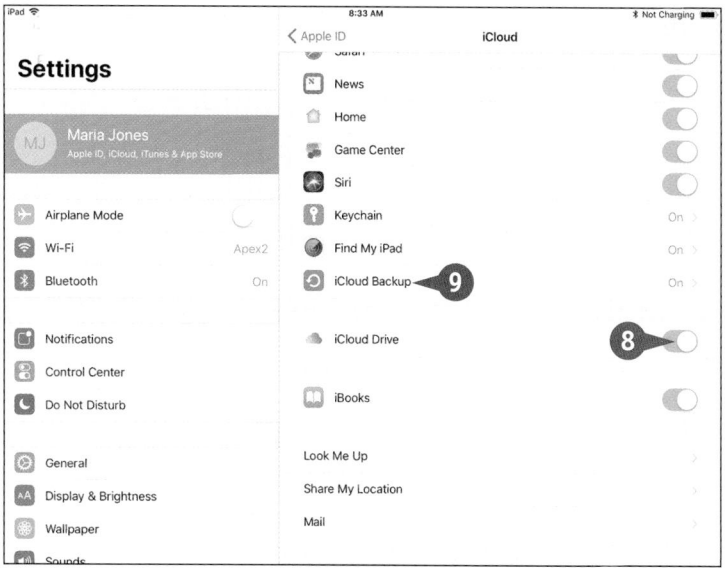

The Backup screen appears.

10 Set the **iCloud Backup** switch to On (◯).

B The Last Successful Backup readout shows when you last backed up your iPad to iCloud.

11 Tap **Back Up Now**.

Your iPad starts performing a backup to iCloud.

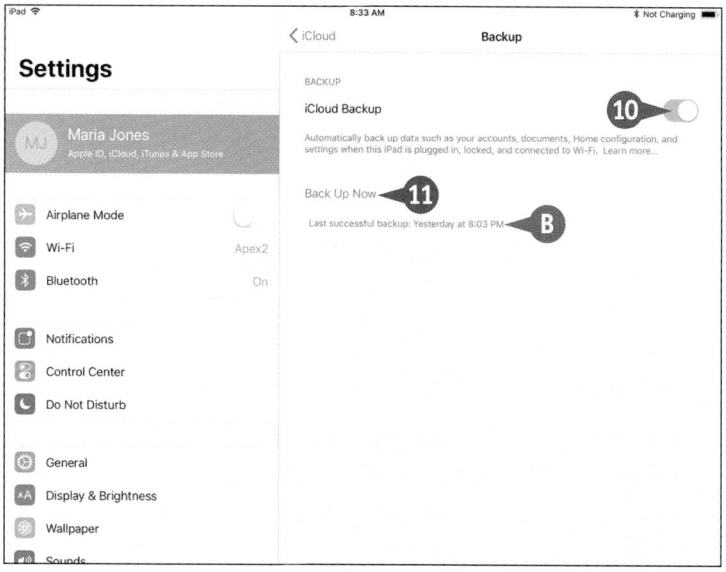

TIP

How do I restore my iPad from its iCloud backup?

First, reset the iPad to its factory settings, as explained in the section "Restore Your iPad to Factory Settings," later in this chapter. To do this, you must first turn off Find My iPad. When the iPad restarts and displays its setup screens, choose your language and country. On the Apps & Data screen, tap **Restore from iCloud Backup**, and then tap **Next**. On the Apple ID screen, enter your Apple ID, and then tap **Next**. On the Choose Backup screen, tap the backup you want to use — normally, the most recent backup — and then tap **Restore**.

Restore the Operating System Using iTunes

If your iPad's operating system becomes corrupted, you can restore it by connecting the iPad to your computer and using iTunes. Restoring the iPad erases all its contents, so use this troubleshooting move only after other moves have failed.

When restoring the iPad, iTunes checks for an updated version of its software. If a new version is available, iTunes downloads and installs it automatically. The download may take minutes or hours, depending on the speed of your Internet connection.

Restore the Operating System Using iTunes

1. Connect your iPad to your computer via the USB cable.
2. Click **iPad** ( ) on the navigation bar.

   The iPad-management screen appears.
3. Click **Summary**.

   The Summary screen appears.
4. Click **Restore iPad**.

Note: If a message appears saying *Find My iPad must be turned off before iPad can be restored*, tap **Settings** ( ) on your iPad, tap **iCloud** ( ), tap **Find My iPad** ( ), and set the **Find My iPad** switch to Off ( ).

iTunes displays a message prompting you to back up the settings for the iPad before restoring.

5. Click **Back Up**.

Note: If you have backed up the iPad very recently, you may prefer to click **Don't Back Up**.

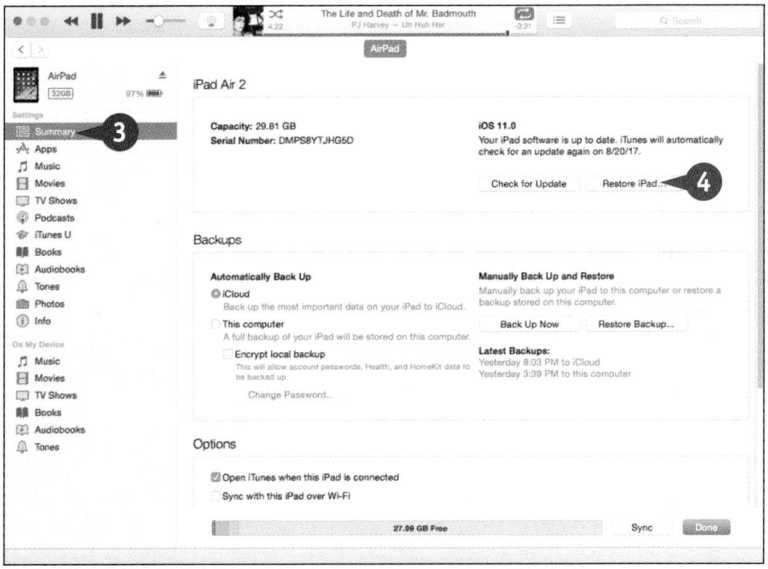

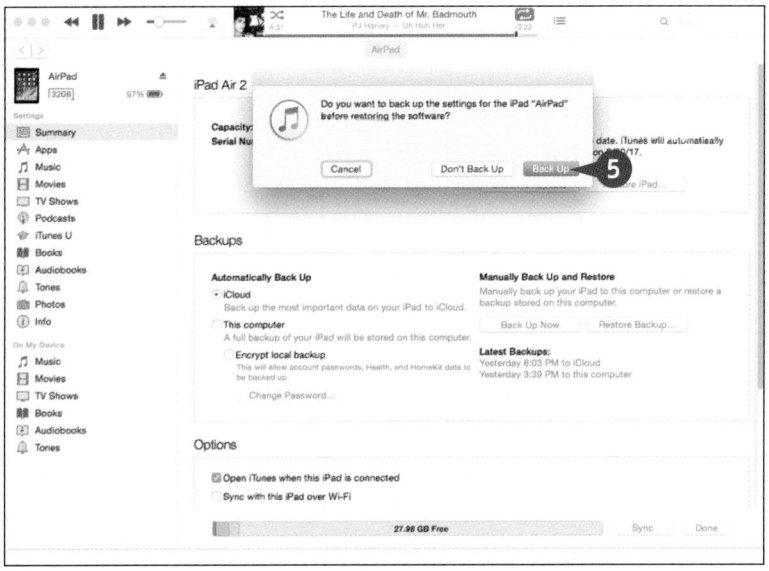

iTunes displays a message confirming that you want to restore the iPad to its factory settings.

6 Click **Restore**.

iTunes backs up the iPad if you chose to do so.

iTunes restores the iPad software.

Your iPad restarts and completes the restoration.

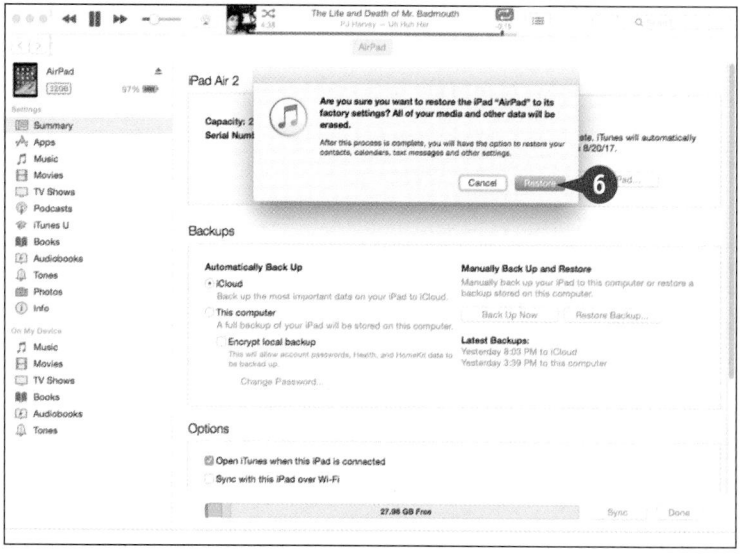

The Welcome to Your New iPad screen appears.

7 Click **Restore from this backup** (○ changes to changes to ◉).

8 Click the pop-up menu (⬍) and choose the iPad backup to restore.

9 Click **Continue**.

iTunes restores the data in the backup to your iPad.

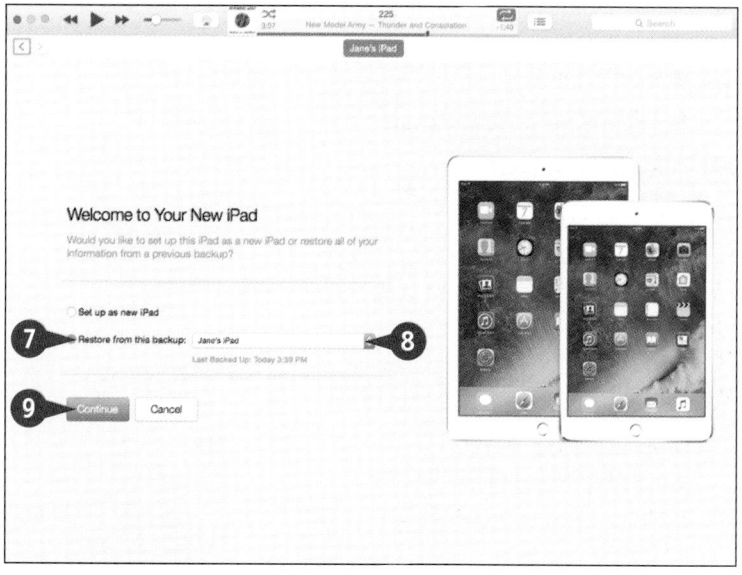

TIP

Can I restore the iPad software to an earlier version?

Yes, if you have the software file. iTunes stores the current version in the ~/Library/iTunes/iPad Software Updates folder on the Mac or the \Users*username*\AppData\Roaming\Apple Computer\iTunes\iPad Software Updates folder on a Windows PC's system drive, such as C:. Each time iTunes downloads a new version, it deletes the old version, so you must copy the current version to a folder of your own if you want to keep it.

To choose which file to use, press Option+click **Restore iPad** on a Mac. In Windows, press Shift+click **Restore iPad**. In the dialog that opens, click the appropriate file.

Restore Your iPad to Factory Settings

If your iPad starts malfunctioning and iTunes will not recognize it, you can restore the iPad to its factory settings. Restoring the iPad to factory settings deletes all the media and data the tablet contains and returns all the settings to their default values, wiping out your accounts and customizations.

Normally, you restore your iPad to factory settings only when it is suffering severe problems that you cannot resolve otherwise or before you sell or give away your iPad.

Restore Your iPad to Factory Settings

1. Press **Home**.

   The Home screen appears.

2. Tap **Settings** ( ).

   The Settings screen appears.

Note: If your iPad is not responding to the Home button or your taps, press and hold **Sleep/Wake** and **Home** for about 15 seconds to reset the iPad.

Note: If you are restoring factory settings in preparation for selling or giving away your iPad, tap **Apple ID**, tap **iCloud** ( ), tap **Find My iPad** ( ), and then set the **Find My iPad** switch to Off (changes to). You must do this to enable the new owner to register the iPad and to set up a new cellular service account for a cellular iPad.

3. Tap **General** ( ).

   The General screen appears.

4. Tap **Reset**.

   The Reset screen appears.

5. Tap **Erase All Content and Settings**.

   The first Erase iPad dialog opens.

Note: If you have secured your iPad with Touch ID or a passcode, you must type the passcode after tapping Erase All Content and Settings.

6. Tap **Erase**.

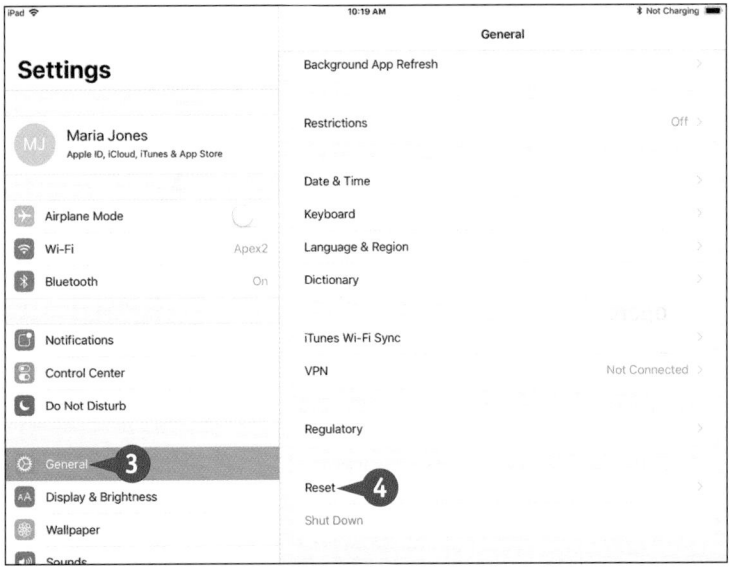

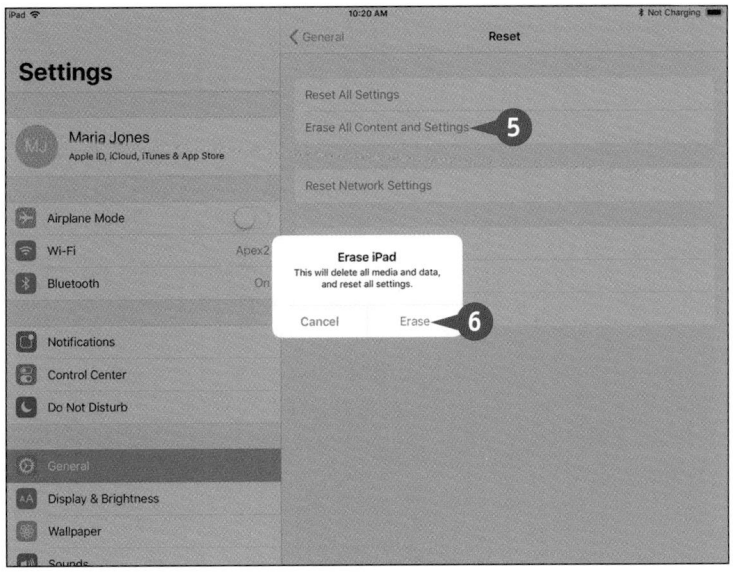

The second Erase iPad dialog opens, double-checking you are sure you want to erase all settings.

7 Tap **Erase**.

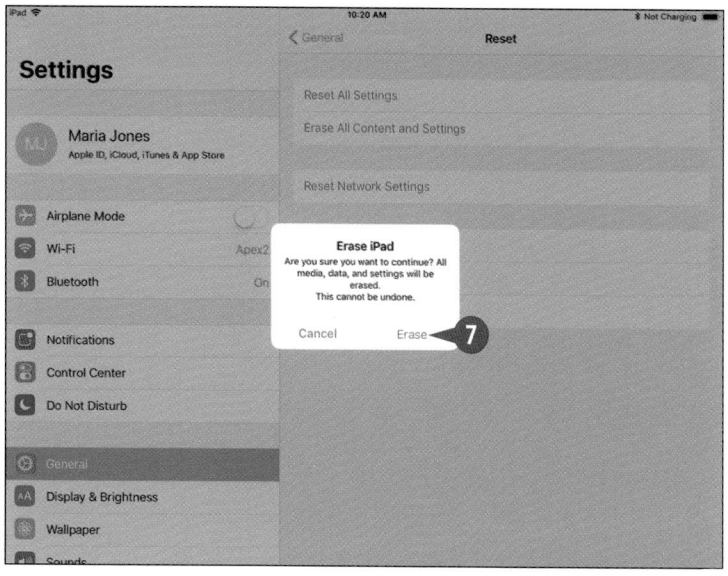

The Apple ID Password dialog opens.

8 Type your Apple ID password.

9 Tap **Erase**.

The iPad erases all your content and settings and restores itself to the factory settings. This takes several minutes.

When the operation is complete, the Hello screen appears, and you can set up your iPad as explained in Chapter 1.

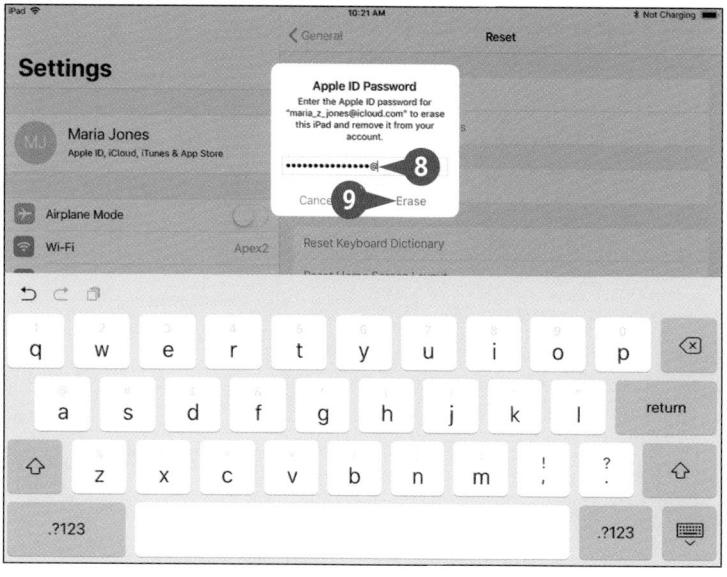

TIP

What does the Reset All Settings command on the Reset screen do?

The Reset All Settings command restores all the iPad settings to their defaults, but it does not erase your data. Use this command when the iPad settings have become confused and you cannot correct them manually. After using this command, you will need to set the iPad settings again, either by restoring them using iTunes or by setting them manually, in order to get the iPad working the way you prefer.

The other commands on the Reset screen enable you to reset your iPad's network settings, the keyboard dictionary, the Home screen layout, and the Location and Privacy settings.

Troubleshoot Wi-Fi Connections

Normally, your iPad automatically reconnects to Wi-Fi networks to which you have previously connected it, and maintains those connections without problems. But you may sometimes need to request the network address for your iPad again, a process called *renewing the lease on the IP address*. You may also need to tell your iPad to forget a network and then rejoin the network manually, providing the password again.

Troubleshoot Wi-Fi Connections

Renew the Lease on the IP Address of Your iPad

1. Press **Home**.

   The Home screen appears.

2. Tap **Settings** (⚙).

   The Settings screen appears.

3. Tap **Wi-Fi** (📶).

   The Wi-Fi screen appears.

4. Tap **Information** (ⓘ) to the right of the network for which you want to renew the lease.

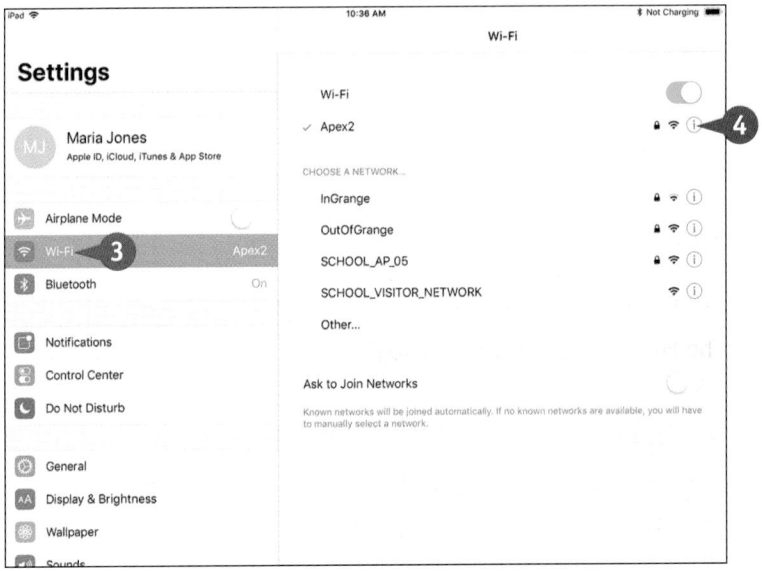

   The network's screen appears.

5. Tap **Renew Lease**.

   The Renew Lease pop-up button appears.

6. Tap **Renew Lease**.

7. Tap **Wi-Fi** (<).

   The Wi-Fi screen appears.

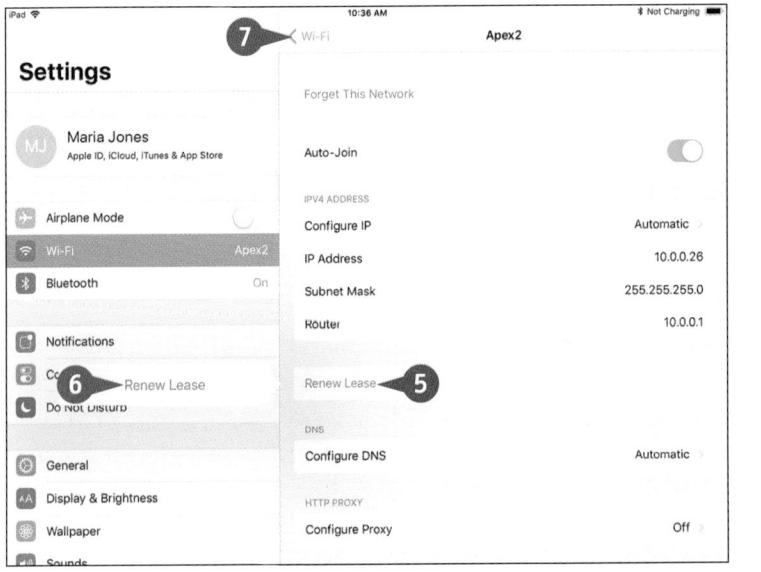

Note: If the IP Address readout shows an IP address starting with 169, your router may be misconfigured. 169 at the start indicates the device has a self-assigned IP address, which usually means it cannot get an address from the router.

Forget a Network and Then Rejoin It

1. On the Wi-Fi screen, tap **Information** (ⓘ) to the right of the network.

Note: Forgetting a network on your iPad causes other devices that use the same iCloud keychain to forget the network too.

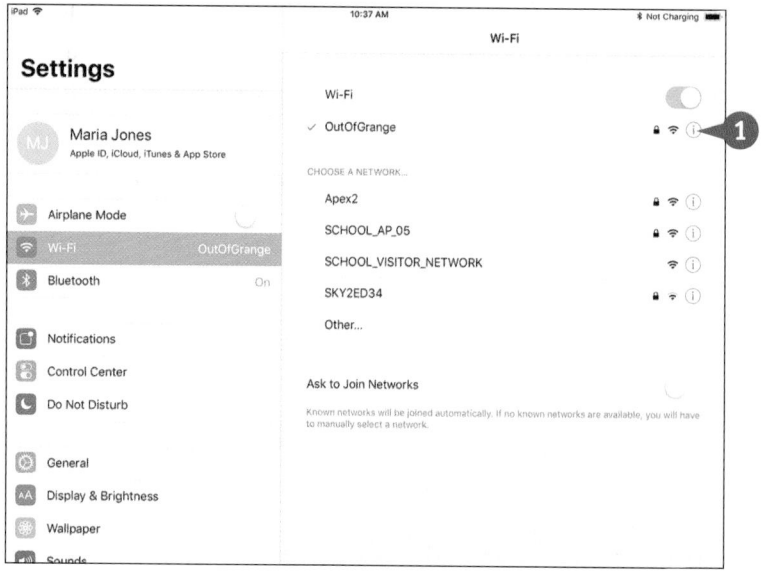

The network's screen appears.

2. Tap **Forget This Network**.

The Forget Wi-Fi Network dialog opens.

3. Tap **Forget**.

The iPad removes the network's details.

The Wi-Fi screen appears again.

4. Tap the network's name.

The Enter Password dialog opens.

5. Type the password for the network.

6. Tap **Join**.

The iPad joins the network.

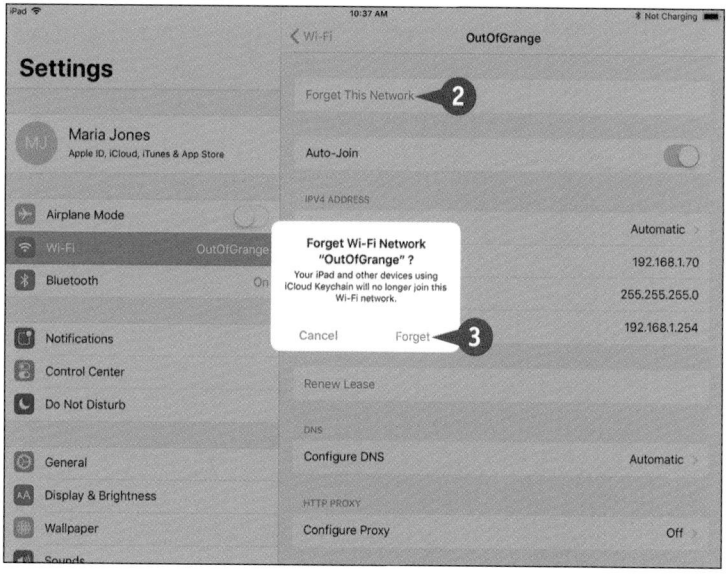

TIP

What else can I do to reestablish my Wi-Fi network connections?

If you are unable to fix your Wi-Fi network connections by renewing the IP address lease or by forgetting and rejoining the network, as described in this section, try restarting your iPad. If that does not work, press **Home**, tap **Settings** (⚙), tap **General** (⚙), and then tap **Reset** to display the Reset screen. Tap **Reset Network Settings**, type your passcode if prompted, and then tap **Reset** in the Reset Network Settings dialog. After this, you will need to set up each connection again manually.

Locate Your iPad with Find My iPad

You can use the Find My iPad feature in iCloud to locate your iPad when it has been lost or stolen. You can also display a message on the iPad or remotely erase the data on the iPad. To use Find My iPad, you must first set up your iCloud account on your iPad and enable the Find My iPad feature.

On a computer, you can use Find My iPad in a web browser to locate your iPad. On iOS, use the Find My iPhone app instead. You cannot use an Android device.

Locate Your iPad with Find My iPad

Turn On the Find My iPad Feature

1. Set up your iCloud account on your iPad as discussed in the section "Set Up and Configure iCloud" in Chapter 2.
2. Press **Home**.

   The Home screen appears.
3. Tap **Settings** ( ).

   The Settings screen appears.
4. Tap **Apple ID**, the button that shows your Apple ID name.

   The Apple ID screen appears.
5. Tap **iCloud** ( ).

   The iCloud screen appears.
6. Tap **Find My iPad** ( ).

   The Find My iPad screen appears.
7. Set the **Find My iPad** switch to On ( ).

   Note: If a confirmation dialog appears, tap **Allow**.

   iCloud turns on the Find My iPad feature.
8. Set the **Send Last Location** switch to On ( ) if you want your iPad to send its location to Apple when the battery runs critically low. Sending the location is usually helpful.

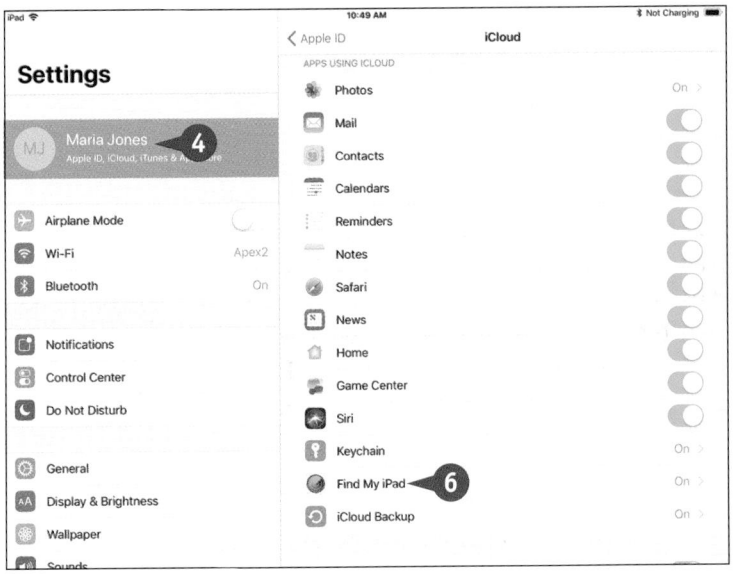

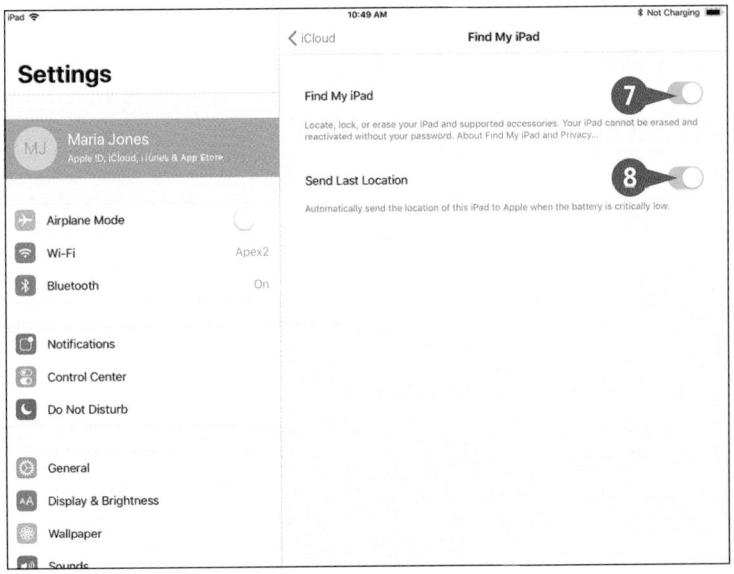

Locate Your iPad Using Find My iPad

1. On a computer, open a web browser, such as Chrome, Firefox, Internet Explorer, Microsoft Edge, or Safari.
2. Click the Address box.
3. Type www.icloud.com and press Enter in Windows or Return on a Mac.

   The Sign in to iCloud web page appears.
4. Type your username.
5. Type your password.
6. Click **Sign In** (→).

Note: If you have set up two-factor authentication on your Apple ID, the Two-Factor Authentication screen may appear. Click the device to use for verification, and then enter the code sent to the device on the Enter Verification Code screen. In the Trust This Browser? dialog that opens, click **Trust** or **Don't Trust**, as appropriate.

The iCloud apps screen appears.

Note: If iCloud displays the page you last used, click **iCloud** to display the iCloud apps screen.

7. Click **Find iPhone**.

Note: If iCloud prompts you to sign in again to use Find My iPhone, type your password and click **Sign In**.

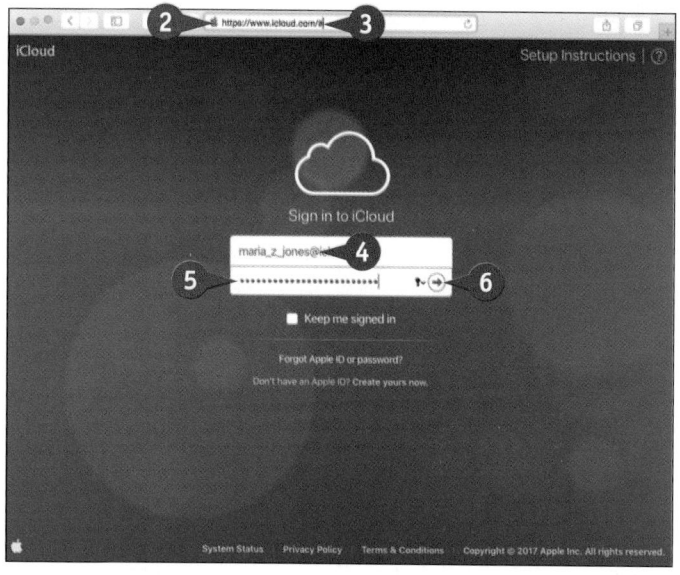

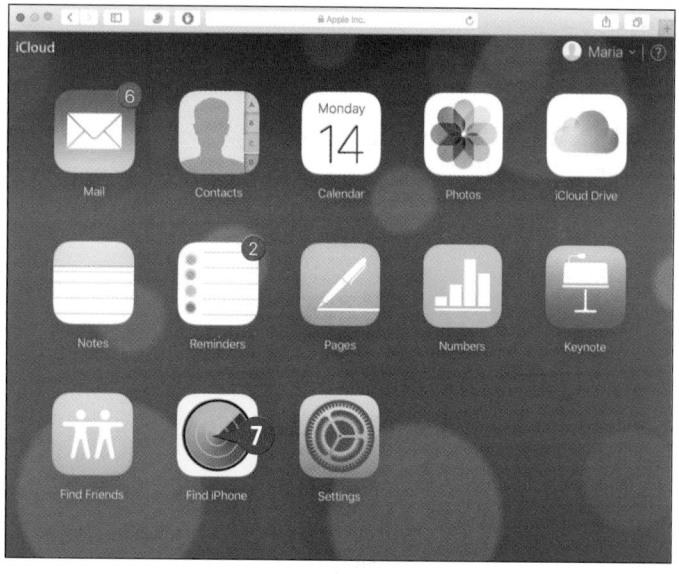

TIP

Is it worth displaying a message on my iPad, or should I simply wipe it?
Almost always, it is definitely worth displaying a message on your iPad. If you have lost your iPad and someone has found it, that person may be trying to return it to you. The chances are good that the finder is honest, even if he has not discovered that you have locked the iPad with a passcode. That said, if you are certain someone has stolen your iPad, you may prefer simply to wipe it, using the technique explained next.

continued ►

Locate Your iPad with Find My iPad (continued)

If Find My iPad reveals that someone has taken your iPad, you can turn on Lost Mode to lock it remotely and turn on tracking. You can also wipe the iPad's contents to prevent whoever has taken it from hacking into your data. Understand, though, that wiping your iPad prevents you from locating the iPad again — ever — except by chance. Wipe your iPad only when you have lost it, you have no hope of recovering it, and you must destroy the data on it.

Locate Your iPad with Find My iPad (continued)

The iCloud Find My iPhone screen appears.

8 Click **All Devices**.

The All Devices list appears.

9 Click your iPad.

A Your iPad's location appears.

The Info dialog appears.

10 If you want to play a sound on the iPad, click **Play Sound** ( ). This feature is helpful for locating your iPad if you have mislaid it somewhere nearby.

B A message indicates that the iPad has played the sound.

Use Lost Mode

1 Click **Lost Mode** ( ) in the Info dialog.

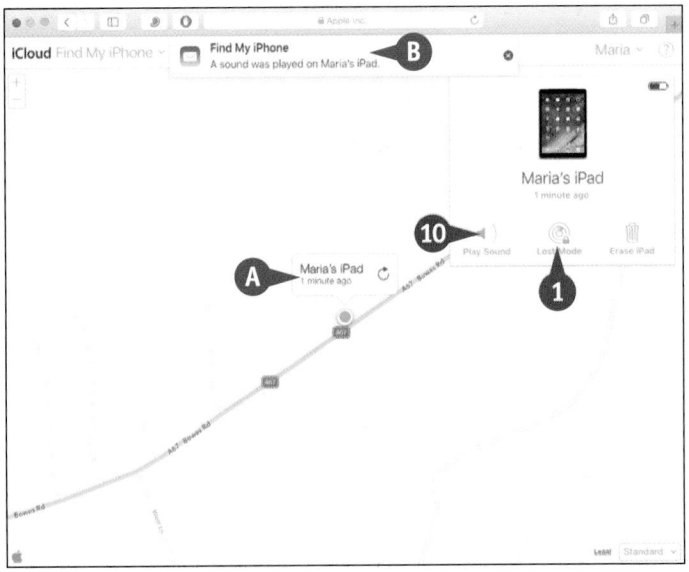

The Lost Mode dialog appears, prompting you to enter a phone number where you can be reached.

2. Optionally, click **Number** and type the number.
3. Click **Next**.

   The Lost Mode dialog prompts you to enter a message.
4. Type a message to whoever finds your iPad.
5. Click **Done**.

   iCloud sends the Lost Mode command to the iPad, which displays the phone number and message.

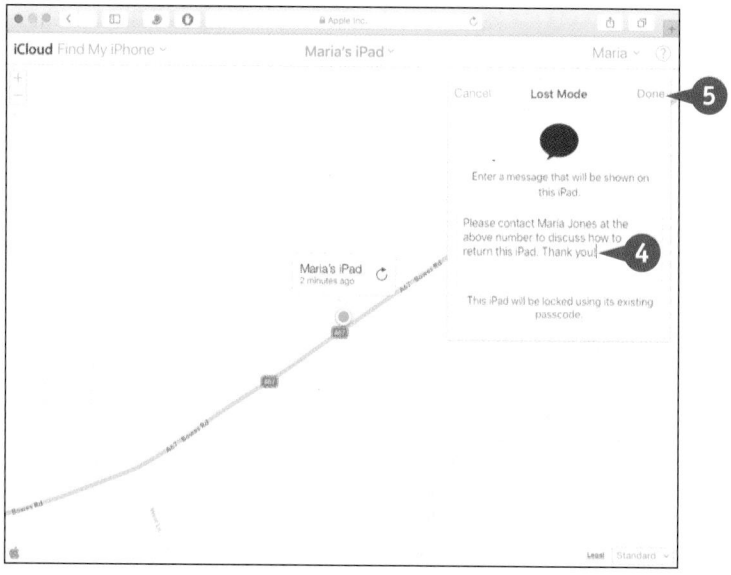

Remotely Erase the iPad

1. Click **Erase iPad** ( ) in the Info dialog.

   The Erase This iPad? dialog opens.
2. Click **Erase**.

   The Enter Your Apple ID Password dialog appears.
3. Type your password.
4. Click **Erase**.

   iCloud sends the erase command to the iPad, which erases its data.

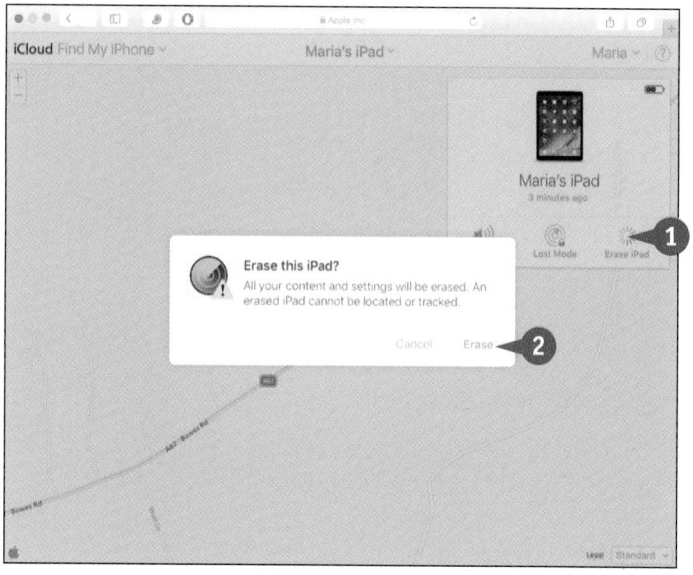

TIP

Can I remotely wipe the data on my iPad if I do not have an iCloud account?
Yes. You can set a passcode for the iPad, as discussed in the section "Secure Your iPad with Touch ID or a Passcode" in Chapter 2, and then set the **Erase Data** switch on the Touch ID & Passcode screen to On ( ). This setting makes the iPad automatically erase its data after ten successive failed attempts to enter the passcode. After five failed attempts, the iPad enforces a delay before the next attempt; further failures increase the delay.

Index

A

Accessibility features, configuring, 82–87
Accessibility screen, displaying, 82–83
accessing
    screenshots, 181
    websites with bookmarks, 186–187
activating iPad, 12–15
adding
    emojis to messages, 138
    family members to Family Sharing, 67
    items to folders, 155
    locations to Locations list, 171
    people to VIP list, 107
    web pages to Reading lists, 190
AirDrop, sharing items via, 126–127
Airplane Mode, 118–119
AirPlay
    launching, 250–251
    playing music and videos using, 250–251
    using devices, 35
alarms, setting in Clock app, 236
albums
    browsing photos using, 268–269
    creating, 270–271
    sharing via iCloud, 274–275
alerts
    choosing options for calendar events, 110–111
    defined, 47
Always Bcc Myself option, 103
APN Settings screen, 125
App Store, 164–165
App Switcher, 156–157
Apple, storage information by, 79
Apple ID, 164–165, 169
Apple Music Radio, 258–261
Apple Pay, 238–239
Apple Pencil, 7
Apple SIM, 8–9
Apple TV, 248–249, 252–253
applying
    bold, italics, and underline, 178
    changes, 26
    filters to photos, 300–301
    italics, 178
    underline, 178
apps. *See also specific apps*
    about, 150
    applying bold, italics, and underline, 178
    choosing
        notifications for, 46–47
        which to sync, 26
    customizing Home screen and Dock, 152–153
    cut, copy, and paste text, 176–177
    displaying settings for, 41
    entering text quickly, 174–175
    finding, 164–165
    getting, 31
    launching, 30–31, 36
    location services and, 5
    managing
        Apple ID, 169
        automatic downloads, 168–169
    multitasking with split-screen views, 158–163
    organizing with folders, 154–155
    reinstalling, 167
    removing, 167
    replacing text with suggested words, 179
    switching quickly between, 156–157
    unresponsive, 157, 306–307
    updating, 166
Ask Before Deleting switch, 105
Ask to Join Networks switch, 131
aspect ratio, 295
audio
    choosing devices for playing, 121
    configuring settings for, 256–257
AutoFill, for forms, 192–193
automatic downloads, managing, 168–169
automatic updates, installing, 11

B

back camera, 6
Background App Refresh, 122–123
backups
    sync options for, 25
    using iCloud, 314–315
    using iTunes, 312–313
    which to use, 21
badge, 47
banner, 47

battery
for Apple Pencil, 7
extending runtime of, 310–311
Bedtime feature (Clock app), 237
bit rate, converting songs to higher, 25
blocking
cookies, 195
senders, 146–147
blue sector (Maps app), 231
Bluetooth
connecting devices, 120–121
turning off, 310–311
Bluetooth keyboard, 88
bold, applying, 178
bookmarks
accessing websites with, 186–187
changing, 189
creating, 188–189
Bookmarks screen, 186
browsing
contacts, 208–209
events in Calendar app, 214–215
files, 170–171
photos
using albums, 268–269
using Years, Collections, and Moments, 264–265
shared photos, 266–267
web. *See* web browsing

C

Calendars app
about, 113
browsing events, 214–215
choosing
alert options for events, 110–111
default calendars, 112–113
creating events, 216–217
invitations, 218–219
Camera app
Grid feature, 289
Self-timer feature, 288
sending photos/videos, 137
taking
HDR photos with, 286, 287
photos with, 284–287
video, 302–303
taking square photos with, 287
Time-Lapse feature, 290–291
cameras, 6, 285. *See also* Camera app; Photos app
capitalization, controlling, 75
capturing videos, 302–303
carriers, connecting to different, 124
cellular access points, specifying, 125
Cellular and Wi-Fi model, 5
cellular data, controlling, 122–123
changes, applying, 26
changing
bookmarks, 189
colors in photos, 298–299
font in iBooks app, 281
Reminder lists, 223
screen brightness, 51
types of passcodes, 63
charging, 311
choosing
accounts with Notes app, 224–225
alert options for calendar events, 110–111
apps to sync, 26
Control Center settings, 58–59
date settings, 68–69
default calendars/time zones, 112–113
devices for playing audio, 121
groups of contacts to display, 209
hardware keyboard, 88
how to display contacts, 108–109
how you receive e-mail, 100–101
items to download automatically, 168
items to sync, 24–27
Language & Region settings, 69
Location settings, 54–55
Locking settings, 58–59
Messages settings, 144–145
music to sync, 26
Notes settings, 114–115
notifications for apps, 46–47
photos, 276
Privacy settings, 54–55
region settings, 68–69
Sounds settings, 48–49
text, 176
time settings, 68–69

Classic Invert, 85
Clipboard, 177
Clock app, 236–237
closing unresponsive apps, 306–307
Collections, browsing photos using, 264–265
colors, adjusting in photos, 298–299
combining contacts, 209
commands, for Siri, 72–73
commitments, tracking with Reminders app, 220–223
communicating
    about, 92, 116
    adding emojis to messages, 138
    Airplane Mode, 118–119
    blocking senders, 146–147
    choosing
        alert options for calendar events, 110–111
        default calendars and time zones, 112–113
        how to display contacts, 108–109
        how you receive e-mail, 100–101
        settings for Messages, 144–145
        settings for Notes, 114–115
    connecting
        Bluetooth devices, 120–121
        to different carriers, 124
        to networks via VPN, 134–135
        to Wi-Fi networks/hotspots, 130–133
    controlling
        background refresh, 122–123
        cellular data, 122–123
        e-mail display, 102–103
        instant messages, 140–141
    creating signatures, 98–99
    FaceTime, 148–149
    iMessage features, 138–139
    muting conversations, 142
    organizing e-mail messages by threads, 104–105
    sending text/multimedia messages, 136–137
    setting default e-mail account, 98–99
    setting up
        Exchange Server accounts, 96–97
        Mail accounts, 94–95
        VIP inbox, 106–107
    sharing
        Internet access, 128–129
        items via AirDrop, 126–127
        locations, 143
        specifying cellular access points, 125
        unblocking senders, 146–147
composing photos using Grid feature, 289
computers
    choosing items to sync with, 24–27
    copying music to iPad from, 245
    synchronizing iPad with via Wi-Fi, 28–29
configuration profile, 135
configuring
    Accessibility features, 82–87
    audio settings, 256–257
    brightness, 50–51
    display, 50–51
    Display Accommodations, 84
    Do Not Disturb Mode, 60–61
    hardware keyboard, 89
    iCloud, 42–45
    Interactive Accessibility features, 86–87
    Keyboard settings, 175
    Multitasking, 158
    Night Shift, 50–51
    Parental Controls, 64–65
    Photo Stream, 273
    restrictions, 64–65
    Search, 56–57
    Siri, 78–79
    Visual Interface Accessibility settings, 85
    Zoom settings, 82–83
connecting
    Bluetooth devices, 120–121
    to different carriers, 124
    hardware keyboard to iPad, 89
    to hotspots, 130–133
    to networks via VPN, 134–135
    Wi-Fi, 130–133, 320–321
contacts. *See also* Contacts app
    choosing how to display, 108–109
    unblocking, 147
    using in Maps app, 234–235
Contacts app
    browsing contacts, 208–209
    creating new contacts, 210–211
    searching for contacts, 209
    sharing contacts vie e-mail or iMessage, 212–213
Continuity, 90

Control Center
choosing settings, 58–59
using, 34–35
controlling
Apple ID, 169
automatic downloads, 168–169
Background App Refresh, 122–123
capitalization, 75
cellular data, 122–123
e-mail display, 102–103
essential settings, 34
frames for Time-Lapse feature, 291
instant messages, 140–141
layouts, 75
Music app playback, 247
music playback, 35
read receipts, 145
Reading lists of web pages, 190–191
controls, 8–9
conversations, muting, 142
converting songs to higher bit rate, 25
cookies, 195
coprocessors, 5
copying
music from computer to iPad, 245
text, 176–177
Cover Sheet, 32–33
creating
albums, 270–271
bookmarks, 188–189
events in Calendar app, 216–217
folders, 154
lists of reminders, 222
music playlists, 254–255
new contacts, 210–211
reminders, 220–221
shortcuts, 175
signatures, 98–99
crescent moon symbol, 61
cropping photos, 294–295
currency symbols, inserting, 74
curved arrow button, 225
cutting text, 176–177

D

Data Roaming feature, 122
date, choosing settings for, 68–69
deleting
albums, 271
apps, 167
conversations, 141
file attachments, 205
files, 173
filters from photos, 301
instant messages, 140
items from folders, 155
items from Reading list, 191
playlists, 255
shared albums, 267
VIPs, 107
Details screen, displaying in Messages, 142
devices
AirPlay, 35
size of, compared with screen size, 4
dictating text using Siri, 74–75
digital books, reading with iBooks app, 280–281
dimming screen, 310
directions, finding with Maps app, 232–233
disabling Night Shift from Control Center, 35
display, configuring, 50–51
Display Accommodations, configuring, 84
displaying
Accessibility screen, 82–83
contacts, 108–109
Details screen in Messages, 142
events in Calendar app, 215
iPad screen on TV, 251–252
messages on iPad, 323
movies on TV, 251–252
settings for apps, 41
Settings screen, 40–41
Share sheet, 276
web pages, 191
Do Not Disturb Mode, 60–61
Do Not Track feature, 194
Dock
customizing, 152–153
using, 36–37

documents, adding in notes, 229
domain names, 97
downloading iTunes, 10–11
dynamic range, 286

E

effects, sending messages with, 139
e-mail
    choosing how you receive, 100–101
    controlling display of, 102–103
    forwarding messages, 198–199
    organizing messages
        in mailbox folders, 200–201
        by threads, 104–105
    reading messages, 196–197
    renaming accounts, 95
    replying to messages, 198–199
    sending
        messages, 72, 99, 202–203
        messages using Siri, 72
    setting default accounts, 98–99
    sharing
        contacts via, 212–213
        photos via, 276–277
    viewing file attachments, 204–205
    writing messages, 202–203
emojis, adding to messages, 138
emoticons, inserting, 75
enabling
    Handoff, 90
    Multitasking, 158
    On My iPad Account feature, 115
    Night Shift from Control Center, 35
encryption, 313
Enhance feature, 296–297
entering text quickly, 174–175
Erase Data feature, 63
essential settings, controlling, 34
events
    browsing in Calendar app, 214–215
    choosing alert options for calendar, 110–111
    timing in Clock app, 237
Exchange Server, setting up accounts, 96–97
external speakers, playing music on, 250–251

F

FaceTime, chatting with, 148–149
factory settings, restoring to, 318–319
Family Sharing
    adding family members to, 67
    setting up, 66–67
favorites, using in Maps app, 234–235
file attachments, viewing, 204–205
files, opening, 37
Files app, 170–173
filling in forms using AutoFill, 192–193
filters, applying to photos, 300–301
Find My iPad feature, 322–325
finding
    apps, 164–165
    directions with Maps app, 232–233
    events in Calendar app, 215
    locations with Maps app, 230–231
    movie information, 76
    restaurants, 76
    settings, 40–41
    sports information, 76
folders
    moving e-mail messages to, 200–201
    organizing apps with, 154–155
Follow Focus feature, 82
font, changing in iBooks app, 281
forgetting networks, 321
formatting, in Notes app, 225, 226
forms, filling in using AutoFill, 192–193
forwarding
    e-mail messages, 198–199
    instant messages, 140
Fraudulent Website Warning feature, 194
front camera, 6

G

gestures, multitasking, 159
getting apps, 31
getting started
    about, 2
    activating iPad, 12–15
    choosing items to sync, 24–27
    Control Center, 34–35
    controls, 8–9

Cover Sheet, 32–33
downloading iTunes, 10–11
installing iTunes, 10–11
interface, 30–31
launching apps, 30–31
models, 4–7
setting up
iPad, 12–15, 16–23
iPad as new using iCloud, 16–19
iPad from iCloud backups, 20–21
iPad using iTunes, 22–23
iTunes, 10–11
synchronizing iPad with computer via Wi-Fi, 28–29
Today view, 32–33
Global Positioning System (GPS), 230, 311
Grid feature, 289

H

Handoff, 90–91
handwritten messages, sending, 138
hardware keyboard
choosing, 88
configuring, 89
connecting to iPad, 89
using, 175
HDR feature, 286, 287
hearing aids, setting up, 87
heartbeats, sending, 139
Hide Alerts, turning on, 142
History, 186
Home screen
customizing, 152–153
setting wallpaper, 52–53
hotspots, connecting to, 130–133

I

iBooks app, reading digital books with, 280–281
iCloud
backing up using, 314–315
configuring, 42–45
restoring using, 314–315
setting
backups iPad up from, 20–21
iPad up as new using, 16–19
setting up, 42–45
storage capacity, 45
iCloud Keychain, 19
icons, moving, 152–153
identifying items on-screen using VoiceOver, 80–81
iMessage
features of, 138–139
sharing contacts via, 212–213
in-app purchases, 65
increasing storage capacity, 26
inserting
currency symbols, 74
emoticons, 75
punctuation, 74
quotes, 75
SIM card, 9
standard symbols, 74
tables in notes, 228
installing
automatic updates, 11
iTunes, 10–11
Instant Markup feature, 180–181
instant messages
managing, 140–141
sharing photos via, 276–277
Interactive Accessibility features, configuring, 86–87
interface, 30–31
Internet, sharing access to, 128–1293
invitations, in Calendar app, 218–219
IP address, 320
iPad. *See also specific topics*
activating, 12–15
charging, 311
connecting
Bluetooth devices, 120–121
hardware keyboard to, 89
to other carriers, 124
enabling Handoff on, 90
locating lost, 322–323
securing with Touch ID or passcodes, 62–63
setting up
about, 12–15
from iCloud backups, 20–21
as new using iCloud, 16–19
using iTunes, 22–23

iPad *(continued)*
specifying cellular access points, 125
synchronizing with computer via Wi-Fi, 28–29
unlocking, 33
using with Macs, 90–91
iPad Pro, 7
italics, applying, 178
iTunes
backing up using, 312–313
downloading, 10–11
installing, 10–11
restoring
operating system using, 316–317
using, 312–313
setting
iPad to sync with via Wi-Fi, 28
iPad up using, 22–23
setting up, 10–11
updating software using, 309
iTunes Match, 246

J

JavaScript programming language, 194

K

keyboard
hardware, 88–89, 175
splitting, 174
undocking, 174
Keyboard settings, configuring, 175

L

Language & Region settings, choosing, 69
launching
AirPlay, 250–251
apps, 30–31, 36
layouts
controlling, 75
keyboard, 89
Load Remote Images, turning off, 103
locating lost iPad, 322–323
Location Services, apps and, 5
Location settings, choosing, 54–55
locations
adding to Locations list, 171
finding with Maps app, 230–231
organizing, 173
sharing, 143
Lock screen, 52–53
Locking settings, choosing, 58–59
locking volume, 257
Look Me Up By Email feature, 43
Lost Mode, 324–325

M

Macs
connecting to Personal Hotspots, 129
enabling Handoff on, 90
receiving text messages from, 91
sending text messages from, 91
setting up iTunes on a, 11
synchronizing reminders, 221
using iPad with, 90–91
Mail app, 94–95. *See also* e-mail
mailbox folders, organizing e-mail messages in, 200–201
malware, 194
manual sync, performing via Wi-Fi, 28–29
Maps app
contacts, 234–235
favorites, 234–235
finding
directions with, 232–233
your location with, 230–231
meetings, setting up using Siri, 73
messages, 138. *See also* e-mail; instant messages; text messages
Messages app, choosing settings for, 144–145
models, 4–7
Moments, browsing photos using, 264–265
movies. *See also* videos
finding information on, 76
time-lapse, 290–291
moving
e-mail messages to folders, 200–201
files, 173
icons, 152–153
notes, 227
photos, 265
multimedia messages, sending, 136–137
multitasking, with split-screen views, 158–163

music
- asking Siri about, 77
- choosing which to sync, 26
- controlling playback, 35
- copying from computer to iPad, 245
- creating playlists, 254–255
- playing using AirPlay, 250–251

Music app
- navigating, 242–245
- playing music, 246–247
- setting preferences, 242–245

muting conversations, 142
My Photo Stream, turning on, 272

N

navigating
- Music app, 242–245
- to web pages, 184–185

networking
- about, 116
- adding emojis to messages, 138
- Airplane Mode, 118–119
- blocking senders, 146–147
- choosing settings for Messages, 144–145
- connecting
  - Bluetooth devices, 120–121
  - to different carriers, 124
  - to networks via VPN, 134–135
  - to Wi-Fi networks/hotspots, 130–133
- controlling
  - background refresh, 122–123
  - cellular data, 122–123
  - instant messages, 140–141
- FaceTime, 148–149
- iMessage features, 138–139
- muting conversations, 142
- sending text/multimedia messages, 136–137
- sharing
  - Internet access, 128–1293
  - items via AirDrop, 126–127
  - locations, 143
- specifying cellular access points, 125
- unblocking senders, 146–147

networks
- forgetting, 321
- rejoining, 321
- troubleshooting, 13

Night Shift
- configuring, 50–51
- enabling/disabling from Control Center, 35

Notes app
- choosing settings for, 114–115
- using, 224–229

notifications
- choosing for apps, 46–47
- receiving, 33
- types of, 47

O

Office 365, setting up an account, 97
On My iPad Account feature, enabling, 115
online payments, 238–239
opening
- bookmarked pages, 187
- Bookmarks screen, 186
- Camera app, 288
- Clock app, 236
- Control Center, 34
- Dock, 36
- files, 37, 170–171
- Files app, 170
- items in folders, 155
- Notes app, 224
- Reading lists, 191
- Reminders app, 220
- Safari, 184
- Siri, 72
- web pages, 185

operating system, restoring using iTunes, 316–317
organization. *See* Apple Pay; Calendars app; Clock app; Contacts app; Maps app; Notes app; Reminders app
organizing
- apps with folders, 154–155
- e-mail messages
  - in mailbox folders, 200–201
  - by threads, 104–105
- locations, 173
- tags, 173

P

Parental Controls, configuring, 64–65
passcodes
    about, 193
    changing types of, 63
    securing iPad with, 62–63
passwords
    for notes, 115
    storing, 193
pasting text, 176–177
payment terminals, 239
payments, sending to contacts, 139
PCs, connecting to Personal Hotspots, 129
people, adding to VIP list, 107
Personal Hotspots, 128–129
personalizing
    about, 38
    adding family members to Family Sharing, 67
    choosing
        app notifications, 46–47
        Control Center settings, 58–59
        date settings, 68–69
        Location settings, 54–55
        Locking settings, 58–59
        Privacy settings, 54–55
        region settings, 68–69
        Sounds settings, 48–49
        time settings, 68–69
    configuring
        brightness, 50–51
        display, 50–51
        iCloud, 42–45
        Night Shift, 50–51
        Parental Controls, 64–65
        restrictions, 64–65
        Search, 56–57
    Dock, 37
    finding settings, 40–41
    Home screen and Dock, 152–153
    securing iPad with Touch ID or passcodes, 62–63
    setting Home/Lock screen wallpaper, 52–53
    setting up
        Do Not Disturb Mode, 60–61
        Family Sharing, 66–67
        iCloud, 42–45
Photo Booth app, taking photos with, 292–293
Photo Stream, configuring in Windows, 273
photos. *See also* Camera app; Photo Booth app; Photos app
    adding in notes, 229
    adjusting colors in, 298–299
    for contacts, 211
    sending, 137
Photos app
    adjusting colors in, 298–299
    applying filters, 300–301
    browsing
        photos using albums, 268–269
        photos using Years, Collections, and Moments, 264–265
        shared photos, 266–267
    creating albums, 270–271
    cropping photos, 294–295
    enhancing photos, 296
    playing slide shows, 278–279
    Red-Eye feature, 297
    rotating photos, 294–295
    sending photos/videos, 137
    sharing
        photo albums via iCloud, 274–275
        photos, 272–273, 276–277
        photos via e-mail/instant messaging, 276–277
    straightening photos, 294–295
Picture-in-Picture feature, 162–163
playing
    music
        in Music app, 246–247
        using AirPlay, 250–251
    slide shows, 278–279
    videos
        in TV app, 248–249
        using AirPlay, 250–251
playlists, creating, 254–255
pop-up features, 161
Portable Hotspots, 91
predictive text, 174
preferences, setting in Music app, 242–245
Privacy settings, 54–55, 65
processors, 5
projector, playing photos on, 279
public albums, 275
punctuation, inserting, 74

Q

Quote Level button, 179
quotes, inserting, 75

R

read receipts, controlling, 145
reading
    digital books with iBooks app, 280–281
    e-mail messages, 196–197
    messages in threads, 105
Reading list, maintaining of web pages, 190–191
receiving
    AirDrop items, 127
    notifications, 33
    text messages from Macs, 91
Red-Eye feature, 297
Reduce Motion feature, 85
regions, choosing settings for, 68–69
reinstalling apps, 167
rejoining networks, 321
reminders, setting using Siri, 73
Reminders app, tracking commitments with, 220–223
remotely wiping iPad, 325
renaming e-mail accounts, 95
renewing lease on IP address, 320
repeating events, 217
replacing
    default apps, 153
    text with suggested words, 179
replying to e-mail messages, 198–199
resending messages, 141
Reset All Settings command, 319
resizing video windows, 163
responding, to messages, 139
restaurants, finding, 76
restoring
    to factory settings, 318–319
    operating system using iTunes, 316–317
    using iCloud, 314–315
    using iTunes, 312–313
restrictions, configuring, 64–65
Retina display, 6
ringtones, setting for callers, 49
rotating photos, 294–295

S

Safari
    opening, 184
    security for, 194–195
    web browsing with, 184–185
Satellite map, 231
screen
    dimming, 310
    size of, compared with device size, 4
screenshots, 180–181
scrolling photos, 269
Search, configuring, 56–57
searching
    for contacts, 209
    using Search, 56–57
security
    encryption, 313
    for notes, 115
    for Safari, 194–195
    storing passwords, 193
    Touch ID for, 15
    with Touch ID or passcodes, 62–63
    Wi-Fi hotspots, 133
self-timer feature, 288
senders, 146–147
sending
    e-mail messages, 72, 99, 202–203
    handwritten messages, 138
    heartbeats, 139
    messages with effects, 139
    multimedia messages, 136–137
    payments to contacts, 139
    photos, 137
    sketches, 138
    taps, 139
    text messages
        about, 136–137
        from Macs, 91
        using Siri, 73
    videos, 137
setting(s)
    alarms
        in Clock app, 236
        using Siri, 72

setting(s) *(continued)*
audio, 256–257
automatic upload to Photo Stream, 273
choosing
for Messages, 144–145
for Notes, 114–115
default e-mail accounts, 98–99
displaying for apps, 41
finding, 40–41
Home screen wallpaper, 52–53
iPad to sync with iTunes via Wi-Fi, 28
Mail to organize e-mail messages by threads, 104
meetings with Siri, 73
preferences in Music app, 242–245
reminders using Siri, 73
ringtones for callers, 49
setting Lock screen wallpaper, 52–53
Travel Time item for events in Calendar app, 219
Settings screen, displaying, 40–41
setup
Apple Pay, 238
Bluetooth devices, 120–121
communications. *See* communicating
Do Not Disturb Mode, 60–61
Exchange Server accounts, 96–97
Family Sharing, 66–67
hearing aids, 87
iCloud, 42–45
iPad
about, 12–15
from iCloud backups, 20–21
as new using iCloud, 16–19
using iTunes, 22–23
iTunes, 10–11
Mail accounts, 94–95
Office 365 accounts, 97
Personal Hotspots, 128–129
repeating events in Calendar app, 217
VIP inbox, 106–107
VPN connections, 134–135
World Clock, 236
Share sheet, displaying, 276
Share Song button (Apple Music Radio), 261
Share Station button (Apple Music Radio), 261
sharing
contacts, 212–213
Internet access, 128–129
items via AirDrop, 127
locations, 143
photo albums via iCloud, 274–275
photos
about, 272–273
from Photo Booth, 293
via e-mail/instant messaging, 276–277
shortcuts, creating, 175
signatures, creating, 98–99
SIM card, 8–9
Siri
about, 17
commands for, 72–73
configuring, 78–79
dictating text using, 74–75
gathering and sharing information using, 76–77
Siri & Search button, 109, 111
size
for e-mailing photos, 277
screen compared with device, 4
sketches
adding in notes, 229
sending, 138
sleep mode, 59, 311
Slide Over view, 159
slide shows, playing, 278–279
Slide-Over view, 37
Smart Case, 59
Smart Connector, 88
Smart Cover, 59
Smart Invert, 85
Smart Keyboard, 7, 88
Smart Typing feature, 82
software, updating, 308–309
sorting contacts, 209
Sound Check feature, 257
Sounds settings, choosing, 48–49
specifying cellular access points, 125
split-screen views, multitasking with, 158–163
splitting keyboard, 174
sports information, finding, 76
square photos, taking, 287
standard symbols, inserting, 74

starting FaceTime calls, 148–149
stopping
    sharing locations, 143
    unresponsive apps, 157
    using Bluetooth, 121
    using Personal Hotspot, 129
    using wireless networks, 131
Stopwatch (Clock app), 237
storage capacity
    about, 5
    iCloud, 45
    increasing, 26
storing passwords, 193
straightening photos, 294–295
styles, in Notes app, 225, 226
stylus, 7
Summary tab, 24–25
switching
    Apple ID, 169
    between cameras, 285
    quickly between apps, 156–157
    between Reminder lists, 222
synchronizing
    choosing
        apps for, 26
        items for, 24–27
        music for, 26
    iPad with computer via Wi-Fi, 28–29
    options for, 29
    reminders, 221

T

Table Commands button, 229
tables, inserting in notes, 228
tags, organizing, 173
Tapback feature, 139
taps, sending, 139
text
    cutting, copying, and pasting, 176–177
    dictating using Siri, 74–75
    entering quickly, 174–175
    replacing with suggested words, 179
    selecting, 176
text messages
    receiving from Macs, 91
    sending
        about, 136–137
        from Macs, 91
        using Siri, 73
threads, organizing e-mail messages by, 104–105
time, choosing settings for, 68–69
time zones, choosing default, 112–113
Timer (Clock app), 237
timing events in Clock app, 237
Today view, 32–33
Touch ID, 15, 62–63, 193
touch screen, 6
tracking commitments with Reminders app, 220–223
transferring Clipboard contents to computer, 177
transit directions, 233
translating, 77
Travel Time (Calendar app), 219
troubleshooting
    App Store, 165
    Apple Music Radio, 259
    backups
        using iCloud, 314–315
        using iTunes, 312–313
    battery runtime, 310–311
    devices, 251
    iMessage, 213
    locating lost iPads, 322–325
    networks, 13
    restoring
        to factory settings, 318–319
        operating system using iTunes, 316–317
        using iCloud, 314–315
        using iTunes, 312–313
    software updates, 308–309
    unresponsive apps, 157, 306–307
    Wi-Fi connection, 320–321
turning off
    AirDrop, 126
    Airplane Mode, 119
    Bluetooth, 310–311
    GPS feature, 311
    Grid feature, 289
    Load Remote Images, 103
    VoiceOver, 81
    Wi-Fi, 310–311
    Zoom feature, 83

turning on
AirDrop, 126
Airplane Mode, 118, 119
Do Not Disturb Mode, 61
Find My iPad feature, 322
Grid feature, 289
Hide Alerts, 142
My Photo Stream, 272
Night Shift, 51
VoiceOver, 81
Zoom feature, 83
TV, playing photos on, 279
TV app, 248–249
typing web addresses, 185

U

unblocking
contacts, 147
senders, 146–147
underline, applying, 178
undocking keyboard, 174
unlocking iPad, 33
unresponsive apps, closing, 306–307
updating
apps, 166
automatically, 11
software, 308–309

V

vCard, 213
versions (operating system), 317
videos. *See also* movies
adding in notes, 229
capturing, 302–303
playing
in TV app, 248–249
using AirPlay, 250–251
resizing windows for, 163
sending, 137
Viewer feature, 204
viewing
contents of mailboxes, 197
file attachments, 204–205
VIP inbox, 106–107, 197
VIPs, removing, 107
Visual Interface Accessibility settings, configuring, 85
VoiceOver, identifying items on-screen using, 80–81
volume, locking, 257
Volume Up/Down buttons, 9
VPN, connecting to networks via, 134–135

W

walking directions, 233
wallpaper
Home screen, 52–53
Lock screen, 52–53
web addresses, typing, 185
web browsing
accessing websites with bookmarks, 186–187
creating bookmarks, 188–189
filling in forms using AutoFill, 192–193
maintaining a Reading list of web pages, 190–191
with Safari, 184–185
security for Safari, 194–195
web pages
adding to Reading lists, 190
displaying, 191
maintaining Reading lists of, 190–191
navigating to, 184–185
opening, 185
websites, accessing with bookmarks, 186–187
Wi-Fi
connecting to networks/hotspots, 130–133
synchronizing iPad with computer via, 28–29
troubleshooting connections, 320–321
turning off, 310–311
Wi-Fi only model, 5
Windows, configuring Photo Stream in, 273
wiping iPad, 323
Wolfram Alpha Computational Knowledge Engine, 77
World Clock, 236
writing
e-mail messages, 202–203
notes, 226–227

Y

Years, browsing photos using, 264–265

Z

Zoom settings, configuring, 82–83